Managing Change, Creativity and Innovation

Managing Change, Creativity and Innovation

Constantine Andriopoulos and Patrick Dawson

Los Angeles • London • New Delhi • Singapore • Washington DC

SAGE Publications Ltd
1 Oliver's Yard
55 City Road
London EC1Y 1SP

SAGE Publications Inc.
2455 Teller Road
Thousand Oaks, California 91320

SAGE Publications India Pvt Ltd
B 1/I 1 Mohan Cooperative Industrial Area
Mathura Road
New Delhi 110 044

SAGE Publications Asia-Pacific Pte Ltd
33 Pekin Street #02-01
Far East Square
Singapore 048763

Library of Congress Control Number: 2008927208

British Library Cataloguing in Publication data

A catalogue record for this book is available from
the British Library

ISBN 978-1-4129-4852-4
ISBN 978-1-4129-4853-1 (pbk)

Typeset by C&M Digitals (P) Ltd, Chennai, India
Printed in Great Britain by TJ International Ltd, Padstow
Printed on paper from sustainable resources

Mixed Sources
Product group from well-managed
forests and other controlled sources
www.fsc.org Cert no. SGS-COC-2482
© 1996 Forest Stewardship Council
FSC

To four generations of love: Irene, Maria, Apostolos, Manto and Lydia

&

To Arthur, Dee, Nigel, Robin Fulmar, Robin Elliot, Rosie and Gareth Dawson

Contents

**PART 2   CREATIVITY AND CHANGE
          IN ORGANIZATIONS**   **107**

List of Figures and Tables

Figures

Table

Acknowledgements

This book draws on research carried out by the authors in a number of organizations over many years. The first acknowledgement must therefore go to the organizations that we have worked with. Their time and expertise has been critical in helping us to deconstruct and demystify processes of change, creativity and innovation. We would like to acknowledge the openness of these companies in allowing us access to do research, as well as the enthusiasm of many people in relaying their work experience and in being available for individual and group interviews. We would also like to thank our publisher, Sage, especially Kiren Shoman for steering the manuscript along the road to publication, and the anonymous reviewers for their useful thoughts and feedback on how to further improve the text. As the book draws on case material which has been published elsewhere, we would also like to gratefully acknowledge Nicky Burr for gaining permission to republish case material from the *Financial Times,* and Routledge for permission to reproduce a teaching case study from Dawson (2003) *Reshaping Change: A Processual Perspective,* pp. 202–7.

From the courses we have run at undergraduate and postgraduate levels through to conference papers, journal articles and detailed discussions with academic colleagues, we have been able to refine and develop the presentation of what are extensive fields of study, into what we hope is a highly accessible and readable textbook. Our colleagues over the years cannot therefore go without mention. These include: Sue Allen, Alistair Anderson, John Balmer, Geoff Bloor, David Buchanan, Katja Christie, Anne-Marie Coleman, Lisa Daniel, Kate Ellis, Jane Farmer, Laura Galloway, Ross Hunter, Jeff Hyman, Sarah Jack, Janice Kirkpatrick, Jonathan Levie, Lorna McKee, Ian McLoughlin, Shaun Powell, David Preece, Jack Robertson and Dennis Tourish. We would also like to give broad acknowledgement to all our students (undergraduate, postgraduate taught and PhD) for their useful feedback during the many hours spent in lectures, tutorials and in one-to-one debates.

There are a number of close friends who have offered advice and motivation in initiating, writing and completing the book that Costas would like to personally acknowledge. These are: George Athanasopoulos Anthony Koustelos and Alexandros Macridis, Anna Malakate, Nikos Stathopoulos, Alexandros Zangelidis, and David Roche. Also to Virna and Dimitris Kallias and Sofia and Hercules Zissimopoulos for their unending and selfless support. And to Andy Lowe (PhD supervisor), who encouraged research in this area and was able to spark enthusiasm and interest. Also to Marianne Lewis, who has offered considerable insight as an inspiring co-author. Last, but not least, Costas would like to acknowledge the support of his family: Maria and Apostolos Andriopoulos, Yeota Lagiou and Charalambos Gotsis. Thanks, also, to Manto for being a supportive wife and academic colleague who has shown considerable patience and understanding during the project, and for her help with various versions of the manuscript

Partrick would like to give special thanks to the employees at the Taylor Group of companies and to Robbie Taylor who allowed us to collect data for use specifically within this book. To Cameron Allan who agreed to co-author a case and provided some useful comments on the pedagogical aspects of the book, and to colleagues at the University of Aberdeen and the University of Wollongong who provided valuable feedback and source material for the book. A special mention should be made to the memory of Jon Clark (PhD supervisor) who passed away during the writing of this book; he was ever able to stir a response on all aspects of life and academia. Sadly, Di Winstanley – a longstanding friend and colleague from our early days at the University of Southampton – also died during this period. Our walks in the Cairngorm mountains, story telling, Scottish dancing and leisurely meals will always be fondly remembered. As always, the family has been a great bastion of support and special thanks go to the wandering tribe as they make their own way in and around the world.

Part 1

SETTING THE SCENE: THE CHANGING LANDSCAPE OF BUSINESS ORGANIZATIONS

1

Introduction

Change is ongoing in organizations as new ways of working replace, reshape and overlap traditional structures. New working environments are sought where people can contribute their creativity and where new ideas can be nurtured and developed into further innovations that transform organizations and lead to the production of new commodities and the delivery of new services. Change, creativity and innovation represent key processes to organizations operating in the 21st century.

The concepts of change, creativity and innovation have never been more topical, especially given the commercial context of fierce business competition, shorter product life cycles and more demanding customers. Increasingly, long-term commercial success is based on an ability to manage change, to nurture creativity and to promote innovation. These processes interconnect in practice, and yet these areas have each developed their own separate and distinct bodies of knowledge. This separation – that is reflected in an education system that encourages the preservation of clear-cut and distinctive disciplines with specialized languages, academic journals, conferences and communities – may go some way to explaining some of the difficulties faced by practitioners and students of management in seeking to understand the connections between these concepts. The tendency to compartmentalize knowledge and place artificial borders around theoretical fields of study has perpetuated the false divide between theory and practice, and restricted our broader understanding of these central business processes. We seek to address this weakness through providing a more balanced analysis of these separate domains in developing what we hope is an informative and readable text on the subject area.

Rationale of the book

In this book, we argue for a more holistic approach that is able to cut across boundaries and disciplines in furthering our knowledge and understanding of change, creativity and innovation. Our intended audience is students of management in both a formal sense – as students in formal education – and more broadly, in terms of practising managers and those that have a more general interest in business management. We have designed the text to encourage reader engagement through the use of case-study material, interviews, reflective questions and hands-on exercises. At the end of each chapter we present some useful websites, further recommended reading and group discussion work. Our aim is to deliver an accessible account of key academic theories whilst relating these to the practice of management. In pursuit of this aim, we have divided the main body of the text into three distinct sections. Part 1 sets the scene and outlines our intention of presenting an integrative approach that is able to draw from a range of disciplines and fields of research. We commence with a working definition for each of our three key concepts from which an historical overview of business practice and theory development is presented. The section ends with an examination of the growth in creative industries and a consideration of debates around the future of organizations.

Part 2 turns our attention to processes within organizations. It commences with an evaluation of the literature on creativity and the individual, and progresses to issues and questions on team work, leadership, the internal environment, organizational culture and the management of change. Each chapter presents a number of case studies/exercises to get the reader to ponder on their own experiences (and those of others) and to apply these to the theories they have learnt. In the final section of the book, we present more challenging material to encourage readers to critically reflect on a series of ongoing theoretical debates and practical concerns. The book concludes with a short summary chapter that outlines some of the key factors that need to be taken into account when managing processes of change, creativity and innovation.

The changing world of business

Managing change, creativity and innovation is central to the repositioning of organizations in the uptake of new technologies and new techniques, to business developments in the provision of new products and services, and to the formulation and implementation of strategies to secure competitive advantage. Through processes of change companies have rewritten patterns of competition in emerging and existing markets, they have become rule makers and rule breakers, they have developed new ways of operating and competing, they have downsized, re-invented and grown, in search of ways to maintain, regain or sustain their competitive position. Business continuity requires change, and knowledge on how to successfully manage change remains a central resource. But change, however well managed, is not by itself enough. Business success also rests on making the right changes, on choosing the right ideas and implementing innovations that will make a difference. This creative element is critical in turning right ideas into innovations that can extend the competitive position of an organization within existing markets and create new markets. Thus, a key currency in this business world of rapid change is the creative idea that can be translated into new products and services, and into new ways of working with the emergence and development of new forms and types of business organization.

Managing processes of change, creativity and innovation are no longer the concern of a few advanced organizations but are essential to all firms operating in an increasingly competitive business landscape. New products like mobile phones, the internet, e-mail, instant messaging, robots, PDAs and cable television are just a few examples that illustrate how ideas and the people who produce them are a precious resource. Developments in products and services and new ways of doing business have seen the emergence of whole new industries that have created new forms of work and changes in the way many of us manage our finances and communicate. Take, for instance, the internet, which has been one of the truly revolutionary innovations – in both a social and technical sense – that have occurred in recent decades. An idea that was only known to a few people in the early 1990s became so popular that it changed the way we communicate with each other (through the use of e-mail, chat rooms and group messaging), research (with wider and quicker access to worldwide information and data sources), shop (through internet home delivery services and various forms of e-commerce) and engage in home and leisure pursuits (through, for example, computer-supported individual and group activities).

Read the case below and consider the questions that follow in reflecting on your own knowledge and experience of internet shopping.

CASE 1.1 AMAZON REPORTS RECORD CHRISTMAS SALES

(Source: *The Guardian*, 28 December 2005)
http://www.guardian.co.uk/technology/2005/dec/28/news.shopping

The online retailer Amazon was today celebrating record Christmas sales after its UK arm delivered up to 480,000 gifts a day in the run-up to the festive weekend.

On its busiest day, Amazon.co.uk shipped more than 256 tonnes of goods, with a Royal Mail truck leaving one of its three distribution centres every 15 minutes.

December 12 proved to be the busiest day for orders across the company's worldwide business, with customers buying a total of 3.6m items – 41 items every second. More than 108m orders were placed globally during the whole of the holiday season.

The retailer's bestselling book in the UK was *Does Anything Eat Wasps and 101 Other Questions*, which sold more than double the number of copies of last year's top-selling title.

Other top titles included *Is It Just Me Or Is Everything Shit?* by Alan McArthur, and Jamie Oliver's latest cookbook, *Jamie's Italy*.

Madonna led music sales with her *Confessions on a Dance Floor* album, followed by *Now That's What I Call Music! Volume 62* and *Intensive Care*, by Robbie Williams.

(Continued)

(Continued)

Amazon's consumer electronics division was dominated by sales of MP3 players and accessories, with the Logic docking station for iPod music players being the bestseller.

The company has delivered gifts and products free of charge when customers spent at least £15 on its UK website – down from £19 last year – in a bid to combat tough competition among retailers.

In October, the group warned that sales growth across its global operations in the final quarter of this year could be as low as 13% – well below the 31% recorded in the same period of last year.

Amazon.co.uk, which began life as Bookpages in 1996 and was acquired by Amazon. com in early 1998, is unlikely to be the only online retailer to report a bumper Christmas.

In the run-up to the festive season, IMRG, a body representing retail sites, reported a 50% year on year rise in sales in the 12 months to November 2005.

UK internet sales reached a record £2bn during the month, while high-street sales for the same period grew by only 0.9%

Questions

1. Can you think of any reasons (social/technological/market) that led to the increase of online sales?
2. Do you think that Amazon will continue to dominate the e-tailing market? Why or why not?

Managing change, creativity and innovation

Managing change has been the focus of an ever-expanding body of literature that Palmer and Dunford (2008: S20) refer to as a 'sprawl' that provides 'a conceptual challenge to both practice and research'. Effecting organizational change is seen as central to company survival (Child, 2005) and yet how to achieve successful change remains open to considerable debate (Graetz et al., 2002). For some commentators, this diversity in the field presents a challenge to organizational change research (Schwarz and Huber, 2008) and a need to reconsider our current understanding through drawing on more critical insights from areas such as organizational discourse and narrative theory (see Buchanan and Dawson, 2007; Marshak and Grant, 2008). For others, there is a need for more critical perspectives that counterbalance the tendency for management-centric studies that focus on the change agent's perspective, rather than on the actions, meanings and reflections of those experiencing change (Alvesson and Sveningsson, 2008: 6). We support the call for more critical reflection and adopt a processual approach to understanding change (Dawson, 1994). As such, we view change as a movement over time that may involve company-wide transformation through to small-scale incremental change (see also Child, 2005: 288). The stimulus for change may come from a variety of sources and take the form of proactive strategies or reactive responses to internal problems or external business market pressures. As we shall see later, there are many theories and guidelines on how to best manage change (see, for example, Cameron and Green, 2004; Carnall, 2007; Newton, 2007).

Making the right decisions on change also rests on evaluating the current situation and generating and identifying new ideas on the speed, direction and choices for change. It is in this area that creativity is important (see King and Anderson, 2002; Zhou and Shalley, 2007). At its simplest, creativity is the thinking process that drives employees to generate new and useful ideas (see also Henry, 2006). Without the development of new ideas, the ability to respond to dynamic market pressures, or to imagine alternative ways of doing things, organizations may lose their competitive position and become staid and unresponsive to the shifting demands of their customers (Rickards, 1999). Increasingly, managers are realizing that processes of creativity should not be left unmanaged, but that these processes require the creation and maintenance of environments that stimulate and encourage new ideas to flourish (De Brabandere, 2005). For example, companies that take a proactive stance in using customers and suppliers as a key source of inspiration, rather than merely monitoring and imitating what competitors are doing, are those that can gain greater rewards in the marketplace and earn a higher market share with better brand awareness in their respective industries. The business world is full of such examples; take, for instance, the case of Apple Computers, a company that was on the verge of bankruptcy but managed to turn its fortune around by focusing strictly on continuous innovation and high-quality products. Apple, nowadays, has become a household name with its flagship product, the iPod.

This in turn draws our attention to the concept of innovation (Mayle, 2006). Innovation is often conceptualized as the translation of new ideas into commercial products, processes and services (Bessant and Tidd, 2007: 29). In the case of the innovation literature, the emphasis has largely been on science-led innovations with a focus on how to translate innovations in science and technology into commercial applications (see Tidd et al., 2005; Tushman and Anderson, 2004). Entrepreneurship and innovation are often seen to go hand-in-hand as new markets and opportunities are identified and exploited in the pursuit of profits and the drive for growth (Bessant and Tidd, 2007). Market economic forces are seen to promote the need for new products and services in rapidly changing markets and yet, in recent years, social impediments and cultural barriers have been identified as a major, and often overlooked, central determinant of successful change (Furglsang and Sundbo, 2002). For example, Sundbo (2002: 57) argues that the push-oriented technology-market tradition for explaining innovation only provides partial understanding, as it downplays social processes and ignores the need for a more contextual understanding of important internal processes (an area that we examine in some detail in Part 2).

Managing change in the uptake and use of new ways of doing things, generating and selecting ideas, translating ideas into innovations, and moving the organization forward to meet the shifting demands of dynamic business environments, is a complex business. These processes of change, creativity and innovation overlap and interlock, and, as such, decisions to focus on only one element (for example, the creative component of the equation) would limit the potential for radical change in the uptake of new products and services since ideas are only the raw material for innovation and change; they do not by themselves guarantee transformation. Imagine having several ideas that could meet an organization's objective to improve market position, but not having the knowledge and expertise to successfully implement change that will enable the transformation of these ideas into tangible and valuable innovations. For change to occur, attention needs to be given to developing the right organizational conditions, such as leadership style, culture, structures, systems and resources to change raw ideas into marketplace products and services, and also to the question of how to move from an understanding of a need to change into an actual programme for implementing company change. Long-term success is based on the companies' ability to create and sustain such internal practices and processes that enable employees to perpetually generate new ideas and to create cultures of innovation and change that span different disciplines, to facilitate the open exchange of knowledge and information, and to recognize that long-held assumptions and traditions can inhibit new ways of thinking. In our view, change, creativity and innovation are key ingredients to the future commercial success of business organizations, and this book sets out to provide an accessible and readable account that will enable the reader to more fully explore these complex dynamic processes.

RESOURCES, READINGS AND REFLECTIONS

CASE 1.2   SONY CHIEF OUTLINES NEW STRATEGY
BY ANDREW EDGECLIFFE-JOHNSON AND PAUL TAYLOR

(source: *Financial Times* 5 January 2006)

Sir Howard Stringer, Sony's chairman and chief executive, on Thursday set out a plan to integrate the company's video and music content more deeply into its technology, as he outlined four entertainment 'pillars' on which the group would focus. He defended fiercely Sony's ownership of both content and the technology used to capture, store and distribute it. 'No other content company has such a complete understanding of technology and no other technology company has Sony's insight into content,' he said. 'Content and technology are strange bedfellows but we are joined together,' he added. 'Sometimes we misunderstand each other, but isn't that the nature of a marriage?' he asked.

Sir Howard's speech to the Consumer Electronics Show in Las Vegas marked his most detailed strategic announcement since he unveiled a restructuring plan in September. While that announcement focused on financial targets, including plans to reduce costs by $1.72 billion and cut 10,000 jobs, Thursday's speech highlighted new products that would reflect the changing relationship between content and technology. He expressed strong backing for Blu-ray, the Sony-backed high-definition DVD format competing with HD-DVD, backed by Toshiba. In spite of fears of a format war, Sir Howard insisted: 'Blu-ray has momentum and it is happening now.'

Sir Howard – Sony's first non-Japanese leader – said it would concentrate on four categories in pursuing the changing consumer entertainment market: high definition video and audio technology; digital cinema; video gaming and 'e-entertainment'. Sir Howard defined e-entertainment as products reflecting consumers' desire for more choice and convenience in how they access entertainment. 'Content is no longer pushed at consumers, it is pulled by them,' he said. He said the advent of 'higher definition' screens could be more profound than the shift from black and white to colour television, and said Sony was best placed to benefit from consumers upgrading their technology.

Sir Howard, who was promoted to his current job in June, is expected to give more financial detail on the progress of its restructuring later in the month. Analysts hope he may elaborate on which businesses Sony intends to sell as it focuses on fewer activities.

Questions

1. Discuss the pros and cons of the new strategy being adopted by Sony.
2. Is the new initiative triggered by internal or external changes? Defend your ideas.

Chapter questions

The questions listed below relate to the chapter as a whole and can be used by individuals to further reflect on the material covered, as well as serving as a source for more open group discussion and debate.

1. *Change is ongoing in organizations as new ways of working replace, reshape and overlap traditional structures.* Discuss this statement.

2. Discuss the pros and cons of a changing external environment to companies in the contemporary business landscape.

Hands-on exercise

Research one of the acknowledged innovations (e.g., MP3 players, PDA, etc.) and identify:

1. Who are the major players in this industry? (Consider whether the industry is dominated by the companies that you had initially thought of.)

2. What is the size of the market?

3. How many people work in the industry?

4. What potential difficulties do you see for existing companies in this industry?

Team debate exercise   ♀♀♀

Debate the following statement:

> *Long-term success is based on the companies' ability to create and sustain such internal practices and processes that enable employees to perpetually generate new ideas and to create cultures of change and innovation.*

Divide the class into two groups, with one arguing as convincingly as possible for the continual adaptation of internal practices to meet changing business market demands, while the other group prepares an argument proposing that long-term success is achieved by creating structures and cultures that maintain the status quo. Each group should be prepared to defend their ideas against the other group's position by using real-life examples.

References

Alvesson, M. and Sveningsson, A. (2008) *Changing Organizational Culture: Cultural Change Work in Progress*. London: Routledge.

Bessant, J. and Tidd, J. (2007) *Innovation and Entrepreneurship*. Chichester: John Wiley.

Buchanan, D. and Dawson, P. (2007) 'Discourse and audience: organizational change as multi-story process', *Journal of Management Studies*, 44: 669–86.

Cameron, E. and Green, M. (2004) *Making Sense of Change Management: A Complete Guide to the Models, Tools and Techniques of Organizational Change*. London: Kogan Page.

Carnall, C. (2007) *Managing Change in Organizations*, 5th edn. Harlow: Financial Times Prentice Hall.

Child, J. (2005) *Organization: Contemporary Principles and Practice*. Oxford: Blackwell.

Dawson, P. (1994) *Organizational Change: A Processual Approach*. London: Paul Chapman.

De Brabandere, L. (2005) *The Forgotten Half of Change: Achieving Greater Creativity through Changes in Perception*. Chicago: Dearborn.

Furglsang, L. and Sundbo, J. (eds) (2002) *Innovation as Strategic Reflexivity*. London: Routledge.

Graetz, F., Rimmer, M., Lawrence, A. and Smith, A. (2002) *Managing Organisational Change*. Queensland: John Wiley & Sons Australia.

Henry, J. (ed.) (2006) *Creative Management and Development*, 3rd edn. London: Sage.

King, N. and Anderson, N. (2002) *Managing Innovation and Change: A Critical Guide for Organizations*. London: Thomson Learning.

Marshak, R. and Grant, D. (2008) 'Organizational discourse and new organization development practices', *British Journal of Management*, 19: S7–S19.

Mayle, D. (2006) *Managing Innovation and Change*. London: Sage.

Newton, R. (2007) *Managing Change Step by Step: All You Need to Build a Plan and Make it Happen*. Harlow: Pearson Education.

Palmer, I. and Dunford, R. (2008) 'Organizational change and the importance of embedded assumptions', *British Journal of Management*, 19: S20–S32.

Rickards, T. (1999) *Creativity and the Management of Change*. Oxford: Blackwell.

Schwarz, G. and Huber, G. (2008) 'Challenging organizational change research', *British Journal of Management*, 19: S1–S6.

Sundbo, J. (2002) 'Innovation as a strategic process', in L. Furglsang and J. Sundbo (eds), *Innovation as Strategic Reflexivity*. London: Routledge.

Tidd, J., Bessant, J. and Pavitt, K. (2005) *Managing Innovation: Integrating Technological, Market and Organizational Change*, 3rd edn. Chichester: John Wiley.

Tushman, M. and Anderson, P. (eds) (2004) *Managing Strategic Innovation and Change: A Collection of Readings*, 2nd edn. Oxford: Oxford University Press.

Zhou, J. and Shalley, C. (eds) (2007) *Handbook of Organizational Creativity*. New York: Psychology Press.

Recommended reading

- Bessant, J. and Tidd, J. (2007) *Innovation and Entrepreneurship*. Chichester: John Wiley.

- Burnes, B. (2004) *Managing Change: A Strategic Approach to Organizational Dynamics*, 4th edn. Harlow: Financial Times Prentice Hall.

- Henry, J. (ed.) (2006) *Creative Management and Development*, 3rd edn. London: Sage.

Some useful websites

Change

- This UK website of the Office of Government Commerce (OGC) (http://www.ogc.gov.uk/delivery_lifecycle_managing_change_.asp) 'outlines the key considerations for managing successful business change and describes the processes of implementing plans'.

- This US website has a lot of articles, book recommendations and reports on the practice of change management (http://www.change-management.com).

- Students should also look over the more critical and research-based material at journals such as *Journal of Change Management* (http://www.tandf.co.uk/journals/titles/14697017.asp) and the *Journal of Organizational Change Management* (http://www.ingentaconnect.com/content/mcb/023).

Creativity

- *Business Week*'s magazine website focuses on the creative process, innovation and design (http://www.businessweek.com/innovate).

- The Creative Entrepreneurs Club is the network for the Creative Industries in Scotland, regularly organizing events. The website has a very useful directory of creative companies in Scotland (http://www.creativeentrepreneurs.com).

Innovation

- Innovation UK aims to help promote innovation and technology in UK business (http://www.innovationuk.org/).
- Also worth visiting is the UK government's website of the Department of Innovation, Universities and Skills (DIUS) (http://www.dius.gov.uk/).

2

The Process of Change, Creativity and Innovation

Learning objectives

This chapter has seven learning objectives:

1. To introduce the concepts of change, creativity and innovation.
2. To consider the key dimensions of organizational change.
3. To identify the main triggers to change.
4. To outline some of the myths that surround creativity.
5. To clarify notions of the creative process and creative thinking.
6. To briefly examine theories of innovation and to describe different levels and types of innovation.
7. To improve understanding of the complex and processual nature of change, creativity and innovation in organizations.

Introduction

This chapter provides an introduction to change, creativity and innovation – a large area that covers a range of theories and disciplines. Integrating theories and studies from the areas of psychology, economics, sociology and organization studies is not an easy task but is a necessary journey in our search for greater understanding. We are necessarily selective in identifying key studies that explore the concepts of change, creativity and innovation, and we examine the relationships between these processes that mark, what we would argue, is an essential feature of modern competitive business organizations. In this chapter, we commence with a discussion on organizational change in which the main dimensions of the change process are identified and described. Creativity is then considered and some of the myths and problems of identifying exactly what we mean by the term 'creativity' are highlighted. This is followed by a clarification of the concept of innovation and a debate of how this concept relates to the process of creativity and change. Overall, the chapter aims to clarify concepts whilst also illustrating the complex and processual character of change, creativity and innovation.

Organizational change

At a general level, we could formulate a definition of organizational change which encompasses all aspects of change within any form of organization. Under such a broad definition, change initiatives could range from corporate restructuring and the replacement of key personnel through to the minor modification of basic operating procedures within a particular branch or plant. One problem that arises from such commonsense definitions is that organizational change is not differentiated from the more general study of organizations. In other words, the study of organizational change virtually becomes the study of organizations. For our purposes, a simple definition of organizational change is 'new ways of organizing and working'. It is the process of moving from some current state to some future state that, whether planned or unplanned, comprises the unexpected and unforeseen as well as the expected. Integral to our concept of change are notions of uncertainty (the unknowable future) and continuity (as Heraclites commented, 'nothing endures but change'). Change equates with life, with our own personal, social, mental and physical development and with our ability to learn, to adapt, and to play an active role in social and community activities. Institutions, regulatory bodies, laws and social codes all serve to shape our behaviours in providing various rules and codes of social engagement. As such, it is perhaps not surprising that our own experiences of change can also draw to our attention certain recurring patterns and cycles.

Defining organizational change: the key dimensions

Over the last two decades there has been a plethora of organizational change initiatives from the uptake and use of new management techniques to the adoption and use of advanced information and communication technologies. There has also been a growing body of research and literature on the process and outcomes of leading and managing change (Burke, 2002; Burnes, 2004; Carnall, 2007; Dawson, 2003a; Graetz et al., 2002; Hayes, 2002). From the early work of Taylor (1911) who championed the application of the scientific method to the study, analysis and problem solving of organizational problems through to the research studies on innovative forms of organizing (Pettigrew, 2003) and the literature-based books on organizational change and innovation (see, for example, Poole and Van de Ven, 2004; Senior and Fleming, 2005), there has been a continuing interest in novel methods of working and alternative ways of organizing. Although this has resulted in a large body of knowledge on new forms of work organization, our theoretical and conceptual understanding of the change process has not provided any lasting prescriptive answers. As Pettigrew et al. (2003: 351) conclude from their extensive study: 'This constant process of change and renewal means that, whilst scholars and managers can take forward certain key messages, there will always be a need for more research on innovative forms of organizing.'

In defining organizational change, the literature varies in an emphasis on one of a number of dimensions ranging from aspects of leadership and political process through to business market dynamics and advances in technology. Although our simple definition – new ways of organizing and working – provides a useful starting point, it is limited. For example, when conceptualizing organizational change we should differentiate between an individual's decision to use an electronic diary with the decision of some large corporation to de-layer and downsize its worldwide operations. In moving beyond lay definitions, academics have sought to identify a number of defining characteristics that can be used to categorize different types and levels of change. One dimension that relates to the above example is the substantive element of change. This is taken to refer to the essential nature and content of the change in question. For example, are we talking about a cultural change programme, the introduction of new technology or the adoption of just-in-time management techniques?

Two further dimensions that run through a number of common characterizations of change relate to: first, the movement over time from a present state of organization to some future state (Beckhard and Harris, 1987) and, second, the scale or scope of change (Dunphy and Stace, 1990). On the timeframe of change, the question arises as to whether the transition is rapid (Newman, 2000) or occurs incrementally over time (Quinn, 1980). The speed of change (this temporal element) is sometimes linked to the scale and scope of change. For example, *first-order incremental change* is seen to reflect a slow adaptive movement that refines rather than revolutionizes existing structures and operating procedures, whereas *second-order discontinuous change* is seen to be of a higher order of magnitude in transforming the very nature of the organization (Bate, 1994). Furthermore, these changes may be anticipated in terms of incremental fine-tuning through to major company reorientation, or they may be reactive to unanticipated changes in business market activities. Palmer et al. (2006: 79) use the example of 'the catch-up response of other New York banks to install ATM machines following Citibank's lead' as an incremental adaptive change; and the major restructuring of Chrysler under Iacocca as an example of reactive 'frame breaking' change. According to Burnes (2004) the main focus of research has been on the more permanent, influential, large-scale operational and strategic changes that affect organizations.

Another concern of scholars has been the political dimension of change (see Buchanan and Badham, 1999, 2008). They argue that strategies for extensive participation may be used under apolitical programmes of incremental change – as change is accepted and occurs at a more relaxed pace. Whereas under more radical change programmes – where significant change occurs rapidly, is critical to company survival, yet is politicized and contested – change agents will have to take a more proactive political position in adopting what they term as 'power-coercive solutions' (for further discussion of their work see Chapter 10). Essentially, they claim that any form of contested change will necessitate political activity in dealing with opponents and building support for the initiative (Buchanan and Badham, 2008: 246–78).

These four dimensions comprising the *substance of change*, the *scale and scope of change*, the *politics of change*, and the *timeframe of change* have been used in various combinations in the creation of theories and models of change management. For some commentators, the process of change is an ongoing dynamic and for others it represents an episode in the life of an organization. Those that view change as a linear sequence of events tend to advocate stage models of change, as associated with some conventional organizational development models of change (see Aldag and Stearns, 1991: 724–8); whereas more processual accounts emphasize the muddied, incomplete and ongoing dynamic nature of change (Dawson, 2003a, 2003b). Collins provides a critique of the schematic 'recipe' models of change and what he terms as the 'n-step guides for change' in questioning their ability to deliver insight or understanding (1998: 82–99). Although generally supportive of the processual approach, Collins nevertheless questions attempts to use the findings from such an approach to draw out 'practical guidelines' (1988: 80). This tension between the planned, formulaic and practical approaches to change management and the more contextual and processual perspectives is evident within the literature and is taken up again in some of our later chapters.

Factors that promote change

A number of key factors for promoting change have been identified in the literature (Palmer et al., 2006: 49–66). These are seen to consist of elements both within and outside an organization. Some of the main external factors are seen to comprise:

- Government laws and regulations (for example, legislation on age discrimination, world agreements and national policies on pollution and the environment, international agreements on tariffs and trade).

- Globalization of markets and the internationalization of business (the need to accommodate new competitive pressures both on the home market and overseas).

- Major political and social events (for example, some of the changing relationships and tensions between America and the Middle East, and Australia and their East Asian neighbours).

- Advances in technology (for example, companies who specialize in high-technology products are often prone to the problem of technological obsolescence and the need to introduce new technology).

- Organizational growth and expansion (as an organization increases in size so may the complexity of the organization requiring the development of appropriate co-ordinating mechanisms).

- Fluctuations in business cycles (for example, changes in the level of economic activity both within national economies and within major trading blocs can significantly influence change strategies).

Four internal triggers to change, which are generally characterized in this field of study, comprise: technology, primary task (main business), people, and administrative structures (Leavitt, 1964). Interestingly, technology is seen as both an internal and external driver for change. As an internal trigger the concept of technology is often broadly defined to refer to the plant, machinery and tools (the apparatus) and the associated philosophy and system of work organization that blend together in the production of goods or services. Thus a change in an organization's technology may involve the installation of a single piece of equipment or the complete redesign of a production process. The primary product of an organization refers to their core business, whether this is providing a health service, refining oil or developing computer software. People, or human resources, is taken to refer to the individual members and groups of people who constitute an organization. Administrative structures are taken to refer to elements pertaining to the administrative control of work, such as formalized lines of communication, established working procedures, managerial hierarchies, reward systems and disciplinary procedures. Moreover, with the growing business expectation of the need to manage change, the managerial careers and political aspirations of business leaders can also promote visions and strategies for change. Essentially, there are external influences as well as a range of internal factors that all inter-link and overlap in determining the speed, direction and outcomes of organizational change.

CASE 2.1 GOOGLE TAKES ON ITUNES

(Source: *USA Today*, 8 January 2006)
http://www.usatoday.com/tech/products/2006-01-08-google-video_x.htm

Google's much-ballyhooed online video store was scheduled to open Monday after technical glitches prevented the service from getting up over the weekend.

The service, announced on Friday, promises to democratize video sales. Anyone with a video camera and ambition can create a production and make it available for purchase at the Google Video Store. Google takes a percentage of the sale, which Google co-founder Larry Page described Friday as "very low."

Google is attempting to take on Apple's iTunes store and its offerings of TV shows from ABC and NBC with four prime-time hit series from CBS, including CSI, NCIS, Survivor and The Amazing Race. They will be available the day after their initial air date for $1.99 each.

(Continued)

(Continued)

But there's a big difference in usability between the two services. ABC shows such as Lost and Desperate Housewives can be viewed on computers or video iPods, but the CBS shows can be viewed only on PCs connected to the Internet.

The same rules apply for day-after games from the National Basketball Association, which sell for $3.95. "If I can't watch on a plane, what's the point?" asks Charlene Li, an analyst at market tracker Forrester Research.

Google's copy-protection policy is at the discretion of the content owner.

Other offerings, such as reruns of PBS' The Charlie Rose Show and news broadcasts from Britain's ITN are not copy-protected and are encoded in a format that allows for transferring to the video iPod and Sony's PlayStation Portable.

Otherwise, viewing is restricted to Google's video player. Having a model for people who want to download shows and watch offline "is at the very top of our list for the second release," says Google Video director Jennifer Feikin.

Other highlights of the CBS deal include classics such as I Love Lucy, My Three Sons and The Brady Bunch.

Google also announced Friday the Google Pack, a suite of software from Google and others aimed at equipping newly purchased PCs with basics including a Web browser and anti-virus software.

It's seen as a defensive move against Microsoft to keep Google at the top of the mind for PC users.

The software pack is a available for download at pack.google.com

From USA Today, a division of Gannett Co., Inc. Reprinted with permission.

Questions

1. Do you think that Google's move into the online video service is critical? Why or why not?
2. Identify the major drivers for change and in so doing, consider how their strategies are likely to influence and/or be influenced by competitors' actions and responses.
3. In your opinion, what will Google's product offering consist of three to five years down the road?

Creativity

Creativity is a unique human quality that differentiates us from the rest of the animal kingdom (Goldenberg and Mazursky, 2002). The ability of Leonardo da Vinci to imagine a helicopter over 500 years ago, Edison to develop the light bulb and, more recently, Steve Jobs to develop the personal computer – all highlight the importance of creativity to the development of society. However, despite growing academic interest in the nature of creativity there remains no unambiguous, generally accepted definition. In fact, there are almost as many ways of defining creativity as there are writers in the area.

Myths surrounding creativity: towards a definition

The intangible nature of creativity does not lend itself to easy definition. Creating something from nothing, being inspired to compose a symphony of lasting beauty, to imagine the new within the constraints of modern thought, and to think outside of traditional beliefs and conventions, all point to aspects of what we might commonly term 'creativity'. An interest in creating the new and using our imagination for commercial purposes has also captured the attention of a growing business community. For example, Ridderstråle and Nordström (2000: 228, 245), in their book *Funky Business*, note that:

> **We have to start competing on the basis of feelings and fantasy –
> emotion and imagination ... To succeed we have to surprise
> people ... By focussing only on the hardcore aspect of business
> we risk becoming irrelevant. And trust us, irrelevancy is a much
> greater problem than inefficiency.**

Similarly, Senior and Fleming (2005) argue that the increasing business concern with flattening hierarchies and creating more flexible organizational forms (not the simple stripping-out of layers through downsizing) is resultant of the growing business recognition of the need to engage employees. The realization that strategic competitive advantage can be achieved through exploring creative and novel ways of achieving company objectives has led to a focus on cultures that promote shared values and attitudes whilst also encouraging the generation of new ideas (at both the individual and group level). Senior (2002: 351–3) claims that employees should not feel chained by convention but, rather, be able to sponsor new attitudes through the encouragement of flexible thinking:

> **In the future, hierarchical management structures will be less evi-
> dent. The management of intellectual capital will require skills
> that nurture creativity and innovation in workforces rather than
> compliance as in the past ... This is because organizations of the
> future need not just knowledge but knowledge generation and
> transfer, which in their turn require social interaction and
> exchange between organizational members.**

Although creativity has always been considered as an asset for individuals and organizations, it has traditionally been associated with a somewhat mystical process. Before further developing our definition of creativity, we aim to challenge some of the commonly held myths about creativity. These can be summarized as follows:

- *The smarter you are, the more creative you are.* This catchy little phrase suggests that there is a direct correlation between intelligence and creativity. However, those writers who support this notion generally stress that there are limits to this association and claim that once an individual has enough intelligence to do their job there is little or no correlation between the two. In other words, the creative process requires a certain level of intelligence but above a basic level there is little evidence for any significant link between the two (Amabile, 1996).

- *Creativity exists outside of time and circumstance.* This is the notion that creativity is something magical and extraterrestrial. This, however, fails to accommodate the creative process as an ongoing contextual dynamic (processual in character) that is inextricably linked to domains of knowledge that are similarly changing and in process of becoming. It is this dynamic flow between a person's thoughts and the changing social contexts from which they draw and refine their ideas that is an essential part of the creative process. It may appear to come magically 'from out of nowhere', but it is in fact an essential part of the world in which we live. Consequently, most examples of creativity do not fit this magical extraterrestrial ideal but are rooted in historical context.

- *Creative people are high rollers.* The willingness to take calculated risks and the ability to think in non-traditional ways do figure in creativity, but you do not have to be a bungee jumper to be creative (Smith and Reinertsen, 2004).

- *The creative act is essentially effortless.* Although creativity is a complex process, there is a tendency to emphasize what is termed as the *illumination* stage. This downplays the contextual dynamics of change and fails to recognize how most innovations occur after many trials, dead ends and a lot of personal effort (Placone, 1989).

- *Creativity derives only from eccentric personalities.* It is much more useful to consider creativity as arising from a particular behaviour than resulting from a particular product or idea. Under this view, creativity is mistakenly linked with personality.

- *Creativity exists in the arts.* In our everyday view of the world, we often link creativity with literature, music and various forms of the performing arts. Whilst these areas are 'creative', it is more appropriate to consider creativity as a human behaviour, which exists in any human activity; for example, from management consulting to scientific and technical discovery, or from film production to physical education (see Amabile, 1996).

- *Coming up with new ideas is the most difficult part of creativity.* There are many well-known techniques that readily help creative persons generate new ideas. The difficult part of creativity is not simply to arrive at ideas that are new, but to identify those that have value and are realizable (Rogers, 1995).

- *Creative output is always good.* Novel ideas can also be applied to evil and destructive ends just as well as they can be applied to good, responsible and constructive ends (Amabile, 1996).

In tackling these myths we can move closer to what we mean by the term creativity. In our discussion we note that the generation of ideas occurs within a social context and is linked to domains of knowledge and understanding that are also in a constant state of change. Individuals require a certain level of intelligence, be willing to think in non-traditional ways and to be persistent over time.

Finally, we argue that it is not simply the creation of new ideas that is important but the translation of these ideas into realizable products and services.

This broader conceptualization of creativity is a more recent development as the concept was initially linked to specially gifted individuals. Historically, researchers tended to view creative people as lone geniuses, working on creative endeavours in isolation from the rest of the world. Today, there is fairly widespread recognition that creativity should not be considered as a gift of the selected few but rather as something that exists in a wider range of professions and people. In the 1970s, process theories of creativity re-emerged when attention moved away from creative personalities (discussed in Chapter 5) to a concern with the creative process (Nyström, 1979). Interest centred on the process through which individuals apply themselves in searching out possible solutions to a known problem, rather than on the outcome itself. In the case of problem solving, early studies in the 1920s had already shown how individuals tend to broaden their options at the outset before reducing solution possibilities. These early studies developed stage models of the creative process from initial consideration through to final evaluation. For example, Wallas (1926) identified four stages in the creative process, namely:

- Preparation

- Incubation

- Illumination

- Verification

The preparation stage refers to the period when an individual may refine their goals in response to a particular issue or question that they face. This is also the period where relevant material from a wide range of secondary and primary sources is collected. The aim of the preparation stage is for the individual to conduct research (as wide and diverse as possible) in order to broaden their view of the area under investigation. The argument is that one firstly needs to equip oneself with the relevant skills, knowledge and abilities in order to be able to refine the problem under question. In most cases, creating novel and valuable solutions does not arise from working on conventional routines and guidelines.

After the preparation phase, individuals go through what is known as the 'incubation' stage. Here individuals suspend their conscious concentration on the problem and engage in a process of subconscious data processing. All of us have a vast storage space of knowledge in our unconscious minds that interacts with new knowledge and, in so doing, can generate new ideas. The temporary breakout from preconceived ideas or gained knowledge in the incubation stage provides space for experimentation and for approaching the issue in new ways.

Once an individual has successfully passed through the incubation stage, then they will move on to what is sometimes known as the 'Eureka!' moment or 'illumination' stage. This is the period when someone suddenly becomes aware of a core answer to the problem. It is characterized by an unplanned result that derives from a unique combination of ideas or patterns of knowledge that occurs during the incubation stage. It is during this phase that creative individuals must use their logical thought processes to turn the sudden insight into a novel and valuable solution. The translation of a new idea into a realizable solution is known as the 'verification' stage. This is when the individual needs to formally evaluate the resultant outcome against the criteria set at the outset.

Since this early work, there have been a range of studies that have focused on the process of creative problem solving. Basadur et al. (1982), for instance, propose a three-stage model that they label as the 'complete process of creative problem solving'. They argue that creative problem solving follows three stages, comprising: *problem finding, problem solving* and *solution implementation.* They argue that in order for the creative process to begin there needs to be a problem that requires a solution. As such, they suggest that the first, and sometimes most difficult task, is to correctly define the problem. But why is this problem-defining stage so important? This is because the way one approaches a problem will affect the quantity and quality of ideas generated in the stages that follow. A favoured approach at this stage is to try to reframe the problem by incorporating novel and divergent ways of viewing the issue in question. If this process is successful, a new problem statement will be identified that encapsulates all the issues that need to be addressed.

The second stage – problem solving – focuses on generating as many ideas as possible. It is assumed that increasing the number of ideas increases the probability of someone coming up with an idea worth pursuing. The third stage then focuses on the implementation of one of the solutions that was generated from the previous phase. In this final stage, it is important to assess whether the proposed solution meets the criteria set in the problem-finding stage. If this is confirmed, then implementation of the solution may require acquisition of certain resources in order to transform the concept into reality.

During each of these three stages, a two-step process of ideation–evaluation occurs. Ideation refers to the uncritical development of ideas. The main objective is to generate as many ideas as possible by 'freeing' the mind from preconceived beliefs, ideas and knowledge. Evaluation refers to the selection (based on judgement) of the best of the generated ideas. This approach by Basadur et al. (1982) is more sophisticated than the one proposed by Wallas (1926), as it not only distinguishes between the behaviours that occur in creative problem solving but also is concerned with the thought processes involved (ideation and evaluation) at each stage. Both models, however, have only limited empirical support and require further empirical testing and development.

Another model worth considering is Amabile's (1983) five-stage componential model. This model was developed at Harvard during the 1980s and identifies key components of creativity at certain stages of the creative process (see Figure 2.1). Problem or task presentation is identified as the first stage of this process in which the task to be undertaken or the problem to be solved is presented to the creative person. This presentation can arise either from external stimuli (the supervisor may have assigned the task) or from internal stimuli (one may be particularly interested in solving a specific problem). Amabile (1988) notes that motivation in the task domain plays an important role during this initial stage; she argues that if an individual is intrinsically interested in the task, then this will be a sufficient motivator for them to begin the creative process.

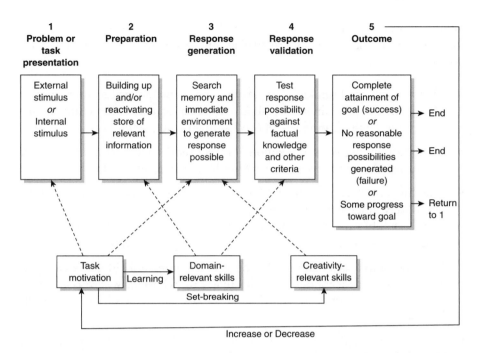

FIGURE 2.1 Componential framework of creativity (*Source*: Amabile, 1983: 367)

Preparation is the second stage prior to the actual development of solutions. At this stage the creative employee develops or reactivates a store of data relevant to the problem or the opportunity identified. During response generation, the individual comes up with a diverse range of possible ideas appropriate to the issue in question. It is at this stage that an individual's creative thinking will determine both the quality and quantity of ideas generated. The fourth stage of response validation refers to the process through which new ideas are checked for their appropriateness and validated. The final stage is concerned with assessing the outcome based on tests performed in the previous stage. If the response is found to be wholly appropriate then the outcome will be accepted and the process ends; if, however, the response is unacceptable or only partially acceptable but shows potential, then the process returns to the initial stage of problem or task presentation. At this second reiteration, the information gained from the initial problem-solving attempt will be added to the existing repertoire of domain-relevant skills. Essentially, this componential framework for creativity identifies five key stages that need to be accommodated in the creative process of identifying and securing novel and practical solutions to defined problems.

Creative thinking

As we have shown, research into individual creativity has focused on either the personality traits associated with creative achievement, or the development of stage models of the creative process. However, there remains an important research question, namely: what kind of thinking is creative and what is not? In attempts to answer this question, academics have proposed that any kind of thinking can be considered as 'creative' as long as one or more of the following conditions are satisfied:

- That the output of thinking has novelty and value, either for the originator of the idea or for their discipline (Amabile et al., 1996; Oldham and Cummings, 1996; Torrance, 1966; Woodman et al., 1993).

- That the thinking is unconventional, in the sense that it requires modification or rejection of formerly accepted ideas (Newell et al., 1962).

- That the output from creative thinking is the result of studying reality and is not purely imaginary. It is recognized that creative discoveries do not emerge full-blown, divorced from any prior knowledge, through mystical insights or causeless intuitions (Locke and Kirkpatrick, 1995).

- That the output of creative thinking can be either individual, challenging one's own preconceptions; or collective (group-based), where one's ideas spark the generation of debate so that the diverse range of viewpoints can be heard.

- That there is a high level of motivation and persistence; with thinking taking place either over a considerable span of time (continuously or intermittently) or at a very high intensity (Newell et al., 1962).

- That the creative output results from freeing oneself from one's own conventional thinking. In this way, individuals see in a deeper or clearer way the structure of the situation that they are trying to understand (Henle, 1962).

- That the initial problem is vague and ill-defined so that part of the task centres on the identification and formulation of the problem itself (Newell et al., 1962).

This of course leaves us with the question posed at the start of this section, namely: what do we understand by the term 'creativity'? Although researchers and theorists in this area have moved from a concern with individual personality traits, to the group and eventually the organizational aspects of creativity, the problem of definition remains. To a large extent, this can be explained by the diversity of studies that have approached this question, drawing on a range of different disciplines and base assumptions. As we have seen, creativity has been considered as a process that sparks emotions. Bruner (1962), for example, uses the 'feel' of the situation as a definition of creativity. As he states, creativity is 'an act that produces effective surprise'. He views the creative product as anything that produces 'surprise' in the creative person as well as a 'shock of recognition'. In other words, that the outcome of the creative process results in something that is suitable to the criteria set by the individual from the outset and is surprising in its appropriateness, ingenuity and, in some instances, simplicity. For others, creativity is a mental ability (Koestler, 1964; Mednick, 1962; Vernon, 1989; Whitfield, 1975). The most prominent definition in this school of thought comes from Weick (1979: 252) who defines creativity as 'putting old things in new combinations and new things in old combinations'. Creativity is proposed to have the capacity of forming associative elements into new combinations, which either meet requirements or have in some way scientific, aesthetic, social or technical value. However, Andrews (1975) adds that the combination of novel and useful ideas does not happen in a vacuum. Therefore, a creative individual must be aware of a specific problem, task or technological 'gap', and must be motivated to work on it. Furthermore, creative individuals must have at their command the discrete bits of knowledge and skills that, in combination, can contribute to the solution. Whitfield (1975) goes on to suggest that such an ability can only really be described in terms of the power to perform a mental or physical act.

Increasingly, authors perceive creativity as a process. For instance, Kao (1989:14) defines creativity as 'a human process leading to a result which is novel (new), useful (solves an existing problem or satisfies an existing need), and understandable (can be reproduced)'. In the same line of reasoning, Woodman (1995: 61) defines organizational creativity as 'the creation of a valuable, useful new product, service, idea, procedure or process by individuals working within a complex social organization'. Attention has generally moved away from individual psychological factors, to a focus on the links between variables related to the individual, the group and the organization and their effects on creative outcomes (Woodman et al., 1993).

So how do we define creativity? Well, for the purposes of this book, a simple definition of creativity is the generation of novel and useful ideas. As our focus is on creativity in organizational settings the book adopts recent perspectives that study creativity at the individual, group and organizational levels. From our perspective, creativity is a process that occurs within society, it is part of individual and group activities that cannot be fully understood without a broader understanding of the dynamic contextual interplay between our social life experiences and our attention to various business tasks and organizational activities. In our focus on business organizations, our aim is to improve understanding and insight into the dynamic and interconnected nature of organizational creativity and change. In pursuit of this aim, the section that follows provides an introduction to the equally contentious concept of 'innovation', but first, reflect on the concept of creativity in light of the case example of Yahoo presented below.

CASE 2.2 YAHOO RAISES PROFILE WITH HOLLYWOOD PUSH

(source: *Associated Press,* 3 April 2005)
http://www.usatoday.com/tech/news/2005-04-03-yahoo-hollywood_x.htm

LOS ANGELES – Five years ago, a handful of companies with names like Pop, Pseudo and Icebox promised a future when original shows produced for the Internet would replace traditional TV viewing. The dot-com bust deflated those grand ambitions. But the vision of creating unique, interactive multimedia programming for a generation weaned on video games is very much alive at Yahoo Inc.

(Continued)

(Continued)

The giant Internet portal isn't talking about its plans for content. But analysts suggest a profound shift may be at work, with Yahoo using its enormous reach to force Hollywood studios, among other video creators, to produce programming with the Internet in mind.

Yahoo can offer up a worldwide audience of more than 300 million – a number that some analysts say could reach 1 billion by the end of the decade.

"Those are numbers that are sufficient to make the likes of Rupert Murdoch salivate and turn green with envy," said David Garrity, an Internet and media analyst with Caris & Co., referring to the man whose News Corp. owns the Fox network and other media outlets.

Yahoo has already forged partnerships to webcast content from other media. It showed the entire debut episode of the Showtime series "Fat Actress," starring Kirstie Alley, at the same time the episode was broadcast on cable.

It also features exclusive behind-the-scenes footage from the Mark Burnett-produced NBC shows "The Apprentice" and "The Contender," and offers material from JibJab, the two guys who created the animated short cartoon that lampooned presidential candidates George W. Bush and John Kerry.

America Online has similarly broadcast the first episode of the WB Television series "Jack & Bobby" and features exclusive musical performances in its "Sessions AOL" series.

Yahoo chairman and chief executive Terry Semel said recently that 75% of users access the portal using high-speed connections, making it possible to stream video of all sorts, including content by individual users.

"Our great attributes are interactive," said Semel, the former co-CEO of Warner Bros. "We have huge audiences who themselves are the programmer."

Among other moves, Yahoo recently signed a deal to buy Canadian photo-sharing startup Flickr Inc., which lets people upload digital photos, publish photos in their blogs and share digital photo albums. Another recently launched Yahoo site lets users search for writings, lyrics, photos and other content authored by people who want others to use their ideas as the basis for new creations – the so-called "Creative Commons." Then there's the newly announced social networking service, Yahoo 360.

It all speaks to Yahoo executives' excitement about "micropublishing" – letting the portal's users create content attractive to fellow users that will encourage people to hang around in Yahoo's virtual world.

It's a vision shared by others who see a future where people aren't just passive viewers of content but participate in creating the "TV shows" of tomorrow.

One company built on the concept is Brightcove, a startup that envisions a day when "Internet Television" offers thousands of channels of content, some produced by traditional TV companies and much produced by individuals as the cost of digital cameras and editing tools drops.

Yahoo fueled speculation that it might try to produce its own original content when it hired former ABC primetime program chief Lloyd Braun in November to run its media group and moved all its content units under one new roof into the former MGM headquarters in Santa Monica.

Yahoo executives insist they don't suffer from Hollywood envy or the desire to take the multimillion-dollar gambles regularly taken by studios.

"When I wanted to move our media companies all into one place, and hire ... creative executives, the intent was not for them to either make movies or start making big television productions," Semel told the investors conference.

"It would be ridiculous and it's not what Yahoo is going to do," he said.

Lauren Rich Fine, an analyst at Merrill Lynch, says Yahoo is attractive to investors for its diversified revenue stream from paid search, advertising and social networking ventures. It simply doesn't aspire to the business model of the traditional Hollywood studio, where only six out of 10 movies make back their investment.

Yahoo says it's in the earliest stages of developing its entertainment strategy and thus would not make an executive available to discuss it with The Associated Press.

But the company has made it clear that one of Braun's mandates is to find new ways for Yahoo's music, games, news, sports, kids and other divisions to draw more visitors.

Moving content off the computer onto cell phones, portable media players and other devices is likely a key goal, many in the industry believe.

"The video experience online and on wireless devices is getting much better," said Bernard Gershon, senior vice president, ABC News Digital Media Group. "People's willingness to pay to access some of that content is definitely improving, and content creators, like us, are actually looking at this medium as a way to produce new and different content."

But it remains too early to tell exactly what direction companies like Yahoo and rivals AOL, MSN and Real Networks will take.

Ultimately, whether Yahoo morphs into an online TV network or produces its own content, its strategy all boils down to keeping visitors within Yahoo's virtual walls as much as possible.

Said Martin Pyykkonen, an analyst with Janco Partners Inc.: "The more content and interesting things they put there, the longer they keep you there, the more opportunities they have to monetize you through advertising."

Questions

1. What is Yahoo's biggest challenge in maintaining its competitive advantage at this point?
2. What should Yahoo's management do to address this challenge?
3. Is the management team attuned to perceiving and pursuing opportunities?
4. Is creativity per se enough?

In the case example above we examined Yahoo and creativity, but along with idea generation is the need to translate these ideas into new products or services. This process of realizing the commercial potential of new ideas is often what people are talking about when they use the term 'innovation'. In the next section, we provide a definition of innovation and explain different processes, levels and types of innovation.

Innovation

Bessant and Tidd (2007: 29) summarize innovation as: 'the process of translating ideas into useful – and used – new products, processes and services'. They support the Department of Trade and Industry (DTI, 2004 quoted in Bessant and Tidd, 2007: 12) definition that, 'innovation is the successful exploitation of new ideas'. For them, innovation can take many forms but these can largely be reduced to four dimensions of change, namely: production innovation (changes to product/services); process innovation (new ways of creating and delivering products/services); position innovation (for example, the watch-making industry and the quartz watch); paradigm innovation (a shift in long-held assumptions about the organization/business; for example, the emergence of low-cost airlines). They view managing innovations as a process ('an extended sequence of activities') involving the generation of innovation possibilities; strategic selection of an innovation from a range of options; and the launching of an innovation – the introduction and implementation process of making it happen in practice (Bessant and Tidd, 2007). They also explain the difference between 'incremental' and 'radical' innovations (2007: 14):

> *running from minor incremental improvements (incremental innovation) right through to radical change ... sometimes they are so radical and far-reaching that they change the basis of society – for example the role played by steam power in the Industrial Revolution or the ubiquitous changes resulting from today's communications and computing technologies.*

Theories of innovation

Theories of innovation have been at the centre of academic concern for a number of decades. Adam Smith's (1998) classic book on how to generate wealth stimulated a raft of research into aspects of innovation and productivity at work (originally published in 1776). Within the field of economics, classical and neo-classical innovation studies have continued to flourish, drawing on the machine metaphor associated with the physical sciences. Free-market forces, such as 'technology push' and 'market pull', are seen to promote appropriate developments for efficient economic alignment. Attention is on discovering the causal connections between various elements for the purpose of building predictive economic models. In contrast, the work of Joseph Schumpeter (1934, 1939) stimulated a more evolutionary perspective in which innovation was identified as a key driver of economic development. New products, processes, markets and forms of organization are seen to promote growth, and yet the question of why some innovations fail whilst others flourish does not lend itself to simple explanation. The call for companies to adapt and to be innovative to survive is frequently made, but what is the nature of the innovation process within organizations that drives company renewal?

Burns and Stalker (1961) conducted an early study into the nature of organizational innovation. Their classic work on *The Management of Innovation* highlights the importance of matching organization structure to business market context. Their work demonstrates the importance of organizational design to a firm's ability to innovate and adapt to a turbulent environment. For example, their study showed how it is possible to construct two ideal types of management system. First, a mechanistic system deemed appropriate for an organization that uses an unchanging technology and operates in a relatively stable market. It is characterized by clear hierarchical lines of authority, precise definitions of job tasks and control responsibilities, a tendency for vertical interaction, an insistence on loyalty to the concern, and an emphasis on task skills and local knowledge rather than general knowledge and experience (Burns and Stalker, 1961: 119–20). Second, an organic form deemed appropriate for an organization that undergoes continual change and operates in a dynamic fluctuating market. This form is characterized by a network structure of control, authority and communication, a reliance on expert knowledge for decision making, the continual redefinition of individual tasks through interaction with others, and the spread of commitment to the firm beyond any formal contractual obligation (Burns and Stalker, 1961: 121–2).

Whilst this distinction has proven influential in the development of organization theory, it has tended to be used as a means of classifying and differentiating between opposing types of industries and company organization (for example, between the bureaucratic mechanistic system of public health services and the loose organic system of high-technology companies), without investigation of the potential for the two structures to co-exist within a single organization. This is perhaps a point that has been lost in the endless summaries of this classic typology. As Burns and Stalker themselves note, 'a concern may (and frequently does) operate with a management system which includes both types' (1961: 122). As such, research and development activities may be organized along more organic forms to stimulate creativity and change, whereas more routine types of work may be better performed under mechanistic structures. But this in turn raises the question of how is innovation different from creativity?

How does innovation differ from creativity?

As a starting point, organizational creativity is often taken to refer to the generation of novel and useful ideas, whereas organizational innovation is used to describe the realization of those ideas (see also Cook, 1998; Jones, 1995; Persing, 1999; Whitfield, 1975). From this position, organizational innovation is defined as the process by which a new element (originating as a creative idea) becomes available within the marketplace or is introduced into an organization with the intention of changing or challenging the status quo (King, 1995: 83). Amabile et al. (1996: 1155) supports this position by stating that 'creativity ... is a starting point for innovation; the first is a necessary but not sufficient condition for the second'. From this perspective, creativity comes first and provides the impetus and content for many forms of innovation. In examining the uptake of technology in the transition from older methods of work to new innovative arrangements that promote creativity, Shoshana Zuboff (1988) argues that there is a choice between *automating* work, which serves to increase managerial control, reduce employee skill requirements and maintain a rigid division of labour with a clear separation between managers and workers; or *informating* work, which facilitates greater collaboration and flexibility through developing the intellective skills of employees, and enabling them to gain and use their knowledge about production and distribution services. She contends that whilst the strategic decision to adopt information technology is usually based on the immediate savings from a reduction in labour costs (through the elimination of jobs), the option of using technology to inform work is likely to improve the quality of working life and productivity in the longer term.

Zuboff's work also spotlights how the uptake and use of innovations within organizations often reflect a complex interplay between social, economic and political factors. Strategic choices are played out in context and over time and, as such, innovations are often reconfigured and reconstituted within the organizations where they are introduced. This point is well illustrated by Fleck and his colleagues, who in discussing developments in Computer Numerical Control (CNC), Computer-Aided Production Management (CAPM), office automation and robotics, conclude that (Fleck et al., 1989: 23):

> *Our historical analyses of the actual development process shows that while the dreams and philosophies of the promoters of technologies may inspire the initial form of a technology, as soon as it is adopted and implemented within industry it becomes subject to a much wider range of forces. These include the objectives and strategies of industrial managers and practitioners, the social and productive conditions within the organization, and the practices and relationships between groups of labour, all of which take place within the context of constant shifts in economic and political conditions in society at large. These forces in the implementation process act upon the offerings of promoters and designers. This interaction serves to reconstitute technologies and produce new 'states-of-the-art' and solutions, which are then again modified in response to the industrial conditions they meet.*

Consequently, the process by which creative ideas are realized as innovations within organizations remains a key area of debate and study (see also Fleck et al., 1990). Before returning to some of these issues, it is worth outlining some of the main levels and types of innovation. As already noted, innovations can lie along a continuum from small incremental innovations to large-scale radical innovations, and may take the form of market (position), process or product innovations through to new management systems, ways of working or to what Bessant and Tidd (2007: 29) refer to as paradigm innovations.

Levels of innovation

Innovations can range from fairly small-scale changes to the more radical groundbreaking innovations associated with developments in steam, electricity, transportation and the ubiquitous computer. Numerous gradations could be made along this continuum and therefore, for simplicity, we have listed small, medium and large-scale innovations:

- *Incremental innovations:* these refer to small changes that are generally based on established knowledge and existing organizational capabilities. Refinements and modifications to existing products, such as improvements to television picture quality or the sound performance of existing hi-fi music systems, would be examples of incremental innovations.

- *Modular innovations:* these refer to middle-range innovations that are more significant than simple product improvements. For example, the transition from black-and-white to colour television sets marks a modular innovation in a well-developed product line. Other similar innovations have been the digital sound systems associated with home entertainment systems.

- *Radical innovations:* these typically occur when current knowledge and capabilities become obsolete and new knowledge is required to exploit uncharted opportunities. For example, the introduction of DVD players resulted in substantial internal changes in the organization and control of work (such as in the manufacturing, marketing and sales functions).

In practice, there is often considerable overlap between types of innovation over time. Take, for example, the development of the Walkman personal music system. This innovation was first developed by Sony and has been an outstanding commercial success (radical innovation). However, Sony selected a single platform for its Walkman and has latterly produced more than 30 incremental versions within the same product family (Tushman and O'Reilly, 2002).

Types of innovation

Innovation can also take many different forms, including the following:

- *Product innovations:* this refers to innovations in the development of a new or improved product. Among the many product innovations that occur every year all over the world, there was one which has become a truly outstanding success: Dyson's bagless vacuum cleaner. James Dyson, after five years of hard work and 5,127 prototypes, came up with the world's first bagless vacuum cleaner. The vacuum was so successful that it won the 1991 International Design Fair prize in Japan. The Japanese were so impressed by its performance that the G Force became a status symbol, selling for

$2,000 apiece. In 2000, Dyson revenues were in the area of $345 million with a total net profit of approximately $52.5 million.

- *Service innovations:* this refers to the development of new or improved services. Think about Hotmail. Hotmail was set up with a unique selling proposition: to offer the first free web-based e-mail service, which would provide its end-users with the ability to access their e-mail from any computer in the world. This powerful idea had widespread application and captured a worldwide market. As it turned out, Hotmail's success – in terms of number of users – rapidly promoted brand recognition among users and receivers of Hotmail e-mails. This public awareness made the company widely known not only for its innovation but also for their skill in turning an idea into a realizable service. Their sudden arrival into the highly competitive IT market drew the attention of other major players. As a result, Hotmail was acquired by Microsoft in December 1997 and is now part of the Microsoft Consumer Group with over 60 million users.

- *Process innovations:* these types of innovations centre on improving processes rather than end products or services. Typically, new ways of doing things are introduced into an organization's production or service operations, such as input materials, information flow mechanisms or any other equipment used to produce a good or service (Damanpour, 1991). An example of a company that innovated in the way they serve customers is Netflix. Netflix is the world's largest online DVD movie rental service offering more than one million members access to more than 15,000 titles sent through the mail, with no due dates and no late fees. The company's success was not only based on the most expansive selection of DVDs but also on fast, free delivery. Instead of having one big warehouse for collecting and posting DVDs, the company decided to have 18 shipping centres. As an alternative to using the traditional warehouse system with shelves where, for instance, you could find *The Matrix* in aisle number 10.5, the company came up with a more innovative way of dealing with its inventory without using any shelves. Each morning the US Postal Service would drop off thousands of returned DVDs. Company employees would then scan the disks and collect returns data that computers at Netflix's San Jose headquarters could then match to new orders. What happens next? With each scan, they act on instructions from San Jose to 'ship disk' if a customer wants the film, or 'scan tomorrow' if not. The ones that must be shipped get an envelope and a sticker, the ones that are to be scanned the following day are set aside. The innovativeness of this system made the company more efficient (they can handle around 800 disks per hour) and cheaper (imagine if one had to post DVDs throughout the country).

- *Management innovations:* during the 1980s and 1990s many American and European companies tried to adopt Japanese manufacturing techniques. Their essential aim was to reduce costs, improve quality and increase productivity. For example, although many of the principles of quality management originated in the West, the uptake of this technique was widespread in Japan following the work of Edward Deming and Joseph Juran (see Dawson and Palmer, 1995). Quality management provided Japanese companies with new innovative practices that would radically change their position in world markets. After the Second World War, Japanese mass-manufactured products were generally associated with poor quality. By the 1970s and in the decades that followed, Japan emerged as a powerful economic force in the major industrial markets of the Western world. The decline of the UK motor-cycle industry became a case in point as cheaper yet more reliable high-performance Japanese models entered the conservative and complacent UK motorcycle market.

- *Market or position innovations:* this refers to the creation of new markets and generally overlaps with product and process innovations. New markets may emerge as competitors promote new products and services in their compe-tition for customers. Alternatively, innovations may be developed with the aim of creating a market where one did not previously exist. For example, considerable research effort has been put into the videophone, and yet establishing this market has proven very difficult. In contrast, developments in the video tape recorder centred on technical and presentational issues that, once resolved, found a readily expandable market.

These then are some of the main types and levels of innovation that occur within business environments. It leaves open the difficult question of what constitutes and differentiates innovation, from creativity and from change (see Galavan et al., 2008; Tushman and Anderson, 2004). In our view, there are no clear boundaries between the three as in practice they interlock and overlap over time. This is usefully illus-trated by a study conducted by one of the authors into the uptake of new technol-ogy at a laundry operation in Australia. Once the company had identified the need to replace existing machinery in order to compete within an increasingly competi-tive regional market, the choice on the new systems rested with senior manage-ment. In practice, a senior engineering manager drove the project forward in his enthusiasm to build the most advanced laundry facility in the world. The avail-ability of technology during the task of search and assessment enabled and con-strained the options available in the redesign of plant operations. Whilst attempts were made to go beyond existing techniques, these changes have taken consider-able time and the system continues to be modified to incorporate more advanced technical developments. As an innovative configuration of technologies taken from various parts of Europe, the new computerized laundry facility raised unique problems requiring the local innovation and diffusion of new ideas and solutions (what Fleck, 1991, calls 'innofusion'). Through a process of experimentation and development, a new stock of knowledge was created and new combinations of sys-tems tested to tackle an ever-changing set of requirements. The high level of user-participation (in terms of the engineering function) and employee involvement (in terms of work restructuring) resulted in an increase in productivity that secured the commercial future of the company. In this case, it was not simply the technology that determined innovations in the system's design and new forms of work orga-nization, but it was the interplay between the context in which change was taking place, the generation of new ideas that were realizable, the politics of negotiating acceptable change routes, and the characteristics of the available technology for the design of an integrated laundry facility.

In the case presented below, the example of mobile gaming is used to further illustrate the contextual development of new innovation and also their potential uptake in emerging consumer markets.

CASE 2.3   MOBILE GAMING: SERVING A VOLLEY OF NEW EXPERIENCES BY BEN HUNT

(Source: *Financial Times,* 6 September 2005)

To many of its owners, Sega's Super Real Tennis, which was embedded in Sony Ericsson's K700 mobile phone handset on its release in 2004, was an incidental feature of a device created for an entirely different purpose. But to the wireless gaming industry the game, alongside others that emerged at the same time, represented a breakthrough.

Gaming has been a popular, if unsophisticated element of mobile phones since Nokia first produced its simple and addictive Snake game eight years ago. But until relatively recently – and with the emergence of compelling, entertaining and dynamic games – mobile gaming had appeared to be a frustrated prisoner of its platform; restrained by small screens, low quality graphics, static game play and an economic model limited by price tags that, typically, are a tenth of those for console games. But as the gaming website Gamespot.com pointed out, Super Real Tennis raised the bar: 'this is one of the most playable mobile offerings we've seen – as well as one of the best looking. This is a mobile tour de force that feels more like a full-fledged console game than something that should appear on a mobile phone.'

If mobile gaming is to fulfil its immense promise, both to the computer game development and publishing industry as well as the wireless communications sector, then many more such games have to appear. To developers and publishers, mobile games represent an opportunity to reach markets that other platforms cannot: by the end of this decade 2 billion people will have mobile phones, most of whom would never buy a PlayStation or an Xbox.

To wireless carriers, games comprise an important part of the data offering that they hope will help them sustain revenue growth in the era of 3G. This ambition has been emphasised by a recent 'We Like Play' marketing campaign from 3 UK. 'It's part of a broader position around entertainment, and what we are finding is that the things that are popular can be categorised as entertainment: music, comedy, football and games. Games in the broadest sense have proved compelling on a 3G network,' says Graeme Oxby, marketing director of 3 UK.

Despite 3's positive experience, and the arrival on the market of some first class titles, mobile gaming remains some distance from reaching its potential. According to Informa Media and Telecoms, the research group, only in Asia Pacific, and in particular Japan – where 10 per cent of wireless subscribers pay for games – is the market reaching maturity. More than half the world's gamers are located in that region with a little more than a third in Europe and North America lagging a long way behind. 'The mobile gaming market is in its adolescence phase,' says Lisa Waits, head of Nokia's Snap Mobile, the Finnish giant's multiplayer and community-based gaming program. 'It is not completely nascent, although it is certainly not full-grown. It is already a big money business, with millions – some even say billions – being made in revenue from simple download games to phones.'

This growing-up process has been confirmed by the recent decisions of some of the gaming industry's big hitters to join the fray. '2005 has seen a lot of traditional game and media companies taking actions to enter the space such as Electronic Arts, Yahoo! Real and Time Warner and the strategies for the players in the industry are still bound to change as more surface,' says Ms Waits.

Gerhard Florin, EA's managing director of European publishing, says the company started to take wireless seriously about two years ago and established a studio group to find ways of exploiting new opportunities for franchises such as The Sims and Fifa football. One such opportunity has been to broaden the gaming market to encompass female mobile phone users. 'A huge installed base opens new doors to widen the knowledge of franchises to bring in new games, and especially girls,' he says.

Ms Waits agrees: 'the key is to give a wide demographic a fun, connected experience. It's no longer just about the 15-year-old boy – although you don't overlook them. Everyone has a cellphone, from the 15-year-old to the 85-year-old grandma.' But creating a game is not as simple as taking a PS2 title and shrinking it to fit a 2 inch screen. Ms Waits says the platform requires a different approach. 'An ideal mobile game takes advantage of two key tenets: firstly, it is short and time-filling game play – it is not the place to spend an hour forging swords, choosing your army layout. Secondly, connectivity through the network. We all use mobile phones to connect to other people, through voice, SMS and e-mail, and to overlook that aspect of the mobile platform is to sell it short – by a long shot.'

This is a view shared by Andy Riedel, head of games at InfoSpace, a San Francisco-based development group. He believes that, as the domain of the casual gamer wireless gaming requires a slate of titles that appeals to a broad cross section of the population. 'At InfoSpace we take a broad view of the mobile game. In some cases it is a straightforward puzzle but we are also trying to take on board new types of experiences, based around social networking and communication that appeal to a more even split between men and women,' he says. Through its slate of tournament games, which require registration from players, InfoSpace has been able to track who is playing, and has discovered that its approach has found appeal in markets that gaming often does not reach.

With developers having already proved that mobile phone users will play good games if they are available, the next step is to prove that services can be consistently profitable. This can be a painful, and formidable, process. EA's Mr Florin admits that the company has had 'to learn new ways of distribution, new technologies and find new partners'. Developing The Sims for the console, EA

(Continued)

(Continued)

must prepare its title for just three platforms. But in the mobile world, in which a dozen manufacturers make hundreds of handset models supporting a variety of different operating systems and user interfaces for distribution to dozens of carriers, the number of platforms is legion. And to maximise the market's potential a great many must be catered for. Ms Waits believes that a degree of standardisation is essential. 'Operators, phone manufacturers, publishers and developers need to work together to put some standards together for the industry – in terms of networks, software on the various handsets and across the platforms (wired and wireless) in order for stakeholders to make money,' she says.

The wireless industry has also to prove that substantial numbers of consumers – multiple millions – will repeatedly pay for downloads of games rather than simply sticking to pre-installed titles that most handsets come armed with. Mr Oxby says 3 has learned that consumers need more options than the traditional approach involving paying once and owning the game that has dominated the market. 'What we have done is introduced the concept of rental games in the market. Before we started all games were downloadable and had to be paid for once and that is a natural barrier to the occasional gamer. So we make them available on a rental basis 50p for three days,' he says. 3 found that this approach – allied to a broad range of games aimed at the widest possible audience – has helped it to double downloads.

Mr Riedel believes that the industry must continue to look at inventive payment methods to entice more gamers. He suggests options such as offering gamers an 'all you can eat' option by which they might, for example, buy a 20 dollar pre-pay voucher when they buy their handset. Alternatively he suggests handsets might install a free demonstration version of a game that will entice users to buy the rest once they have tried it.

The industry might face teething problems and a few growing pains, but those involved remain excited at the potential of wireless. 'Consumer expectations in the mobile space will transform expectations in the fixed space,' says Ms Waits. 'And, everything will be connected – fixed and wireless. We can each move from platform to platform seamlessly. At least this is what we hope for in 10 years.'

Questions

1. Based on the discussed definitions of innovation, would you classify mobile games as innovative? Why or why not?
2. Would you classify a mobile game as incremental or radical innovation? Defend your position.
3. Are the concepts of change, creativity and innovation relevant to this particular company? Discuss.

Conclusion

The pace and pattern of change associated with the modern business world and recent developments in communication and information technologies, all highlight the centrality of change, creativity and innovation. However, major transformations are not new: the Industrial Revolution, the growth of towns, cities and commerce and new forms of energy and transportation have been a constant source of change to the way we organize both our work and non-work activities. What is new is the way we now think about business products and services, and the way we organize work and interact with the world around us. E-mail, for example, is now a common form of communication even between those who may work within the same building. Although this is a 'lean' form of communication (Panteli and Dawson, 2001) it increasingly dominates as a central work communication medium. The uptake of this technology has redefined the nature of our working relationships and, some would argue, has led to a reduction in employee performance whilst increasing levels of interpersonal conflict, frustration and the overall workloads of staff. Whether or not such assertions are valid, there is general agreement that change is an integral part of our lived experience of work. Yet, combined with these processes of change there remains a sense of continuity. Most people still drive to work each day, children go to school and people look forward to traditional celebrations and summer holidays. This notion of change and continuity, of the new replacing the old, is well captured in centuries of literary writing. As Shakespeare writes in his play *The Tempest*: 'We are such stuff as dreams are made on, and our little life is rounded with a sleep'. In this final play, Shakespeare mirrors the role of his main character Prospero in orchestrating a process over which he never appears to have full control. There is a vision, but the route becomes far more muddled and unpredictable than it would at first seem. Prospero wants to manage all his characters and get to an end point, but all along the way it does not quite go as planned, unexpected things happen – and this is something of the journey of change in organizations today. Furthering our understanding of change, creativity and innovation and the way that these overlap and interplay over time, is part of the story that we hope to capture in the pages that follow.

This chapter has provided an overview and introduction to the concepts of change, creativity and innovation. We have shown how change is seen as a movement from some present state to some future state of organization; how commentators perceive creativity as the quality of originality in something developed by the human mind, the mental ability to produce such novelty or the actual activity of producing it; and how innovation is generally seen as the process of translating ideas into new products, processes and services. In managing these processes of change, creativity and innovation, there is rarely a clear starting or end point as they continue within a context in which critical junctures (for example, unforeseen world events, new innovative developments and creative ideas) and major planned investments (translation of creative ideas into planned programmes of change) may further influence the speed, nature and direction of these processes over time. As such, the dynamic interface between these concepts can be seen to represent an ongoing interplay in which new forms and outcomes rest within the unfolding tapestry of company futures.

RESOURCES, READINGS AND REFLECTIONS

Chapter questions

1. Do you agree with the main myths that surround creativity in discussing definitional issues? Why or why not?

2. What are the advantages and disadvantages of the different creative process models?

3. Which are the main types of innovations? Identify relevant examples.

4. Summarize the key dimensions of organizational change. Which one do you think is the most important? Why?

5. Which are the main triggers of change?

Hands-on exercise

Students are allocated to small groups and are required to undertake a study by researching one product innovation of their choice (they should investigate a product, which has become a truly outstanding success based on sales and/or industry awards). Student groups are expected to make a brief presentation of their findings based on the following questions:

1. When was the product introduced in the market?

2. What was so innovative about it? Was the concept behind it unique?

3. Did it solve an existing problem? What was it?

4. Was it the first product in its industry? Did the company enjoy the first mover's advantages (strong sales, favourable reputation, etc.)?

Team debate exercise

Debate Ridderstråle and Nordström's (2000: 228, 245) statement:

> *We have to start competing on the basis of feelings and fantasy – emotion and imagination ... To succeed we have to surprise people ... By focussing only on the hardcore aspect of business we risk becoming irrelevant. And trust us, irrelevancy is a much greater problem than inefficiency.*

Divide the class into two groups. One should argue as convincingly as possible that imagination and fantasy are the most important factors to creating and sustaining a company's competitive advantage. The other should prepare arguments against this, highlighting that a focus on the bottom line and profitability will lead to long-term success. Each group should be prepared to defend their ideas against the other group's arguments by using real-life examples.z

References

Aldag, R.J. and Stearns, T.M. (1991) *Management*. Cincinnati, OH: South-Western College.

Amabile, T.M. (1983) 'The social psychology of creativity: A componential conceptualization', *Journal of Personality and Social Psychology*, 45: 357–77.

Amabile, T.M. (1988) 'A model of creativity and innovation in organizations', in B.M. Staw and L.L. Cummings (eds), *Research in Organizational Behavior*, Vol. 10. Stamford, CT: JAI Press. pp. 123–67.

Amabile, T.M. (1996) *Creativity and Innovation in Organizations* (HBS Note 9-396-239). Cambridge, MA: Harvard Business School.

Amabile, T.M., Conti, R., Coon, H., Lazenby, J. and Herron, M. (1996) 'Assessing the work environment for creativity', *Academy of Management Journal*, 39: 1154–84.

Andrews, F.M. (1975) 'Social and psychological factors which influence the creative process', in I.A. Taylor and J.W. Getzels (eds), *Perspectives in Creativity*. Chicago: Aldine.

Basadur, M., Graen, G.B. and Green, S.G. (1982) 'Training in creative problem-solving: effects on ideation and problem finding and solving in an industrial research organization', *Organizational Behavior and Human Performance*, 30: 41–70.

Bate, P. (1994) *Strategies for Cultural Change*. Oxford: Butterworth-Heinemann.

Beckhard, R. and Harris, R.T. (1987) *Organizational Transitions*, 2nd edn. Reading, MA: Addison-Wesley.

Bessant, J. and Tidd, J. (2007) *Innovation and Entrepreneurship*. Chichester: John Wiley.

Bruner, J.S. (1962) *On Knowing; Essays for the Left Hand*. Cambridge, MA: Belknap Press of Harvard University Press.

Buchanan, D. and Badham, R. (1999) 'Politics of organizational change: the lived experience', *Human Relations*, 52: 609–29.

Buchanan, D. and Badham, R. (2008) *Power, Politics, and Organizational Change. Winning the Turf Game*, 2nd edn. London: Sage.

Burke, W. (2002) *Organization Change: Theory and Practice*. London: Sage.

Burnes, B. (2004) *Managing Change: A Strategic Approach to Organizational Dynamics*, 4th edn. Harlow: Financial Times Prentice Hall.

Burns, T. and Stalker, G. (1961) *The Management of Innovation*. London: Tavistock.

Carnall, C. (2007) *Managing Change in Organizations*, 5th edn. Harlow: Financial Times Prentice Hall.

Collins, D. (1998) *Organizational Change: Sociological Perspectives*. London: Routledge.

Cook, P. (1998) 'The creativity advantage – is your organisation the leader of the pack?', *Industrial and Commercial Training*, 30 (5): 179–84.

Damanpour, F. (1991) 'Organisational innovation: a meta-analysis of effects of determinants and moderators', *Academy of Management Journal*, 34: 555–90.

Dawson, P. (2003a) *Understanding Organizational Change: The Contemporary Experience of People at Work*. London: Sage.

Dawson, P. (2003b) *Reshaping Change: A Processual Perspective*. London: Routledge.

Dawson, P. and Palmer, G. (1995) *Quality Management: The Theory and Practice of Implementing Change*. Melbourne: Longman.

Dunphy, D. and Stace, D. (1990) *Under New Management: Australian Organizations in Transition.* Sydney: McGraw-Hill.

Fleck, J. (1991) 'Information-integration and industry – a digest of the development of information-integration: beyond CIM', *PICT Policy Research Papers.* London: ESRC.

Fleck, J., Webster, J. and Williams, R. (1989) 'The dynamics of IT implementation: a reassessment of paradigms and trajectories of development', PICT Working Papers Series No. 14, University of Edinburgh.

Fleck, J., Webster, J. and Williams, R. (1990) 'The dynamics of information technology implementation: a reassessment of paradigms and trajectories of development', *Futures,* (July/August): 22 (6): 618–40.

Galavan, R., Murray, J. and Markides, C. (2008) (eds) *Strategy, Innovation and Change: Challenges for Mangaement.* Oxford: Oxford University Press.

Godenberg, J. and Mazursky, D. (2002) *Creativity in Product Innovation.* Cambridge: Cambridge University Press.

Graetz, F., Rimmer, M., Lawrence, A. and Smith, A. (2002) *Managing Organizational Change.* Queensland: John Wiley & Sons Australia.

Hayes, J. (2002) *The Theory and Practice of Change Management.* Basingstoke: Palgrave.

Henle, M. (1962) 'The birth and death of ideas', in H.E. Gruber, G. Terrell and M. Wertheimer (eds), *Contemporary Approaches to Creative Thinking.* New York: Atherton Press.

Jones, A. (1995) 'TNT – providing customers with solutions to their problems', *Managing Service Quality,* 5 (6): 13–17.

Kao, J.J. (1989) *Entrepreneurship, Creativity and Organization: Text, Cases and Readings.* Englewood Cliffs, NJ: Prentice Hall.

King, S. (1995) 'Managing creativity and learning', *Management Development Review,* 8 (5): 32–4.

Koestler, A. (1964) *The Act of Creation.* London: Hutchinson.

Leavitt, H.J. (1964) 'Applied organizational change in industry: structural, technical and human approaches', in W.W. Cooper, H.J. Leavitt, and M.W. Shelly (eds) *New Perspectives in Organizations Research.* New York: John Wiley.

Locke, E.A. and Kirkpatrick, S.A. (1995) 'Promoting creativity in organisations', in C.M. Ford and D.A. Gioia (eds), *Creative Action in Organisations: Ivory Tower Visions & Real World Voices.* Thousand Oaks, CA: Sage.

Mednick, S.A. (1962) 'The associative basis of the creative process', *Psychological Review,* 69: 220–32.

Newell, A., Shaw, J.C. and Simon, H.A. (1962) 'The process of creative thinking', in H.E., Gruber, G. Terrell and M. Wertheimer (eds), *Contemporary Approaches to Creative Thinking.* New York: Atherton Press.

Newman, K. (2000) 'Organizational transformation during institutional upheaval', *Academy of Management Review,* 35: 602–19.

Nyström, H. (1979) *Creativity and Innovation.* Chichester: John Wiley.

Oldham, G.R. and Cummings, A. (1996) 'Employee creativity: personal and contextual factors at work', *Academy of Management Journal,* 39: 607–34.

Palmer, I., Dunford, R. and Akin, G. (2006) *Managing Organizational Change: A Multiple Perspective Approach.* New York: McGraw-Hill/Irwin.

Panteli, A. and Dawson, P. (2001) 'Video conferencing systems: changing patterns of business communication', *New Technology, Work and Employment,* 16 (2): 88–99.

Persing, D.L. (1999) 'Managing in polychronic times', *Journal of Managerial Psychology,* 14: 358–73.

Pettigrew, A. (2003) 'Innovative forms of organizing: progress, performance and process', in A. Pettigrew, R. Whittington, L. Melin, C. Sanchez-Runde, F. van den Bosch, W. Ruigrok and T. Numagami (eds), *Innovative Forms of Organizing.* London: Sage. pp. 331–51.

Placone, R. (1989) 'Debunking the creativity myths', *Bank Systems and Technology*, 26 (11): 60–2.

Poole, M. and Van de Ven, A. (eds) (2004) *Handbook of Organizational Change and Innovation*. New York: Oxford University Press.

Quinn, J. (1980) *Strategies for Change: Logical Incrementalism*. Homewood, IL: Irwin.

Ridderstråle, J. and Nordström, K. (2000) *Funky Business*. Stockholm: Bookhouse Publishing AB.

Rogers, E. (1995) *Diffusion of Innovations*, 4th edn. New York: The Free Press.

Schumpeter, J.A. (1934) *The Theory of Economic Development*. Cambridge, MA: Harvard University Press.

Schumpeter, J.A. (1939) *Business Cycles: A Theoretical, Historical, and Statistical Analysis of the Capitalist Process*. New York: McGraw-Hill.

Senior, B. (2002) *Organizational Change*, 2nd edn. London: Pitman.

Senior, B. and Fleming, J. (2005) *Organizational Change*, 3rd edn. London: Financial Times Prentice Hall.

Smith, A. (1998) *Oxford World's Classics: Adam Smith, The Wealth of Nations*. Oxford: Oxford University Press.

Smith, G.S. and Reinertsen, D.G. (2004) 'Shortening the product development cycle', in R. Katz (ed.), *The Human Side of Managing Technological Innovation*. New York: Oxford University Press.

Taylor, F. (1911) *The Principles of Scientific Management*. New York: Harper.

Torrance, E.P. (1966) *The Torrance Tests of Creative Thinking: Norms-Technical Manual*. Lexington, MA: Personnel Press.

Tushman, M.L. and O'Reilly, C. (2002) *Winning through Innovation: A Practical Guide to Leading Organizational Change and Renewal*. Cambridge, MA: Harvard Business School Press.

Tushman, M. and Anderson, P. (2004) (eds) *Managing Strategic Innovation and Change: A Collection of Readings*, 2nd edn. New York: Oxford University Press.

Vernon, P.E. (1989) 'The nature–nurture problem in creativity', in J.A. Glover, R.R. Ronning and C.R. Reynolds (eds), *Handbook of Creativity*. New York: Plenum Press.

Wallas, G. (1926) *The Art of Thought*. London: Cape.

Weick, K. (1979) *The Social Psychology of Organizing*. Reading, MA: Addison-Wesley.

Whitfield, R.R. (1975) *Creativity in Industry*. Harmondsworth: Penguin Books.

Woodman, R.W. (1995) 'Managing creativity', in C.M. Ford and D.A. Gioia (eds), *Creative Action in Organisations: Ivory Tower Visions & Real World Voices*. Thousand Oaks, CA: Sage.

Woodman, R.W., Sawyer, J.E. and Griffin, R.W. (1993) 'Toward a theory of organisational creativity', *Academy of Management Review*, 18: 293–321.

Zuboff, S. (1988) *In the Age of the Smart Machine*. New York: Heinemann.

Recommended reading

Change and innovation

- Poole, M. and Van de Ven, A. (eds) (2004) *Handbook of Organizational Change and Innovation*. New York: Oxford University Press.

- Senior, B. and Fleming, J. (2005) *Organizational Change*, 3rd edn. London: Financial Times Prentice Hall.

- Tushman, M. and Anderson, P. (eds) (2004) *Managing Strategic Innovation and Change: A Collection of Readings*, 2nd edn. Oxford: Oxford University Press.

Creativity and innovation

- Amabile, T.M. (1989) *Growing Up Creative.* New York: Crown Publishing Group, Inc.

- Kaufman, J.C. and Baer, J. (2005) *Creativity across Domains: Faces of the Muse.* Mahwah, NJ: Lawrence Erlbaum.

- Watkins, M. (2003) *Managing Creativity and Innovation.* Boston, MA: Harvard University Business Press.

Some useful websites

Please note: the websites listed at the end of Chapter 1 are also relevant here.

Change

- The Division of the Organization Development and Change website of the Academy of Management is a useful source of reference material and academic activities (http://division.aomonline.org/odc/).

Creativity

- This website has lots of links to interesting tools and techniques, articles and other information relevant to creativity (http://www.creativeideas.org.uk).

Innovation

- Professor Christensen's website is designed to help organizations become more innovative with resources such as articles, research papers, etc. (http://www.innosight.com).

3

An Historical Overview of Business Practice and Theory Development

---

Learning objectives

This chapter provides an historical backcloth on developments in business practice and organization theory. The Industrial Revolution – as a seedbed for change, creativity and innovation – is used as our starting point in a rather quick Cook's tour of business practice and theory development. Owing to the breadth of material, we have been selective in focusing our attention on the main topic concerns of this text. The three key learning objectives of the chapter are:

1. To provide an historical overview of practical management concerns and the way that these relate to developments in management theory. The aim is to provide an historical contextual map that facilitates some broader thinking as students progress through the main chapters of this book.

2. To identify and summarize key links between historical and contextual concerns and the formulation of new theories and concepts. Our intention is to reflect on how these relate to our thinking about change, creativity and innovation.

(Continued)

(Continued)

3. To provide a critical analysis of some more recent areas of concern, such as the process of managing innovation and change in competitive environments, understanding the relationship between the technical and social dynamics in creative and innovative processes, and making sense of recent developments in theories that seek to explain business innovation.

Introduction

The main aim of this chapter is to provide a broad historical context in which current concerns and ideas can be assessed and understood in the light of previous business developments and academic debates. We also seek to clarify the interplay between theories and practice which we view as intertwined and ongoing rather than as distinct and separate bodies of knowledge.

Over the last 50 years the number of books, studies, video presentations and articles on innovation and change has grown significantly, with a greater concern on creativity and the creative organization emerging over the last two decades. Interest in these areas is not new, however, and dates back to early concerns about how best to manage and get the most out of employees at work. With the growing volume of research into organizations many might assume that we should now be well equipped to tackle a vast array of management issues. But is there a sound and deep knowledge base to help guide our organizations through the turbulent landscape of change? Do we fully understand the nature of creativity and processes of innovation? In addressing these questions, we will briefly overview the development of some key management theories within the context of wider societal change and innovations at work (see also Tidd et al., 2001). Our intention is to map out a fairly broad historical terrain in charting the development of our theoretical knowledge, whilst also considering the implications of this for understanding change, creativity and innovation.

The British Industrial Revolution

The British Industrial Revolution (*c.* 1730–1850) provides us with a useful starting point, as it is during this period that new management problems emerged following the rapid expansion of the newly industrialized towns and the rise in factory organization. As people moved off the land into the growing urban centres around Glasgow, Manchester and Newcastle, new forms of industrial organization developed. The rise in commerce and the opening of markets combined with innovations in the use and application of technology. The railways provided the necessary infrastructure for the comparatively rapid transportation of goods and people to further stimulate economic growth and new business activities. The steam engine that powered the locomotives revolutionized the textile industry and heralded an era of mass production in which goods, previously the preserve of the rich, became affordable to a new consumption-oriented middle class. Mechanization of tasks previously carried out by skilled craftsmen and women marked a radical departure from old ways of working (as illustrated in the textile industry with the introduction of Hargreave's spinning-jenny). In the early cotton, flax and woollen mills machine accidents and industrial diseases were commonplace through poor working conditions, fatigue and ill treatment (Henriques, 1979: 76). Within the factories of this new industrial era the transformation of raw materials into products was largely accomplished by machines rather than by the hands of the skilled worker.

These innovations did not represent the outcome of rapid technological advance, but rather resulted from the bringing together of knowledge, skills and ideas that had been around for decades and even centuries, in new, creative and innovative ways. For example, the development of the steam engine drew on the knowledge of control mechanisms long associated with the craft of creating accurate mechanical time pieces (clocks and watches), the boiler expertise from the brewing industry and the piston technology associated with military cannons. It was in combining these previously discrete forms of knowledge and expertise that marked a radical innovation that was instrumental in moving Britain from a primarily agricultural to an industrial nation. Throughout this period, there was a complex ongoing interplay between socio-political, technological and economic factors in the design, development and introduction of new forms of work organization. The use of steam power to drive machinery was utilized in new forms of transportation that were in turn supported by the abundance of rich mineral resources, especially coal and iron ore. The development of railways, the construction of bridges and tunnels and the building of steam-powered ships, were all part of the new Industrial Revolution that swept across Britain and stimulated international trade. In its wake came a new breed of creative entrepreneur who grappled with the problem of how best to manage their new commercial enterprises.

Industrial organization and the co-ordination and control of work

For the new entrepreneurs and factory owners, the question on how best to co-ordinate and control the work of labour became a central issue. Their objective of profitability drew their attention to systems that would ensure that workers produced commodities that provided them with a good financial return. Employers were interested in forms of work organization that would ensure that workers' capacity to work was transformed into actual work, and that the value of the work created by employees exceeded the wages paid out for their labour. On this count, it was Taylor's (1911) principles of scientific management that provided a blueprint on how best to organize work. His main focus rested on the development of new forms of organizing that improved profitability for the employer and simultaneously increased the take-home earnings of employees. He advocated that the systematic study of work tasks by what he termed 'first-class' workers, would provide information that could be used to design work systems to ensure that employees worked to their full capacity. For Taylor, the main problem centred on setting an acceptable work standard by getting agreement between employers and employees on what constitutes a 'fair day's work'; and then to design and implement a system of motivation that would prevent 'soldiering' (what he deemed as a tendency for employees to take it easy and avoid work).

Born in America (1856, died 1917) as part of an affluent Philadelphian family, Taylor developed a five-step process for the co-ordination and control of work that rested on:

1. Identifying 10–15 of the most productive workers.

2. Studying their work behaviours and, in particular, their methods of working and their use of implements in carrying out tasks.

3. Timing the movements made in the completion of tasks in order to identify and select the most efficient methods for carrying out tasks.

4. Designing a work system that is streamlined in ensuring that all unnecessary movements are eliminated.

5. Equipping employees with the best implements to carry out a prescribed set of movements in the accomplishment of clearly defined work tasks.

It was the job of management to select and train employees, to provide good working conditions and equipment, and to determine the most appropriate methods of work through the systematic analysis of job tasks. A clear standard of work performance should be set and any employee not meeting that standard should be financially penalized. The differential piece-rate system proposed by Taylor comprised: setting a low rate up to a set standard (based on time-and-motion studies), after which a bonus would be payable on reaching the standard with a higher rate payable above that set standard. His work culminated in a set of principles of scientific management that promoted the replacement of guesswork and rules of thumb with a more scientific approach to the organization and control of work. His aim was to enable each employee to reach their highest level of efficiency that would not only maximize output and increase productivity but also enable employees to benefit from higher levels of pay (advocating a 30–100 per cent increase in pay for a two-to-fourfold increase in productivity).

Taylor promoted these ideas by embarking on a consultancy career and in the publication of *A Piece Rate System* in 1895, *Shop Management* in 1903, and his most famous book *The Principles of Scientific Management* in 1911 that was serialized in *The American Magazine*. Through employing his methods in the Manufacturing Investment Company (in which he invested $45,000 of his own money), he demonstrated how the introduction of a differential piece-rate system reduced labour costs and led to a threefold increase in output. His work in the Bethlehem Iron Company and the Ball-Bearing Company was used to further illustrate the benefits of this approach; for example, the Ball-Bearing case was used to show how 35 employees – following the application of scientific management techniques to the redesign of work – could achieve work previously done by 120.

This change and innovation in the way work is organized replaced 'rule-of-thumb' methods with standard rates of output fixed to set financial rewards. It assumed that workers would, given the opportunity, restrict output – work-avoidance strategies that Taylor referred to as 'systematic soldiering' – and thus sought to control and regulate work behaviour through an individual reward system that promoted economic self-interest (Knights and McCabe, 2003: 13). However, the approach over-emphasized the economic orientation of industrial workers and, as a consequence, failed to recognize the importance of *non-monetary incentives*, especially following economic growth and the movement away from subsistence levels of income among the working population. Nevertheless, various elements of scientific management remain influential in the organization and design of work (see, for example, Graetz et al., 2002: 89–94; Littler, 1982), particularly in the development and use of continuous-flow assembly lines in the automotive industry (Walker and Guest, 1952).

The continuous-flow assembly line refers to the industrial arrangement of machines, equipment and workers that allows for the continuous flow of work-pieces along an assembly line in the mass manufacture of products. All movement of material is simplified, with no cross-flow or backtracking, and the worker remains in position on the line carrying out a simplified set of repetitive tasks. By 1913–14, Ford's new plant in Highland Park, Michigan, was able to deliver parts, sub-assemblies and assemblies (themselves built on subsidiary assembly lines) with precise timing to a constantly moving main assembly line, where a complete chassis was turned out every 93 minutes. With the mass production of his Model T, Henry Ford demonstrated how this method of large-scale manufacture could be used to produce goods previously unavailable, too costly and simply unimaginable to the average working family. During this period, wages increased and markets multiplied with the mass production of standardized affordable goods, as Clutterbuck and Crainer (1990: 32–3) note:

> *Mass production, Ford rightly perceived, was the key to achieving uniform products. He believed in providing the market with what it wanted – an affordable practical car ... In 1914 Ford promised that if people bought more than 300,000 Model Ts he'd return $50 to every purchaser. Sales hit 308,000 and Ford distributed $15 million.*

Throughout the 20th century the manufacture of automobiles has been a key industry that has served as a leading example of technological advancement, innovation and change. Touraine's (1955) study of Renault and the American study by Walker and Guest (1952), all drew attention to employee experience of working under automotive assembly-line production. For Blauner (1964), job fragmentation and the simplification of tasks resultant of technological progress could be linked to worker alienation. He investigated four industries which represented different levels of technological sophistication; these were: printing, cotton-spinning, motor cars and petrochemicals. He found that under traditional craft-style industries work retained social meaning, while under mass production (the automotive assembly line) jobs became meaningless and employees felt increasingly isolated, self-estranged and powerless (alienated) from the work they were performing. This concern with the human side of work resulted in the development of theories and intervention programmes that were aimed at tackling this growing problem of worker alienation and motivation.

Change and the human aspects of work

After the Second World War, with the growth in size of the industrial enterprise, economic prosperity and unionization, the 'problem' of dissatisfaction, alienation and industrial unrest became an organizational concern. Essentially it was argued that with the advent of relatively full employment since the late 1940s, people were able to find employment and switch jobs (the job mobility of labour increased) and consequently workers felt less compelled to submit to the authority of management (Roethlisberger, 1945: 283–98). Changes in the functional organization of work, and the substantial growth in the collective organization of employees and the power of the shop steward, had shifted attention towards leadership and the management of human relations. The classic study by Roethlisberger and Dickson (1950) into the Western Electric Company, Hawthorne Works in Chicago, is well documented in the organizational behaviour texts (see, for example, Huczynski and Buchanan, 2006). Their studies were used to show the benefits of 'democratic' leadership which encouraged employee participation in decision making. The importance of consulting and listening to employees prior to embarking on change and the need to provide open and accurate information, are central tenets to this approach. In viewing industrial organization as a complex social system, the study draws attention to technical innovations and the problems of employee resistance:

> *Distrust and resistance to change ... was expressed whenever changes were introduced too rapidly or without sufficient consideration of their social implications; in other words, whenever the workers were being asked to adjust themselves to new methods or systems which seemed to them to deprive their work of its customary social significance. In such situations it was evident that the social codes, customs, and routines of the workers could not be accommodated to the technical innovations introduced as quickly as the innovations themselves, in the form of new machines and processes, could be made ... Not only is any alteration of the existing social organization to which the worker has grown accustomed likely to produce sentiments of resistance to the change, but too rapid interference is likely to lead to feelings of frustration and an irrational exasperation with technical change in any form. (Roethlisberger and Dickson, 1950: 567–8)*

The social context of change and the meanings that employees attach to their work remain an important area of concern (see McCabe, 2007) and yet, following this piece of research, attention switched from more sociological concerns (social relationships and meanings) towards a barrage of psychological studies that examined job satisfaction, motivation and leadership. Knights and McCabe (2003: 19) argue that the Hawthorne studies provided fertile ground for the development of 'management innovation based on a neo-behaviourist model' and that the 'Hawthorne understanding of worker subjectivity was much more complex than the conceptualisations that flowed from those in the new-human relations' school' that was to dominate thinking in North America. Within Europe, the influence of human relations is evident in the work carried out by the Tavistock Institute of Human Relations that was established in post-war Britain. Over the years, this consulting and research organization has produced a considerable body of research on the design of work structures.

Sleepers wake: the spectre of technology and innovation

During the 1940s and 1950s, the Tavistock Institute in the UK embarked on a series of studies into technology and innovation at work. They were concerned with improving the social aspects of working environments whilst at the same time accommodating the use of advanced technologies in the production of goods and services. In reporting on a study into the long-wall method of coal mining, Trist and Bamforth (1951: 37) conclude that:

> *The fact that the desperate economic incentives of the between-war period no longer operate means a greater intolerance of unsatisfying or difficult working conditions, or systems of organization, among miners, even though they may not always be clear as to the exact nature of the resentment or hostility which they often appear to feel. The persistence of socially ineffective structures at the coalface is likely to be a major factor in preventing a rise of morale, in discouraging recruitment, and in increasing labour turnover.*

They discovered that the long-wall method of production (through the use of technology in the form of mechanization) was not securing the economic benefits anticipated. On the basis of some of their early results (monitoring factors, such as output, absenteeism and turnover), Trist and Bamforth set out to test two hypotheses: first, that output shortfall was essentially a technical problem associated with innovation and, second, that it was the social shortcomings of the long-wall method of coal mining that was restricting output. In testing these hypotheses Trist and Bamforth note that prior to mechanization the *technical* process of coal-getting had the following cycle of stages:

- *Preparation*: coal cut by hand or undercut and blown down into cleared space.

- *Getting*: coal loaded for removal to surface.

- *Advancing*: roof supports, etc., moved forward.

The form of work organization – the *social* aspect of coal-getting – that accompanied this process was termed 'composite work organization'. Here one or two self-selected miners worked under their own supervision with picks at the face (up to 11 yards in length) doing all the tasks necessary for each cycle. Both miners were paid on the one 'pay note'. However, with mechanization – which involved the use of pneumatic drills and electrical coal cutters to replace picks and the use of conveyor belts to remove coal from the face – a new technical process of coal-getting process emerged known as the 'long-wall method'. This enabled the length of face that could be worked at any one time to be increased (80–100 metres, hence the term long-wall). Under this method, a new form of work organization was adopted where the tasks involved in each cycle were broken down to constitute the work of separate shifts. In addition, miners were subjected to close supervision in order to ensure appropriate co-ordination of each stage in the cycle of operations.

From their analysis, the Tavistock researchers argued that there was a misalignment between the technical and social aspects of work. This had resulted in a divisive payment system and an over-specialization of work tasks. This in turn caused sectional bargaining and competition between shifts, supervisory friction and the need for management to continually negotiate separate wage agreements. These findings were further supported by an examination of an alternative social system that had emerged elsewhere. This modified version – that had been recommended by Lodge, the Union of Miners – was found to be far more productive than long-wall methods. The coal-mining operation in Durham involved 'composite working' on 'short walls' by a team of around 40 self-selected miners who carried out all the tasks necessary for the production cycle. Each shift picked up where the other shift left off, then allocated tasks accordingly and operated a single wage agreement.

The existence of another form of *social system* in combination with a similar *technical system* led the Tavistock researchers to argue that whilst the nature of production technology did not directly determine the form of work organization, some forms of work organization provided a 'better fit' than others. In this case the socio-technical system that produced the best fit was where composite working was adopted since this was more likely to lead to higher productivity than forms of work organization that broke work down into specialized tasks and subjected employees to direct forms of supervision.

On the basis of these studies, it was argued that change initiatives which focus on either the purely technical or social aspects of work are likely to have limited 'success' as they create a situation where the whole is sub-optimized for developments in one dimension. In Sweden, for example, the success of the work redesign programme at their Kalmar plant in the 1970s provided a practical example of Social Technical Systems (STS) theory, which was further supported by Uddevalla in the 1980s (prior to their displacement in the 1990s). Since these early achievements, one major criticism of the STS approach has been that whilst it purports to view organizations as organic open systems, key proponents of this approach have tended to look inwards and have consequently ignored the external business market environment. In spite of these criticisms, activity has continued in this area and with the growing uptake of team-based manufacturing, many of these original STS ideas have been further developed (Willcocks and Mason, 1987).

In Australia, the work of Richard Badham has rekindled interest in modern socio-technical approaches through claiming that it is not only necessary to address the interdependent and interpenetrating nature of the technical and the social, but also the change process through which these elements are reconfigured (Badham, 1995: 81). He forwards a configurational process model where technology is viewed as malleable and socially shaped. Under this model, there are technological configurations (the technical and non-human elements), operator configurations (the social and human elements of work), and configurational entrepreneurs (people involved in the change process) who configure emerging forms through championing certain developments and/or obstructing others. Unlike the traditional STS approach, Badham forwards a more contextual and negotiated model in which individuals and groups may shape processes and outcomes of change (Badham, 1995). This shift in emphasis moves attention from a concern with resolving the tensions between human needs and the technical system of operation, towards the contextual process by which these systems come to be designed, implemented and used. However, this perspective maintains a prescriptive intent and action agenda towards both understanding and managing the process in a particular direction (in this the researcher becomes an active change agent and consultant). In this focus, there can be a tendency towards less theoretical and more prescriptive models, which may mask a more rigorous analysis of the contextual shaping process and limit theoretical insight (Knights and Murray, 1994: 12).

Fit for purpose: the rise of contingency theory

A theory that has sought to look beyond the organization in accommodating the need for companies to adapt to changing business environments is the contingency approach. Originating in the 1960s from the classical studies of Burns and Stalker (1961), Lawrence and Lorsch (1967) and Thompson (1967), this influential approach advocates that the best way to organize depends on the circumstances. The basic theoretical tenet is that, whilst there is no one best way of organizing, it is possible to identify the most appropriate organizational form to fit the context in which a business has to operate (Wood, 1979: 335). Regaining strategic fit with the arrival of a new organizational order is the emphasis of a number of contingency models for managing innovation and change. The contingent factors which are deemed to be of primary significance include either single variables, such as technology (Perrow, 1970; Thompson, 1967; Woodward, 1980), or the environment (Burns and Stalker, 1961; Lawrence and Lorsch, 1967), or a range of variables, such as in the ambitious study (Pugh and Hickson, 1976) which examined the relationship between contextual factors and structural variables (for a critique see Wood, 1979).

A seminal study carried out by Joan Woodward and her team identified 11 different types of production system (technology) that are used by organizations. She grouped these into three main categories, namely: unit and small-batch production systems; large-batch and mass-production systems; and automated continuous-process production systems. Woodward discovered that commercially successful organizations using these production systems tended to have adopted a particular kind of organization structure (she found that successful firms in each technical category had structural characteristics near the average for the category as a whole). She argued that the more technically advanced firms found within the process industry tend to exhibit more harmonious and collaborative systems of employee relations, and that these relations were likely to characterize organizations of the future (Woodward, 1980: 233).

In analysing production systems, Woodward utilizes Robert Dubin's (1959) distinction between, first, the tools, instruments and machines of manufacture (the 'tool' level); and, second, the body of ideas which provide the rationale for the work methods employed and supports the managerial function (the 'control' level) (Woodward, 1980: 248). This led her to further develop her work through the construction of fourfold typology of management control systems, which can be located along two continua. First, the degree to which management control systems were integrated or fragmented; that is, the degree to which control was centralized or spread out across several divisions or departments. Second, the extent to which management control systems were human (personal) or machine-based (mechanical); that is, the degree to which control over employees was exercised directly by supervisors and managers or built into the production itself.

From her studies, Woodward found a strong statistical correlation between the type of production system, type of management control system and commercial success. She concluded that the firms that were most successful were those that adapted their management control system to suit their production system. As such, unit or small-batch production systems were best suited by an integrated personal control system. For example, a small business producing single or small runs of products where an owner-manager would control all aspects, functions and employees. Large-batch or mass-production systems were best suited to fragmented control systems of a personal or mechanical type. For example, the larger organization where management functions are distributed across departments and where employees are controlled by direct supervision or machines. Finally, process production systems were best suited to integrated mechanical control systems. For example, organizations such as oil refineries where management functions are highly centralized and employees highly skilled.

Woodward noted how these more advanced forms of organization were likely to exhibit the following characteristics:

- *Automated tasks:* key operations, such as the transforming of raw materials, would be incorporated into the system of production. The work tasks of operators would therefore largely centre on monitoring and preventive maintenance in ensuring the smooth and continual operations of production.

- *Multi-skilled workers:* flexible and multi-skilled work teams would be best suited to carrying out work tasks; for example, in control room operations or as maintenance crews. Moreover, these teams would be self-supervising since the key managerial decisions which might require direct management control – such as what work to do, when to do it, how fast to work – are in effect 'built-in' to the system of production.

- *Harmonious employee relations:* the absence of direct supervision of the workforce eliminates a major source of industrial conflict (visible managerial authority), and in situations where employee contributions are valued, industrial relations are likely to be far more harmonious.

These studies highlight how structural adjustment should be contingency driven. They claim that a change in organizational circumstance (business market or production system) is likely to cause an imbalance reducing performance and signalling the need for an adjustment of organizational form in order to restore effectiveness. The emphasis that contingency models place on strategies for gaining an effective fit between organizational structure and functional performance has been criticized in the literature (see McLoughlin and Clark, 1994). For example, Child (1972) questions the contingency-based concept of environment that ignores the role of companies in moulding the views of politicians, influencing legislation and actively shaping the business environment in which they operate, whereas Woodward's use of the concept of technology has been criticized for being 'technological determinist' and downplaying the significance of contextual and social factors (MacKenzie and Wajcman, 1985). In short, contingency theories have been criticized for underplaying choice and failing to account for differences between participants through their focus on the technical problem of matching situations to organizational form (see also Aldrich, 2008: 19–24; Child, 1988: 13–18; Clegg, 1988: 7–12; Karpik, 1988: 25–8).

In search of excellence: recipes for success

In conjunction with the persistence of new forms of scientific management, human relations, socio-technical systems and contingency approaches to innovation and change, a range of consultant-led approaches to managing these processes have also been developed. Following the publication of Peters and Waterman's (1982) best-selling book *In Search of Excellence: Lessons from America's Best-Run Companies*, there has followed a whole plethora of recipe books on how to successfully manage change. Some of the more popular publications have been written by what Huczynski (1993) terms the 'management gurus' and 'celebrity professors' – such as Handy (1984, 1994, 1996, 1999), Kanter (1985, 1990), Kotter (1995, 1996, 2002) and Peters (1989, 1993, 1997) – as well as those associated with particular movements, such as Crosby (1980), Deming (1981) and Juran (1988) with Quality Management, and Shonberger (1982) with Just-In-Time (JIT). Although it is not possible to detail all these developments here, it is worth drawing out some of the main themes and approaches that have been promoted by some of the more popular management gurus.

The book by Peters and Waterman was a landmark publication in capturing the imagination of American managers who were quick to digest proposals that offered a Western route to competitive success, particularly in the light of articles in the *Harvard Business Review* during the 1970s which drew attention to the productivity gap between American and Japanese workers (see Burnes, 2000: 75–81) and the success of Japanese manufacturing in the uptake of JIT techniques and quality management (Mitroff and Mohrman, 1987). In using the well-known McKinsey Seven S Framework (strategy, structure, systems, staff, style, shared values, and skills), the authors argued against too much analysis and planning (although recognizing that there is the need for some planning) as this can serve simply to block action. They identified eight major determinants of organizational excellence, namely that:

1. Organizations should have a bias for action through encouraging innovation and through active response to problem situations.

2. Organizations should develop closer relationships with their customers.

3. Organizations should foster and support the entrepreneurial spirit among their staff and aim to increase the level of responsible autonomy among their employees.

4. Employees should be treated with respect and dignity in order to ensure productivity through people.

5. All employees should be driven by the values of the organization.

6. Companies should do what they know best and should restrict diversification.

7. Flat organization structures and slimmed-down bureaucracies enable greater flexibility and provide for more rapid communication.

8. Simultaneous loose-tight properties should be established through high levels of self-supervision and the development of a common cohesive organizational culture.

As Peters and Waterman conclude: 'We find that autonomy is a product of discipline. The discipline (a few shared values) provides the framework. It gives people confidence (to experiment, for instance) stemming from stable expectations about what really counts' (1982: 322).

This work, in putting forward a simple recipe for achieving organizational excellence, has proven to be very influential in spite of it being viewed as a poor piece of research (Collins, 1998; Guest, 1992). Guest provides a damning critique of this study at both a conceptual and methodological level. Methodologically, the selection of excellent companies is questioned as being little more than an ad hoc grouping of senior executives and journalists and, conceptually, it is criticized for assuming that managers can control their own destiny without due regard to various business market and contextual influences (Guest, 1992). Collins (1998: 45) also points out how a number of these companies have since 'fallen from grace' and that it is unclear, 'whether what Peters and Waterman have trumpeted as excellence in management, leading to business success, might more usefully be considered as business success built upon such features as geographic advantage, trade protection, or any one of dozens of environmental and contextual factors'.

During the 1990s, the codified blueprints for implementing particular techniques, such as World Class Manufacturing, TQM and Best Practice

Management, largely replaced the broader 'excellence-recipes' of the 1980s. But once again, the complexities of managing large-scale transitions that incorporate cultural as well as structural change are largely downplayed. It would seem that the lessons of the past are forgotten under the dazzling banners of new methods and techniques for organizational success. For example, Tom Peters continued to promote actions for success in books, such as *Thriving on Chaos* (1989), *Liberation Management* (1993) and *The Circle of Innovation* (1997). A theme running through this and much of the guru management literature is the need for managers to act as leaders of change and to be proactive in the search for strategies that will make organizations more competitive (Ulrich and Lake, 1991: 77–92; Vesey, 1991: 23–33). A central premise is that companies that are unable to manage ongoing change will cease to exist (Gray and Smeltzer, 1990: 615–16; Peters, 1989). Typically, what is advocated is a revolution in the world of management, through the adoption of policies which discard traditional hierarchical structures, rigid bureaucratic systems and inflexible work practices (Dunphy and Stace, 1990: 11–12). For example, Rosabeth Moss Kanter, in her popular book *When Giants Learn to Dance*, claims that competitive corporations of the future must develop a strategic business action agenda towards 'flatter, more focused organizations stressing synergies; entrepreneurial enclaves pushing new stream businesses for the future; and strategic alliances or stakeholder partnerships stretching capacity by combining the strength of several organizations' (1990: 344).

The new bias for organizational action rests with an emergent breed of manager whose job involves successfully managing strategic change in work structures, process and product technologies, employment relations and organizational culture. These managers are expected to compete in the new 'corporate olympics' and balance the apparent contradictions between, first, centralizing resources whilst creating autonomous business units and, second, replacing staff through 'lean' restructuring programmes yet maintaining employee-centred personnel policies (Kanter, 1990: 17–31). According to Kanter, the seven managerial skills required of these new business athletes comprise: an ability to achieve results without relying on organizational status; to be self-confident and humble; to maintain high ethical standards; to attain co-operative competitiveness; to gain satisfaction from results rather than financial rewards; to be able to work across functions and find new synergies; and the need to be aware of the process, as well as the outcomes, of change (1990: 359–65).

The intention behind the listing of managerial competencies is to help managers become 'masters' rather than 'victims' of change. However, due to an overreliance on metaphors, Kanter presents little of any real use to the discerning manager. As Gabor and Petersen (1991: 98) note: 'clichés and banalities depicted by chapter headings ... detracts measurably from Ms Kanter's fervent and sincere hope that America's business community will be energised to change direction to compete and succeed in the current and future global business climate'.

The call for action is also evident in the work of John Kotter (1995, 1996) who provides a recipe for successful change and suggests that failure to be proactive is likely to result in business failure. He claims (1995) that it is important to push people out of their comfort zones in promoting the significance of change and that it is often complacency and a fear of the future which inhibits successful company transformation. As Kotter states:

> *A strategy of embracing the past will probably become increasingly ineffective over the next few decades. Better for most of us to start learning now how to cope with change, to develop whatever leadership potential we have, and to help our organizations in the transformation process. Better for most of us, despite the risks, to leap into the future. And to do so sooner rather than later. (1996: 185–6)*

From identifying eight major reasons why transformation efforts fail, Kotter (1996) then turns this around and offers eight key steps to ensuring successful change (this is discussed further in Chapter 7). These involve: establishing a sense of urgency, forming a powerful guiding coalition, creating a vision, communicating that vision, empowering others to act on the vision, planning and creating short-term wins, consolidating change improvements, and institutionalizing the new approach. Kotter uses this eight-step model to 'successful' change in a fable about a penguin colony with Rathgeber (2006), where the essential message is how to succeed under conditions of change. For Kotter (1996), successful change is marked by a clear vision which is relentlessly communicated to everyone, people are rewarded throughout the change process, any change obstacles are removed, and change outcomes are anchored into the corporation's culture. The focus is on embracing the future rather than living on past success. Similarly, Hamel and Prahalad (1994) argue that the downfall of companies can often arise from the unsupported belief by senior management that past strategies (which proved successful) can and should be sustained into the future. They suggest that the seeds of company failure are often sown during the years of company success and point out that the top companies today are often not those who were the top companies 10 or 20 years ago. Two key elements that they identify in competing for the future are: first, the counter-intuitive claim that the need for continuity is embedded in change. In other words, that due to the ongoing nature of change (regulatory change, product and competitor change, and so forth) continuity of the company will necessitate change. Second, that companies require foresight to influence the future world of business. This may be through creating new markets, services or products, or simply by changing the rules of the game (Hamel and Prahalad, 1994). For these authors, it is the creation of new ideas, their development and use, and the ongoing management of innovation and change that are all central to business success.

In looking towards the future, all these commentators emphasize the need to question cherished assumptions and to critically reflect on the way things are currently done. As Nordström and Ridderstråle (2001: 245) suggest, irrelevancy may become a much greater problem than inefficiency and signal the need to break away from the straitjacket of traditional ways of thinking. They highlight the place of imagination and emotion, and stress the importance of knowledge. These authors also draw attention to the need for creativity, innovation and change in securing competitive survival and highlight how our assumptions based on past experience may limit our vision of the future (Nordström and Ridderstråle, 2001, 2004).

Academic critique and guru influence: making sense of a changing world

Jackson (2001: 178–9) argues that in turbulent times organizations will search out new ideas in order to survive and that the guru literature has significantly influenced the uptake of new management initiatives. He identifies four main approaches to explaining the rise of the management guru and their influence on the widespread adoption of new business innovations. The first of these is the *rational approach* where the new ideas put forward by the guru closely align with the needs of managers, as in the arrival of Peters and Waterman's (1982) *In Search of Excellence* that provided simple answers and a positive message for corporate America (Freeman, 1985: 348). The second is a *structural approach* where the new ideas are seen to serve the political socio-economic context of the time, as characterized by a renewed interest in entrepreneurial values in the Reagan (US) and Thatcher (UK) era (Jackson, 2001: 25–6). The third draws on institutional theory (Powell and DiMaggio, 1991) and is labelled as the *institutional/ distancing approach* (see also Burgoyne and Jackson, 1997). This approach posits that during times of uncertainty there can be a tendency for organizations to imitate others due to pressure either from 'institutional' (not wanting to appear different) or 'competitive' (not wanting to lose market position) elements, and that both pressures 'can prove to be highly persuasive, generating strong mimetic behaviour and creating isomorphic tendencies within and across specific institutional fields' (Jackson, 2001: 27). The fourth approach explains how managers may look to a charismatic business guru for guidance (as an act of faith) during times of intense competition and uncertainty – the *charismatic approach*.

Jackson (2001) usefully highlights the influence of management innovations and the guru literature on the world of business. He demonstrates how the critical limitations of much of this work have not made it any less influential in the uptake and implementation of new ideas and management fashions. Although academics have variously discredited and dismissed this work, this has not prevented a growing appeal and interest among business leaders (Jackson, 2001: 8–9). For these reasons, Jackson (2001) calls for academics to engage with managers in order to improve the quality of management and organizational learning through more critical dialogue and debate. As he concludes:

> *One of the primary motives for writing this book was an attempt to facilitate what I felt was a much needed yet all too rare dialogue between academics and practitioners about management gurus and management fashions. I hope that the rhetorical critiques that are presented in this book might serve to stimulate*

> *discussion about the sources and underlying appeal of these and other management guru-inspired management fashions. I also hope to encourage some critical reflection on the quality of managerial and organizational learning that management fashions have been responsible for generating, either directly or indirectly. I have come across numerous practitioners who share the same kinds of concerns and are asking the same kinds of questions about the management guru and management fashion phenomenon as many of my academic colleagues. In light of these common interests, it is somewhat unfortunate that there has been little evidence of these two communities talking across their respective boundaries. (Jackson, 2001: 173–4)*

There has been a tendency for the critical narratives of the academic to run in parallel to the narratives of the management guru, and to be in the background (through retrospective analysis) rather than at the forefront of new business ideas (see also Collins, 2000, 2001). Academic research is clearly presenting some useful and challenging ideas, but the influence of these ideas on business remains questionable. For some commentators, there is a growing disjunction between critical academic theories and practical management guides. As Knights and McCabe (2003: 176–7) reflect:

> *Despite flaws in the dreams that the gurus peddle, each new guru or manager finds a way to expound the same unitary dream. Such dreams provide some managers with much needed solace from the difficulties in which they find themselves ... There is then a critical limitation within the guru literature and in the discourse of the managers who imbibe it, in that it seeks to promote unity and equality in a world that is frequently divided and undoubtedly unequal.*

There have been a number of more critical perspectives on innovation and change that have questioned the guru literature and the more normative approaches that offer n-step guides and recipes for success (see, for example, Collins, 1998, 2000; Pettigrew et al., 2003). Simple management recipes have been criticized for trying to present neat sequential prescriptions for organizations whilst giving little attention to the potential diversity of organizational forms and the complex issues of managing large-scale change (Dawson, 1994). This inability to deliver practical long-term solutions is seen to highlight a problem with management books that identify and codify supposedly best-practice strategies for achieving organizational effectiveness based on anecdotal evidence or commonsense interpretations of organizational life (see also Abrahamson, 1991, 1996; Abrahamson and Fairchild, 1999; Huczynski, 1993; Pascale, 1990). As some of these issues are dealt with in Chapter 10 they need not detain us here; however, it is worth commenting on two studies that draw attention to the problems of guru approaches that tend to overstate the role of managers and the sequential nature of change, whilst understating processual aspects and the influence of employees as shapers and mediators of change (Balogun, 2006). In a piece of processual research, Alvesson and Sveningsson (2008) set out to counterbalance the predominance of anecdotal or management-focused case studies in capturing different interpretations and sense-making experiences of change among a range of stakeholders. They advocate the benefits of more processual in-depth research but note the sparseness of such studies and a tendency to focus on positive examples of 'successful' change rather than on the lessons that can be learnt from failure (2008: 148). Although most change initiatives fail (Sorge and van Witteloostuijn, 2004), managers are keen to present themselves in a positive light as part of an ongoing political process (see Buchanan and Badham, 2008). In their detailed investigation of a cultural change programme in a high-tech firm, Alvesson and Sveningsson (2008) found that while most employees were positive to the ideas and values encapsulated in the project, in practice there was a mismatch between ideal values and actual experience. In making sense of this initiative, professional employees at the 'coal-face' spotlight the unresolved contradictions and the thinness of symbolic support to the non-verbal aspects of the culture change programme. In other words, although most employees felt that the high ideas espoused were worth striving for, their experience of change contrasted with these and led to scepticism. A lack of engagement between groups (for example, senior management, engineering employees and the HR group) drew attention to the problem of transferring ownership of change beyond the initiators of the programme. The role of HR staff in being 'mailpersons' highlighted the problems to this rather linear approach – following a stage model framework – that was impersonal and lacked opportunities for employee engagement.

Drawing on the work of Latour (1986, 1988, 2005) they contrast a *diffusion* model of planned change in which senior managers direct and propel change (and where subordinates accede to these demands as passive intermediaries); to a *translation* model in which movements of ideas or objects reside in the sense-making of people who are the active mediators of change (Alvesson and Sveningsson, 2008: 29). In supporting a translation approach, they criticize much of the literature for assuming that culture can be managed by a grand technocratic approach in which the manager can control and direct outcomes. The main problems with this perspective are seen to rest on: a heavy emphasis placed on management as the architects of change in which their decisions are unquestioningly cascaded down the hierarchy (managerialism); a trivialization of complex issues and attempts to find quick fixes (through, for example, simplified representations of teamwork and leadership); a strong emphasis on planning and design; and a marginalization of the social and emotional aspects of change (Alvesson and Sveningsson, 2008).

In his analysis of management fads and buzzwords, Collins (2000: 41) forwards a scathing critique of the gurus' pronouncements on practical advice:

> *'Gurus' as we have seen, offer 'practical' advice on how best to run organizations. Yet their advice is 'spuriously practical'. It is weak conceptually, theoretically and empirically, yet has a certain immunity to criticism because the users of 'guru theory' are discouraged from questioning the assumptions which underpin it. Once unpicked, however, it becomes apparent that rather than offering guidance to management, rather than offering a cohesive assessment of the very real problems of managing, the 'guru' practical advice serves only to befuddle and to overwhelm managers in a welter of contradictory advice.*

Knights and McCabe (2003) are also critical of the rationalist managerialist approach to innovation and change and, in particular, to the sovereignty given to management. They are also critical of commentators they categorize as holding a critical control perspective – such as Boje and Windsor (1993), McArdle et al. (1995), Parker and Slaughter (1993) and Tuckman (1994) – for their tendency to be 'convinced that TQM increases the scope and diversity of management control'. For Knights and McCabe (2003: 51–3), this understates and downplays the complex power and identity relations that are an integral part of the lived experience of change. Like Alvesson and Sveningsson (2008), they call for a greater recognition of employees as shapers of change (mediators rather than intermediaries) in being able to resist, evade and transform the strategies imposed upon them and not simply being seen as passive recipients. They also draw attention to the import of identity theory and the wider political economy and call for a more politicized processual approach to understanding change:

> *Managers may be able to deploy a ... discourse to deflect attention from the inherent contradiction in workplace relations but the effect on employees is likely to be superficial or short-lived if the innovation is accompanied by redundancy (McCabe et al., 1998) or a more general insecurity. Given the contractual nature of employment, the vagaries of capitalism and the structural inequalities of power, such inconsistencies cannot simply be talked away ... It has to be remembered that relations of power, privilege, identity and inequality are reflected in, and reinforced by, organizational life and it would take more than communication or employee involvement to resolve the contradictions of such a system. (Knights and McCabe, 2003: 60)*

The work of Alvesson and Sveningsson (2008) and Knights and McCabe (2003) is part of a more general movement towards more fluid, dynamic and process-based approaches (see Tsoukas and Chia, 2002). Although there is variety and debate within such approaches there is support for more process-oriented perspectives. We in turn advocate a version of the processual approach that views creativity, innovation and change as an ongoing dynamic rather than a final end state (see also Dawson, 2003a, 2003b). Although there are recognizable outcomes and achievable milestones, these represent moments in a process that continues *ad infinitum*. From this perspective there can never be a simple magic bullet for company success, as the context in which these processes are managed are themselves open to continual change.

Theory and practice: a reappraisal

> *I believe that organization theory always has been and always will be multiplicitous because of the variety of other fields of study that it draws on for inspiration and because organizations cannot be explained by any single theory ... In organization theory, perspectives accumulate, and over time they influence one another*

> *... This interaction among perspectives produces continuous change which is one reason why it is so difficult to make a case for any particular way of sorting through the ideas and perspectives of organization theory. (Hatch, 1997: 4)*

The ongoing debate between theory and practice continues in the field of business and management (Tsoukas and Knudsen, 2005) from an early concern with the control and co-ordination of work to more recent debates around management fashions and critical process-based views of organizing and strategizing (see also Hatch and Cunliffe, 2006). New problems emerge that require our attention, theories develop and are revised, new guidelines supersede older versions, and in the process we contribute to the development of new bodies of knowledge. These bodies of knowledge serve to inform our understanding and encourage us to further explore and investigate areas of emerging interest. In the search for more comprehensive theories that explain our phenomena of interest, we refine, replace, enhance and develop new concepts that we seek to further explore and test in fieldwork studies. The academic takes time in reflecting on the literature, analysing new data and formulating conceptual frameworks that help explain complex processes associated with people and organizations. In conjunction with our theoretical pursuits, managers seek solutions, frameworks and models, to help them solve problems and to guide them in the difficult task of managing business organizations. They have little time for complex conceptual schemes and are attracted by simplified tool kits that will service their immediate needs and provide a way forward. There is a place for both the academic scholar and business practitioner and, as Jackson (2001) points out, there is a need for greater collaboration and dialogue between these two groups.

It is perhaps not surprising that in a time of rapid and dynamic change there is a growing need for simple solutions to complex problems and some tension between our theoretical understanding and practical needs. This is not necessarily a bad thing, as it draws attention to the value of reflective dialogue and the need to engage in debates about the relationship between theory and practice. Business and management is well positioned to address such issues and hopefully, as this chapter has shown, there has been a longstanding relationship between these two elements. As the much-quoted dictum of Levin states: 'there is nothing so practicable as a good theory', and yet there remains a tendency for academics to dismiss the value of distilling practical guidelines from their work. A commonly held view is that even to attempt such an objective devalues the critical academic scholarship of such work. It is not by chance, however, that many of the management gurus have a credible academic background and found themselves tilted towards more practical concerns of business leaders following their close engagement with senior executives (see, for example, the work of Peter Drucker (1981), Gary Hamel and Rosabeth Moss Kanter). On the flip side, it is a little paradoxical that whilst detailed processual studies are able to identify some of the critical limitations of linear stage models to the practice of change and innovation, they are generally viewed as being too theoretical to be of practical use to the business managers – once again drawing us back to this debate between theory and practice.

So what is it we can learn from this historical overview of business practice and theory development? First, that there is an ongoing dynamic between theory and practice and that whilst the differences may never be resolved, it is the existence of this tension that promotes new ideas, the development of new theories and the uptake of new business practices. Second, that the separation of these two 'worlds' is as much to do with people and an absence of dialogue as it is to do with fundamental differences in interests and concerns. Third, that any attempt to distil out general lessons or practical guidelines from complex data will necessarily be selective, in the use and refinement of data; and partial, in the creation of condensed and accessible versions for business use. Such a presentation will need to address broader and more general issues and, in so doing, necessitates a reduction in theoretical sophistication.

This of course leaves open the question as to whether such attempts are of value or whether they simply undermine the data that they seek to represent. For us, the answer is that there is value in such attempts, but recognition should also be given to the limitations of these heuristics or 'rules of thumb' for business managers. The research already referred to by Alvesson and Sveningsson (2008) provides a useful illustration of this. From their study of a cultural change project they identify 15 practical lessons for working with change that they divide into five overall themes comprising: framing context, organizing change work(ers), content, tactics and process (2008: 175–80). In framing context, they argue for the need for endurance and a long-term view, to work with realistic aims, and to recognize that change is about self-transformation and not simply the imposition of predefined ideas. In organizing for change there is a need to address issues of identity and, when appropriate, revise the basic image of change, to maintain a view of the whole project and to gain involvement and a 'strong sense of a "we" in change work' (2008: 177). In the content of change, they call for a focus on meanings more than values, and to avoid promoting the self-evidently good, such as respect for people or quality. Tactically, they emphasize skilful attention to emotions and symbolism, and the need to combine pushing for change with a dialogue for change. Process activities involve keeping the culture theme on the agenda, paying careful attention to the way messages are received, interpreted and made sense of, and to connecting to people's experience in a positive sense. They conclude by stressing the need to recognize that some changes simply produce negative responses and cynicism among employees.

We commend the push to link theory and practice in the further development of our knowledge and understanding of management and organization in a rapidly changing business world. We also see value in carrying out more scholastic research, to identify and study problems and issues faced by modern business, and to analyse and comment upon the emergence of management fads and fashions. With the continuing development in technology, with globalization and opening-up of markets in international trade and commerce, and in the rapid changes in business market activities and customer demands, there remains plenty of room to research, debate and reflect upon the theory and practice of change, creativity and innovation.

Conclusion

Classical management theorists and early modernists nearly always focused on how to stabilize, routinize, and rationalize organizational knowledge about effective organizational performance. In stability-oriented frameworks such as these, changes were seen as the intended result of doing more of a good thing – more routine, more structure, more rationality. A change-centred perspective, however, has gradually swept away the dominance of stability-centred views, and all ... perspectives of organization theory now embrace more dynamic ideas that celebrate organizational processes. (Hatch, 1997: 350–1)

This chapter has provided an overview of a number of key theoretical developments that have emerged in an attempt to make sense of concepts, issues and the 'problems' and 'opportunities' that face those who seek to manage the complex processes of creativity, innovation and change. With the movement from a primarily agricultural to an industrial economy the new industrializing countries faced the issue of how best to co-ordinate and control operations within large-scale factories. From drawing on Adam Smith's *Wealth of Nations* to Taylor's *Principles of Scientific Management*, new practices were introduced and adapted in a range of different business environments. Within manufacturing, the continuous flow assembly line further divided work up into ever-simpler tasks. Workers were likened to automatons in the mass manufacture of automobiles that became an engine for economic growth and industrial development. Symmetry, formality and rigidity became associated with this classical school of thought that also permeated literary styles of the time and architectural forms. But this emphasis on technical efficiency and the structure of organizations (the skeleton of organizational form) ignored the human aspects of work (the living tissue of employees) and was questioned in the changing context of the inter-war and post-war period.

The economic growth stimulated by post-war reconstruction created a period of relatively full employment. Furthermore, returning soldiers who had been trained in warfare and had experienced the devastation of war expected to be treated with a certain amount of dignity at work. In the very different contextual conditions of the 1940s and 1950s, the growing unrest, industrial sabotage, absenteeism and militancy at work, created a new concern for business managers. Studies conducted at this time identified the importance of the social and human dimensions to work, drawing attention to factors such as, leadership style, motivation, social relations at work and job design (for example, job enlargement/rotation). With developments in technology and the mechanization of business operations, the need to accommodate both the social and the technical in reconfiguring work was highlighted in a number of studies carried out by the Tavistock Institute.

By the 1960s and 1970s, the emphasis was not only on the internal workings of organizations but also on their business market environments. Strategy and 'fit' became a focus and concern for contingency theorists who variously emphasized technology, size or a combination of contingent variables. Performance and efficiency in managing companies for competitive success was central to debates, models and prescriptive frameworks. Structural, human and environmental issues were variously accommodated in a growing range of empirical studies examining business organization. Within America, business became a growing area of academic interest and scholarly activity, and throughout the 1980s and 1990s there has been a significant expansion in business-related courses in America and Europe, that have since the late 1990s and 2000s expanded throughout Asia and northern Europe.

Developments in communication and information technologies and the growing array of new management techniques (such as just-in-time management, business process re-engineering, cellular manufacture, computer-aided manufacture, lean production systems, total quality management, and so forth), have all drawn attention to the rapidity of innovation and change at work. New theories have emerged and the promotion of new ideas (whether fads or fashions) have combined with an unprecedented growth in consultant activity and the rise of the guru professor. Popular management books are commonplace in main communication hubs, such as central railway stations, international airports and motorway services. Following the appeal of *In Search of Excellence* (Peters and Waterman, 1982), there has been a growing raft of management fashions promoted by gurus such as Hamel (2000), Hammer and Champy (1993), Handy (2001), Kanter (1990) and Kotter and Rathgeber (2006). They present simple recipes for success and call for managers to be proactive and to develop appropriate competencies to be masters rather than victims of change. From Hamel and Prahalad's (1994) advice on competing for the future through to Kotter's (1996) eight-step model of successful change, there are a range of new management thinkers who highlight the competitive threat of irrelevancy and the need to be creative and innovative (Nordström and Ridderstråle, 2004, 2007).

A more critical literature has also developed alongside these bestsellers that has sought to explain the rise and popularity of the management guru (Collins, 2000; Jackson, 2001), as well as the problems and pitfalls of simple recipes of success (Dawson, 2003a). For example, Alvesson and Sveningsson (2008) and Knights and McCabe (2003), both criticize the spurious character and questionable value of the practical advice offered by the management guru. They are critical of the sovereignty given to management and to the stage model approach that downplays the complex and processual nature of change. This separation in the literature – between more critical studies in management and the celebrity professors – also flags an ongoing debate between theory and practice. This tension between attempts to improve our theoretical understanding and the more practical needs of business is useful as it not only draws attention to central questions that need addressing, but it also stimulates an interest in these areas among academic scholars and business managers. Although the dialogue between these two groups remains limited, there is a growing debate around some of these key issues. From our own processual perspective, we support attempts to link theory and practice in furthering our knowledge and understanding of the complex processes associated with a change, creativity and innovation.

Within these debates, technology is also seen as a key driver and shaper of change in the modern business world; for example, with rapid forms of electronic communication through the internet and e-commerce activities, many companies have shifted their service operations through the establishment of call centres outside of their home country where they can employ skilled labour at far lower cost. These trends and patterns of innovation and development raise the question of converging forms of organization in a post-industrial world shaped by the ubiquitous computer. Interestingly, in their most recent book *Funky Business Forever*, Nordström and Ridderstråle (2007) argue that technology is necessary but not sufficient for business success. They argue that temporary monopolies based on being the fittest (as in Ikea, Dell Computers and RyanAir), or around the principle of attraction (as in BMW and Apple), are the two key elements to competitive advantage. In contrast, academic studies continue to highlight the importance of context in explaining creativity, innovation and the configuration and reconfiguration of organizational arrangements within particular localities (Alvesson and Sveningsson, 2008). The paradox and juxtapositions of renewal for continuity and stability for innovative change raises the notion of working with people in the creation of new ideas, in the translation of ideas into products or services, and in the ongoing management of change processes within organizations. In the chapter that follows, we examine these issues in relation to the growth and development of 'creative industries' before examining these processes at the level of the individual, group and organization.

RESOURCES, READINGS AND REFLECTIONS

CASE 3.1   THE BRITISH RAIL CASE STUDY: LEARNING FROM THE PAST? BY PATRICK DAWSON

(*Source*: Dawson, 2003b: 202–7)

In 1971 British Rail (BR) decided to invest 13 million pounds (1971 prices) in a new computer system to improve the performance of its freight operations. Having considered a variety of options, including the possibility of developing a system 'in-house', BR decided to purchase software already developed and proven in railway freight operations in North America. The system in question was known as 'TOPS' (Total Operations Processing System).

The decision to computerise was based on two factors:

1. The severe economic crisis facing British Rail's freight business due to competition from road haulage and the decline of the industries which traditionally were the railway's principal source of freight revenue (coal, iron and steel).

(Continued)

(Continued)

2. The identification of inefficiencies in the day to day supervision of freight operations stemming from inaccurate and out of date information about the whereabouts of freight resources – empty wagons, locomotives and freight trains.

Prior to computerisation information on the disposition of freight resources and the operating situation was reported through a hierarchical structure, consisting of supervisors in local marshalling yards, who reported to divisional control rooms who in turn reported to regional control rooms. A central control room at BR Headquarters in London oversaw operations as a whole. The principal methods of communicating information were 'manual' involving either telephone or telex reports of such things as the numbers of empty wagons 'on hand' in a marshalling yard or the 'consist' of a freight train en route. Much of this information was inaccurate, not least because of the manipulation of information by marshalling yard supervisors. For example, empty wagons were frequently in short supply and in order to satisfy the daily requirements of local customers supervisors under-reported the number of wagons 'on-hand' and over-reported the number of 'empties' required.

This resulted in a gross oversupply and under-utilisation of resources. In 1971 there were well over half a million wagons on the BR network, only 80% of which was accounted for in daily reports from supervisors. Similar problems were involved with locomotives, and these along with empty wagons, were frequently 'hidden' in remote sidings by supervisors in order that they could respond to unexpected changes in local requirements. As a result, although a vast amount of information was being passed day-to-day on the disposition of freight resources, very little of this bore any relation to the reality of the operating situation at 'ground' level. Moreover, there were inevitable delays in passing information on by 'manual' methods. In the context of 'time-sensitive' railway operations much of this information on the whereabouts of resources was invalid by the time it reached its destination. As a result senior operations management were simply unaware of much of what was happening and spent most of their time in a 'reactive' role attempting to establish what had happened and why.

The economic circumstances of the freight business meant that a solution to the problem of supervising freight operations had to be found if rail freight was to remain competitive and in business. The TOPS system offered a potential solution. Each local marshalling yard was to be equipped with an on-line terminal linked to a mainframe computer at BR Headquarters. Marshalling yard staff would be required to provide information to 'TOPS clerks' who would input information via the local terminals. This information provided a 'real-time' picture of the operating situation in any particular area. Because the information was communicated by electronic means direct to a central computer and could be easily accessed the 'inbuilt' delays and inaccuracies inherent in the old 'manual' reporting system could be avoided. Further, because the TOPS system kept tabs on each individual wagon, locomotive and train, it was impossible to 'hide' resources as had previously been practised. Moreover, because the system could cross check reports from local terminals almost instantaneously any attempt to input misleading information was rejected by the computer.

The decision to computerise the control of freight operations involved considerable uncertainty and risk. There was no guarantee that the system would arrest the decline of the freight business and every possibility that the implementation of the system would run into difficulties, with the risk of delays and the escalation of the costs of the project. Despite the advantages of buying-in an already proven technological innovation, successful adoption of the new technology still depended on solving a number of technical, personnel, industrial relations, and managerial problems. The situation was summed up in 1981 by one senior freight operations manager in BR who described TOPS as BR's most speculative investment since the Beeching Report and restructuring in the 1960s.

Given the critical economic position of the freight business, there was considerable concern at Board level that computerisation should be completed within a four year time-scale and within budget. The scale of the project was enormous. In technical terms it meant adapting the TOPS software to suit BR's operations, providing a network of computer terminals in 150 locations around the country, installing a new mainframe computer centre, and upgrading BR's existing telecommunications system. In personnel terms there was a major task of educating all levels of freight operations staff from shunters to headquarters management in the capabilities and use of the system, and in providing specialist training for the staff who would make day-to-day use of the system. In industrial relations terms it meant gaining the acceptance of the new technology by the rail unions in a climate that had previously proved resistant to rapid change. Finally, there was the question of how the introduction of the new technology should be managed. Should traditional practice be followed where each specialist department was allocated responsibility for the aspects of the project which concerned them (eg: computing to Management Services, retraining to Personnel etc.) and each BR Region was given the responsibility for the management of change in its own local areas – or – should a new approach be tried?

It was the risk of delay through inter-departmental rivalries and Regional/ Headquarters conflict which was most feared by management. Despite nationalisation, geographical identities remained strongly rooted in the organisational culture, and at corporate level functional specialisms jealously guarded their areas of expertise. There was every possibility that the whole project would founder on the rocks of inter-management squabbles. However, the BR chief executive gave the project high-level support and appointed a senior operations manager to head-up an implementation team. Given the high stakes involved other departments made no effort to take responsibility for the various aspects of implementation, and in the ensuing vacuum the project manager was able to assemble a 'task force' in the form of a cross-functional team which assumed complete control of the entire project. Computing, telecommunications and operations specialists were seconded from their departments, whilst the training function and Regions were virtually by-passed altogether. Instead a number of

(Continued)

(Continued)

operations staff and a year's intake of graduate trainees were co-opted to form a team which would act as a mobile training force, travelling around the country to retrain staff. The 'task force' was presented to the rest of the organisation as a 'fait accompli' and, with the support of the Chief Executive, set about bending normal rules and procedures and upsetting the traditional customs of the organisational culture with a view to the introduction of the TOPS system without delay.

The two principal non-technical tasks facing the 'task force' were in gaining the acceptance of the new technology by staff and management, and convincing the unions of the need for rapid change. In relation to the first task, the initial step was to create within the implementation team itself an almost unbounded enthusiasm for and identification with the achievement of change. The team was run on almost militaristic lines and a number of devices, including a special 'TOPS logo', a 'TOPS tie'. a 'TOPS Newsletter', and a package of training graphics featuring a character called 'TOPS Cat' were employed to foster a 'corporate identity' for the project. In the words of one of the 'task force' members, "if you weren't fired with enthusiasm for the project you were fired from the project". Faced with such commitment backed by high-level management support, local personnel saw little opportunity or point in resisting change. Where they did, the project team ignored any protestations and carried on regardless. The use of the mobile team proved a masterstroke in providing a training package which could combine classroom theory with 'hands on' experience on the job. Any resistance to the new reporting procedures required for computerisation by the staff – many of whom had spent years working by traditional methods – were more readily overcome.

In terms of the trade unions there was no opposition in principle to the computerisation, not only because the introduction of TOPS promised to save the jobs that would be lost if the freight business went to the wall, but also, because it involved the creation of new jobs, at least in the short term. Whilst consulting with the rail unions from a very early stage, management studiously avoided entering into any time-consuming national negotiations over extra payments for using the new technology. Further, no attempt was made by management to develop the potential use of the TOPS systems for keeping tabs on train crews. It was certain that the 'Big Brother' connotations of such a use would have brought vigorous union opposition, in particular from the train driver's union ASLEF. As a result union leaders were 'won over' to the system and were happy to cooperate in its speedy introduction. Indeed, national officers of the unions were instrumental in resolving some of the small localised disputes which did occur during the implementation programme. In retrospect, the view of many national officials was that if management had introduced such a system sooner much of the market which had already been lost may have been saved.

The TOPS computerisation project was completed on time and within budget in October 1975. A far more efficient utilisation of freight resources was achieved and operational control considerably improved. In particular, it became clear that management for the first time had an opportunity to play a 'proactive' role in the planning and control of freight operations. As one operations manager put it 'we now had a production line we could control'.

Questions

1. What would you identify as the critical factors that contributed to the successful implementation of the TOPS system?
2. What were the advantages and disadvantages of the 'task force' approach?
3. How important is context and culture in understanding change?
4. Are there any general lessons that can be learnt from this case study on the process of organizational change?

Chapter questions

The questions listed below relate to the chapter as a whole and can be used by individuals to further reflect on the material covered, as well as serving as a source for more open group discussion and debate.

1. How relevant is Taylor's principles of scientific management to modern business organizations?

2. What has been the main contribution of human relations theory?

3. The market environment, technology and the social aspects of work all have to be taken into account in the effective design of organizations – do you agree?

4. Consider whether there can ever be an authentic list of key ingredients for the 'successful' management of change.

5. Most of us are familiar with the saying that 'the more things change, the more they stay the same' (*plus ça change, plus c'est la même chose*). What are your views on this saying?

6. Consider the claim that employee resistance is simply an obstacle to be overcome in managing large-scale change.

7. What is the relationship between theory development and management practice?

8. How important has been the rise and popularity of the management guru to our knowledge and understanding of management and organization?

9. Consider whether the main limitation of the more critical literature is their failure to address the practical problems of business management?

Hands-on exercise

Research the airline industry and consider the issues of change from the perspective of the short-haul competitively priced airlines and the larger operators such as Qantas and British Airways. Keep in mind the following questions when collecting data and media material:

1. What determines who are the major players in this industry? (Consider the issues of market entry and compare and contrast short-haul and long-haul operations and customer expectations and demands.)

2. Identify possible niche opportunities in exploring the nature of the business of air transportation.

3. How vulnerable is this industry to external events and critical junctures? (For example, oil prices, health scares, terrorist activity and so forth.)

4. What potential difficulties do you see for existing companies in this industry?

Team debate exercise

Debate the following statement:

> *It is perhaps ironic that the more we study change the less we seem to learn as the popularity of shortcut answers frequently call testimony to the short-sighted character of many change management decisions. Long-haul frameworks which do not provide neat solutions to complex problems may be far less attractive and easy to package, but they do offer more insight on the process of change. (Dawson, 2003a: 9)*

Divide the class into two groups. The first group should argue for the importance of identifying lessons for the practical management of change and provide some general guidelines on how best to manage change. The second group should question the value of such 'recipes' and draw attention to the high level of failed change initiatives and the unpredictability of change.

References

Abrahamson, E. (1991) 'Managerial fads and fashions: the diffusion and rejection of innovations', *Academy of Management Review*, 16: 586–612.
Abrahamson, E. (1996) 'Management fashion', *Academy of Management Review*, 21: 254–85.
Abrahamson, E. and Fairchild, G. (1999) 'Management fashion: lifecycles, triggers, and collective learning processes', *Administrative Science Quarterly*, 44: 708–40.
Aldrich, H. (2008) *Organizations and Environments*. Stanford: Stanford University Press.
Alvesson, M. and Sveningsson, S. (2008) *Changing Organizational Culture: Cultural Change Work in Progress*. London: Routledge.

Badham, R. (1995) 'Managing sociotechnical change: a configuration approach to technology implementation', in J. Benders, J. de Haan and D. Bennett (eds), *The Symbiosis of Work and Technology*. London: Taylor & Francis.

Balogun, J. (2006) 'Managing change: steering a course between intended strategies and unanticipated outcomes', *Long Range Planning*, 39: 29–49.

Blauner, R. (1964) *Alienation and Freedom: The Factory Worker and his Industry*. Chicago: University of Chicago Press.

Boje, D. and Windsor, R. (1993) 'The resurrection of Taylorism: TQM's hidden agenda', *Journal of Organizational Change Management*, 6 (4): 57–70.

Burnes, B. (2000) *Managing Change: A Strategic Approach to Organizational Dynamics*, 3rd edn. London: Pitman.

Burns, T. and Stalker, G.M. (1961) *The Management of Innovation*. London: Tavistock.

Buchanan, D. and Badham, R. (2008) *Power, Politics, and Organizational Change: Winning the Turf Game*, 2nd edn. London: Sage.

Burgoyne, J. and Jackson, B. (1997), 'The arena thesis: management development as a pluralistic meeting point', in J. Burgoyne and M. Reynolds (eds), *Management Learning: Integreting Perspectives in Theory and Practice*. London: Sage. pp. 54–70.

Burgoyne, J. and Jackson, B. (1997) 'The arena thesis: management development as a pluralistic meeting point', in J. Burgoyne and M. Reynolds (eds), *Management Learning*. London: Sage. pp. 55–70.

Child, J. (1972) 'Organization structure, environment and performance: the role of strategic choice', *Sociology*, 6: 1–22.

Child, J. (1988) 'On organizations in their sectors', *Organization Studies*, 9: 13–18.

Clegg, S.R. (1988) 'The good, the bad and the ugly', *Organization Studies*, 9: 7–12.

Clutterbuck, D. and Crainer, S. (1990) *Makers of Management. Men and Women Who Changed the Business World*. London: Macmillan.

Collins, D. (1998) *Organizational Change: Sociological Perspectives*. London: Routledge.

Collins, D. (2000) *Management Fads and Buzzwords: Critical–Practical Perspectives*. London: Routledge.

Collins, D. (2001) 'The fad motif in management scholarship', *Employee Relations*, 23: 26–37.

Crosby, P. (1980) *Quality is Free: The Art of Making Quality Certain*. New York: Mentor.

Dawson, P. (1994) *Organizational Change: A Processual Approach*. London: Paul Chapman.

Dawson, P. (2003a) *Understanding Organizational Change*. London: Sage.

Dawson, P. (2003b) *Reshaping Change: A Processual Perspective*. London: Routledge.

Deming, W.E. (1981) *Japanese Methods for Productivity and Quality*. Washington, DC: George Washington University.

Drucker, P. (1981) *Managing in Turbulent Times*. London: Pan Books.

Dubin, R. (1959) *The Sociology of Industrial Relations*. Englewood Cliffs, NJ: Prentice Hall.

Dunphy, D. and Stace, D. (1990) *Under New Management: Australian Organizations in Transition*. Sydney: McGraw-Hill.

Freeman, F. (1985) 'Books that mean business: the management best seller', *Academy of Management Review*, 10: 345–50.

Gabor, S.C. and Petersen, P.B. (1991) 'When giants learn to dance: mastering the challenges of strategy, management, and careers in the 1990s', Book Review, *Academy of Management Executive*, 5: 97–9.

Graetz, F., Rimmer, M., Lawrence, A. and Smith, A. (2002) *Managing Organisational Change*. Queensland: John Wiley.

Gray, E.R. and Smeltzer, L.R. (1990) *Management: The Competitive Edge*. New York: Macmillan.

Guest, D. (1992) 'Right enough to be dangerously wrong: an analysis of the in search of excellence phenomenon', in G. Salaman (ed.), *Human Resource Strategies*. London: Sage.

Hamel, G. (2000) *Leading the Revolution*. Boston, MA: Harvard Business School Press.

Hamel, G. and Prahalad, C.K. (1994) *Competing for the Future*. Boston, MA: Harvard Business School Press.

Hammer, M. and Champy, J. (1993) *Reengineering the Corporation: A Manifesto for Business Revolution*. New York: HarperBusiness.

Handy, C. (1984) *The Future of Work*. Oxford: Blackwell.

Handy, C. (1994) *The Empty Raincoat*. London: Hutchinson.

Handy, C. (1996) *Beyond Certainty: The Changing World of Organizations*. Boston, MA: Harvard Business School Press.

Handy, C. (1999) *The New Alchemists*. London: Hutchinson.

Handy, C. (2001) *The Elephant and the Flea*. London: Hutchinson.

Hatch, M.J. (1997) *Organization Theory: Modern Symbolic and Postmodern Perspectives*. Oxford: Oxford University Press.

Hatch, M.J. and Cunliffe, A. (2006) *Organization Theory: Modern Symbolic and Postmodern Perspectives*, 2nd edn. Oxford: Oxford University Press.

Henriques, U.R. (1979) *Before the Welfare State. Social Administration in Early Industrial Britain*. London: Longman.

Huczynski, A. (1993) *Management Gurus: What Makes Them and How to Become One*. London: Routledge.

Huczynski, A. and Buchanan, D. (2006) *Organizational Behaviour: An Introductory Text*, 6th edn. Harlow: Financial Times/ Prentice Hall.

Jackson, B. (2001) *Management Gurus and Management Fashions*. London: Routledge.

Juran, J.M. (1988) *Quality Control Handbook*. New York: McGraw-Hill.

Kanter, R.M. (1985) *The Change Masters: Corporate Entrepreneurs at Work*. London: Allen & Unwin.

Kanter, R.M. (1990) *When Giants Learn to Dance: Mastering the Challenges of Strategy, Management, and Careers in the 1990s*. London: Unwin Hyman.

Karpik, L. (1988) 'Misunderstandings and theoretical choices', *Organization Studies*, 9: 25–8.

Knights, D. and McCabe, D. (2003) *Organization and Innovation: Guru Schemes and American Dreams*. Maidenhead: Open University Press.

Knights, D. and Murray, F. (1994) *Managers Divided: Organisation Politics and Information Technology Management*. Chichester: John Wiley.

Kotter, J. (1995) 'Leading change: why transformation efforts fail', *Harvard Business Review*, 73 (2): 59–67.

Kotter, J. (1996) *Leading Change*. Boston, MA: Harvard Business School Press.

Kotter, J. (2002) *The Heart of Change: Real Life Stories of How People Change their Organizations*. Boston, MA: Harvard Business School Press.

Kotter, J. and Rathgeber, H. (2006) *Our Iceberg is Melting*. London: Macmillan.

Latour, B. (1986) 'The power of association', in J. Law (ed.), *Power, Action and Belief: A New Sociology of Knowledge?* London: Routledge & Kegan Paul.

Latour, B. (1988) *The Pasteurization of France*. Cambridge, MA: Harvard University Press.

Latour, B. (2005) *Reassembling the Social*. Oxford: Oxford University Press.

Lawrence, P. and Lorsch, J. (1967) *Organization and Environment*. Harvard: Harvard University Press.

Littler, C. (1982) *The Development of the Labour Process in Capitalist Societies*. London: Heinemann.

MacKenzie, D. and Wajcman, J. (1985) *The Social Shaping of Technology*. Milton Keynes: Open University Press.

McArdle, L., Rowlinson, M., Proctor, S., Hassard, J. and Forrester, P. (1995) 'Employee empowerment or the enhancement of exploitation', in A. Wilkinson and H. Willmott (eds), *Making Quality Critical*. London: Routledge.

McCabe, D. (2007) *Power at Work: How Employees Reproduce the Corporate Machine*. Abingdon: Routledge.

McCabe, D., Knights, D., Kerfoot, D., Morgan, G. and Willmott, H. (1998) 'Making sense of quality – towards a review and critique and quality initiatives in financial services', *Human Relations,* 51: 389–411.

McLoughlin, I. and Clark, J. (1994) *Technological Change at Work*, 2nd edn. Buckingham: Open University Press.

Mitroff, I. and Mohrman, S. (1987) 'The slack is gone: how the United States lost its competitive edge in the world economy', *Academy of Management Executive*, 1: 65–70.

Nordström, K. and Ridderstråle, J. (2001) *Funky Business*, 2nd edn. London: Financial Times Prentice Hall.

Nordström, K. and Ridderstråle, J. (2004) *Karaoke Capitalism: Management of Mankind*. London: Financial Times Prentice Hall.

Nordström, K. and Ridderstråle, J. (2007) *Funky Business Forever: How to Enjoy Capitalism*. London: Financial Times Prentice Hall.

Parker, M. and Slaughter, J. (1993) 'Should the labour movement buy TQM?', *Journal of Organizational Change Management*, 6 (4): 43–56.

Pascale, R. (1990) *Managing on the Edge*. New York: Touchstone.

Perrow, C. (1970) *Organizational Analysis*. Belmont: Wadsworth.

Peters, T. (1989) *Thriving on Chaos*. London: Pan Books.

Peters, T. (1993) *Liberation Management: Necessary Disorganisation for Nanosecond Nineties*. London: Pan Books.

Peters, T. (1997) *The Circle of Innovation*. New York: Alfred A. Knopf.

Peters, T. and Waterman, R. (1982) *In Search of Excellence: Lessons from America's Best-Run Companies*. New York: Harper & Row.

Pettigrew, A., Whittington, R., Melin, L., Sanchez-Runde, C., van den Bosch, F., Ruigrok, W. and Numagami, T. (eds) (2003) *Innovative Forms of Organizing*. London: Sage.

Powell, W. and DiMaggio, P. (eds) (1991) *The New Institutionalism in Organisational Analysis*. London: University of Chicago Press.

Pugh, D. and Hickson, D. (1976) *Organizational Structure in its Context: the Aston Programme* I. London: Saxon House.

Roethlisberger, F. (1945) 'The foreman: master and victim of double talk', *Harvard Business Review*, 23 (3): 283–98.

Roethlisberger, F. and Dickson, W. (1950) *Management and the Worker. An Account of a Research Program Conducted by the Western Electric Company, Hawthorne Works, Chicago*. Boston, MA: Harvard University Press.

Schonberger, R.J. (1982) *Japanese Manufacturing Techniques: Nine Hidden Lessons in Simplicity*. New York: The Free Press.

Smith, J. (1987) 'Elton Mayo and the hidden Hawthorne', *Work, Employment and Society*, 1: 107–20.

Sorge, A. and van Witteloostuijn, A. (2004) 'The (non)sense of organizational change: an essay about universal management hypes, sick consultancy metaphors, and healthy organization theories', *Organization Studies*, 25: 1205–31.

Taylor, F. (1911) *The Principles of Scientific Management*. New York: Harper.

Thompson, J.D. (1967) *Organizations in Action*. New York: McGraw-Hill.

Tidd, J., Bessant, J. and Pravitt, K. (2001) *Managing Innovation: Integrating Technological, Market and Organizational Change*, 2nd edn. London: John Wiley.

Touraine, A. (1955) *L'evolution du Travail ouvrier aux usines Renault*. Paris: Centre National de la Recherche Scientifique.

Trist, E. and Bamforth, K. (1951) 'Some social and psychological consequences of the longwall method of coal-getting: an examination of the psychological situation and defences of a work group in relation to the social structure and technological content of the work system', *Human Relations*, 4: 3–38.

Tsoukas, H. and Chia, R. (2002) 'On organizational becoming: rethinking organizational change', *Organization Science*, 13: 567–82.

Tsoukas, H. and Knudsen, C. (2005) *The Oxford Handbook of Organization Theory*. Oxford: Oxford University Press.

Tuckman, A. (1994) 'The yellow brick road: total quality management and the restructuring of organizational culture', *Organization Studies*, 15: 727–51.

Ulrich, D. and Lake, D. (1991) 'Organizational capability: creating competitive advantage', *Academy of Management Executive*, 5 (1): 77–92.

Vesey, J.T. (1991) 'The new competitors: they think in terms of "speed-to-market"', *Academy of Management Executive*, 5 (2): 23–33.

Walker, C.R. and Guest, R.H. (1952) *The Man on the Assembly Line*. Boston, MA: Harvard University Press.

Willcocks, L. and Mason, D. (1987) *Computerising Work: People, Systems Design and Workplace Relations*. London: Paradigm.

Wood, S. (1979) 'A reappraisal of the contingency approach to organization', *Journal of Management Studies*, 16: 334–54.

Woodward, J. (1980) *Industrial Organization: Theory and Practice*, 2nd edn. Oxford: Oxford University Press.

Recommended reading

- Alvesson, M. and Sveningsson, S. (2008) *Changing Organizational Culture: Cultural Change Work in Progress*. London: Routledge.

- Collins, D. (2001) 'The fad motif in management scholarship', *Employee Relations*, 23: 26–37.

- Jackson, B. (2001) *Management Gurus and Management Fashions*. London: Routledge.

- Tsoukas, H. and Chia, R. (2002). 'On organizational becoming: rethinking organizational change', *Organization Science*, 13: 567–82.

Some useful websites

There are a number of websites for guru management speakers and celebrity professors that can be found from a simple Google search. Some of these may also change over time; two that may be of interest that were running at the time of drafting this text relate to Peter Drucker and the funky business books of Kjell Nordström and Jonas Ridderstråle.

- Peter Drucker, who is sometimes referred to as the father of modern management, continues to influence thinking through the establishment of *The Drucker Institute* at the Claremont Graduate University on website http://www.druckerinstitute.com/; also see www.drucker.cgu.edu.

- Kjell Nordström and Jonas Ridderstråle represent a new generation of European-based business gurus. They work as professional public speakers in the field of strategic management. The 2005 Thinkers 50, the bi-annual global ranking of management thinkers, ranked Nordström and Ridderstråle at number nine internationally and number one in Europe. They are listed on the International Speakers Bureau website where short videos are available. See: http://www.internationalspeakers.com/speakers/ISBB-553F9B/ and http://www.internationalspeakers.com/speakers/ISBB-553D66/Dr._Jonas_Ridderstrale/.

- For the more historical and critical literature on theory development and business management, then the European Group of Organization Studies (EGOS) at http://www.egosnet.org/index.shtml and Critical Management Studies (CMS) at http://www.criticalmanagement.org/ provide a good starting point. Also, journals such as *Organization Studies* and the *Journal of Management Studies* provide more critical academic articles.

4

Growth in the Creative Economy and the Future of Organizations

Learning objectives

This chapter has four key learning objectives:

1. To acknowledge the factors which make change, creativity and innovation a key priority in today's competitive business landscape.
2. To identify and describe a range of different creative industries that constitute the new creative economy.
3. To evaluate the importance of creative industries to national economies and to explore the number and type of people who are involved in them.
4. To analyse the major trends that affect creative industries.

Introduction

Creativity plays a central role towards economic competitiveness in advanced economies. Several countries pride themselves on being 'creative' economies that develop, attract and retain creative individuals and nurture creative organizations (Florida, 2004). For the purposes of this book, we define creative organizations as: *any business entity whose main source of income comes from the production of novel and appropriate ideas to tackle clients' problems or opportunities identified.* Creativity is therefore increasingly high on the agenda of politicians and policy makers. The UK government, for instance, views creative talent as one of Britain's most distinctive and marketable strengths, and proposes that creativity is fundamental to the future health of the UK economy. Encouraging people into careers within creative industries has also become an important part of policy with growing emphasis being placed on creating and supporting a culture where creativity can thrive, particularly in the development of an education system that facilitates the generation and realization of ideas from an early age. Capturing the economic value of creativity in terms of the returns from the creative economy is therefore a subject that is receiving increased attention. This chapter aims to shed some light on the importance of creative industries, by discussing the economic value of the creative industries to the global and UK economy.

Why is now more than ever before the age of creativity?

Although forward-looking CEOs and policy makers have long considered creativity as an essential ingredient to economic competitiveness, it seems that now, more than ever before, is the age of creativity. Why is this the case? Let us consider some current trends:

- *Technology.* The rapid technological advancements, such as new design software and the extensive use of the World Wide Web have changed the way work is done, forms of communication and the nature of business market activities (Castells, 2000). Özsomer et al. (1997) propose that a new business era, in which information technology is changing the way we work and live, has emerged (see also Preece et al., 2000; Stewart, 1994). The information revolution has created a business environment with shorter product cycles, increased segment fragmentation, and increased interdependence of world markets. Such environmental dynamism increases the need for creativity and change – the ability of a firm to continuously introduce new products and production processes that capitalize on market opportunities (Castells, 2001). These contextual conditions require companies to support a culture of creativity in order to nurture and facilitate the generation and realization of ideas in their working environments.

- *More unpredictable and demanding customers.* It is also commonly accepted that customers today are more knowledgeable about what products and service are available and, hence, they are becoming more demanding and less 'loyal' to particular brands. Nevertheless, customers still remain at the heart of any organization (Mohanty, 1999) and, therefore, companies need to keep abreast of changing customer requirements. Demographic changes are also leading to a growing diversity in the profile of customers (for example, ethnicity and age profiles) that makes customizing to individual differences essential for gaining and sustaining a competitive edge. These trends drive organizations to change from stabilized bureaucratic forms to more adaptive modes of organizing in order to better meet the changing needs of existing and future potential customers.

- *Global competition.* Kao (1996) proposes that global competition is placing competitive pressure on national economies and that this is noticeable in areas such as their ability to mobilize ideas and encourage creativity in support of creative industries. Increasingly, we live in an interlinked economy with blurred business boundaries and this situation requires organizations to continually monitor and evaluate real-time business market change (see Giddens and Hutton, 2001). Organizational and market knowledge is used as a resource to make decisions and to foster quick innovations that support a constant stream of new and improved products, processes and services, in order to ensure company survival and to maximize value for their key stakeholders (Irani et al., 1997).

- *Knowledge.* The advances in communication and information technology help organizations to learn and compete at a faster pace. Thus, developing and sustaining organizational knowledge, ensuring that organizational memory is enriched and maintained, are all pivotal priorities in today's competitive marketplace (Castells, 2001: 52). Creativity is based on combining disparate sources of information and transforming the raw data (with which many organizations become bogged down) into valuable insights. Raw facts, data and information are limited unless they are translated into an order that makes sense or can be used to create connections that lead to the development of new concepts/ideas. Over the last decade, organizations have increasingly adopted team-centred structures in order to improve the way in which knowledge is developed, disseminated and applied in their working environments.

- *Change.* The rapid technological advancements and the fierce competition for market share have contributed to the increasing pace of change in the business landscape (Ridderstråle and Nordström, 2004). A term such as 'paradigm shifts', 'managing in chaos' or 'white-water change' draws our attention to the rapidity of business sector change (Harvard Business Review, 2005). Organizations need to be prepared to rearrange their resources to meet these new demands (Martin, 2006). The prevailing forces of organizational change, including globalization and the supply of new products and services at much faster speeds and lower costs, have all been evident for some time. Morgan (1991) and Peters (1997) reiterate the view that the world of business is now in a permanent state of flux where constant change is the only strategy for survival for both the individual and the organization. As such, organizational survival can often rest on a company's ability to quickly transform market opportunities into tangible bottom-line results to manage change successfully.

- *Higher employee expectations.* Highly skilled employees working within creative environments increasingly look for autonomy so that they can exercise personal initiative. Such high-calibre employees are extremely job mobile and require more than monetary compensation from their work (O'Toole, 1974). Nishibori (1972) argues that human work should always include creativity (the joy of thinking), physical elements (the joy of physically using the hands and body in working) and social aspects (the joy of sharing with colleagues at work, including the 'ups' and the 'downs'). More so than ever before, organizations today are required to continuously identify ways for motivating, developing and retaining their talented people.

- *The importance and dominance of design.* In an unpredictable business environment, the need to stand out from the crowd by adding value is central (Ridderstråle and Nordström, 2000). Under such intense market conditions competitive advantage can be fostered if companies see design as an integral part of business strategy.

There are several examples of companies that have grown because they have listened to what their customers want and designed products with desirable consumer features. Take the OXO peelers designed by Smart Design Inc. (a new product development consultancy based in New York): they conducted a thorough research of the market through talking with consumers, chefs and retailers, as well as studying competitive products. From their analysis the designers decided upon the necessary criteria for a new product that included a large handle that was easy to grip firmly and did not cause unnecessary strain. They came up with a very comfortable handle that was also aesthetically pleasing, almost 'inviting' people to touch it. This product has been very popular and provides a good example of the synergy between creativity and design that can lead to commercial success.

National prosperity is created

A nation's competitive advantage depends on the capacity of its industry to innovate continuously. Companies can achieve competitive advantage by serving the needs of unpredictable, sophisticated and demanding customers, competing against strong domestic and international rivals, and by recognizing new opportunities or markets. Within the creative economy, a common strategy for sustaining competitive advantage centres on the continuous identification and exploitation of new technologies and markets in the development and commercialization of new products and services (Chandy and Tellis, 1998). The value of creative organizations in the global economy is considerable (see Figure 4.1). For example, in 1999 the annual revenue of the 15 creative sectors worldwide was estimated to be in the region of $2.24 trillion. The United States is the world's leading creative economy with $960 billion in revenue, accounting for more than 40 per cent of the global total.

In the UK, the value of the creative sector to gross domestic product (GDP) is substantial (Department for Culture, Media and Sport, 2001). The creative industries in the UK employ around 1.3 million people and generate revenues

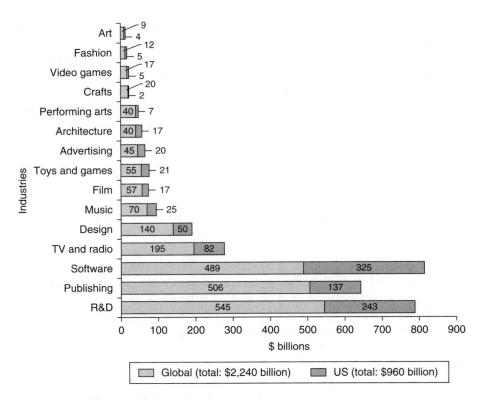

FIGURE 4.1   The creative economy – market size (1999)
(*Source:* Howkins, 2002: 116)

in the area of £112.5 billion. Britain's reputation in the fields of creativity and quality also assists its exports. The total value of exports is in the area of £10.3 billion and the creative industries account for over 5 per cent of GDP. The first *Creative Industries Mapping Document*, which was published in 1998 as a means to raise awareness of the creative industries and their contribution to the British economy, spotlights the importance of this industry to the UK economy. At this time, UK creative industries generated a total of £57.5 billion (Figure 4.2), whilst in 2001, revenues almost doubled to £112.5 billion, substantiating the high economic value of creative industries to the UK economy.

The creative industries are also important employers in the UK economy. Figure 4.3 highlights the trends for share of total employment in the creative industries. A total of 1,322,000 people were employed in the creative industries in 2001, as opposed to 966,000 in 1998. Employment in the creative industries grew at a rate of 5 per cent per annum, compared to 1.5 per cent for the whole economy in the period 1997–2001.

But, why are businesses located in certain nations more capable than others to continuously innovate? Porter (1990) modelled the effect of the local business environment on competition in terms of four interrelated attributes (see Figure 4.4). Porter claims that these attributes combine to produce a dynamic and stimulating competitive business environment. These attributes comprise:

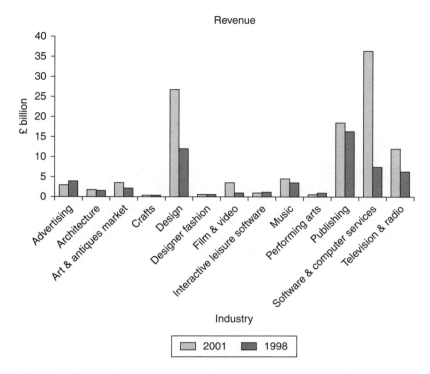

Revenue

FIGURE 4.2   Creative industries in the UK – revenues
(*Source:* Department for Culture, Media and Sport, 2001: 0 03)

1. *Factor conditions.* These refer to the cost, quality and availability of inputs, such as the development of a skilled well-educated labour force, the availability of venture capitalists to fund new initiatives, and the local market costs for key resources. Today's global and sophisticated business landscape forces nations to invest in the creation of a highly specialized workforce that is very difficult to imitate (such as highly trained scientific staff working in biotechnology companies, research institutions specializing in nanotechnology, and so forth).

2. *Demand conditions.* These refer to the composition and sophistication of local customers. Local demand conditions help build competitive advantage when sophisticated customers communicate emerging needs and/or when they pressure companies to meet ever higher standards, which in turn forces them to innovate faster.

3. *Related and supporting industries.* These refer to the extent and sophistication of local suppliers and related industries. The close proximity of suppliers and end-users contributes to the constant flow of communication and ongoing exchange of ideas and innovations. Exposure to emerging technologies, manufacturing techniques and new markets may help companies to plan new products.

4. *Firm strategy, structure and rivalry.* The nature and intensity of local competition influences how companies are created, organized and managed. Strong

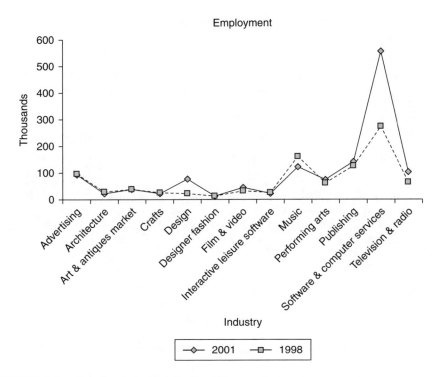

FIGURE 4.3   Creative industries in the UK – employment
(*Source*: Department for Culture, Media and Sport, 2001: 0 04)

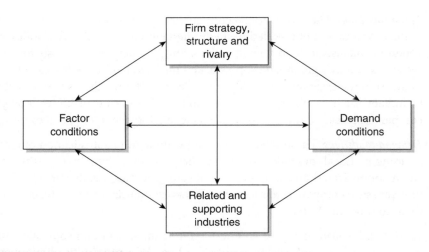

FIGURE 4.4   Determinants of national competitive advantage
(*Source*: Porter, 1990: 77)

competition among local firms may be a powerful stimulus to the creation
and persistence of competitive advantage. Take, for example, the computer
companies based in Silicon Valley: local companies not only have to focus

on increasing productivity but also on their ability to innovate and be creative in driving the direction and pace of change (Porter, 1998).

Let us now have a closer look at how the creative industries contribute to the economy.

Advertising

Advertising is a process through which companies promote their goods or services to their target customers. Advertising agencies in particular are involved in managing clients' marketing activities and communication plans. This entails activities such as identifying consumers' needs, creating the advertisements and promotions, handling PR campaigns, media planning, buying and evaluation and, finally, production of advertising materials. In most cases, the client is a business, but it can also be a government, a charity or a museum. Advertisements can promote messages relevant to building and maintaining brand awareness or, from a charitable point of view, may aim to educate people on the consequences of specific actions, such as alcohol and drug abuse.

The worldwide market for the conception and development of advertising campaigns is in the area of $45 billion. There are three main advertising centres in the world, namely: New York, Tokyo and London. The US market dominates; large American companies are their main clients and it is worth $20 billion. The UK is the fourth largest advertising market in the world in terms of revenues after the US, Japan and Germany. The UK advertising industry employs around 92,800 people (June 2000) of which approximately 57 per cent are female and 35 per cent are part-time.

Today, advertising is faced with new opportunities as well as new challenges. Traditional forms of advertising are being supplemented by the development of new media agencies focusing on the internet or digital media. Also, new internet start-ups are spending a lot of their initial funding on traditional advertising as a means of increasing their brand awareness. In the period 1997 to 2000, when a number of new dot.com companies emerged, there was heavy investment in advertising in order to differentiate themselves in what was then the underdeveloped digital (consumer) market. Their advertising campaigns were mainly focused on creating a unique and recognizable brand image. Today, advertising has to be very creative in order to convince consumers that the products/services they promote are distinctive and of value. Fallon Worldwide, in Minneapolis, raised the bar on creativity with their action-film campaign for BMW North America. The first five short films were released in spring 2001, where BMW 5 and 7 series' performance, handling and reliability are demonstrated. The films have been directed by some of Hollywood's finest, including Ang Lee (director of the Oscar-winning *Crouching Tiger, Hidden Dragon*) and Guy Ritchie (director of *Lock, Stock, and Two Smoking Barrels*). Clive Owen starred in these six- to nine-minute films, with guest appearances from Mickey Rourke and Madonna. The first series of five films was viewed 14.5 million times in the first 46 days after release. This figure increased by about

50 per cent with the release of the second series of another three short films for the launch of BMW's new Z4 roadster. These were produced by Ridley Scott (director of *Gladiator*), directed by John Woo (director of *Mission Impossible II*) and Tony Scott (director of *Spy Game*), with guest stars ranging from Gary Oldman and Madonna to James Brown. The films were successful both in generating brand awareness and eventually sales, as well as from a creative point of view. The short films have received several awards, such as 'Best of Show' honours at Cannes, the Clios and the One Show, as well as taking top prizes at several film festivals.

Architecture

Architects' artistic creativity and commercial expertise are behind the building and construction industry. This industry ranges from award-winning architects or architectural practices who design the most outstanding buildings, to the hundreds of thousands of architects, surveyors, builders, project managers and owners who design and construct the remainder. Currently, there is a trend for a polarization between large architectural practices and sole practitioners/ micro-practices across the UK. More specifically, large practices (practices with 11+ staff) earn 64 per cent of all the fee earnings of this industry. This happens because large practices are in the position to offer a variety of services, such as feasibility studies and interior design – services that the sole practitioners cannot afford to offer.

There are approximately 20,900 architects in full-time employment in the UK (2000). It is worth mentioning that architecture is still a male-dominated profession as only 12 per cent of architects are women. It is estimated that architecture firms' turnover was around £1.7 billion in 1998. Some £68 million of architectural fee income was earned abroad. The most important markets abroad are in the United States and countries in the Pacific Rim, such as Japan, Hong Kong, Malaysia and South Korea. In the majority of cases, it is the larger architectural practices that are involved in international projects (some have branches in these other countries).

An architectural practice with a presence abroad is RMJM. RMJM was founded in 1956 as a partnership between Sir Robert Matthew and Stirrat Johnson-Marshall. The current limited company was formed in 1986 in Edinburgh and London, and since then it has increased substantially both in the UK (Cambridge and Glasgow) and abroad (Hong Kong, Bangkok, Manila, Singapore and Dubai). The company is ranked 17th largest in the world with over 600 staff. The company's projects include the new University of Lincolnshire, Glaxo Wellcome's new World Headquarters, New Zealand House, Microsoft Research building in Cambridge, as well as the Tron Theatre in Glasgow.

There are many well-known architects for the forward-looking nature of their design. Frank Gehry, the American architect, is famous for his unique and revolutionary approach to architecture with highly acclaimed designs, such as the Guggenheim Museum Bilbao and the recent Experience Music Project (EMP) museum in Seattle. When Frank Gehry met with co-founders Paul Allen (Microsoft co-founder, EMP museum) and Jody Patton (EMP museum) he was taken up with their drive and passion to share their creative inspiration of music with others. The inspiration for his design came directly from music. Gehry bought numerous electric guitars, took them back to his office and cut them into pieces. The guitar pieces comprised the basis upon which Gehry came up with his initial design. Influenced by the colours in this initial model, Gehry's final design brilliantly shows the red and blue hues of electric guitars.

Another famous architect is Sir Norman Foster of the Foster & Partners studio in London, which has established an international reputation with buildings such as the new German Parliament in the Reichstag in Berlin, as well as the Great Court for the British Museum and Headquarters for HSBC in Hong Kong and London. The success of the practice is the result of design excellence achieved through active collaboration with clients and specialists and the perpetual pursuit of quality. This notion is strongly inherent in the belief that the quality of design (the form of a building, interior workspace, and so forth) directly affects the quality of the way people work and live. Foster & Partners have received more than 260 awards and citations for design excellence, and have won over 55 national and international design competitions.

Art and antique

This industry includes paintings, sculpture, jewellery, printmakers, fine furniture, other fine art and collectibles. The American market dominates the art industry; it is estimated to be in the area of £6,396 million. On the other side of the Atlantic, the UK market is worth £5,254 million and employs around 38,000 people. The dealer market employs around 20,000 people and the auction market around 17,000. The market is dominated by London and New York. The famous Sotheby's and Christie's auctioneers dominate the auction market. Christie's is the world's largest auction house with revenues in the area of $2.3 billion. People who view themselves as professional artists (their primary occupation) exhibit their work in galleries, auctions, specialist fairs, department stores and currently through the internet (companies such as eBay and Sothebys.com provide a different platform for bidding within which collectors can buy or sell their collectibles).

Crafts

This industry includes the creation, production and exhibition of crafts, such as ceramics, textiles, jewellery/silver, metal and glass. The UK market is estimated to be in the area of £400 million, employing around 24,000 people. Craftspeople often display their work in shows, festivals and exhibitions around the country (there were 2,000 craft events in the UK in the year 2000). The problem with this industry, is that it is very difficult to assess its contribution to the economy since craftspeople often have several jobs, their business' turnover falls below the VAT threshold level, and most of them are sole practitioners. Furthermore, craft activities usually involve labour-intensive processes with low return, forcing many craftspeople to have other jobs in order to supplement their craft income. These are also challenging jobs as craftspeople generally need to create, produce and distribute their crafts, while at the same time they are responsible for the actual running of their business.

Design

Industrial design is defined by the Industrial Design Society of America (IDSA) as: 'the professional service of creating and developing concepts and specifications that optimize the function, value and appearance of products and systems for the mutual benefit of both user and manufacturer'. The challenge of the design profession is that creative employees need to come up with ideas that are aesthetically pleasing, that function, but that also fulfil a need. Creative employees in this sector offer the following services: Brand and Corporate Identity, Exhibitions, Interiors, Literature, Multimedia, New Product Development, Packaging, Product TV Graphics and Websites. Design firms in the UK generated a fee income of £26.7 billion in 2000, while fees earned by UK design firms abroad amounted to £1 billion in 2000. There are 4,000 design firms in the UK, where the larger consultancies (with a turnover of more than £31 million) account for around 86 per cent of the sector's total turnover. The total number of people employed in the UK design consultancy sector is around 76,000, while the gross number of people employed in design-related activities in the UK is estimated at about one million.

British designers are featured among the winners in a variety of international design competitions, such as New York Clio's, D&AD, Germany's Red Dot awards for design innovation and the European Design Prize. The work of many leading British designers is exhibited in the Museum of Modern Art, New York. One award-winning design firm is Wolff Olins. The company was founded in London in 1965 and is now one of the world's largest corporate identity and branding consultancies. The company was initially involved in the creation and/or management of corporate identity and brands, but lately has added new services to its existing ones. For instance, the company now offers consulting to companies that need assistance in terms of their own vision, culture and image. The company employs people in five different countries around the world in offices in London, Barcelona, Lisbon, New York, San Francisco and Tokyo in four main skill groups, namely, designers, consultants, project managers and support people. Its cross-industrial and multinational clientele includes companies like First Direct, Q8, 3i, Goldfish, Channel 5, BT, Orange, Boerhringer Ingelheim, and others. There are also design consultancies, which are based outside London with international reputations, like Graven Images, a cross-disciplinary consultancy established in Glasgow in 1986. The company currently employs 20 staff in two major activities, namely graphic and interior design. In terms of graphic design, the company has expertise in corporate identity, annual reports, packaging, and so forth. As far as the interior services are concerned, the company targets the corporate, retail and leisure sectors. Graven Images' diverse clientele includes the British Council, Barclays Plc, Babtie Group, DTI, Royal Mail, and others.

Fashion

Mintel defines 'designer fashion' as encompassing four key sectors:

1. *Couture:* the original designer market dominated by French-based brands, like Dior, Chanel, Givenchy and YSL.

2. *International designers:* labels usually dominated by one name, such as Ralph Lauren, Giorgio Armani, Donna Karan or Calvin Klein (CK).

3. *Diffusion:* designers producing 'high-street' ranges for specific retailers; for instance, Jasper Conran at Debenhams.

4. *High fashion:* new designers who are up and coming usually endorsed by celebrities.

Designer fashion is one of the most visible of the creative industries. It includes clothing, but also accessories, watches, perfumes, etc. The leading companies of this industry are based in Paris, New York, Milan and Geneva:

- *LVMH,* which includes fashion and leather goods brands (Dior, Givenchy, Kenzo, Christian Lacroix, Fendi, Thomas Pink, Louis Vuitton), perfumes and watches (TAG Heuer, Ebel, Zenith).

- *Hermès,* which includes fashion brands like Hermès, Gaultier, John Lobb.

- *Prada,* which includes Prada, Helmut Lang, Jill Sander and Church.

- *Richemont,* which includes fashion brands (Dunhill, Chloé, Old England, Hackett London), jewellery (Cartier, Van Cleef & Arpels) and watches (Cartier, Vacheron Constantin, Piaget, IWC, Baume & Mercier).

In 1996, British fashion companies grossed approximately £600 million (£200 million at home and £400 million abroad). The UK fashion market is the fourth largest in the world, worth £900 million after the US (£5.2 billion), Italy (£1.5 billion) and France (£900 million). It is estimated that 1,000 to 1,500 people are employed directly in the UK fashion industry with another 10,000 people employed in machining, pattern-cutting, manufacture, marketing, distribution and retail. Young British designers have an excellent reputation abroad and some of them are currently working in international fashion houses. For instance, Stella McCartney, the daughter of ex-Beatle Sir Paul and Linda McCartney, was appointed chief designer at the French couture house Chloé.

The largest fashion company in the UK is Paul Smith, which in 2000 made £6.2 million profit on sales of £48.1 million. Born in Nottingham, Paul Smith founded the fashion house in 1974 and was knighted in November 2000 for his services to the fashion industry. His fashion is distinctive because of its sharp tailoring and extraordinary fabrics. Today, Paul Smith Ltd boasts a chain of around 225 shops, 200 of which are in Japan.

Another example of a successful fashion entrepreneur is Shami Ahmed. Ahmed is the founder of the Joe Bloggs clothing empire. He started in business with his parents when he was only 14 years old. Shami Ahmed was born in Karachi, Pakistan, but when he was two years old his parents moved to Britain. His father was an engineer turned businessman, first running a clothes market stall in Burnley, later a jeans shop in Manchester. He first started working for his father's business at the age of eight when he used to help with the invoices. From the age of 12 he became actively involved in the business, and from the age of 15 he was very seriously involved after leaving school without any qualifications. Within two years, he was running the family business, which had a workforce of three and annual sales of less than £200,000. In 1986, aged just 24, he launched his own brand of jeans: The Legendary Joe Bloggs Inc. Co. He thought Joe Bloggs, as it is better known, was 'truly British and common sounding' and he wanted his own label because he was 'tired of being dictated to buy the big names'. Today the company has annual sales of more than £50 million and employs a workforce of 300, while its customers include Warner Brothers.

CASE 4.1   RESTYLING THE OLD PATTERNS BY BOYD FARROW

(Source: *Financial Times*, 26 July 2004)

Last month Ben Sherman, the British fashion brand beloved by 1960s Mods and endorsed by Liam Gallagher, was sold for £80 million to the American giant Oxford Industries, which produces clothes for the Tommy Hilfiger and Nautica labels.

Ben Sherman was rescued from receivership in 1993 by a management team backed by 3i and Irish venture capitalist firm Enterprise Equity. The Oxford deal netted Enterprise £11.6 million profit – the most successful return on any of its investment in its 17 years. Yet it is the only clothing brand Enterprise has backed. 'Fashion is too dangerous,' says Bob McGowan-Smyth, Enterprise's chief executive, 'Ben Sherman was a quality brand based on solid foundations and it had three top-quality managers in place. You cannot afford just to be flavour of the week which is what "fashion" is seen to be.' Bluntly, the notion that the fashion sector represents an unpalatable investment risk is the single biggest obstacle between fashion businesses in need of capital and investors who could provide it. Keith Benson, a fashion industry veteran, now working for the DTI Business Link's *Access to Finance* initiative, says: 'the fashion sector has a lousy reputation for attracting private investors of any sort. Few angels are willing to even invest the £15,000 to £30,000 required by a fledgling designer.'

So what are the issues that fashion entrepreneurs need to address to close the culture gap with the City and/or other investors? First is the quality of management. This applies as much to designers straight out of college as to companies with years trading in an industry traditionally built around owner-managers. 'Fashion is unlike other industries – the road map is less clear,' says Karen Frank, who is eyeing UK fashion brands on behalf of private equity investors. 'Often strong management is missing, even when a company gets to have £15m turnover. Or companies do not have a growth plan in place before they set out.'

Suran Goonatilake, entrepreneur-in-residence at the Centre For Fashion Enterprise financed by the London Development Agency (LDA), says: 'the failure is usually on the management side, which is easy to remedy by training.' Second, there is the appropriate source of funding. Benson says: 'the first port of call is the banks, but they are completely risk-averse. Generally, they are not even interested in the DTI's own small firms loans guarantee scheme, when it comes to fashion.'

Friends and family, and successful industry names that have subsequently become angel investors are other obvious early resorts. However, this is considerably easier for serial entrepreneurs who already have a reputation and a network of contacts. The more ambitious, or those with some record of trading, might be tempted to approach smaller private equity and venture capital groups. But it will not be an easy sell. Even the venture capital group 3i, which has stakes in more than 1,800 businesses, has less than half-a-dozen fashion investments. Patrick Sheehan, managing director of technology at 3i, says: 'when we're looking at a company starting up it is a very risky proposition. So there has to be a large opportunity for us, but also we have to understand why that large opportunity exists.'

To underline the low-risk approach, when 3i co-led the £72.6 million buy-out of Swedish concern Gant a year ago, 3i cited Gant's 'strong brand proposition based on a stable design concept and low fashion risk' as factors. Hugh Lenon, managing partner of Phoenix Equity Partners, has a different take: 'people say that venture capitalists ignore this sector but it could be lack of supply not demand. The number of companies we've looked at must now run into three figures. There are a large number of surprisingly small companies that are unprofitable. Others are large and profitable but too expensive. Companies in the middle ground with real potential are few and far between.'

There are around 300,000 people employed in the UK clothing and textile industries, producing £16.5 billion worth of goods annually, of which £6 billion is exported. Most of the 11,000 companies in this sector are small, with an average size of 25–30 employees. Because of the funding gap between the start-ups and the mid-sized companies, Graham Hitchen, head of Creative London, part of the LDA, has been in discussions with mid-size private equity fund managers. The aim is to knit together the first development seed capital fund for the fashion business. Another LDA-funded business initiative, the London Fashion Forum, has taken a short-term let off Carnaby Street to showcase new designers and manufacturers. Two of these have since struck a deal with House of Fraser. And Nesta, the National Endowment for Science, Technology and the Arts, offers early-stage funding to a cross-section of science, arts and other creative industries. Benson says that of the 30 start-ups he has on his books, only two are in a position to approach a medium-level venture capitalist, hoping to raise £120,000 each.

(Continued)

(Continued)

The third issue for funding is that fashion businesses are advised to be clear about the integrity of their brands and how they could be grown. Goonatilake says: 'venture capitalists think luxury goods are not good returns. In fact, there can be a 95 per cent margin on good luxury brands.' Timothy Maltin, the entrepreneur who raised private equity to acquire British fashion house Hardy Amies in 2001, says established fashion brands that can be expanded across a range of products can be attractive. 'However, a lot of British fashion brands have been created from scratch recently, then spread out too quickly.' Phoenix Equity Partners created Equinox Luxury Holdings to acquire luxury branded businesses, including shoe brand Jimmy Choo. Lenon says: 'we look for strong brands that have the ability to grow globally. Brands imply stability and durability. We're not interested in "fashion" companies.'

Overall then, the climate is probably tougher for fashion funding than for other creative sectors. Investment can be raised, but both sides must go into it with clarity. Maltin adds: 'investors in the fashion sector need to take the medium-term view. It needs significant investment – not just money, but time. But with fashion they can at least see a well-made garment and appreciate what they are investing in.'

The essentials:

- Experienced management is your strongest asset.
- Start-ups are probably better off targeting specialist development funds, rather than private equity houses.
- Brand extensions are attractive, but risky.

Final thought: 'if they truly believe there's a market for what they are creating they must work with the financial people or whoever they have to get the product out there. Historically, too many companies fail because the creative and the corporate sides don't communicate' – Karen Frank, private equity investor.

Questions

1. What are the critical challenges raised in this case?
2. In your opinion, which of the identified challenges can be overcome? Illustrate your answers by using relevant examples.
3. What do you think that the government should do in order to minimise the culture gap .between fashion entrepreneurs and the City and/or other investors?
4. In December 2005, the clothing and design group Tommy Hilfiger has agreed to be taken over by private equity firm (Apax Partners) in a deal worth £923 million. What do you think makes 'Tommy Hilfiger' an attractive business for investors? Defend your position.

Film

This creative industry includes the production, distribution and exhibition of feature films (long and short), adverts, as well as training, promotional and educational videos. Film companies reach their audiences in a variety of ways: through the cinema, television, video and more recently through DVDs.

The UK film industry has grossed £3.6 billion in 1998. The value of the production sector alone is calculated to be £1.6 billion from TV advertisements, pop and corporate videos. Recent British blockbusters include *Four Weddings and a Funeral* in 1994, which grossed £160 million, and *Mr. Bean* with £150 million. Regarding distribution, there is a domination of US companies (UIP, Buena Vista, Fox and Warner Brothers). In terms of exhibition, in 1999 there was a growth of screens in the UK (789 more screens than in 1994), which was the result of multiplex developments. There are about 33,000 people working in film and video activities and there are a further 11,500 people who are estimated to be self-employed. Globally, the film industry is estimated at around $57 billion a year (calculating sales from cinema, TV and video). The Indian film industry, popularly known as Bollywood, dominates the global film industry. It produces the largest number of films in the world (around 1,000 movies per year), followed by the Americans (467 films in 2002).

The biggest commercial success comes from 20th Century Fox's *Titanic*, whose budget was in the area of $200 million and which has grossed over $1.8 billion. On the other hand, there are films that have used their limited resources creatively to come up with a blockbuster. For instance, the low-budget horror film, *The Blair Witch Project*, was one of the biggest success stories in film history in terms of the ratio of production cost to revenue. Costing only $35,000 to create, it generated $48 million in its first week of general release (on 1,101 screens) in July 1999, and its eventual worldwide box office totalled $245 million. How did they do it? Without a script, with unknown actors/actresses, directing and producing at the helm, but with a lot of enthusiasm, dreams and ingenuity they managed to make their film a not-so-ordinary Hollywood story. People behind the film used guerrilla marketing techniques such as word-of-mouth and the internet to promote their movie around the globe.

Music

The music industry has the following main activities: songwriting and composition, performance, as well as the production, distribution and retailing of sound recordings. The global turnover of the music industry is estimated to be around $70 billion. The music industry in the UK grossed £4.6 billion in 1998. There are approximately 122,000 people employed in the music industry. Their roles vary from composers and songwriters to promoters and managers. The music industry includes self-employed, part-time and multiple job-holders, which makes it difficult to calculate the total employment. The majority of music businesses (between 80 and 90 per cent) are micro-businesses employing up to nine people.

The music publishing industry follows similar patterns. There are five major companies, which dominate the market (75 per cent of the UK's recorded music market and 80 per cent of the global market): Universal Music Group, Sony, Bertelsmann Music Group (BMG), EMI and Warner Music Group. The retail market consists of some 6,400 over-the-counter retail outlets, ranging from specialist chains (e.g., Virgin, Tower Records or HMV), to independent specialists, multiple retailers (e.g., Woolworth's) or supermarkets (e.g., Tesco).

The record of achievements for the UK music industry is strong. Specifically, in 1998, the UK was the nationality of origin of 22 per cent of the top 100 European hit singles and of 31 per cent of hit albums. There are many UK artists who have enjoyed substantial success around the globe: Robbie Williams, Craig David, Coldplay and Oasis. A recent British music phenomenon has been the popular girl group 'Spice Girls'. The Spice Girls were initially formed in 1994 and then signed to Virgin Records in 1995. The group released their first single in July 1996 and by Christmas of that year had become a major international pop group. They managed to establish themselves as one of the world's biggest pop bands by selling 35 million albums and over 25 million singles worldwide in four and a half years. They also starred in their own movie, *Spiceworld* (1997), and the epitome of their success is the way they have managed to become the focus of so many discussions about the changing pop arena.

Performing arts

Creative companies in this sector are involved in live performances of ballet, contemporary dance, drama, music, theatre and opera. Their core activities are focused on the production and performance in the UK and abroad. New York's Broadway and London's West End are the centres of the English-language performing arts. The global performing arts industry is estimated to be worth around $40 billion in box-office revenues. In the UK, the industry has grossed around £470 million in the period 1998–9. The industry employs around 74,300 people as actors, entertainers, performers, stage managers, producers and directors.

The live performing arts continue to be highly appreciated abroad, with whole productions and individual performers in demand. Plays, particularly, are often taken up abroad with a flow of royalties back into the UK. For instance, Lord Lloyd-Webber's *Phantom of the Opera* brought him over £2 million a week in royalty fees from four productions in the US. Critical acclaim is also seen in the fact that international film actors are keen to work in the UK: in 2005–6 these have included Rob Lowe in *A Few Good Men* and Woody Harrelson in *The Night of the Iguana*.

Publishing

The publishing sector capitalizes on its employees' ability to write, design, produce and sell publications that satisfy the UK and global markets. The UK publishing industry is worth around £18.5 billion and employs 141,000 people. It encompasses three main sectors: books and learned journals, newspapers and magazines. Within these three main sectors there are various divisions. For instance, regarding books, there are different categories, such as general books (fiction and non-fiction), children's books, educational publishing, academic and professional publishing including journals. The newspaper industry is divided into national press (daily and Sunday titles) and regional press (morning, evening, Sunday, paid weekly and free weekly titles). Within the magazine industry there are divisions between consumer, business-to-business and customer magazines. Although these three main sectors in publishing have by tradition been primarily engaged in paper publishing, they are increasingly becoming involved in digital media development.

The UK publishing industry continues to be highly appreciated abroad. The Harry Potter books by J.K. Rowling, for instance, have sold more than 41.4 million copies in 200 countries and have been translated into approximately 40 languages. The success was so big that the UK company Electronic Arts produced computer and video games based on J.K. Rowling's Harry Potter books, in agreement with Bloomsbury (Harry Potter's publisher) and Warner.

Research and development (R&D)

People working in the R&D industry usually undertake scientific and technical research and development activities carried out in companies, universities or research organizations (excluding academic research on non-scientific and non-technical areas). There are two ways of measuring the R&D sector: first, by expenditure on R&D and, second, by the number of patents granted. The OECD reported $495 billion gross spending on R&D in 1998. The leading market is still the United States with $250 billion in 2000, a substantial increase from roughly $5 billion in 1953. In terms of the fruits of the research, there has been a growth in the number of patents awarded. For instance, in 1999 the three main patent offices in Washington, Tokyo and Munich awarded around 329,000 patents and America awarded around 169,000 patents in 1999 to both domestic and foreign applicants (see Figure 4.5). The company that has registered the most American patents (3,288 US patents) for 10 consecutive years is IBM. IBM is the world's largest information technology company, as well as the world's largest business and technology services provider ($36 billion). Their mission is to create, develop and manufacture the industry's most advanced information technologies, such as computer systems, software, networking systems, storage devices and microelectronics. Their aim is to translate their extensive R&D experience into products or services that offer value to their customers worldwide.

In the UK, the British patent office has registered around 8,000 patents, with an investment in R&D of around 1.8 per cent of gross national product in 1999. These figures suggest that British companies are not only investing less money in R&D than the US, but are also less commercially oriented and produce fewer patents.

Software

This industry involves the design and development of computer programs. The global software industry is estimated to be around $489 billion. The main markets constitute the USA (which is worth around $325 billion) and Europe. The UK market is worth £36.4 billion (1999) employing around 555,000 people.

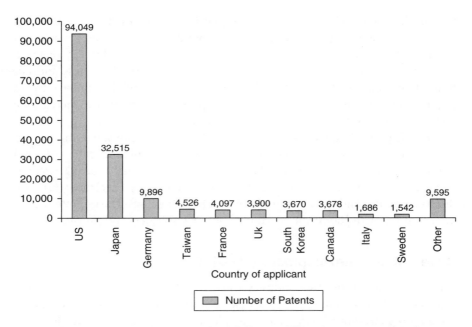

FIGURE 4.5   Patents registered by the US Patent Office, by country of applicant
(*Source:* Howkins, 2002: 109)

One of the most successful companies in software development for the last three decades has been the Microsoft Corporation. Founded by Bill Gates and Paul Allen in 1975, Microsoft is the worldwide leader in software, services and internet technologies for personal and business computing with revenues of $28.37 billion for year 2002, and employing more than 50,000 people in 78 countries and regions. Gates left Harvard to devote his energy to Microsoft with the vision that the computer would be a valuable tool on every office desktop and in every home. Microsoft started by developing software for personal computers. Gates's creativity, enthusiasm, ingenuity and long-term vision for personal computing has driven the company to continually advance and improve software technology, and strive to make personal computing easier, more cost-effective and more enjoyable for people to use.

Another more recent pioneer in the field of software development is Sabeer Bhatia, the co-founder of Hotmail Corporation. He founded the company in 1996, and as President and CEO he guided Hotmail's rapid rise to industry leadership and its eventual acquisition by Microsoft in 1998. Today, Hotmail remains the world's largest e-mail provider with over 50 million registered users in 230 countries. Bhatia's visionary contribution to the internet revolution has earned him widespread acclaim.

Toys and games (excluding video games)

Core activities in the toys and games industry include the design, manufacture and marketing of games and toys ranging from traditional to high-tech.

Companies in this industry market various toy products worldwide through sales to retailers and directly to consumers. Their primary markets include infants, pre-school children, girls and boys. The global toy industry (excluding video games) is estimated to be worth around $60 billion. The toy industry has been quite stable and large although it has been affected by the growth of video games. It is dominated by two publicly held US toy makers: Mattel (Barbie, Hot Wheels, Fisher-Price toys) and Hasbro (G.I. Joe, Tonka, Playskool), which are followed by Japan's Bandai Co. (Digimon) and Sanrio (Hello Kitty), as well as Denmark's LEGO Company. US chains also lead the global toy retail market. More specifically, Wal-Mart Stores is the number one toy seller, having surpassed Toys 'R' Us in 1999. Other leaders are discount stores, including Kmart and Target.

A very interesting example of a toy 'phenomenon' is the board game *Cranium*. It is the idea of two ex-Microsoft executives, Richard Tait and Whit Alexander, who started the company in 1998. Their goal was to apply the innovative product development methods they learned at Microsoft to build great products that would deliver incredibly funny and rewarding moments. Cranium Inc.'s founders used consumer views, reactions and perceptions collected during prototype play tests with original game concepts. The result of the whole process was the board game, *Cranium*. *Cranium*'s collection of activities included sketching, sculpting, humming, whistling, and even spelling words backwards, which proved to be a lot of fun. A word-of-mouth hit, the game quickly became the fastest-selling independent board game in history. Just three years later, over 800,000 copies of *Cranium* have been sold and the game has brought outrageous fun to millions of people on every continent. Following their early success, Cranium launched different editions for the UK, Australian and German markets, and two editions for Canada (English and French Canadian) with content geared specifically for each country.

TV and radio

The TV and radio industry includes activities, such as production, programming, packaging, broadcasting and transmission. The global TV revenues are in the area of $195 billion, coming from advertising, subscription, TV licensing fees, sponsorship and government grants. The US TV market is estimated to be around $72 billion, while the UK market is worth £6 billion. Although, there is a slight decline in terrestrial TV, BBC and ITV have a large share of the television audience. Satellite and cable companies are growing since the cost of switching to digital is now within the reach of most consumers. The TV and radio industry employs around 102,000 (2000) people, with half of these tending to be freelancers.

Although this is another under-represented industry in terms of ethnic minority, some creative entrepreneurs with ethnic minority backgrounds have been very successful. For instance, Mr Waheed Alli, who was born in November 1964 in south London, is a television producer, entrepreneur, and politician. He is the son of a Trinidadian nurse and a Guyanese mechanic. He was the brains behind Channel Four's *Big Breakfast*. He was brought up in south London and after leaving school at the age of 16 he got his first job as a £40-a-week researcher on a magazine called *Planned Savings*, before going on to work for the late Robert Maxwell's publishing companies. In the mid-1980s, Alli, living in fashionable Islington, got a job in the City and began earning big money. But he got bored of investment banking and formed a television production company with Charlie Parsons, a rising star of television. They teamed up with Bob Geldof in 1992 to form Planet 24 Productions, and through a series of shrewd deals – including their audacious win of Channel Four's breakfast slot – made a lot of money. Nowadays, TV producers find it increasingly difficult to create new, exciting programmes with loyal fans. It is not only the willingness, the enthusiasm or the financial back-up that one must have, the most important component is the idea – producers need to come up with a unique idea that has not been featured in the past or with a twist of an old idea that will be popular.

The highest rated programmes today are the so-called 'reality shows', such as *Big Brother*. The uniqueness of *Big Brother*, and ultimately its success, is based on the following factors:

- The viewers can watch how the contestants are interacting with the other members of the house; there are cameras recording every moment of the contestants' lives.

- The contestants do not have any contact with the outside world except those allowed by the editorial team.

- Although the contestants are required to nominate members to be voted out of the house, the audience has the final word for deciding who must leave the Big Brother house.

Although the show is based on a very simple idea (put 12 contestants in a house for three months and ask the TV audience to evaluate who should win based on their behaviours), the aforementioned twists have made this programme a global bestseller.

Video games

The video game industry has grown a lot in the last 20 years. This industry includes video games for the console market, such as Nintendo, Sega, Sony and recently Microsoft, as well as games for the computer market. The console games tend to be more expensive than the PC games because the publishers of the console games have to pay a royalty fee to the hardware manufacturers. For instance, the console games are in the price range from £29.99 to £39.99, while the games for the computer market are in the area of £24.99 to £29.99.

The global market for video games is estimated to be worth around £10.6 billion. Electronic Arts, headquartered in Redwood City, California, is the world's leading video games publisher. Founded in 1982, Electronic Arts announced revenues around $2.5 billion for the year 2003. The company develops, publishes and distributes interactive software worldwide for video game systems, personal computers and the internet.

The UK video game industry has grown rapidly with the launch of the console machines in the mid-1990s. The industry has reached an unprecedented record with revenues in the area of £1 billion. The UK market is now the third largest in the world and, including console sales, is now estimated to be worth over £2 billion, with around 3.2 million consoles bought in 2002, 44 per cent more than 2001. In 2002, two new consoles were launched: Microsoft's *Xbox*, which has sold around 680,000 and Nintendo's *GameCube*, which has sold over 489,000 consoles. This gives a total of almost 5.5 million installed consoles in the UK.

The UK games industry employed around 21,500 people in 1999, the majority of whom are involved in the production and retail of new games. The sophistication of game development and the ongoing demand for new features by consumers has forced game developers to grow their companies in terms of staff numbers. Consequently, half of the UK studios now employ more than 100 staff. There are also people who are employed in the retail sector, publishing as well as distribution; the remainder are involved in activities such as packaging, legal services, press and print. British video game developers have an excellent reputation abroad. For instance, two video games, namely *Colin McRae* and *TOCA* published by Codemasters, have sold jointly around 4.2 million. Also, action games, such as *Goldeneye 007* (Rare) and *Tomb Raider* (Eidos) have sold 7 and 21 million copies, respectively, worldwide.

CASE 4.2   COMPETITION IN CREATIVE INDUSTRIES

(Source: *Financial Times*, 5 November 2002)

Two weeks ago, the government warned that the competitiveness of a creative industry worth more to the UK economy than either film or television was at risk. Stephen Timms, the e-commerce minister, was wheeled out to wring his hands in public at the prospect. You missed the story? No, you didn't, because no UK national newspaper bothered to run it. The industry in question, you see, is video games software. The perception in Britain is that developing games is not a proper occupation for grown-ups, and is certainly not a 'serious' industry. However, the numbers suggest otherwise. The UK has the largest games industry in Europe employing some 20,000 people, and *Screen Digest* estimates that UK-developed games generated more than £1.1 billion in retail sales outside the UK in 2000, delivering a positive trade balance of £186 million. The UK, furthermore, has a reputation for creating outstanding games software that goes back to the days of 8-bit consoles and legendary developers such as Archer MacLean and David Braben. Last year *Grand Theft Auto III*, developed by DMA Design and published by Rockstar Games, topped the list in the US. The UK-developed *Who Wants to be a Millionaire?* beat fierce US and Japanese competition to top the UK charts that year.

So what is the problem? Essentially, UK games software started as a cottage industry and is now experiencing serious growing pains. The Department of Trade

(Continued)

(Continued)

and Industry is sufficiently concerned to have commissioned a report on the industry's future from Spectrum Strategy Consultants. It concludes that while UK games developers are the tops, a weak publishing and distribution side that could lead to it becoming 'simply a creative and technical bodyshop for overseas publishers and developers is undermining the industry'. The statistics tell the tale: UK-developed games account for 15.6 per cent of global sales; games released by UK publishers account for only 5.7 per cent of the global total. So is the UK games industry set to mirror the fate of the film industry, exemplified by the closure of FilmFour this year, the last UK-owned and vertically integrated film group with financial muscle? The question is all the more poignant with the world-wide video games business undoubtedly set for a golden age: software revenues of £11 billion in 2001 are set to rise to £20 billion by 2007, and that could easily be an under-estimate.

Roger Bennett, director-general of Elspa, the games publishers' trade association, is hugely optimistic about the industry: 'there is no question that this is now a mass market,' he says. But there will have to be changes if the UK is to make the most of its gaming assets. The *Spectrum Report* warns: 'the UK is at a turning point in its development and there are no global parallels within the games sector for it to follow. No other country has such a globally strong development sector with a comparatively weaker native publishing sector.'

Finance is the main problem. UK investors are reluctant to invest in games software, possibly because it seems frivolous or because of the industry's previously lurid commercial track record. Either way, the UK investment community has shown little interest in the sector, leaving small UK publishers to slug it out with overseas rivals many times their size. There is, for example, only one UK publisher, Eidos, in the global top 15, dwarfed by the likes of Electronic Arts of the US and Square of Japan. There are, however, five French companies there including Infogrames, Europe's largest. Bennett says this is because of the willingness of French investors to support local publishers.

The problem has been exacerbated by rapid advances in technology, which mean games today are created by teams of specialists – artists, mathematicians, graphics experts and programmers. Each game may take 18–24 months to create and cost between £1 million and £2 million. Developers are heavily dependent on advances from publishers. But the cost of an individual game is still around £40. The Spectrum report calculates that in 1992 a publisher had to sell just over 72,000 units to recoup a £200,000 advance to a developer. Today, they have to shift 227,000 units to recover an outlay of £1 million. So developers and publishers are increasingly dependent on big hits like Grand Theft Auto or sure-fire successes based on expensively acquired licences such as Harry Potter. Ensuring at least one hit means multiple projects have to be on the go simultaneously, a daunting project for underfinanced developers and publishers.

What is to be done? Ben McOwen Wilson, lead author on the *Spectrum Report*, says the industry and the government must work together to improve the image of the games industry and to pump-prime the under-developed domestic games investment industry. He argues for a two-pronged approach, with the UK continuing to attract the level of inward investment it is receiving from overseas publishers while attracting, promoting and ensuring the success of domestic games industry funding schemes such as Fund4Games, run by investment management company Noble Fund Managers. The government says its sponsorship of the *Spectrum Report* was an indication of how seriously it takes the industry's predicament. So there is everything to play for. But those who have witnessed the UK frittering away its advantages in other creative businesses will not be holding their breath.

Questions

1. What are the critical challenges relevant to the creative industries raised in this case?
2. Do you see any similarities or differences with the challenges identified in Case 4.1?

Creative industries: potential for growth

Although the creative industries are already receiving increased attention by forward-looking investors and policy makers, as the future unfolds it is expected that their value will further increase. Utilizing technology developments, traditional advertising agencies are looking to capitalize on using new advertising space through new media and internet options. Traditional auction houses are also using the internet to provide a different platform for bidding within which collectors can buy or sell their collectibles. Moreover, the generation of new technologies, such as new advanced game consoles and wireless gaming on mobile phones, will create new markets for industries such as interactive leisure software. E-commerce will also continue to challenge the traditional ways of delivering music to the consumer. Apple Computers has been one of the first companies to acknowledge this trend. Apple is trying to gain market share through their iTunes, an online service, which features hundreds of thousands of songs from major music companies including BMG, EMI, Sony Music Entertainment, Universal and Warner Bros. Some other trends and opportunities that are likely to influence potential growth within this area are lifestyle trends and changing demographics. Consumer expenditure on products and services associated with creative industries continues to increase and it remains a dynamic area of future potential growth.

Conclusion

In this chapter we have concentrated on the significance of the growth and future anticipated growth of creative industries for the UK economy. Historically, creative industries in the UK have been less important than in other developed nations. Countries such as America have long understood the value of new ideas and they have been quick to capitalize on the economic returns from turning ideas into commercial goods and services. However, in the last decade the UK government has identified the importance of the creative industries, especially as a means for generating jobs and providing the engine for new economic growth. As such, the future for the UK's creative economy looks promising, as the international competition to meet growing consumer demand intensifies business activities in what is an increasingly global and local marketplace.

RESOURCES, READINGS AND REFLECTIONS

CASE 4.3   A DIRE GLOBAL IMBALANCE IN CREATIVITY
BY RICHARD FLORIDA

(Source: *Financial Times,* 20 July 2005)

There is much talk of the internationally destabilising effects of the 'twin deficits' in America's domestic budget and foreign trade. But there is a third deficit, which may prove much more troubling. This deficit, which I call the talent deficit, will affect not just the US but also the UK, Germany, Japan and other traditional economic powers. For decades, these powers have taken for granted their net gains in the circulation of more than 150 million members of the global creative class: including scientists, engineers, entrepreneurs, artists, musicians and entertainers, and knowledge-based professionals in fields such as law, finance and medicine. The creative class accounts for between 30 and 40 per cent of the workforce in the advanced nations. In the US, it earns a staggering 50 per cent of all wages and salaries – as much as the manufacturing and services sectors combined.

The advanced nations have been living far beyond their capacity to generate talent and have essentially been borrowing from other places to fuel their growth and prosperity. This talent deficit is now growing for two reasons. First, around the world, a large share of the existing creative workforce is ageing and set to retire. Second, the advanced countries are not producing the talent they need in critical areas of science and technology. In the US, for example, more than 40 per cent of scientific and engineering talent will leave the workforce in the next decade or so, according to the National Science Foundation. More than 50 per cent of US computer scientists and nearly a quarter of its science and engineering workforce hail from abroad. Entrepreneurs from China and India accounted for almost a third of high-tech start-ups in Silicon Valley in the 1990s – companies that generated $20 billion (£11.5 billion) in sales and 70,000 jobs.

The flow of global talent has long provided the US its edge in high-technology, as people such as Sergey Brin, the Moscow-born co-founder of Google, and Sabeer Bhatia, Hotmail's co-founder, who grew up in Bangalore, emigrate to

America. Yahoo's Jerry Yang of Taiwan, Pierre Omidyar, the French-born founder of eBay, and Linus Torvalds, the open-source software luminary from Finland, are just a few of the migrants who have helped revolutionise the global economy.

In the creative age, the ability to address this deficit by competing for and cultivating top talent will outstrip the competition for jobs, technology and investment. The US seems to have forgotten its core advantage in attracting top talent; its restriction of immigration and growing social intolerance suggest that it is retreating from global competition and culture. Partly as a result, the competition is heating up. Countries from Sweden to Spain, Canada to New Zealand are increasing their efforts to attract talent – from high-tech workers to filmmakers, established scientists and promising graduate students. Australia and Canada have become particularly aggressive in the competition for talented immigrants. Both already have a higher proportion of foreign-born residents than the US – 22 per cent and 18 per cent respectively. Foreign students make up greater shares of the student body in these two countries and in several others than they do in the US. Taiwan, Korea, India and China are doing everything they can to retain top talent and lure expatriates back home by increasing investments in science and creativity and offering better pay and opportunities.

Many traditional economic powers, especially European ones, are experiencing a backlash against foreign influence. Ironically, these places are virtually dependent on immigrants as replacement workers – not just for low-end jobs but for critical high-skilled occupations in everything from software and information technology to biotechnology, the arts, entertainment and even sports. If they wish to succeed in the growing global competition for talent, economic capitals the world over must act now. Aggressively recruiting foreign students and highly skilled workers must be coupled with increased investment in education to develop and harness creative talent. Laws and social practices that discriminate – whether against specific religions, ethnicities, age groups or sexual orientations – must be eradicated, so that all may contribute their ideas to a place's economic ecosystem. Most of all, politicians and business leaders in the advanced nations must develop concrete strategies that enable people to see clearly how they can benefit from the global creative economy. Only by doing so can they overcome the growing opposition to foreign talent and immigration. If they fail to adapt their countries in such a way, the traditional powers will begin to see their industries suffer, their economies stall and their societies fracture. At that point, they will have far more to worry about than just a talent deficit.

Questions

1. What will be the main challenges for creative companies in Britain and America in the near future? How do these compare with developments in countries like China and India?
2. If you had your own creative business, what would you do to prepare for these challenges? Devise an action plan.
3. What do you think governments should do?

Chapter questions

1. Do you agree with the classification of the aforementioned creative sectors? Why or why not?

2. Do you think that there are other sectors that should be included? Use examples to illustrate your points.

3. Why are the creative sectors important to the health of a nation's economy?

4. In your opinion, what factors account for the increased policy attention given to these creative sectors?

Hands-on exercise

Students are allocated to small groups and are required to undertake a study by researching one creative sector of their choice and making a brief presentation on:

- the regional variations of the industry of their choice (based on the number of companies formed, revenues and job creation);

- different regional policies that contributed to the variation of economic activity.

Answer the following small quiz. Read the following statements carefully and circle the correct answer:

Statements		
1. Creativity plays a central role to economic competitiveness in advanced economies.	*True*	*False*
2. A creative organization is defined as: *'Any business entity whose main source of income comes from the production of novel and appropriate ideas to tackle clients' problems or opportunities identified'.*	*True*	*False*
3. In 1999, the annual revenue of the 15 creative sectors worldwide was estimated in the region of $2.24 billion.	*True*	*False*
4. The creative industries in the UK employ around 1.1 million people and generate revenues in the area of £50.5 billion (2001).	*True*	*False*
5. The UK is the fourth largest advertising market in the world in terms of revenues after the US, Japan and Germany.	*True*	*False*
6. The Indian film industry, popularly known as Bollywood, dominates the global film industry. It produces the largest number of films in the world (around 1,000 movies per year), followed by the Americans (467 films in 2002).	*True*	*False*

7.	There are 400 design firms in the UK.	*True*	*False*
8.	The company that has registered the most American patents (3,288 US patents) for 10 consecutive years is Microsoft.	*True*	*False*
9.	The internet and new technology will have a direct effect on some of the aforementioned creative industries.	*True*	*False*
10.	In the last decade the UK government has identified the importance of the creative industries as a means of generating jobs and providing the engine for new economic growth.	*True*	*False*

Answers

1: True; 2: True; 3: False; 4: False; 5: True; 6: True; 7: False; 8: False; 9: True; 10: True.

Team debate exercise

Debate the following statement:

Policy makers should focus on encouraging more entrepreneurial activity to the most profitable creative sectors.

Divide the class into two groups. One should argue as convincingly as possible that concentrating on one profitable creative sector is the most important factor for economic growth and job creation. The other should prepare its arguments against this, highlighting that only a focus on all identified sectors will enhance the health of a nation's economy. Each group should be prepared to defend their ideas against the other group's arguments by using real-life examples.

References

Castells, M. (2000) *The Information Age; Economy and Society and Culture. Vol. 1: The Rise of the Network Society*, 2nd edn. Oxford: Blackwell.

Castells, M. (2001) 'Information technology and global capitalism', in W. Hutton and A. Giddens (eds), *On the Edge: Living with Global Capitalism*. London: Vintage.

Chandy, R.K. and Tellis, G.J. (1998) 'Organizing for radical product innovation: the overlooked role of willingness to cannibalize', *Journal of Marketing Research*, 35: 474–87.

Department for Culture, Media and Sport (1998) *Creative Industries Mapping Document*. London: DCMS.

Department for Culture, Media and Sport (2001) *Creative Industries Mapping Document*. London: DCMS.

Florida, R. (2004) 'America's looming creativity crisis', *Harvard Business Review*, (October): 122–36.

Giddens, A. and Hutton, W. (2001) 'In conversation', in W. Hutton and A. Giddens (eds), *On the Edge: Living with Global Capitalism*. London: Vintage.

Harvard Business Review (2005) *The Essentials of Managing Change and Transition*. Boston, MA: Harvard Business School Press.

Howkins, J. (2002) *The Creative Economy*. London: Penguin Books.

Irani, Z., Sharp, J.M. and Kagioglou, M. (1997) 'Improving business performance through developing a corporate culture', *TQM Magazine*, 9: 206–16.

Kao, J.J. (1996) *Jamming: The Art and Discipline of Business Creativity*. London: HarperCollins Business.

Martin, G. (2006) *Managing People and Organizations in Changing Contexts*. Oxford: Butterworth-Heinemann.

Mohanty, R.P. (1999) 'Value innovation perspective in Indian organizations', *Participation and Empowerment: An International Journal*, 7 (4): 88–103.

Morgan, G. (1991) *Images of Organization*. Thousand Oaks, CA: Sage.

Nishibori, E.E. (1972) *Humanity and Development of Creativity*. Tokyo: Japan Productivity Center.

O'Toole, J. (1974) *Work in America. Special Task Force to Secretary of Health Education and Welfare*. Cambridge, MA: MIT Press.

Özsomer, A., Calantone, R.J. and Di Bonetto, A. (1997) 'What makes firms more innovative? A look at organizational and environmental factors', *Journal of Business and Industrial Marketing*, 12: 400–16.

Peters, T.J. (1997) *The Circle of Innovation*. London: Hodder & Stoughton.

Porter, M. (1990) 'The competitive advantage of nations', *Harvard Business Review*, (March–April): 73–93.

Porter, M. (1998) 'Clusters and the new economics of competition', *Harvard Business Review*, (November–December): 77–90.

Preece, D., McLoughlin, I. and Dawson, P. (eds) (2000) *Technology, Organizations and Innovation: Critical Perspectives on Business and Management, Vols I–IV*. London: Routledge.

Ridderstråle, J. and Nordström, K. (2000) *Funky Business: Talent Makes Capital Dance*. Edinburgh: Pearson Education.

Ridderstråle, J. and Nordström, K. (2004) *Karaoke Capitalism: Management for Mankind*. New York: Financial Times Prentice Hall.

Stewart, T.A. (1994) 'The information age in charts', *Fortune*, 4 April: 75–9.

Recommended reading

- Florida, R. (2002) *The Rise of the Creative Class*. New York: Basic Books.

- Kline, S., Dyer-Witheford, N. and de Peuter, G. (2003) *Digital Play. The Interaction of Technology, Culture and Marketing*. Montreal: McGill-Queen's University Press.

- Press, M. and Cooper, R. (2003) *The Design Experience: The Role of Design and Designers in the 21st Century*. London: Ashgate.

- Ridderstråle, J. and Nordström, K. (2000) *Funky Business: Talent Makes Capital Dance*. Edinburgh: Pearson Education.

- Ridderstråle, J. and Nordström, K. (2004) *Karaoke Capitalism: Management for Mankind*. New York: Financial Times Prentice Hall.

Some useful websites

@

- The website for PDMA (Product Development and Management Association) provides lots of articles, book suggestions and information on product development (http://www.pdma.org).

- IDSA's (Industrial Designers Society of America) website provides lots of articles, book suggestions and information on people, companies and best practices on industrial design (http://www.idsa.org).

- The DMI's (Design Management Institute) website offers some interesting articles (http://www.dmi.org, registration is needed).

- The Design Council's website offers a variety of publications, reports, case studies, links and interviews around design, its process and its impact to business performance (http://www.designcouncil.org.uk).

- The Department for Culture, Media and Sport website with several reports, publications and links related to the creative industries in the UK (http://www.culture.gov.uk/about_us/creativeindustries/default.htm).

- The website by the Scottish Enterprise also provides some interesting facts about the creative industries in Scotland (http://www.scottish-enterprise.com).

- This is a website from UCLA's Anderson School of Management with a lot of interesting research papers, links and information on the management of entertainment and media companies (http://www.anderson.ucla.edu/x1030.xml).

- This website from Professor Richard Florida provides a listing of his publications and insights into his research findings (http://www.creative class.org).

Part 2
CREATIVITY AND CHANGE IN ORGANIZATIONS

5

The Individual: Promoting Critical Thinking

Learning objectives

After reading this chapter you will:

1. Understand individual creativity.
2. Appreciate the relationship between personality and creative achievement.
3. Be able to explain the cognitive factors that predict creative achievement.
4. Be able to examine the basis of knowledge and its contribution to individual creativity.
5. Be able to differentiate between intrinsic and extrinsic motivation and understand how they both influence individual creativity.

Introduction

Creative thinking is among the most significant of all human activities. As individuals, creativity surrounds us from the moment that we wake in the morning until we sleep at night. The cars we drive to work in, the software applications that we use, the newspapers or magazines that we read, as well as the movies, books or music that entertain us in our spare time, all engage our creative minds. A commonly held myth about creativity is the notion that creative people behave in unique ways to the rest of us. Our undergraduate and postgraduate students always surprise us at the beginning of our course on 'change, creativity and innovation', by always referring to well-known individuals when they are asked to identify creative people; mainly because they are characterized by eccentric and distinctive personalities. In this chapter, we aim to shed some light on individual creativity (the person behind a creative idea or a product) and show how creative behaviour is not only affected by personality factors, but is the outcome of a complex interaction between an individual and his/her contextual and social influences (Woodman et al., 1993). The chapter aims to answer two pertinent questions, namely:

- Why are some individuals more likely to make interesting contributions (or advance knowledge in their respective industries/professions) than others?

- Why do some people generate more breakthrough ideas than others?

In an attempt to answer these questions we will explore four main topics, comprising: cognitive style and abilities (e.g., making remote associations); personality traits (e.g., risk taking, non-conformism); relevant knowledge (e.g., building understanding and insight); and the motivation required to innovate. Based on our understanding of these four elements, we forward some specific human resource practices that can be used to promote processes of change, creativity and innovation in the workplace.

Cognitive factors

A useful opening question to this section is: why do scholars in this area continually list cognitive abilities as correlates of individual creativity? The simple answer to this question is that many studies show how individuals high on general cognitive ability tend to achieve better results on measures of job knowledge, skills and techniques (Ree and Earles, 1996), and they are good at processing information (Schmidt et al., 1981). Majaro (1992), for example, proposes that *mental flexibility* is an important cognitive feature associated with creative achievement. A creative mind must be able to deal with complexity, discriminate options and to be open to new ideas and not constrained by habit. Creativity-relevant processes involve breaking out from existing perceptual and cognitive sets in order to create 'space' for new problem-solving strategies (Taggar, 2002). Moreover, people who are open to new experiences tend to be more imaginative and willing to consider issues or problems from a broader range of perspectives (Costa and McCrae, 1992).

Mednick (1962) identifies the ability to *link remote associations* across elements as a cognitive style that contributes to creativity. The main problem that most of us face is our natural tendency to see what we are taught to see (James, 1983). Whilst it is important for individuals to gain an in-depth knowledge of their particular fields in order to have the necessary expertise to be creative, this does not mean that an individual's focus should be narrow and constrained. On the contrary, the ability to make connections in new ways is a necessary precursor for creativity (Sternberg and Lubart, 1991). Creative individuals approach their work settings with a broad range of interests that encourage them to seek out resources from 'wide' constituencies. This enables them to recognize relationships among apparently unconnected bits of information (Amabile, 1983; Cummings and Oldham, 1997; MacKinnon, 1962). Eckert and Stacey (1998), for example, illustrate how employees in a variety of creative activities try to recognize similarities and connections as well as to modify or combine existing ideas into novel solutions (see Figure 5.1). These can take the form of new products, musical compositions, new graphic logos, and so forth.

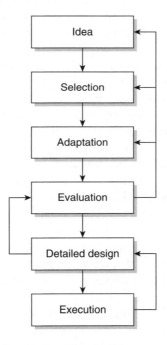

FIGURE 5.1   Direct use of a source of inspiration
(*Source*: Eckert and Stacey, 1998: 14)

Context is important and the quest for new ideas may take different forms in different industries. For instance, product designers derive most of their ideas from other artefacts, fine art, or by looking at nature and its motifs, colours or patterns (Eckert and Stacey, 1998). Engineers or scientists in R&D departments may be looking for analogies from other situations where there is a solution; they may then modify this solution to enable the generation of novel or useful ideas. Bransford and Stein (1984) provide several examples where analogy has been used in order to generate a new invention. For instance, they refer to Gutenberg's printing-press invention, which was inspired by his observation of a wine-press and the punches used for making coins. Gutenberg used this knowledge in tackling the different 'problem' of publishing and ended up providing the market with a highly desirable solution. According to Eckert and

Stacey (1998), the adaptation of a source of inspiration to a design can take the following forms:

- *Literal* – meaning that the design is kept as close as possible to the original source.

- *Abstraction* – when certain features are isolated or highlighted.

- *Association* – when the designer comes up with an idea loosely connected to the source.

Another cognitive feature that has been found to be relevant to creativity is *suspension of judgement.* Majaro (1992) argues that creative individuals are highly tolerant of uncertainty and are able to hold back from accepting the first solution that comes to mind, especially if it is not considered appropriate in the sense of rightness or elegance. As the creative process can be prematurely curtailed if an idea is 'placed in the dock' too early, individuals may inadvertently limit their options by trying to identify quick solutions to problems. They may not give their ideas time to develop and they may quit too soon (Lizotte, 1998). Likewise, Ray and Myers (1986) stress the importance of what they call the 'voice of judgment'. In simple terms, it is 'the voice inside' that provides us with a running commentary on our actions. The collective judgement of society as a whole, including rules of fashion, social class and etiquette, all affect our thinking. Creative individuals need to reflect on their thoughts in assessing whether their ideas are being constrained by biases, preconceptions or time limitations. The more individuals become aware of these barriers, the more likely they are to move forward in their creative thinking. We find that final-year undergraduate students find this quite hard to apply in practice. In doing their dissertations, they often generate theoretical models or frameworks very early on in the process and this can limit their thinking. The challenge that these students face is to remain open to other stimuli whilst having to collect, analyse and write-up data to meet submission deadlines. The observation of this working habit should not be considered as something that only happens in the context of a dissertation project, but as something that may occur in a range of working environments, especially where uncertainty dominates and deadlines are pressing.

MacKinnon (1960) and Majaro (1992) also identify *originality of thinking and freshness* as a cognitive characteristic needed for innovative solutions to be developed. These scholars consider originality as the ability to give unusual answers to questions or atypical responses to specified problems. They propose that employees who consistently generate a richer list of unusual perceptions are likely to be those people who demonstrate a higher level of original thinking. Design companies often embrace an array of techniques to encourage employees to come up with unusual responses to their clients' problems. For example, once per month, Design Continuum (a Boston-based new product design consultancy) invite all their staff during lunchtime to participate in a fun activity, where one chooses randomly one word and the rest search for images, synonyms, articles, and so forth, that they feel best describe or correspond to these stimuli. The objective of this exercise is to encourage creative individuals to think of something original or fresh. Such activities assist employees to think of concepts or ideas that are outwith their specialization or normal area of interest.

Implications for human resource management

Our understanding of cognitive factors suggests that the following human resource practices may promote creativity in the workplace:

- *Managers should hire individuals who are able to generate alternatives and engage in divergent thinking.* Accessing a variety of alternatives (based on changing requirements and emerging opportunities) makes them more likely to make connections that may lead to creative output.

- *Managers should encourage employees to try new things.* To develop new products or processes, individuals must be encouraged to engage in activities (e.g., flexible thinking, experimenting with ideas, examining possibilities, searching for analogies) that could lead to creative outcomes.

- *Managers should set some creativity goals* that are related to creative activities and/or outcomes (e.g., ideas that are novel and useful). When individuals know that creativity is needed and valued by an organization, they are more likely to act creatively (Manske and Davis, 1968).

- *Managers must allow their employees to initiate their own projects* that, whilst related to their own interests, are also aligned to organizational goals. The development of new ideas without the burden of ongoing firm activities may allow employees to develop unique insights whilst pursuing their own interests.

Apart from these four cognitive abilities of *mental flexibility, remote associations, suspension of judgement* and *originality of thinking,* the literature suggests that highly creative individuals are also characterized by a number of dispositional traits that predict creative achievement.

Personality traits

In studying the creative personality, researchers initially set out to identify the personality traits of the creative person. Scholars listed personality correlates of creativity, as well as biographical data that would predict the potential for creative behaviour (Hall and MacKinnon, 1969; MacKinnon, 1960, 1962). Researchers tried to shed some light on this area by focusing on direct influences in the family environment and situations that positively link with creative individuals. Interestingly, the findings indicate that creative individuals do not always emerge from the most nurturing of environments (Goertzel et al., 1978; Simonton, 1984). On the contrary, the potential for creativity is often influenced by the diverse range of experiences an individual encounters. Diverse events, as well as exposure to challenging experiences, often strengthen a person's ability to carry on in the face of obstacles (Simonton, 1994) and to feel less restricted by commonly held views.

Other research has focused on particular occupations (e.g., students, R&D scientists) in their search for personality traits that may be associated with creative achievement (Amabile, 1988; Barron and Harrington, 1981; Welsh, 1975). This focus on personality traits as predictors of creative achievement has experienced something of a revival in recent years (Simonton, 1999a). For example, Csikszentmihályi (1990) conducted a longitudinal study of artists in their early 20s that sought to understand why some of them created work that would be considered 'creative' while others did not. The first follow-up of these young artists occurred a few years after they graduated from art school, while the second follow-up occurred 18 years after the initial research. In terms of personality traits, Csikszentmihályi (1990) found that the most creative students tended to be sensitive, independent, unconcerned with social norms and social acceptance. Taken as a whole, the main personality traits that are linked to creative achievement include: risk-taking, self-confidence, tolerance of ambiguity, need for achievement, autonomy and non-conformity – and each of these are briefly discussed below.

Risk-taking: it is generally acknowledged that creativity requires a risk-taking personality (Glassman, 1986; Michael, 1979; Sternberg et al., 1997). Creative individuals are more willing to take a stand and challenge the status quo. Consequently, there is a popular belief that creative individuals are high risk-takers. However, this is not necessarily true; successful creative professionals usually take calculated risks, which they believe they understand and have the ability to manage. They acknowledge the risks associated with their work and are therefore acting proactively by cautiously calculating risk elements against potential benefits of engaging in more creative endeavours.

Self-confidence: research has revealed how creative individuals tend to have a high regard of themselves. For instance, in studies conducted by Buel (1965) and MacKinnon (1960), creative individuals used a large number of favourable adjectives when asked to describe themselves. It is often the employees' own belief in the worth and validity of their creative efforts that helps them override periods of frustration during the creative process (MacKinnon, 1962). Thus creative employees tend to have faith in their own abilities and skills in order to face the open-ended problems that they often encounter and for which, usually, there is no set answer (see Keller and Holland, 1978).

Tolerance of ambiguity: early studies in this area suggest that highly creative employees are more likely to tolerate ambiguity than other employees. MacKinnon (1960), for instance, illustrates how such employees are likely to acknowledge complexity and even disorder without becoming overly anxious. MacKinnon (1962) attempts to explain this personality trait by proposing that it is not so much that creative employees like chaos *per se*, but that they are challenged by the richness of the disorder and complexity that presents them with opportunities to form new orders and ways of doing things. This feeling of comfort with ambiguity can result in creative employees bringing together previously unrelated pieces of information or messages into new forms (McGrath, 2000).

Need for achievement: creative people are generally ambitious individuals with a strong passion to achieve (Barron, 1966; Buel, 1965; MacKinnon, 1959, 1962). Motivation derives from an inner need to accomplish a combination of personal and economic goals. Moreover, this need for achievement often combines with a desire for autonomy in testing their own ideas and being forward in promoting new perspectives (MacKinnon, 1960, 1962).

Autonomy and non-conformity: creative individuals desire autonomy in their work and social environment (Buel, 1965; McDermid, 1965) and this is often associated with the personality trait of non-conformity. Creative employees usually show high levels of social independence and a lack of concern for social norms (Keller and Holland, 1978). MacKinnon (1960, 1962) notes that creative individuals' independence in thought and action contributes significantly to creative achievement. This personality trait, triggered by the need for social independence, was taken a step further by Majaro (1992), who suggests that creative employees are more likely to take an active role and challenge authority; for example, by demanding more information and explanation than other less creative individuals.

This list of key personality traits can help us identify individuals that exhibit creative characteristics. The identification of these personality traits is also of significance since they are vital to individual development. Take, for example, an individual who shows an early openness to new experiences. In such a case, it is possible to further nurture this potential and facilitate the development of a richer and more diverse associative network (Simonton, 1999b). Nevertheless, the view that personality traits are a good predictor of creative achievement does have a number of limitations. First, there is no real evidence to suggest that there is a single 'creative personality'. People of all personality types, attitudes and dispositions, may not only be creative but become successful creative individuals. Second, personality theories are rather static and tend to ignore the dynamic social–cultural influences that shape creative processes. Third, the list of key traits is ambiguous. Some of these characteristics have been derived from biographies and autobiographies of creative individuals who have been successful. Such individuals often portray themselves as geniuses, eccentric and unique. Others have originated from attempts to portray an ideal type of 'creative individual' that markedly differs from the key characteristics of an 'average person'. This false dichotomy discounts the possibility of 'average individuals' also being creative and, as such, conflicts with the findings from other empirical research that will be discussed later in this chapter. Finally, academic studies that have focused on identifying personality traits typically attempt to differentiate the so-called 'creatives' from the 'non-creatives'. This, however, has proven problematic as some of the personality traits concerned are situation-specific and thus represent unstable features at the more general level. Once again, the 'either/or' scenario limits analysis and polarizes views.

To sum up, much of the early work into individual creativity has focused on identifiable personality traits. The position held was that – all other conditions being equal – those individuals who exhibit the traits of risk-taking, self-confidence, tolerance of ambiguity, need for achievement, autonomy and non-conformity, are more likely to generate creative outcomes or make contributions that are creative than individuals whose personalities reflect other characteristics. But as already noted, this position has been criticized for its failure to take account of contextual and processual factors in the dynamic interplay between individuals, groups and society. This limitation to a purely personality-based explanation of creativity has led to a reconsideration of more process-based accounts. Personality *per se* is not a panacea for creative achievement; what individuals also need to have is knowledge relevant to their respective domain (Amabile, 1983).

Implications for human resource management

Our understanding of personality traits suggests that the following human resource practices may promote creativity:

- *Managers should hire individuals who are more predisposed to be creative.* Managers may screen potential candidates for high innate levels of creativity by going through their previous work or by asking them to make a presentation of a recent project.

- *Managers should allow their employees discretion in structuring their job activities.* Individuals should be given autonomy in how they allocate time to job tasks, and control over how their work is planned and conducted. They should also follow their own ideas and interests without being too concerned about how others view them.

- *Managers should encourage their employees to take risks.* Individuals should be encouraged to take risks and break out from routine and safe ways of doing things since creativity usually happens through a trial-and-error process.

- *Managers should celebrate 'small wins'.* It is not only important to encourage experimentation with new ideas but also to praise and support efforts. Recognition of 'successes' in the work being done will build self-worth and improve the confidence of employees.

CASE 5.1   NEW MEDIA ARE JUST THE TICKET FOR BUS, TUBE AND TAXI BY ROBERT WRIGHT

(Source: *Financial Times,* 29 November 2005)

The common phrase 'you've got a face like the back end of a bus' is fast becoming a compliment rather than insult. Or at least it should be, given the evolution of buses' backs into advertising displays adorned by giant images of the likes of Jose Mourinho, Sharon Osbourne and Kylie Minogue. In a more high-tech example of the evolution of London's transport network into mobile canvases for advertisers, passengers riding the escalators at Tottenham Court Road underground station are greeted by 66 moving images cascading down the walls. The area is the first on the underground to be equipped with the technology which London Underground officials predict will soon become standard – poster sites with a plasma screen and broadband internet connection, rather than pasted-up paper.

The experiment is one of many ways transport operators in London are contriving to deliver more active, more interesting or more eye-catching advertising to travellers in London who, research shows, have developed a particularly high resistance to the messages which regularly bombard them. Passengers on buses are now often treated to TV clips giving news headlines and other information mixed in with advertising. In March, Cabvision launched a system which starts a television screen automatically when a passenger enters the taxi. Viacom, which installed the screens at Tottenham Court Road, has also tested moving, digitally-produced adverts on the side of buses. Bus stops are increasingly used to deliver digital information and advertising.

The question is whether advertisers will think the extra attention they gain by targeting consumers through such media merits the extra they will be asked to pay to appear on them. 'It's just a question of striking a balance between how much they will charge you and how much it's worth to you', says Jo Sutherland, communications planning director at Carat Media, an advertising planning and buying agency.

There is little doubt on the issue in the mind of Chris Townsend, director of group marketing for Transport for London (TfL), who is in charge of the changing technology of advertising at London Underground, the TfL subsidiary which runs underground trains and stations. The changes represent the biggest transformation ever in the more than 100 years that adverts have appeared on the underground, he says. It should significantly increase the rates London Underground can charge advertisers. That should be important for media buyers since the underground is already one of the UK's most valuable outdoor advertising estates. There are well over 1 billion journeys on the system annually – more than on the entire national rail network. As well as the measures already introduced or under trial, Mr Townsend hopes it will soon be possible to undertake cross-track projection – beaming frames from adverts through trains as they go down tunnels to give passengers the illusion of seeing a moving advert projected on the tunnel wall. The changes should increase revenue because they will greatly improve the quality of material shown, Mr Townsend believes. 'We're re-evaluating the opportunity to use new technology to amass revenue for London Underground and TfL', he says. 'We're particularly interested in having the very latest broadband communications feeding into plasma screens – and potential cross-track projection'.

Research on the escalator panels at Tottenham Court Road has shown far higher recall afterwards than normal for advertisements on escalator panels. 'We had a particular advertising campaign by "O" that showed a wonderful effect flowing from the top plasma screen down to the bottom one that looked like flowing water', he says. The campaign had particularly high recall rates among customers. 'We will certainly be able to charge a premium rate, particularly where there's a moving

(Continued)

(Continued)

video opportunity', Mr Townsend says. He hopes to gain an extra advantage from using new, more interactive advertising technology by interspersing the adverts with travel information, that potentially helps advertisers by drawing passengers' attention to the screens. The technology should also cut London Underground's costs. The main cost in setting up sites will be to install the screens and broadband connection. After that, it will be possible simply to send out advertisements from one central computer. Mr Townsend says: 'Once you have a very simple broadband connection, you then don't need to use human resources to place out posters in panels. Once it's installed, there's a lot less maintenance to change the advertising'.

Yet the advertising industry may still take some convincing. Ms Sutherland at Carat says cross-track projection has been under discussion for at least six years but constantly seems to be held up by concerns over safety. That is particularly the case over its potential use in stations, where it might confuse some passengers and prevent them paying attention to the platform edge. 'Doing attractive, high-impact ads with the underground is quite an issue', she says. 'You don't want to stop people. It has to be interesting enough for people to look at, but not so interesting that they're going to stop'. The underground is already one of the most expensive places to advertise, she points out, and this might discourage advertisers from paying a further premium for more sophisticated adverts. Advertisers might, however, be interested in the possibility offered by new technology of having their advert on display only at appropriate times of day. 'If you're a beer brand, you could just be up at night', she says.

There are similar issues for all forms of transport advertising. One of the most successful initiatives to reach travellers in London, Ms Sutherland suggests, is Waterloo station, where a digital screen placed above the train information screens tells commuters about television programmes airing that evening. 'You don't really have a choice of anything else to do', she says of the reasons why passengers will look at the screens.

Bus stops – which increasingly feature sophisticated, interactive advertising – also benefit from a captive audience. This is the same reason for the strong opportunity faced by Cabvision, which has placed digital screens in more than 1,000 London taxis since launching in March this year. The service offers passengers a choice of seven channels where five-minute programmes are split into two-and-a-half minute segments with an ad break. The taxis used are soundproofed and there is high-quality sound; while the sound can be muted, the screen cannot be turned off entirely. 'If you're a mobile phone company and you want to put an ad on a screen in a taxi to sell to a businessman, it might work', Ms Sutherland says. The risk, however, remains that on many forms of transport the advertising-led TV channel will be just another medium to ignore. 'People in buses are chatting', Ms Sutherland says of buses with TV screens. 'They're not at the front gathered round a TV commercial.' The challenge, she says, will be to decide how to use the proliferating media opportunities. 'There are hundreds of different ways you can reach people', she says. 'As a planner, you're trying to find the right one. You can waste a lot of money on low-impact media.'

Mr Townsend at TfL accepts media buyers face a challenge in learning how to use the new media. But he remains convinced, based on experience at Tottenham Court Road, that new digital screens have an ever more important part to play in grabbing a jaded London public's attention. 'Where you can use the medium creatively, you can maximise impact', he says.

Questions

1. Can a business succeed without 'outside the box' thinking? Why or why not?
2. 'Traditional ways of advertising are still effective'. Evaluate this statement.
3. Which of the identified creative strategies do you think will be the most effective in capturing the audience's attention? What kind of criteria have you used to assess their effectiveness?

Knowledge

Taggar (2002) argues that one cannot be really creative unless one possesses an adequate amount of knowledge in the particular area under investigation, and that one also has the necessary skills to generate and implement ideas in that area. In this respect, people often confuse the concepts of data, information and knowledge. Data is defined by Zack (1999: 46) as 'observations or facts out of context'. Let us give you an example to illustrate the point.

Read the following words:
simple, not, phenomenon, linear, or, is, creativity, a

Some of you may find it difficult to understand what the words above try to convey and some of you may find it even useless or annoying. You may feel like that because the words are out of context and most probably they are meaningless to you. The difference between data and information is that the latter must be perceived as 'data within some meaningful context, often in the form of a message' (Zack, 1999: 46). Therefore, information is considered more useful than data since it is context-specific and explicit.

Read the following words again:
creativity is not a simple or linear phenomenon

The above sequence of words seems more logical because it puts the words in a context that gives them meaning. This in turn makes them easier to understand and store in one's memory.

Several scholars and practitioners often use the terms 'information' and 'knowledge' interchangeably, even though the two entities are far from identical. Davenport and Prusak (1998: 5) define knowledge as:

A fluid mix of framed experiences, values, contextual information, and expert insight that provides a framework for evaluating and incorporating new experiences and information. It originates and is applied in the minds of the knower. In organizations, it often becomes embedded not only in documents or repositories but also in organizational routines, processes, practices and norms.

There are two types of knowledge, namely, formal and informal (Sternberg and Lubart, 1995). Formal knowledge, or otherwise defined as 'explicit', is the knowledge of a discipline or occupation (Nonaka and Takeuchi, 1998). It is the knowledge that you can gain by reading books, magazines, academic journals, or by attending lectures, seminars, etc. This knowledge may consist of facts, theories, principles, opinions, theoretical frameworks, techniques or paradigms. For instance, the creative act of writing a book demands that its authors possess a good grasp of the knowledge related to the issues that the book will cover. Informal or tacit knowledge, on the other hand, is the knowledge that you acquire by being in the relevant discipline or occupation. This is the knowledge that operates at a subconscious level in the human mind and therefore may be very difficult for one to become aware of and make explicit (Polanyi, 1958).

Formal or explicit knowledge

Nonaka and Takeuchi (1995) define formal or explicit knowledge as knowledge that can be articulated and may range from grammatical statements, mathematical expressions and specifications to manuals. Hence, formal knowledge can be transmitted more easily and formally between individuals. Choo (1998) proposes that explicit knowledge is knowledge that manifests itself through language, symbols, objects and artefacts. Therefore, it can take the form of chemical and mathematical formulas, patents, business plans, software code, databases, blueprints and statistical reports. Choo (1998) argues that nowadays firms tend to depend heavily on formal or explicit knowledge collected, documented and stored in formal databases during their decision-making processes.

Why is this type of knowledge important to creativity? In order to be creative in any discipline or occupation that you may choose to follow, knowledge is important. Imagine the catastrophic consequences of working as an architect if you do not know the structures that can support a building. Why is it important to creative achievement? First, knowledge acts as a store of building data for novel combinations, which means that without 'input' there can be no 'output' because there is nothing to 'build upon' (Whitfield, 1975). There is no point in taking risks or investing resources and time into things that have already been invented. Second, knowledge makes you aware of the current thinking in your own field or discipline. This may be the basis upon which new thinking can be developed in order to introduce novelty. Knowledge can be extremely useful when you constantly question current thinking rather than take it for granted. One may use experimentation and research skills to reorganize current knowledge into new forms, shapes and processes. The ones who update their knowledge are more likely to think about issues, which are currently important for the industry within which they work. This leads to the third benefit, which is to consider knowledge as a source of opportunity to be further exploited. Knowledge not only comprises a basis for new ideas, it also prevents mistakes from happening again by reminding people of regular 'traps' that occur in their respective industries or fields. Lastly, knowledge enhances creative individuals' morale since it enables them to add more interesting perspectives to what they are currently doing and produce more creative work for which they may be rewarded.

Informal or tacit knowledge

Informal knowledge is the knowledge that one acquires by being part of a relevant discipline or occupation. The notion of tacit knowledge was first introduced by Polanyi, a philosopher who argues that an individual can know more than he/she can tell (1966: 136). Based on Polanyi's thinking, Nonaka (1994) goes one step further and uses tacit knowledge to indicate particular knowledge that is hard to express. Sternberg and Lubart (1995) point out that this is knowledge that is rarely taught and often not documented. The importance of this type of knowledge has been identified by Kasperson (1978), who studied scientists from university and industry R&D laboratories. He points out how the more creative scientists were different from the less creative scientists in the way that they handled informal sources of information. For instance, the more creative scientists placed greater emphasis on interacting with other scientists in conferences or seminars and read outside of their main field of study (Pruthi and Nagpaul, 1978). To illustrate the importance of informal knowledge, let's take the example of an entrepreneurial team that wants to commercialize their idea. The first thing that they may have to do is to attract investors. Informal knowledge regarding the different venture capitalists (financial institutions that fund new business ventures) is important in order to secure funds to bring the entrepreneurial idea into fruition.

Csíkszentmihályi (1988) reinforces the importance of informal knowledge in a field or occupation and more specifically its impact on creativity, by suggesting that it provides an opportunity to engage with key gatekeepers. The gatekeepers may be individuals or organizations that control or influence the progress of a field. These 'boundary-spanning individuals' play an important function in the organization, since, by crossing departments or disciplines, they create channels to the outside world that enable them to be kept up to date with their respective markets or developments (Tushman, 1977). The ability of a firm to identify the value of new, external information and the need to incorporate and apply this to commercial ends is vital to innovative capabilities – often labelled as a firm's absorptive capacity (Cohen and Levinthal, 1990). However, a company's absorptive capacity is not simply the sum of the absorptive capacities of its employees, nor is it simply the acquisition or assimilation of information; rather it rests on an ability to identify and exploit information in a meaningful way. As such, gatekeepers play two important roles. First, they act as environmental monitors, identifying new information that is valuable to the organization. Second, they act as translators in relating information that is not closely linked to the activities of their company into a form that is understandable to the appropriate research groups.

Knowledge for creativity?

Amabile (1983) highlights the importance of knowledge for creativity by suggesting that domain-relevant skills influence the creative employee's set of possible solutions from which new answers are synthesized. They also provide information against which generated solutions are evaluated. Such domain-relevant skills include familiarity with the area as well as factual knowledge. This can take the form of facts, principles and viewpoints about a diverse range of issues in the domain, knowledge of different paradigms, and aesthetic criteria. For instance, an architect's domain-relevant skills may include the person's inner talent for imagining visually realistic representations of abstract images, the factual knowledge of art and architectural history, and the knowledge of the site where a building will be based. For example, in their article 'Building the innovation factory' Hargadon and Sutton (2000) describe four processes for creating and applying knowledge towards innovation. This is what they label as the 'knowledge-brokering' cycle. The companies and employees in their study use proven products, technologies and business practices, and recognize that old ideas can be the central source for new ideas. Specifically, the four stages of this 'knowledge-brokering' cycle are:

1. *Capturing good ideas.* This is not only about identifying and filing prospective ideas, but also about experimenting with them and trying to figure out how and why they work. The 'brokers' tend to create a substantial collection of ideas that may lead to innovations.

2. *Keeping ideas alive.* The next stage involves trying to keep the ideas alive because if ideas are forgotten they cannot be used. In this respect, most innovative companies tend to collect interesting and inspiring stuff to be used in brainstorming sessions or when their staff feel stuck. These can range from collections of physical things like objects, magazines or books, to intranet databases, where employees can search and consult previous projects, memos, reports or presentations.

3. *Imagining new uses for old ideas.* The third stage entails people acknowledging novel uses for ideas that they have gathered and kept alive. In his book *How Breakthroughs Happen*, Hargadon (2003) gives the example of the Reebok Pump shoe, which was designed by Design Continuum, a full-service product design firm. The firm was approached by Reebok to design a shoe that reduced injuries by providing more support. Some designers of the assigned team, who had worked on hospital equipment, had the idea of modifying medical IV bags to make an inflatable insert. This insert could be inflated and deflated so that support on the ankle of the basketball shoe could be achieved. This is a prime example of imagining (and in this case commercializing with great success) a new use for an established idea.

4. *Putting promising concepts to the test.* The last stage of the knowledge-brokering process involves turning a generated idea into a real product, process or business model. This is the time when prototypes, experiments and pilot tests shape the concepts further or help determine whether the generated ideas have any commercial value. The primary goal of this stage is to identify the best idea for solving the problem or opportunity identified.

Is knowledge always conducive to processes of change, creativity and innovation?

Despite general recognition that knowledge is a key input to creative achievement, current writings suggest that knowledge can be a double-edged sword (Andriopoulos, 2003). On the one hand, past successes and failures comprise a precious pool of knowledge for everyone within a company. People who aim to generate innovative ideas need to know the basic knowledge of the field in order to move beyond the status quo. In other words, it is hard to conceive any creative behaviour that is somehow 'knowledge free' (Stein, 1989). Yet, on the other hand, within the development of novel and unique ideas there is a hidden danger of conditioning in the sense that previous patterns of thought/knowledge provide individuals or teams with easy solutions to current problems. Sternberg and Lubart (1995) point out how existing knowledge may interfere with an ability to see things in new ways and create novel combinations. Similarly, Gordon (1961: 95) suggests that an

> *... expert tends to discuss the problem in the language of his own technology. This language can surround the problem with an impenetrable jacket so nothing can be added or modified. The result is that it becomes impossible to view the problem in a new way.*

Bengtson (1982) also refers to the problem of the expert becoming enslaved by their own pattern of thoughts; what he regards as 'expertitis'. On this subject, Sternberg et al. (1997) suggest that people are not generally creative in every field but rather in the area of their specialization. However, they argue that the accumulation of extensive knowledge in a specific field requires a considerable amount of time. Hence, 'expertitis' is a problem more evident in people who have been in a specific field for a long time and may find it harder to adjust to new changes. In such cases, experts find it hard to accommodate change because they either resist it in any form or shape, or because they remain insensitive to new developments in their field.

The creative process requires employees to be inquisitive and continuously seize new areas of knowledge (Andriopoulos, 2003). Knowledge should not be viewed as a resource only to be acquired and retained but as something to be used in order to connect it with something else (James, 1907). Experimentation and research to reorganize current knowledge into new forms, shapes and processes is central to not only increasing the wealth of knowledge, but also to promoting creative thinking. In short, creative individuals need to be reminded that they have to constantly question the 'status quo' rather than take it for granted.

Implications for human resource management

Our understanding of knowledge suggests that the following human resource practices may promote creativity and innovation:

- *Managers should provide different opportunities for ongoing learning.* Creative individuals should be given the opportunity to progressively acquire skills and expertise through different activities, including conference or seminar attendance, visits to other companies, professional involvement, external training courses, and so forth.

- *Managers should maintain a portfolio of projects* that require a different mix of skills and diverse viewpoints. When individuals are involved in different projects across a range of fields, they can see how ideas in one industry may be applied to others.

- *Managers should establish and manage effective mentoring relationships* with all employees so that the growth of necessary skills is encouraged. It is important to develop a formal system through which ongoing advice is given or knowledge is disseminated by the more senior members of the organization.

Motivation

Motivation is the distinguishing factor between what a creative individual can do and what they actually do (Amabile, 1990). Personality traits, cognitive factors and knowledge directly affect what one can do, but it is one's motivation that determines the extent to which one fully applies one's skills (Amabile, 1997). Paradoxically, motivation is one of the oldest managerial problems and one that is increasingly becoming more difficult to manage. Both psychologists and management academics have always been intrigued by the mystery of 'motivation'; what makes people 'tick' in the workplace. Many studies focus on the issues that motivate people; for example, challenging tasks or colleagues, personal development, rewards (either monetary or verbal), and so forth. In the section that follows we will look in more detail at the different types of motivation and their link to individual creativity.

The word 'motivation' originally comes from the Latin word *'movere'*, which means 'to move' (Kreitner et al., 2002). Motivation has been studied with reference to motives, needs, drives and goals or incentives (McKenna, 2000). To begin with, Armstrong (2001: 156) suggests that motive is 'a reason for doing something'. Extant studies have identified different motives that may stimulate creative acts. Ford (1995: 22), for instance, notes that 'creative people are on average more professionally oriented and interested in attaining status and power when compared with their less creative counterparts'. The discovery of something novel stimulates the pleasure centres in the brain (Csíkszentmihályi, 1997). People enjoy things that provide them with an opportunity to discover or design something new. This is what makes a creative act, no matter where it occurs or what form it takes, such a rewarding experience. Ford (1995) adds that apart from achieving personal goals, there are also two other motives that mobilize individual creativity. First, there are motives related to expectations regarding personal capabilities. For instance, creative individuals are interested in showing how 'smart' they are when they find solutions to problems. Second, there are emotions that directly influence motivation. Emotions are of high importance since they are indicators of behaviours within the working environment. Some emotions, such as satisfaction or interest, can generate stimulation and hence focus effort towards achieving the identified goal. Other emotions, such as depression or boredom, may discourage people from getting involved in certain activities.

Types of motivation

Amabile's ongoing research in the area of creativity (1979, 1990, 1997, 1998) shows that there are two basic types of motivation; namely: extrinsic and intrinsic. Extrinsic motivation, as the word suggests, comes from outside a person – it is tangible, for example, in receiving monetary rewards or punishments (a carrot-and-stick-type motivation). Intrinsic motivation refers to an internal desire to do something, it is driven by deep interest and involvement, by curiosity, enjoyment, or simply a personal sense of challenge.

Although creative individuals differ from one another in a variety of ways, they all generally love what they do (Csikszentmihályi, 1997). Creative individuals are motivated by the opportunity to pursue their passions that triggers creative discovery. Many creative individuals devote long hours in their pursuits because they enjoy what they do (Robinson and Godbey, 1999). It is often the experience and the quality of the experience that keeps the creative person going in difficult times.

The importance of task in motivating creative individuals has been a research focus for scholars in this area. For instance, Hackman et al. (1975) note that employees who have more complex jobs tend to be more motivated, satisfied and productive than those engaged in simple, routine tasks. Complex jobs give employees the discretion to focus simultaneously on multiple dimensions of their work, it permits them to conduct their activities without extensive external controls or constraints, and it may also enhance their interest in persisting with novel approaches.

Jones and McFadzean's (1997) research adds that creative employees should be encouraged to challenge their assumptions and perceptions regarding procedures, products and processes. Creativity is fostered when individuals and teams have relatively high autonomy in the day-to-day conduct of their work and a sense of ownership and control over their own ideas (Amabile, 1996). Amabile and Gitomer (1984), pursuing the same line of argument, suggest that individuals generate more creative work when they believe that they have a choice in how to go about achieving the tasks that they have been assigned. Intrinsically motivated people show greater commitment and devote more time towards completing the task at hand (Amabile et al., 1994; Mainemelis, 2001). Using a similar argument, Ruscio et al. (1998) suggest that motivated individuals tend to show deeper levels of commitment to problems at hand by concentrating their time and energy on solving them, minimizing distractions and by feeling totally immersed in their work. The notion of immersion in one's work ('I lost track of time') is also identified by Mainemelis (2001) as an important factor of individual creativity. He defines this as 'timelessness', when time appears distorted, a sense of mastery of the task is achieved and, finally, a sense of transcendence of both time and task is experienced. He further stresses the importance of timelessness to creativity by proposing that 'it leads to a context of highly focused, imaginative, and quality work' (Mainemelis, 2001: 559). Timelessness is also an experience that re-creates itself, meaning that the more one experiences timeliness, the more one learns how to create and protect a space within a workday for experiencing timelessness and achieving focus in this process (Massimini and Delle Fave, 2000; Seligman and Csíkszentmihályi, 2000).

Up to a certain point, intrinsic motivation is affected by a person's personality (Amabile et al., 1994). Csíkszentmihályi (1990) points out how intrinsic motivation often relates to the values exhibited by creative individuals. For instance, he notes that young art students place social and economic values in much lower esteem, while they support aesthetic values more than average college students. More specifically, his study highlights how the more creative an artist becomes the less interested they become in money and status, placing higher value on their domain interest, which in this case is art.

Amabile's ongoing research in the area of creativity (1979, 1990, 1997, 1998) shows that although part of intrinsic motivation resides in one's personality, the person's social environment can also have a significant impact on an individual's intrinsic motivation. Amabile (1997: 46) proposes the following intrinsic motivation principle:

Intrinsic motivation is conducive to creativity. Controlling extrinsic motivation is detrimental to creativity, but informational or enabling extrinsic motivation can be conducive, particularly if initial levels of intrinsic motivation are high.

This principle suggests that employees will be most creative when they feel motivated primarily by the interest, satisfaction and challenge of the work itself – and not by external pressures. In her journal article: 'Motivating creativity in organizations: on doing what you love and loving what you do', Amabile (1997) attempts to give an explanation of the factors that determine whether extrinsic motivation combined with intrinsic motivation are more or less likely to affect creativity in a positive or negative manner. In her work, Amabile proposes three important determinants: the person's initial motivational state, the type of extrinsic motivator used, and the timing of the extrinsic motivation. She argues that the initial level of intrinsic motivation is of vital importance. For example, if one is deeply involved in the work because it is appealing or personally challenging, then that high degree of intrinsic motivation may be unaffected by any undermining effects of extrinsic motivators. On types of extrinsic motivators, Deci and Ryan (1985) note how 'informational extrinsic motivators' can promote positive creative outcomes. These types of motivators consist of reward, recognition and feedback that either give reassurance on one's competence or provide information on how to strengthen performance. In addition, 'enabling extrinsic motivators' can also promote individual creativity. These include reward, recognition and feedback that directly increase the person's involvement in the work itself. On the other hand, 'non-synergistic extrinsic motivators', which are controlling extrinsic motivators, rarely combine positively with intrinsic motivation, since they often threaten a person's perception of autonomy (Deci and Ryan, 1985). It is common sense to believe that one should be rewarded for exhibiting a behaviour that is in accordance with an organization's or society's goals and not to be rewarded for behaviours that are outside of this. However, considerable evidence suggests that rewards or incentives have a counterproductive effect on creativity since one may be encouraged to get involved in the creative act to get the reward, rather than to focus on the creative process and its output. For instance, the most usual extrinsic motivator employers use is money, which does not necessarily stop people from being creative. In this situation, Amabile (1998) found that money does not motivate creative individuals, especially when the financial incentive is perceived as a means of bribing or controlling. She concludes by suggesting that money by itself does not make employees passionate about their jobs. In contrast, students who told stories focusing more on their passion of making art, tended to follow through what they were doing even if they were not extrinsically 'successful'.

Implications for human resource management

Our understanding of motivation suggests that the following human resource practices may promote creativity and innovation:

- *Managers should provide a mix of rewards* that focus both on intrinsic (e.g., greater autonomy) and extrinsic motives (e.g., pay increases).

- *Managers should offer jobs that are complex, demanding and of interest to employees.* These types of jobs allow employees to experiment with new ways of doing things, to take risks and act creatively.

- *Managers should periodically review employees' job activities and interests* so that they are made aware of different fields of interest. When employees are matched with assignments that they regard as interesting, they are more likely to focus all their attention on the task at hand.

Conclusion

In this chapter we have focused on creative thinking and the individual, the person who is behind a new product or new idea. We sought to identify whether there are any characteristics that relate to the uniqueness of such individuals. Our review of the extant literature identified several cognitive factors that are linked to creative achievement. These include: mental flexibility, the ability to link remote associations, the suspension of judgement and the originality of thinking and freshness. On turning our attention to personality traits, we demonstrated how the profile of the 'highly creative' individual is often associated with a preference for risk-taking, a tendency for being confident, a tolerance for ambiguity, a need for achievement and autonomy, and a non-conformist tendency.

Our discussion then turned to the role of knowledge as an important determinant of creative achievement. As Simonton (2000: 153) notes, 'creative individuals rarely generate new ideas de novo, but rather those ideas must arise from a large set of well-developed skills and a rich body of knowledge relevant to the respective domain'. We not only highlighted the significance of formal and informal knowledge, but also stressed the dangers of routines and habits if there is too much focus on the status quo. We also examined the influence of motivation on creative output. Although personality traits, cognitive factors and knowledge directly affect what one *can* do, motivation is likely to be the factor that will determine what one *will* do. The componential theory of individual creativity by Amabile (1983, 1996) suggests that task motivation, domain-relevant skills and creativity-relevant processes are all essential components for individual creativity. This research highlights how the observed differences among creative and non-creative individuals often arise from the different levels of attribution that individuals possess towards these components. In the final analysis, being creative is more than a cognitive or dispositional attribution. It is an activity that develops over time (Simonton, 2000: 153) and a process that happens in interpersonal work settings. The popular image of the lone genius is highly inappropriate and can no longer be regarded as the profile of the creative individual. In this respect, the next chapter focuses on the nature of the interpersonal interactions of individuals within teams and shows how these may enhance or inhibit processes of change, creativity and innovation.

RESOURCES, READINGS AND REFLECTIONS

CASE 5.2   MINIATURE COULD BE HOLLYWOOD'S NEW MONSTER HIT
BY JOSHUA CHAFFIN

(Source: *Financial Times,* 12 December 2005)

As president of marketing at Universal Pictures, Adam Fogelson has been toiling for months to make *King Kong*, a three-hour, $200 million monster of a film, one of the biggest blockbusters of all time when it opens on Wednesday. But across town, his father, Andrew, has been working towards a very different purpose: he is searching for the next small thing. That is, he is seeking to develop a repertoire of tiny films that he believes could generate sizeable returns.

The elder Mr Fogelson already has one miniature hit under his belt. His first project, *Indigo*, a tale of children with spiritual powers, cost just $500,000 to make and $60,000 to market and distribute. Yet it has gone on to earn more than

$3 million, and counting, since its January release. Mr Fogelson acknowledges that this is 'lunch money' in a town that tends to measure success by box office bulk rather than return on investment. Yet he is not chasing conventional Hollywood glory. He has already served as head of marketing at Warner Brothers and Columbia Pictures in the 1970s, and then as president of PolyGram Films. Instead, he is determined to test a thesis about Hollywood's changing economics.

Mr Fogelson accepts that studios will continue to churn out *King Kong*-sized movies that they can propel around the world with their formidable distribution and marketing machines. But he believes that technology is opening the industry to a new generation of pint-sized productions aimed at narrow but passionate segments of the audience. 'The middle is a bad place to be' he explains, setting out his vision. 'You either have movies made for everybody who can walk – say, where the target audience is 'ambulatory' – or you make target-specific movies that ought to be marketable at a fraction of the cost.'

It is an intriguing idea at a time when Hollywood is at a crossroads. Attendance is down 8 per cent so far this year as the studios grapple with competition from video games, the internet and other entertainment options. At the same time, the emergence of new digital technologies, such as video-on-demand, is prompting film executives to rethink business models that have sustained them for years. Under the old assumptions, a film the size of *Indigo* would have little chance of ever making it to the silver screen – let alone the video store – because of the costs associated with its distribution and marketing. But *Indigo*'s odyssey demonstrates technology's power to break down the film industry's barriers to entry – not to mention the value of clever marketing.

It began when two New Age producers brought the film to Mr Fogelson two years ago. *Indigo* tells the tale of an 'Indigo child' endowed with psychic gifts who is reluctantly adopted by her cynical grandfather and subsequently inspires his spiritual awakening. At first glance, it did not appear to have the makings of a hit. One reviewer called the acting 'cardboard dry, and occasionally nauseating'. But there was something that intrigued Mr Fogelson. *Indigo* had been made for an audience that had been largely overlooked by the mainstream film industry. 'When it comes to these New Age people, they are dramatically underserved' he says. There was also another hidden asset he saw in *Indigo*: Neale Donald Walsch, the film's star and co-writer. Mr Walsch is the author of a dozen best-selling books about God and spirituality and commands a devoted following in the New Age community. As such, he provided *Indigo* with a natural marketing hook among the film's target audience.

Mr Fogelson's initial plan was to sell the film directly to video, where he believed it would find a small but devoted following. But when he approached a friend in distribution, he was rebuffed. *Indigo*, like other films, needed to play in a cinema and generate some buzz before the distributor would accept it. 'They said it wasn't worth it to them unless it had theatrical release', Mr Fogelson recalls.

In the past, this might have killed the project. Even without the big studios' lock on most cinema screens, the mere cost of printing and distributing the movie would have been prohibitive. At $2,000 each, the bill for just 30 prints, for example, would

(Continued)

(Continued)

have equalled *Indigo*'s entire marketing and distribution budget. But the *Indigo* team got around the problem by filming in digital. As a result, rather than make prints, they could have the film stamped on to discs for a few cents apiece, then transmitted to cinemas with digitally equipped screens. It was a breakthrough that allowed Mr Fogelson to approach cinema chains with an offer they could not refuse. He asked if he could hire their digital screens for just one *Indigo* showing at a time when no one was around. 'Give me the deadest Saturday morning you've got, where if a bomb goes off, nobody would get hurt', he pleaded. With nothing to lose, AMC, one of the largest US exhibitors, eventually agreed to a screening on Saturday January 29, at the inauspicious time of 11am.

Meanwhile, Mr Walsch and his co-writer, James Twyman, set about drumming up enthusiasm in the New Age community. Their budget may have been the equivalent of a rounding error on the $34 million that the big Hollywood studios spent to market each of their films in 2004. But it was sufficient because they were targeting a narrow audience with which they were well acquainted. They previewed the film at a festival in Santa Fe, New Mexico, a hub for spiritual types, while mining e-mail lists from Mr Walsch's foundation and other like-minded organisations. One of Mr Twyman's savvier innovations was the creation of a World Indigo Day, in which hundreds of churches around the world were encouraged to say a special prayer for 'Indigo children'. The New Age holiday conveniently coincided with the film's release. 'Not only did we start selling out all the screenings, we started getting calls from other venues asking if they could show it – churches, bookstores, what have you', Mr Fogelson says.

When all was said and done, *Indigo* had played on 604 screens that day and managed to gross $1.19 million, reaching 17th place on the weekend box office charts. More important, the screening secured a DVD distribution deal, where the filmmakers stand to reap as much as half the profits of every disc sold. Since April, 80,000 have been shipped. 'Suffice it to say, we are going to make a ton of money', Mr Fogelson says. That success raises the question of what relevance a film such as *Indigo* might have for big studios built for mega-productions capable of generating $1 billion or more through toys, DVD sales and other ancillary revenue streams.

Mr Fogelson imagines a day when studios might launch dozens of niche films alongside their *King Kong*s. A small portfolio of niche productions could also serve as an interesting off-the-books investment as the internet emerges as a new low-cost way to distribute and market films. In the meantime, Mr Fogelson is busy searching for other untapped audiences – although he won't say which – in hopes of bringing them their own *Indigo*s, and proving a point to his son. 'We want to bring entertainment to people in a way that Hollywood right now hasn't the time or inclination to do', he says.

Hollywood's changing economics

- Technology is opening the movie industry up to a new generation of pint-sized productions aimed at narrow but passionate segments of the audience.
- Andrew Fogelson's hit movie *Indigo* cost just $500,000 to make and $60,000 to distribute. Its New Age audience was underserved, Mr Fogelson judged, and distribution could be achieved with relatively little outlay.

- The Indigo team filmed in digital so that the movie could be stamped on to discs for a few cents apiece, then transmitted digitally to cinemas.
- Mr Fogelson believes that underserved audiences will be more willing to attend films because of the community experience: 'if people come for the community, then the sound and the pictures don't have to be so good.'

Questions

1. Was Andrew Fogelson creative? What kind of cognitive factors and personality traits has he exhibited so far?
2. What role have intrinsic motivation and extrinsic motivation played in Andrew Fogelson's new venture?
3. In your view, is there a 'big idea' behind pint-sized productions?
4. How and why was Andrew Fogelson able to make his initial idea work? Defend your position by comparing this case to other examples of technological innovations.

Chapter questions

The questions listed below relate to the chapter as a whole and can be used by individuals to further reflect on the material covered, as well as serving as a source for more open group discussion and debate.

1. Which are the main cognitive factors that may predict creative achievement? Use examples from your personal life to illustrate your points.

2. Do you think that knowledge is beneficial to creativity and innovation? Why or why not?

3. In your opinion, which is the most important type of motivation? Discuss your answer by using relevant examples.

Hands-on exercise

Students are required to find a magazine or newspaper article about a creative individual of their choice and discuss whether:

1. The individual of their choice exhibits the cognitive abilities as discussed in this chapter.

2. The individual of their choice exhibits the main personality traits that have been linked to creative achievement.

3. Knowledge of their specific domain was critical to their success.

4. The individual is intrinsically or extrinsically motivated.

Team debate exercise

Debate the following statement:

Knowledge is a double-edged sword.

Divide the class into two groups. One should argue as convincingly as possible that knowledge of one's field is the most important ingredient in moving beyond the status quo and coming up with new and useful ideas. The other should prepare its arguments against this, highlighting that focusing on the past and/or current knowledge may interfere with one's ability to see things in new ways and create novel combinations. Each group should be prepared to defend their ideas against the other group's arguments by using real-life examples.

References

Amabile, T.M. (1979) 'Effects of external evaluation on artistic creativity', *Journal of Personality and Social Psychology*, 37: 221–33.

Amabile, T.M. (1983) *The Social Psychology of Creativity*. New York: Springer-Verlag.

Amabile, T.M. (1988) 'A model of creativity and innovation in organisations', in B.M. Staw and L.L. Cummings (eds), *Research in Organizational Behaviour*, Vol. 10. Stamford, CT: JAI Press. pp. 123–67.

Amabile, T.M. (1990) 'Within you, without you: the social psychology of creativity and beyond', in M.A. Runco and R.S. Albert (eds), *Theories in Creativity*. Thousand Oaks, CA: Sage.

Amabile, T.M. (1996) *Creativity in Context*. Boulder, CO: Westview Press.

Amabile, T.M. (1997) 'Motivating creativity in organizations: on doing what you love and loving what you do', *California Management Review*, 40 (1): 39–58.

Amabile, T.M. (1998) 'How to kill creativity', *Harvard Business Review*, 76 (6): 76–87.

Amabile, T.M. and Gitomer, J. (1984) 'Children's artistic creativity: effects of choice in task materials', *Personality and Social Psychology Bulletin*, 10: 209–15.

Amabile, T.M., Hill, K.G., Hennessey, B.A. and Tighe, E.M. (1994) 'The work preference inventory: assessing intrinsic and extrinsic motivational orientations', *Journal of Personality and Social Psychology*, 66: 950–67.

Andriopoulos, C. (2003) 'Six paradoxes in managing creativity: an embracing act', *Long Range Planning*, 36: 375–88.

Armstrong, M. (2001) *A Handbook of Human Resource Management*. London: Kogan Page.

Barron, F.X. (1963) 'The needs for order and for disorder as motives in creative activity', in C.W. Taylor and F.X. Barron (eds), *Scientific Creativity: Its Recognition and Development*. New York: John Wiley.

Barron, F (1966) 'The psychology of the creative writer', *Theory into Practice*, 5: 157–9.

Barron, F. and Harrington, D.M. (1981) 'Creativity, intelligence and personality', in L.W. Porter and M.R. Rosenzweig (eds), *Annual Review of Psychology*, 32. Palo Alto, CA: Annual Reviews. pp. 439–76.

Bengtson, T. (1982) 'Creativity's paradoxical character', *Journal of Advertising*, 11: 3–9.

Bransford, J. and Stein, B.S. (1984) *The IDEAL Problem Solver*. New York: W.H. Freeman.

Buel, W.D. (1965) 'Biographical data and the identification of creative research personnel', *Journal of Applied Psychology*, 49: 318–21.

Choo, C.W. (1998) *The Knowing Organization*. New York: Oxford University Press.

Cohen, W.M. and Levinthal, D.A. (1990) 'Absorptive capacity: a new perspective on learning and innovation', *Administrative Science Quarterly*, 35: 128–52.

Costa, P.T. and McCrae, R.R. (1992) *Revised NEO Personality Inventory Manual*. Odessa, FL: Psychological Assessment Resources.

Csíkszentmihályi, M. (1988) 'Society, culture and person: a systems view of creativity', in R.J. Sternberg (ed.), *The Nature of Creativity*. New York: Cambridge University Press.

Csíkszentmihályi, M. (1990) 'The domain of creativity', in M.A. Runco and R.S. Albert (eds), *Theories of Creativity*. Thousand Oaks, CA: Sage.

Csíkszentmihályi, M. (1997) 'Happiness and creativity', *The Futurist*, 31 (5): 8–12.

Cummings, A. and Oldham, G.R. (1997) 'Enhancing creativity: managing work contexts for the high potential employee', *California Management Review*, 40 (1): 22–38.

Davenport, H.T. and Prusak, L. (1998) *Working Knowledge*. Boston, MA: Harvard Business School Press.

Deci, E.L. and Ryan, R.M. (1985) *Intrinsic Motivation and Self-Determination in Human Behavior*. New York: Plenum Press.

Eckert, C.M. and Stacey, M.K. (1998) 'Fortune favours only the prepared mind: why sources of inspiration are essential for continuing creativity', *Creativity and Innovation Management*, 7: 9–16. (With thanks to Blackwell).

Ford, C.M. (1995) 'Creativity is a mystery', in C.M. Ford and D.A. Gioia (eds), *Creative Action in Organisations: Ivory Tower Visions & Real World Voices*. Thousand Oaks, CA: Sage.

Glassman, E. (1986) 'Managing for creativity: back to basics in R&D', *R&D Management*, 16: 175–83.

Goertzel, M.G., Goertzel, V. and Goertzel, T.G. (1978) *Three Hundred Eminent Personalities*. San Francisco: Jossey-Bass.

Gordon, W.J.J. (1961) *Synectics: The Development of Creative Capacity*. New York: Harper & Row.

Hackman, J.R., Oldham, G., Janson, R. and Purdy, K. (1975) 'A new strategy for job enrichment', *California Management Review*, 17 (4): 57–71.

Hall, W.B. and MacKinnon, D.W. (1969) 'Personality inventory correlates of creativity among architects', *Journal of Applied Psychology*, 53: 322–6.

Hargadon, A. (2003) *How Breakthroughs Happen*. Boston, MA: Harvard Business School Press.

Hargadon, A.B. and Sutton, R.I. (2000) 'Building the innovation factory', *Harvard Business Review*, 78 (3): 157–66.

James, W.B. (1907) *Pragmatism*. New York: The American Library.

James, W.B. (1983) 'An analysis of perceptions of the practices of adult educators from five different settings' *Proceedings of the 24th Adult Education Research Conference*. Montreal: Concordia University/University of Montreal.

Jones, G. and McFadzean, E.S. (1997) 'How can Reboredo foster creativity in her current employees and nurture creative individuals who join the company in the future?', *Harvard Business Review*, 75 (5): 50–1.

Kasperson, C.J. (1978) 'An analysis of the relationship between information sources and creativity in scientists and engineers', *Human Communication Research*, 4: 113–19.

Keller, R.T. and Holland, W.E. (1978) 'A cross validation study of the Kirton adaption–innovation inventory in three research and development organizations', *Applied Psychological Measurement*, 2: 563–70.

Kreitner, R., Kinicki, A. and Buelens, M. (2002) *Organizational Behaviour*. Maidenhead: McGraw-Hill.

Lizotte, K. (1998) 'A creative state of mind', *Management Review*, 87: 15–17.

MacKinnon, D.W. (1959) 'The creative worker in engineering', *Proceedings: Eleventh Annual Industrial Engineering Institute*. pp. 88–96.

MacKinnon, D.W. (1960) 'Genvs architectvs creator varietas Americanvs', *AIA Journal*, (September): 31–5.

MacKinnon, D.W. (1962) 'The nature and nurture of creative talent', *American Psychologist*, 17: 484–95.

MacKinnon, D.W. (1978) *In Search of Human Effectiveness: Identifying and Developing Creativity*. Buffalo: Creative Education Foundation.

Majaro, S. (1992) *Managing Ideas for Profit – The Creative Gap*. London: McGraw-Hill.

Mainemelis, C. (2001) 'When the muse takes it all: a model for the experience of timelessness in organizations', *Academy of Management Review*, 26: 548–65.

Manske, M.R. and Davis, G.A. (1968) 'Effects of simple instructional biases upon performance in the unusual uses test', *Journal of General Psychology*, 79: 25–33.

Massimini, F. and Delle Fave, A. (2000) 'Individual development in a bio-cultural perspective', *American Psychologist*, 55: 24–33.

McDermid, C.D. (1965) 'Some correlates of creativity in engineering personnel', *Journal of Applied Psychology*, 49: 14–19.

McGrath, J.E. (2000) 'The study of groups: past, present and future', *Personality and Social Psychology Review*, 4: 95–105.

McKenna, E. (2000) *Business Psychology and Organizational Behaviour: A Student's Handbook*. Hove: Psychology Press.

Mednick, S.A. (1962) 'The associative basis of the creative process', *Psychological Review*, 69: 220–32.

Michael, W. (1979) 'How to find – and keep – creative people', *Research Management*, (September): 43–5.

Nonaka, I. (1994) 'A dynamic theory of organizational knowledge creation', *Organization Science*, 5: 14–37.

Nonaka, I. and Takeuchi, H. (1995) *The Knowledge-Creating Company: How Japanese Companies Create the Dynamics of Innovation*. Oxford: Oxford University Press.

Nonaka, I. and Takeuchi, H. (1998) 'A theory of the firms' knowledge-creating dynamics', in A. Chandler, P. Hagstrom and O. Solvell (eds), *The Dynamic Firm: The Role of Technology, Strategy, Organisation and Regions*. Oxford: Oxford University Press.

Polanyi, M. (1958) *Personal Knowledge: Toward a Post-Critical Philosophy*. Chicago: University of Chicago Press.

Polanyi, M. (1966) *The Tacit Dimension*. New York: Doubleday.

Pruthi, S. and Nagpaul, P.S. (1978) 'Communications patterns in small R&D projects', *R&D Management*, 11: 37–40.

Ray, M. and Myers, R. (1986) *Creativity in Business*. New York: Doubleday.

Ree, M.J. and Earles, J.A. (1996) 'Predicting occupational criteria: not much more than g', in I. Dennis and P. Tapsfield (eds), *Human Abilities: Their Nature and Measurement*. Mahwah, NJ: Lawrence Erlbaum.

Robinson, J. and Godbey, G. (1999) *Time for Life: The Surprising Ways Americans Use Their Time*. University Park, PA: Pennsylvania State University Press.

Ruscio, J., Whitney, D. and Amabile, T.M. (1998) 'Looking inside the fishbowl of creativity: verbal and behavioral predictors of creative performance', *Creativity Research Journal*, 11: 243–63.

Schmidt, F.L., Hunter, J.E. and Pearlman, K. (1981) 'Task differences as moderators of aptitude test validity in selection: a red herring', *Journal of Applied Psychology*, 66: 166–85.

Seligman, M. and Csikszentmihályi, M. (2000) 'Positive psychology: an introduction', *American Psychologist*, 55: 5–14.

Simonton, D.K. (1984) *Genius, Creativity, and Leadership: Historiometric Inquiries.* Cambridge, MA: Harvard University Press.

Simonton, D.K. (1994) *Greatness: Who Makes History and Why.* New York: Guilford Press.

Simonton, D.K. (1999a) 'Creativity and genius', in L.A. Pervin and O. John (eds), *Handbook of Personality Theory and Research.* New York: Guilford Press.

Simonton, D.K. (1999b) *Origins of Genius: Darwinian Perspectives on Creativity.* New York: Oxford University Press.

Simonton, D.K. (2000) 'Creativity: cognitive, developmental, personal, and social aspects', *American Psychologist*, 55: 151–8.

Stein, B.S. (1989) 'Memory and creativity', in J.A. Glover, R.R. Ronning and C.R. Reynolds (eds), *Handbook of Creativity.* New York: Plenum Press.

Sternberg, R.J. and Lubart, T.I. (1991) 'An investment theory of creativity and its development', *Human Development*, 34: 1–31.

Sternberg, R.J. and Lubart, T.I. (1995) *Defying the Crowd.* New York: The Free Press.

Sternberg, R.J., O'Hara, L.A. and Lubart, T.I. (1997) 'Creativity as investment', *California Management Review*, 40 (1): 8–21.

Taggar, S. (2002) 'Individual creativity and group ability to utilize individual creative resources: a multilevel model', *Academy of Management Journal*, 45: 315–31.

Tushman, M.L. (1977) 'Special boundary roles in the innovation process', *Administrative Science Quarterly*, 22: 587–605.

Welsh, G. (1975) *Creativity of Intelligence: A Personality Approach.* Chapel Hill, NC: University of North Carolina Press.

Whitfield, R.R. (1975) *Creativity in Industry.* Harmondsworth: Penguin Books.

Woodman, R.W., Sawyer, J.E. and Griffin, R.W. (1993) 'Toward a theory of organisational creativity', *Academy of Management Review*, 18: 293–321.

Zack, M.H. (1999) 'Managing codified knowledge', *Sloan Management Review*, 40 (4): 45–58.

Recommended reading

Creativity

- Amabile, T.M. (2001) 'Beyond talent: John Irving and the passionate craft of creativity', *American Psychologist*, 56: 333–6.

- Root-Bernstein, R. and Root-Bernstein, M. (2000) *Sparks of Genius: The Thirteen Thinking Tools of the World's Most Creative People.* New York: Houghton Mifflin.

Knowledge

- Davenport, T. (2005) *Thinking for a Living: How to Get Better Performance and Results from Knowledge Workers.* Boston, MA: Harvard Business School Press.

- Hennessey, B.A. and Amabile, T.M. (1987) *Creativity and Learning.* Washington, DC: National Education Association.

Some useful websites

Creativity

- On this website you can find information about tools, strategies and techniques that one can use to be more creative (http://www.innovationtools.com).

Knowledge

- This website provides some useful articles, case studies and other information related to knowledge management and innovation (http://www.knowledge board.com).

6

The Group: Nurturing Team Work

Learning objectives

After reading this chapter you will:

1. Appreciate the importance of the team in today's complex working environments.
2. Understand the differences between a group and a team.
3. Be able to explain the stages of the group development process.
4. Understand the main reasons why teams fail.
5. Be able to explain the variables related to creative team inputs, processes and outcomes as well as the moderating factors that may affect team performance.
6. Acknowledge the importance of team problem solving.
7. Understand the value of brainstorming and its influence on the generation of ideas.
8. Be able to discuss the advantages and disadvantages of three different team problem-solving techniques, and to consider the suitability of these techniques for different problem-solving situations.

Introduction

If we are to compete in today's world, we must begin to celebrate collective entrepreneurship, endeavors in which the whole of the effort is greater than the sum of individual contributions. We need to honor our teams more, our aggressive leaders and maverick geniuses less. (Reich, 1987: 78)

It is not uncommon for Western cultures to overemphasize the importance of the individual in many aspects of life; from football teams to corporate boards. There are thousands of articles in magazines, newspapers and books, which herald the personal triumph of individuals. There are many living examples that illustrate this point. Who has not heard of the football player David Beckham, or the eccentric and flamboyant Dennis Rodman with his on-the-court and off-the-court adventures? In the corporate world, who has not heard of Bill Gates of Microsoft or Sir Richard Branson of Virgin? The examples are endless.

The mistake that we often make is to forget that these individuals are not alone in their pursuits. Typically, they are part of a team which supports, nurtures and often delivers their vision and goals. But why do we often choose to ignore the teams behind the triumphant individuals? Part of it is inherent in our upbringing. From our early years we learn which behaviours are acceptable (and therefore are usually reinforced) and which we should avoid in order to steer clear of punishment. Part of it is also the result of our education system, which focuses on individual performance; a phenomenon that continues quite often in the workplace where it is the individual who is mainly assessed and rewarded, even in situations where collaborative team work is encouraged. Within our culture, we are fascinated by 'heroes' and 'heroines', by the power of the individual to make a difference. But is this focus on individualism appropriate? Does it provide a true reflection of the importance of the individual to change, creativity and innovation? Let us consider the following facts:

- Michelangelo could not have painted the Sistine Chapel without the help of a group of artisans.

- Thomas Edison, the American inventor who generated an astonishing array of inventions like the telegraph, telephone, light bulb and phonograph, had a team of 14 people to help him implement his dreams in his Menlo Park laboratory in New Jersey.

- Bill Gates managed to become the richest man in the world by starting a business from scratch just three decades ago. In his journey to 'success', there were a lot of people who 'bought' into his vision and made his dreams a reality.

In this chapter we aim to introduce the concept of the team and to explain in more detail different aspects of creative team working. We begin by comparing and contrasting various definitions of 'group' and 'team'. We then discuss key stages in team development and the main reasons why teams 'fail'. The last section explores creative team working in which we identify key attributes that may enhance or impede team working in the development of innovative products/ services.

What is a group and how is it different from a team?

A *group* can be defined as two or more individuals, interacting and interdependent, who work together to achieve particular objectives. Groups can take two forms: they can be either formal or informal. Formal groups tend to have specific tasks to perform and their responsibilities and behaviours are often set by the organizational goals (Huczynski and Buchanan, 1991). Frontline hotel employees are an example of a formal group. They all have their own roles and responsibilities in terms of delivering a service, but they all have one common goal in mind: to provide a desired standard of customer experience. In contrast, informal groups are characterized by a lack of formal structure and are generally not organization-led (Huczynski and Buchanan, 1991). Interestingly, Katzenbach and Smith (1993) after several years of researching different types of teams (they interviewed hundreds of people in more than 50 teams in 30 companies from a diverse range of sectors) concluded that successful groups are different from teams and that the two concepts should not be used interchangeably.

According to Katzenbach and Smith (1993: 112), a team can be defined as:

> **A small number of people with complementary skills who are committed to a common purpose, performance goals and approach for which they hold themselves mutually accountable.**

Take any team that you can think of, whether this is a football team, a pop group or a space mission. It is quite clear that each member has a specific role that he/she plays within that team. In a football team, there are players who are defending the team from its opponents; in a pop band, there are members who are playing musical instruments, while others are singing; in a space mission, there are people who are navigating the space craft and others who are conducting experiments or observing natural phenomena. Individuals in these situations know that they are part of something bigger and that they should not risk the end-result – for example, a goal, a good performance or new findings – for personal gratification. Katzenbach and Smith (1993) summarize the key differences between a working group and a team in Table 6.1.

Why do people join teams?

Today, the corporate world and society at large is characterized by ongoing technological, economic and political change. Within this ever-changing environment, individual efforts are often not enough to tackle complex tasks in the pursuit of commercial objectives. Take, for example, an aspiring music band trying to 'make it big' in the music scene. Obviously, the recruitment

TABLE 6.1　The key differences between a working group and a team

Working Group	Team
• Strong, clearly focused leader	• Shared leadership roles
• Individual accountability	• Individual and mutual accountability
• The group's purpose is the same as the broader organizational mission	• Specific team purpose that the team itself delivers
• Individual work products	• Collective work products
• Runs efficient meetings	• Encourages open-ended discussion and active problem-solving meetings
• Measures its effectiveness indirectly by its influence on others	• Measures performance directly by assessing collective work products
• Discusses, decides and delegates	• Discusses, decides and does real work together

Source: Katzenbach and Smith (1993: 113).

and retention of the most appropriate and talented members is the first challenge for the band, but not the last. There are several people who are working 'backstage' and whose contribution is of significant importance to the success of the band. Its members need to collaborate with music producers, they need to work side-by-side with a good manager, who takes care of their financial resources and negotiates deals with record companies and manufacturers of merchandising (T-shirts, posters, etc.), an agent who schedules concerts in the most promising clubs and organizes events around the world, video directors who produce the video clips, graphic designers who design logo gear, and so forth. Like music bands, most projects, nowadays, require the co-ordinated contributions of many talented people. Whether the goal is to create popular music, to introduce a 'blockbuster' in the market or to build a global business, one individual can rarely achieve it on his/her own, regardless of how talented or energetic he/she might be. Although collaboration may not always be desirable, it is often unavoidable. Robbins et al. (1994) identify four reasons why employees join teams:

- *Security.* Individuals feel that by joining a team they become stronger; it helps them deal with their own insecurities, and enables them to be more resistant to external threats. Joining a team is particularly important to new employees in any organizational setting since they rely on the reassurance and support of team members to deal with the stress associated with a new job.

- *Self-esteem.* Individuals who participate in teams get a strong sense of self-worth by voicing their opinions and by assisting team members in finding suitable solutions to the problems at hand. The more people value the group that they join, the more their own confidence is likely to grow.

- *Power.* It has been proposed that people can achieve more by belonging to or leading a team. A team, for instance, usually has more bargaining power to negotiate issues with senior management than an individual employee.

- *Goal achievement.* Individuals can achieve personal and organizational goals by being part of a team. In today's workplace, individuals need to combine their talent, power or knowledge to achieve their personal goals.

The team development process

Similarly to organizations and products, work teams also have their own development process. During the period when researchers used to refer to groups and teams interchangeably, Tuckman and Jensen (1977) proposed that team development involved five stages, namely: forming, storming, norming, performing and adjourning. Let's look more closely at each of these five stages.

The *forming* stage focuses on the initial setting up of teams in which members try to figure out what they are supposed to be doing. This stage is characterized by ambiguity in terms of the team's goal, structure and direction. Hence, most of the team members are inclined to hide their feelings.

The second stage is *storming*. This is the time when members accept the fact that there is a team for the first time, but they often experience tremendous conflict while they try to determine how they fit into the evolving power structure of the team. Hence, *storming* is a stage where team members often express strong views; and this, sometimes, may lead to an open rebellion. This is the reason why many teams stall during the early stages of their development.

The *norming* stage is where initial relationships develop and the team members begin to organize themselves. At this stage, the group identifies a set of expectations and agrees on acceptable behaviour. These expectations are defined as behavioural norms. The outcome of the *norming* stage is that team members understand their roles and a 'we' attitude is initiated. This is what we refer to as 'team cohesiveness'. From this stage onwards team members try to find solutions to the problems in hand by discussing them openly with each other. The task is no longer an individual challenge; it is rather a challenge that, synergistically, the whole team needs to address.

The next stage, *performing*, is characterized by an emerging sense of team loyalty, where there is contribution by all team members and where conflicts are resolved constructively and efficiently. Team members feel that an atmosphere of openness and trust is developed, and hence they tend to commit to the team's goals.

The last stage, of *adjourning*, occurs when teams have reached their goals or when the task is completed (temporary committees, task forces, and so forth) and team members are moving on to meet the next challenge. At this stage, reactions of team members are likely to differ: some team members may feel proud of the end product that the team has achieved, or they may feel sad because the team with which they have developed rapport is going to disband; others may be judgemental and criticize the effectiveness of the team.

These stages of forming, storming, norming, performing and adjourning provide a useful framework to aid our understanding of the dynamics of the team development process. However, it must be noted that although researchers agree on the importance of the team development process and its stages, there is disagreement on the nature of these stages, their sequence and their length.

Why do teams fail?

In recent years, management theorists and practitioners have overemphasized the importance of teams, often viewing team working as the panacea for a myriad of management problems. Teams have been used to combat a wide range of workplace issues ranging from performance improvements to organizational change initiatives. In practice, however, teams have not always succeeded in securing their objectives and hence it is worth examining some of the reasons why teams fail.

Reasons for team failure can include the following (Adams, 2001; Isaksen and Lauer, 2002; Yeung and Bailey, 1999):

- *Hidden agendas.* This refers to the belief that some team members are building their own empires or are using team members to advance their own careers instead of utilizing them as a means for achieving the team's and organization's goals.

- *Lack of understanding.* Misunderstandings and misconceptions regarding the credibility of team members and the expected outcomes of the collaboration can arise when team members are brought together for the first time.

- *Lack of leadership.* This situation usually occurs when the team leader does not have the appropriate skills to lead a team, or where team members do not acknowledge an individual as their leader.

- *Wrong mix of team members.* As we have already discussed, team work requires an appropriate mix of expertise, skills and personalities. A team that is unevenly balanced can face either the danger of generating too many ideas or no ideas at all.

- *Unhealthy team environment.* The team may not be effective if team members feel that the expectations set either by the client or the team leader are unrealistic. In such cases, many problems arise due to the fact that some (or all) team members cannot cope with the resultant uncertainty and stress.

- *Treating a team like a group.* Some organizations label a group as a team, but then treat the team as nothing more than a collection of people.

Psychological phenomena that can cause teams to fail

It is important to note that even if the team leader and the team members do their best, there are psychological events that can cause team performance to deteriorate. These can range from social loafing to a kind of blind conformity and groupthink. These different psychological phenomena and their effects on team working are discussed in the sections that follow.

Blind conformity

It is part of human nature to want to be liked and to be accepted by others (Thompson, 2003). There have been several experiments conducted which have shown how people even tend to engage in illogical or bizarre behaviour in order to guarantee acceptance by a group. For instance, nearly 50 years ago, Solomon Asch (a social psychologist) conducted several laboratory experiments in his studies on conformity – the tendency of a human being to consent, often reluctantly, to a group's view. Asch (1951) demonstrated a negative side of group dynamics by revealing that it is difficult for individuals to resist group views or opinions. A group of seven to nine volunteers were shown a line of certain length (line A) and were then asked to identify the line that was the same length as line A (see Figure 6.1). Within these groups, all members apart from one (the true volunteer) were Asch's confederates or stooges, who were told secretly beforehand to choose the wrong line. The group members were giving their answers in a fixed manner leaving the true volunteer to give his/her choice last. So, when the group was presented with the task, all confederates said that line A was the same length with a line other than line 3 (the obvious right answer!).

FIGURE 6.1   The Asch experiment

Asch conducted the same experiment with approximately 31 subjects. Only 20 per cent of the volunteers remained independent and resisted pressure to conform (and, therefore, gave the right answer). The remaining 80 per cent 'gave in' to the pressure that the group exerted at least once. The disturbing facts from Asch's experiment suggest that it is fairly easy for an individual to consent to a unanimous but incorrect judgement. The point to consider here is that if individuals are inclined to conform due to group pressure to issues where most of us know the answer and are familiar with the task in hand (like the task in the Asch experiment), imagine what may happen to team dynamics when the issue that people are facing may be unfamiliar and/or ambiguous.

Groupthink

In the same line of argument, another psychological event that may potentially lead to team failure is what psychologists label as *groupthink*. Researchers have studied this subject extensively over the past four decades. Janis (1972) conducted research into a number of 'disasters' in American foreign policy (e.g., Korea, Vietnam), in order to uncover the reasons why these committees made such bad decisions. He discovered that group cohesiveness had a negative effect on outcomes. He suggested that the cohesion experienced in these groups prevented contradictory and/or alternative opinions from being considered. The group loyalty in these cases had a negative effect – it stifled discussion and constrained debate – which had a direct effect on the quality of the decision. Buchanan and Huczynski (2003) also argue that groupthink limited decision making in this context because:

- the courses of action were accepted by the majority;

- nobody in these committees was re-examining or coming up with alternative routes to solving the problem; and

- the group failed to make use of expert opinion, and in the case that they did make use of an expert, it was evaluated with a selective bias, ignoring the facts which did not support the group's view.

Janis suggests that groupthink can lead to the deterioration of mental competence, reality appraisal and ethical standing. He has defined groupthink as: 'the psychological drive for consensus at any cost that suppresses dissent and appraisal of alternatives in cohesive decision-making groups' (1972: 8).

There are several differences between groupthink and blind conformity:

- Members of groups are not total strangers.

- Groups victimized by groupthink are friendly and generally tight-knit and cohesive (Kreitner et al., 2002).

Janis (1972) recommends that the following steps be considered in order to prevent groupthink in helping cohesive teams generate sound decisions:

1. Each team member must be encouraged to actively voice their opinions or express their concerns.

2. Leaders should be prepared and must anticipate criticism for their own actions.

3. Get recommendations for the same policy question from different groups with different leaders.

4. Periodically divide the group into subgroups in order to gain a fresh perspective.

5. Invite outsiders that the group trusts and get their reactions.

6. Someone from the group should play the 'devil's advocate' role in order to uncover any unfavourable outcomes to the plan discussed.

7. Reconsider the action plan and look for flaws when the decision is reached.

Social loafing

The last psychological phenomenon that can inhibit team performance is 'social loafing'. Social loafing is defined by Thompson (2003: 100) as: 'the tendency for people in a group to slack off – i.e., not work as hard either mentally or physically in a group as they would alone'.

Within the literature, a range of issues has been identified as potential causes for social loafing. Some of the main reasons have been proposed by Kreitner et al. (2002: 334) and include:

- *Equity of effort:* 'Everyone else is goofing off, so why shouldn't I?' In these cases, team members have the perception that their co-workers are loafing and therefore they should also invest minimum effort to the project.

- *Loss of personal accountability:* 'I'm lost in the crowd, so who cares?' Here, team members feel that the task they are performing is routine (simple or unimportant), making them feel dispensable.

- *Motivational loss due to the sharing of rewards:* 'Why should I work harder than the others when everyone gets the same reward?' This happens when team members are performing part of the whole process and therefore do not feel ownership of the end result.

- *Co-ordination loss as more people perform the task:* 'We're getting in each other's way'. Here, team members may feel that there are more people involved in the task than there should be and hence their contributions tend to be unidentifiable, which makes them feel that their value is undermined.

Creative teams: what do we know?

Today's ever-changing business environment requires people working together to accomplish something beyond the capabilities of individuals working on their own. The factors that determine creative effectiveness at the team level are multifaceted. In the past, a plethora of studies have tried to identify the variables that make or break effective team work and hence often aid or undermine the development of innovative products/services. In order to shed more light in the area of creative teams, we apply the inputs–processes–outcomes (I–P–O) model developed by Hackman and Morris (1975). This prevailing framework in the study of teams, will help us to organize and put together the literature on creative teams. *Inputs* encapsulate all the necessary drivers of a team, such as its material or human resources, while *processes* denote the dynamic interactions among team members as they work together on the way to achieving their goal. *Outcomes* refer to the task and non-task-related results of a team's operation. Figure 6.2 shows the I–P–O model, while findings on each of these aspects are discussed below.

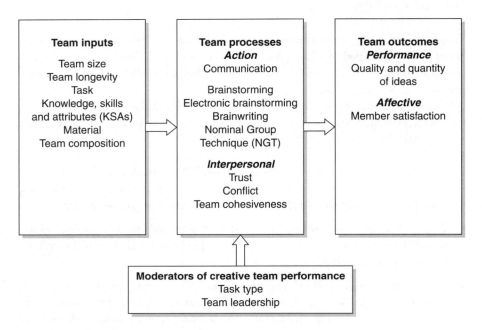

FIGURE 6.2   I–P–O model of creative team functioning

Team inputs

Inputs represent the design and compositional characteristics of a team, such as the size of team, the skills and abilities of team members and how long the team members have worked together. These team inputs influence how teams operate and perform (Hackman and Morris, 1975) and are discussed in more detail below.

Team size

Scholars traditionally described group size as critical to group performance. In particular, research on brainstorming by both Bouchard and Hare (1970) and Renzulli et al. (1974), found that the output of creative ideas on a per-employee basis decreased as team size increased. For instance, they found that for teams consisting of five, seven and nine members, the average output was 66, 44 and 40 ideas, respectively. Thornburg (1991) argues that what he terms the Creative Production Percent (CPP), improves with a decrease in team size until it reaches the group size of two, or dyads. Why does this happen? The dyads experience a unique and exclusive one-to-one capability to share and exchange ideas, and team-level inhibitors – such as social loafing, conformity or production blocking – are less likely to occur (Brajkovich, 2003; Murray, 1964). Interestingly, Thornburg (1991) points out that although dyads are more effective when teams are required to break away from the usual, in other situations they should be considered along with other teams. If we look at different fields around us, we will find an abundance of successful dyads. Think, for instance, about Stanford University classmates Bill Hewlett and Dave Packard (founders of HP) and Larry Page and Sergey Brin (founders of Google). Adams (2001), however, suggests that the creative team should be big enough so that the necessary knowledge, skills and capabilities are present in order to tackle the problem at hand or to seize an identified opportunity, while at the same time it should be small enough for members to work together without any difficulty.

Team longevity

Katz and Allen's (1982) longitudinal research with 50 R&D teams identified an inverse relationship between team longevity and innovativeness. Interestingly, the longer teams worked together, the less innovative they became. The findings from this study suggest that the positive project performance that these teams experienced within the first two years was mainly due to new members coming together and contributing fresh viewpoints or concepts, while developing a better understanding of each other's knowledge, skills and abilities. Katz and Allen's study shows how team performance starts to deteriorate in project teams that continue to work together for longer periods of time. They identify a number of reasons why the performance of long-tenured teams tends to deteriorate:

- The project teams with higher longevity tend to be staffed by older employees. How does this affect team performance? Older employees tend to be less up-to-date in their fields or on new tools (such as new techniques, knowledge and software packages), which limits their knowledge and contribution to new problems.

- As team membership stabilizes, members tend to interact less among themselves as well as with others outside of the organization. Katz and Allen (1982) suggest that a decrease in project performance occurs because team members tend to ignore or become isolated from important sources of knowledge and interaction, which in turn reduces project communication and causes a fall in performance.

Similarly, Nyström (1979) and Payne (1990) suggest that there needs to be a restriction on the life cycle of a team in order to enhance its innovativeness. Many creative companies have encountered this problem and have come up with strategies for preventing this from happening. For example, the award-winning Silicon Valley new product consultancy, Lunar Design, has devised the following strategies to prevent their employees from working with the same group of people or from doing the same kind of work for too long:

- Projects which last for several years are broken down into smaller ones with clear and identifiable goals managed by a project manager. By doing this, Lunar can involve different people according to the requirements of each project and therefore maintain a fresh and diverse team throughout the duration of the project.

- Employees are encouraged to get involved in a wide range of projects, sometimes even at the same time, which helps them to cross-fertilize ideas and therefore increase the set of suggestions to be considered.

- All employees, from newcomers to more senior people, are encouraged to take part and contribute to projects which do not necessarily fit into their existing portfolio of experiences in order to add some new and fresh perspectives to the problems that they face.

Task

Creative work is not limited to a particular occupation but can occur in a diverse range of jobs that require certain types of tasks (Mumford et al., 1997). We typically associate creative work with advertisers, engineers, musicians, film directors, video game developers and scientists. Yet, creative work can occur at any occupation where the tasks at hand involve complex, ill-defined problems, where the result requires the generation of novel and useful ideas (Mumford and Gustafson, 1988). Business problems, for instance, are generally complex, demanding different types of knowledge and skills. Developing and launching a new product or making improvements to an existing product often requires the very careful co-ordination and co-operation of people within departments, across functional divisions, at different hierarchical levels within an organization, and across sites and departments that may form part of an external collaborating company. Typically, many people will be involved in the process from the initial generation of a new idea through to refinement and eventual implementation. Achieving these developments requires team work and the integration of specialized capabilities in order to come up with new ideas, as well as to transform these ideas into viable commercial products or services (Wageman, 1995).

Knowledge, skills and abilities (KSAs)

It is not a cliché to think that if you want great performance you need great people. Individuals participating in high-performing teams must be competent and they must possess the necessary knowledge, skills and abilities to perform the given tasks successfully (Hoegl and Gemuenden, 2001). The greatest benefit of creative teams is that they can bring together hand-picked individuals from a diverse range of backgrounds with the required KSAs to play specific roles. Every day, engineering, design and marketing teams are assembled with the aim of solving problems that can enhance customer experience or improve efficiency in the delivery of a product or a service. Whitfield (1975) states that knowledge acts as a store of building data for novel combinations. In other words, without 'input' there can be no 'output' because there is nothing on which to 'operate'. Solutions to problems do not occur in a vacuum (Mumford, 2000). Sternberg et al. (1997) take this notion a step further by suggesting that people are not generally creative in every field but rather in the area of their specialization. They also add that extensive knowledge of a specific field (otherwise referred to as expertise) requires a considerable amount of time to be accumulated. People who aim to generate innovative ideas need to know the basic knowledge of the field in order to move beyond the status quo. Therefore, Sternberg et al. (1997) note that, in order to move forward, one needs to be aware of what the status quo is. Marks et al. (2001) highlight how team leaders should consider the different KSAs that their team members should have in relation to the different stages of a project. For instance, some team members will be better at defining the problem, others at refining the area under investigation or brainstorming, and some will excel in taking ideas further.

Resourcing the team

Resourcing the team includes everything that the organization has available to assist employees' work. Amabile and Gryskiewicz (1989) note that these resources include an array of elements: sufficient funds, material resources, systems and processes for work in the domain and relevant information. Amabile (1998) points out that managers must decide on the funding and other resources that a team legitimately needs to complete a project. The lack of project resources can constrain employees' creativity. Amabile et al. (1996) add that employees' perceptions of the adequacy of resources may affect people psychologically by leading to beliefs about the intrinsic value of the projects that they have undertaken.

Team composition

The final input variable that has been considered within the team creativity literature is team composition. Most teams struggle to pull together the right skills, knowledge, attitudes, behaviours and problem-solving styles to achieve adequate team diversity and cohesiveness. We use the word 'adequate' to show that a right balance should be achieved in terms of:

- knowledge, skills and attitudes;
- personality traits required in the design of an effective team.

There are many individual characteristics that can potentially affect the creative outcome of a team. Milliken and Martins (1996) distinguish between two types of diversity, namely: observable or readily detectable attributes, such as age, race or ethnic background and gender; and less visible or underlying attributes, such as educational background, functional background, industry experience and organizational tenure. Observable or detectable attributes are more likely to evoke responses from team members since they are mainly influenced by biases or stereotypes (Milliken and Martins, 1996). Kurtzberg and Amabile (2001) suggest that diversity among team members may influence the creative outcome of the team since it affects the context for communication, interaction and collaboration. Paradoxically, diversity can either enhance or hinder creativity. Amabile's (1998) study proposes that when teams include people with different expertise and creative thinking styles, ideas are often combined in exciting and useful ways. Diverse groups are perceived to have more potential in generating alternative orientations for approaching an issue in question, cross-fertilizing team members' ideas and promoting creative thinking (Falk and Johnson, 1977). Thornburg (1991: 326) defines diversity as: 'the number of different orientations brought to bear on a problem and to interact in a problem situation'. Parmerter and Gaber's (1971) research with scientists stresses the importance of having stimulating colleagues within project-based environments, since the presence of diverse stimuli provides fresh insight into existing activities. However, not all studies have found support for diversity in team creativity. Diversity can also hamper creativity, especially if team members are so distant from each other that they find it difficult to communicate and to reach an agreed conclusion.

According to Cummings and Oldham (1997), creative employees need to be surrounded by colleagues who help excite them about their work but do not distract them from it. Homogeneity among group members, while desirable from some perspectives, is not particularly facilitative for creative group outcomes. When a team is too homogeneous (comprised of members with similar educational or cultural backgrounds or within the same age group or from the same gender) it tends to under-perform since the lack of different perspectives inhibits the generation of creative outcomes. A series of studies by Amabile (1983) and Amabile and Glazebrook (1982) also suggest that another normal reaction that dampens creativity, particularly in team situations, is employees' negativity bias in evaluating others' intellectual work, and individuals' tendency to perceive critics as more intelligent than praise-givers. In such cases, team members are more likely to look for flaws in others' ideas and the leader tends to overplay the comments of the critics because the critics are perceived as smarter than the idea generators.

Team processes

Team processes refer to the different ways and means through which creative teams achieve their outcomes (Weingart, 1997). Success does not only depend on each team member's talents and resources but also on the way people interact with each other (e.g, processes) in order to accomplish the task at hand (Marks et al., 2001).

Action processes

Action processes refer to the dynamic activities that team members undertake in order to accomplish the desired goal (Marks et al., 2001). Communication is a key action process in team working. Earlier research (Allen, 1977; Menzel, 1965) as well as more recent studies (Hargadon and Sutton, 1997, 2000), stress the importance of interpersonal interaction as the primary means of collecting information and ideas relevant to a team's project work. Currently, companies are investing heavily in knowledge management systems and intranet websites with very detailed and updated databases to help employees in their search processes. Yet what they often discover is that these databases are used by staff to find out who (within the company) has the relevant knowledge. Once employees have identified who can help, they frequently resort to interpersonal interaction to solve the problems at hand. Face-to-face communication is still the dominant way of exchanging knowledge and ideas within the workplace as issues presented in the written form are often complicated and, hence, require explanation and further discussion (Allen, 1977; Price, 1965).

Creative problem solving is another critical action process in team working. This usually involves three key stages. The first requires team members to clearly define the problem in hand. Once this has been achieved members then generate ideas that could potentially solve the problem. In the final stage, the team has to decide on the most feasible and valuable solution. Taking into account the complexity of creative problem solving, a large volume of research has focused on specific techniques that can enhance creativity in each stage of the team problem-solving process. Most research on team problem solving remains focused on brainstorming, as this is the most widely used technique for generating ideas. Brainstorming has been adopted and implemented by almost every profession, from engineering and construction through to advertising and new product development.

Brainstorming

One of the earliest attempts to develop a structured approach to enhance creative problem solving at team level is brainstorming. In 1938, Alex Osborn – one of the founders and executives of the advertising firm Batten, Barton, Durstine, and Osborn (BBDO) – generated this technique. Osborn discovered that conventional team meetings were inhibiting the generation of new ideas, especially from junior staff. He noticed that junior people were not expressing their thoughts or ideas in front of senior colleagues at these meetings. This observation triggered him to come up with some rules designed to improve team problem solving, by giving people the freedom to speak their minds.

Osborn labelled this process 'brainstorming, using the brain to storm a problem' (Osborn, 1963: 151). Nowadays, brainstorming goes hand in hand with other creative efforts. For instance, The American Heritage Dictionary of the English Language defines brainstorming as: 'a method of shared problem solving in which all members of a team spontaneously contribute ideas'.

Osborn (1963) argues that the creative process involves two steps; first, idea generation and, second, idea evaluation. Brainstorming focuses mainly on the first stage, idea generation, which is further divided into the phases of fact-finding and idea-finding. Fact-finding refers to the phase of problem definition and preparation, while idea-finding is about making inferences from old ideas and combining existing knowledge in new ways to generate new ideas.

Rules for successful brainstorming

Osborn (1963) identified four rules for the effective use of brainstorming. First, during the brainstorming session, *criticism of ideas should be abolished.* In a brain-storming session, participants are not allowed to express any kind of judgement. This allows individuals to contribute their ideas to the problem at hand without being concerned about how others will react to them. Our society, unfortunately, encourages individuals to be critical and judgemental rather than supportive and creative in such circumstances. From our early years at school and throughout university we learn to use our judgement rather than our creativity; we learn to show off our 'smartness' by criticizing other people's ideas. We rarely focus on being constructive in supporting the development of existing ideas. As a result, we tend to apply the more negative elements in critical thinking without due regard to the more positive, critically constructive comments that can help refine and develop a new idea. Too often we equate critical thinking with negative eval-uations and this is supported by, for example, newspaper critiques of movies, the-atre productions, government policies, and so forth. Recently we have even seen the development of TV shows where there is a celebration of critiques in what often takes the form of personal put-downs. For example, *Pop Idol,* the reality entertainment show by Fremantle Media, became an instant hit not only due to its original concept – the televised search for a new national solo pop idol – but because some of the judges have been highly critical of the participants' perfor-mances. On the flipside, creativity theorists suggest that individuals taking part in team problem-solving sessions must change their habits and contribute to the development of a social context that gives free reign to the imagination (Nickerson, 2002), and that this is the basis for effective brainstorming.

The second rule of brainstorming is that participants should welcome *'free-wheeling'.* In other words, the wilder the idea the better. Participants in brain-storming sessions need to be daring in generating wild ideas, no matter how unrealistic or unconventional they may seem. It is through stepping outside of convention and limiting group views that it is possible to generate ideas that go beyond the 'obvious' and shed new light on existing problems.

Third, participants in brainstorming sessions are encouraged to *'go for large quantities of ideas'.* Osborn (1963) found that the greater the number of ideas, the greater is the probability of coming up with a set of new and useful ideas. His rule suggests that quantity of ideas leads to quality. Research has shown that the last ideas on a brainstorming session are on average of higher value than the ideas generated at the beginning of the session (Osborn, 1963). Osborn (1963) also argues that the longer teams are in this phase, the speed of flow tends to accelerate. For instance, a brainstorming team can commence at a comparatively slow pace, coming up with 25 ideas in the first 10 minutes. These ideas will comprise the basis upon which new ideas will be generated. That is why it is normal in the next 15 minutes for the brainstorming team to produce another 80 ideas. As a result, Osborn (1963) recommends that the optimum duration of a brainstorming session should be no more than 30 minutes. Similarly, after being involved in several brainstorming sessions, Parnes and Meadow (1959) conclude that between 30 and 45 minutes is the required time for an effective brainstorming session. The temptation that many brainstorming teams experience is to keep going and trying not to make a note until the last idea is forced out, rather than to stop the session and resume later (De Bono, 1990). Brainstorming sessions can be mentally demanding, and consequently De Bono suggests that if one team needs more time then they should break down the problem into smaller parts and deal with them in separate 45-minute sessions. Similarly, Ricchiuto (1996) stresses the importance of not forcing the brainstorming participants to stay together for a longer period of time because they may end up getting angry and frustrated with the process and consequently resist contributing to another brainstorming session in the future.

Fourth, Osborn (1963) argues that *'combination and improvement need to be sought'* in a brainstorming session. In addition to contributing ideas of their own, participants should build on each other's ideas. Osborn suggests that brainstorming participants may be stimulated by other people's ideas and these in turn may trigger the development of better ideas or the reconfiguration of existing ideas into novel solutions. These four rules are critical to the success of the brainstorming process and for the creative output of team problem solving. The facilitator of a brainstorming session should ensure that all participants are aware of these principles and that the session should remain open and informal (Osborn, 1963).

Since the development of Osborn's brainstorming method, this technique has been widely adopted in both profit and not-for-profit organizations throughout the world. Brainstorming has been used in many different fields, such as: social services, government policies, military affairs, hospitals, education, broadcasting, retailing, advertising, marketing, product design, packaging, transportation, accounting, engineering and journalism (Osborn, 1963). The list is extensive. However, in the early days, many organizations were too quick to regard the brainstorming technique as a panacea to all problems and consequently some organizations turned against this method when they realized that the technique could not provide solutions to all their problems.

Advantages of the brainstorming session

The most frequently observed benefits of a brainstorming session are the following (Brahm and Kleiner, 1996; Kelley and Littman, 2001; Parnes and Meadow, 1959; Sutton and Hargadon, 1996):

- *The generation of hundreds of ideas.* The number of ideas generated in a brainstorming session is beyond question. The central goal behind brainstorming is that it lets ideas flow, no matter how unconventional or unrealistic they may seem.

- *Support the organizational memory.* Brainstorming participants may take advantage of these sessions to retrieve, organize and combine previous knowledge from old problems to existing ones. It can also help to add and store new knowledge to be used in future brainstorming sessions.

- *Impressing clients.* Clients are usually impressed by the ideas, sketches and concepts generated and by observing team members' capabilities and skills. Clients may also collect ideas faster in a brainstorming session than through individual discussions.

- *Improved morale.* The inclusive nature of brainstorming promotes a 'feel-good factor', especially when participants contribute to the success of the company or project. Participants can be inspired by these sessions; they tend to discuss ideas generated from the brainstorming sessions for several days. Also, brainstorming sessions help companies who use them regularly to articulate a very important message: that good ideas may come from any level within the organization.

- *Gain better understanding of each other.* A mix of people from different departments and different levels of management are brought together in a brainstorming setting. This may help those involved to better understand how each other is thinking and the different expertise, passions and goals of team members. This in turn may promote the development of mutual trust and respect for each other. The unrestricted nature of a brainstorming session allows its members to share the experiences, frustrations or blocks that they may encounter in their creative endeavours in a relatively uninhibited fashion.

- *Enjoyment.* Brainstorming is all about generating valuable ideas in a relaxed manner. People have to be reminded that a brainstorming session is not like any other business meeting and that the logic behind it is that 'anything goes'. Brainstorming participants are encouraged to contribute their ideas; they often draw and come up with diagrams, in order to better explain how things may work in the area under investigation, they constantly interrupt each other, and so forth. This process often feels like a form of play and people tend to enjoy it. In practice, brainstorming sessions also demand a lot of hard work since their purpose is to maximize the number of ideas generated by the whole team and, in many cases, this is a challenging task.

- *Personal growth and well-being.* Most of the times participants' thinking processes initially lack robustness; this is because all of us are rarely challenged to stretch our minds beyond conventional wisdom. However, the more individuals experience these sessions the more they become inclined to solve problems creatively. For example, participants often recount that when they walk out of brainstorming sessions they feel richer from the experience. This process of personal development can be of high importance to the individual's thinking skills.

- *Think up improvements.* The systematic use of brainstorming sessions may help a team to identify things that are not going well and, hence, need to be changed or improved. VanGundy (1992) stresses the importance of bringing external people (e.g., suppliers, customers, retailers, etc.) into the organization in order to increase the probability of identifying potential problems that only they may be able to see. By so doing, one may spark new thinking, which in turn may stimulate alternative viewpoints that may trigger a collective solution to the problem.

- *Relatively inexpensive.* Brainstorming is a relatively inexpensive technique that does not require a lot of time in preparation or execution. As we have already stressed, brainstorming should happen whenever required within the workplace in order to instil a belief in the power of generating creative ideas. Through our research, we have seen companies investing heavily in very expensive equipment, such as electronic whiteboards with integrated printers. However, teams may also conduct effective brainstorming sessions by using existing resources. A meeting room equipped with note pads, different colours of markers and sticky note paper, is quite sufficient.

Disadvantages of the brainstorming session

Despite the many virtues that the brainstorming technique may offer to the team involved, it can also have several drawbacks. Two of these are listed below:

- *The generation of ideas without screening them.* Although brainstorming may generate hundreds of ideas, the method does not include any kind of screening or evaluation. That is why brainstorming must always be seen as a technique for finding ideas and therefore as the first part of the overall problem-solving process. The second phase of creative problem solving must be aimed at selecting those ideas that are worthy of further development from the generated pool of suggestions (Nickerson, 2002).

- *It may not always be the answer to your problems.* Brainstorming is not, nor can it ever be, a panacea to all business problems. Brainstorming sessions are more likely to have value if the rules previously outlined are followed. If any of the conditions are not met, then the outcome of the session is likely to be less successful.

Useful guidelines for effective brainstorming

Practitioners and academics have offered useful guidelines for conducting an effective brainstorming session (De Bono, 1990; Kelley and Littman, 2001; Osborn, 1963). These include:

- Warm-up and homework; that is, ensure that participants are prepared.

- Define the problem and consider the use of a skilled facilitator.

- Suspend judgement and consecutively number ideas.

- Cross-pollinate ideas and create an effective setting for idea generation.

The first thing that brainstorming participants need to do is to *warm-up*. All participants, either experienced or novice, must have a warm-up session before they join the brainstorming session. A good idea would be to think about relatively simple things (e.g., a computer screen or a magazine) and start a word game simply to clear the mind and to remind them that evaluation is excluded in brainstorming. Brainstorming members also need to do some *homework* before they start brainstorming. For instance, several NPD consultancies (New Product Development is the term used to explain the process of bringing a new product/service to the market) that we have studied focus a lot of their effort on trying to understand the users' needs by gathering up-to-date consumer data. Typically, they start by examining secondary data; information that has already been collected (in many cases by other researchers and often for another purpose) and is readily available, for example, in the form of magazines or newspapers, or through using the internet to find out more about the client as well as data on competitive products. This knowledge is also often supplemented by visits to supermarkets, toy stores, hardware stores and specialized retail outlets in order to identify the latest developments in engineering and design. Talking to relevant end-users is also important; for example, the normal procedure for an NPD team is to interview or observe current or potential end-users. NPD consultancies claim that this helps the team to get a sense of end-users' experiences with existing products/services and allows them to gain an understanding on how the end-user feels about the proposed product/service. This process not only provides teams with valuable feedback, but also triggers new ideas about enhancing the product experience. The central goal behind the *warm-up* guideline is, therefore, to stretch thinking by enriching understanding and knowledge of the current problem at hand. Imagine if you had to participate in a brainstorming session where you knew nothing about the area in question. Most probably, the quantity of ideas and their quality would be limited by the absence of relevant experience or knowledge.

The second guideline for effective brainstorming is that teams need to *define the problem*. This prescribes that the initial statement that will trigger the discussion must be specific rather than general. The brainstorming participants have to narrow down their focus so that they can start generating ideas on a single issue. Imagine that your team was asked to perform a brainstorming session regarding new services to be offered to air travellers to enhance their travel experience. The first thing that your team needs to do is to try to define the problem as accurately as possible. The better the brainstorming participants are able to articulate and describe the problem, the easier it is to commence the session. Therefore, the first thing that team members may consider is how to break down elements of the 'travel experience' that air travellers go through. For example, we could assume that the passenger is involved in the following main stages: the journey to the airport, finding his/her own way around the airport, checking-in, waiting in the lounge, the actual flight, arriving at the destination, collecting the luggage and also the journey from the airport to the destination. In other words, a passenger goes through a diverse range of stages, each of which the airline could focus on as a means of enhancing the whole 'flight' experience. A well-defined problem statement directs the brainstorming participants to shoot their ideas at a single target.

Although there is a need to be specific, a too narrow focus can also limit idea generation. For example, a brainstorming facilitator who asks participants to think about new internet services that could be made available to first-class air passengers is probably taking a very narrow definition of the travel experience and hence limits participants' creative contribution. Conversely, if the facilitator asks the brainstorming members to contribute ideas related to all air travellers' needs, this also constitutes a bad brainstorming articulation of the topic because it is too general. In this case, the brainstorming team faces the danger of aimless wandering, of having no clear direction on what aspect of the 'travel journey' they should be focusing on. In other words, a too narrow or too broad definition is problematic as it may negatively affect the team's spontaneity. What is there-fore essential is to draw an appropriate framework within which the participants are required to think; skilled facilitators play a key role in this respect.

Another useful guideline is to remind participants that they should *suspend judgement* for the duration of a brainstorming session. The brainstorming ses-sion should encourage an open forum where all ideas, no matter how simple, ridiculous, exaggerated or wild, are expressed. Participants in these meetings should never feel that their ideas may be criticized or laughed at. It is impor-tant to remember that evaluation does not occur during the brainstorming ses-sion and that expressions like 'that would never work here …', or 'we have already tried that unsuccessfully here …', or 'has anyone else tried this before?' should not be allowed because they defeat the purpose of the brainstorming session. Ideas should also be *consecutively numbered* during the brainstorming ses-sion. All brainstorming evangelists suggest that every brainstorming session should make use of an 'idea collector' (most probably the brainstorming facili-tator), whose role is to record the ideas generated in the brainstorming session. We are not referring to note taking; idea collectors should capture the ideas to demonstrate the progress that is being made during the brainstorming session. Numbering ideas has two immediate benefits. First, at any point in the meeting the brainstorming facilitator can inform the participants about the number of generated ideas and may therefore ask them to produce more. Second, it can help brainstorming participants to move back and forth between ideas without losing direction and focus.

Brainstorming participants should also strive to build upon other people's ideas; the goal of the brainstorming session is the *cross-pollination* of ideas among the participants. New ideas are more likely to arise when individuals are exposed to other people's ideas. These ideas can serve as stimuli to one's own imagination. Even the simplest and most obvious ideas that are generated within the brainstorming session, may be combined and hence may lead to the gener-ation of ideas that are unique and valuable. Brainstorming allows participants to experience how different people think and react to the same issue. By so doing, participants are less likely to get bogged down by their own way of thinking, since the process involves mutual exchange of stimuli among team members.

It is also important for anyone involved in a brainstorming session to accept that 'anything goes' in order to create an *effective setting*. Brainstorming participants are usually intrigued by the session's value, but may find it quite hard to express ideas, especially if they perceive them as wild or exaggerated. Participants may also experience a perfectionism complex, which again is likely to stifle their effort and lead members to abandon or not reveal their ideas (Osborn, 1963). To avoid these from occurring, facilitators need to formalize the brainstorming principles, so that people do not feel threatened or apologetic when they generate new ideas, draw sketches from ideas or try to identify emerging patterns. At the same time, participants need to be reminded that they are around friends in a supportive environment. Kelley and Littman (2001) also stress the importance of the physical space during a brainstorming session. They argue that the brainstorming team must use the walls so that the ideas are visible by everyone within the team. Posting ideas on the wall encourages participants to come back to those that seem worthy for further development. This strategy has two clear benefits: first, participants do not forget previous ideas and, second, they can build upon other people's ideas.

Over the years, new techniques have emerged to stimulate the development of new and useful ideas at the team level (both in terms of quantity and quality), but before we review some of these techniques, have a go at the in-class brainstorming exercise below.

IN-CLASS BRAINSTORMING EXERCISE

Problem to consider

Your team (comprising four to eight members) acts as management consultants advising the manager of your local railway station. Recent market research suggests that 60 per cent of travellers from your station to other destinations in the UK are travelling alone, are female and are aged 16–25.

You are required to rethink 'entertaining while waiting' in the railway station in relation to this market segment, and propose innovative solutions. Your team will be given a flipchart and several markers. You are advised to elect a facilitator who will write down the team's ideas on the flipchart. You have 25 minutes to generate 50 ideas relevant to the problem under investigation. Don't forget to follow the discussed guidelines. Enjoy!

Debriefing

Take five minutes in your teams after finishing with the brainstorming exercise to discuss the following questions:

1. Did you think that the brainstorming was successful? Why or why not?
2. How difficult did you find it to suspend judgement while listening to other people's ideas?

Creativity enhancement techniques

Prior research has shown that people participating in face-to-face brainstorming sessions are sometimes afraid of being criticized by the team and hence are unwilling to contribute their ideas. Several academics and practitioners have tried to address the brainstorming shortcomings by introducing other creativity enhancement techniques.

Electronic brainstorming

Electronic brainstorming, the use of computers to interact and exchange ideas, was perceived as a way of making it easier for participants to contribute their ideas, since no one would know whose ideas were whose (Diener, 1979; Thompson, 2003: 106). The principle behind it is that participants contribute their ideas anonymously to a general pool. This technique allows team members to generate a large quantity of ideas by sitting at their own desk and by being electronically connected to other participants. At any time, participants are able to review other people's ideas and use them to further develop new ideas. Although the original systems were designed for participating team members to be in the same room at the same time, they have evolved to enable users to interact with other team members over the Web. Gallupe and Cooper (1993) summarize the five stages of the electronic brainstorming process:

1. *Generating ideas.* Each participant inputs his/her ideas relevant to the topic into the computer at will. Regardless of whether the team participants are in the same room or dispersed throughout the world, they have access to the pool of ideas generated and archived into the computer. Although team members are allowed to talk if they want to during these meetings, most of them choose not to do so since they feel that computers are their primary channels of communication.

2. *Editing ideas.* Ideas are then categorized by key words identified by the team members as relevant to the issue under investigation. The aim is to organize ideas so that team members can identify similar ideas and combine them or eliminate redundant ideas. This will allow the team to go on with the important task of evaluating any promising ideas.

3. *Evaluating ideas.* Ideas are then evaluated and prioritized by each participant anonymously. The computer then collects all these individual rankings and generates a new group ranking that all participants can see. A voting tool can be of importance in assisting the team to reach a consensus on the ideas that are the most valuable. This can also be used as a means of identifying the degree of consensus or conflict among team members to the specific question posed to the team.

4. *Implementing ideas.* Electronic brainstorming cannot implement the best ideas, but it can ensure that several other ideas are considered, articulated and

assessed. Nevertheless, many electronic brainstorming software packages have a 'plan-of-action' tool where action steps are identified and sequenced and responsibilities are acknowledged. Team members are asked to propose action steps for each idea. Every member of the team can see all the actions proposed for each idea. Once this process is complete then the whole team starts to refine the action plan for each idea separately.

5. *Action.* The team ends the session with ideas accompanied by an agreed action plan and allocated responsibilities.

The use of networked computers by a team to assist the generation of ideas may offer the following benefits:

- *Simultaneous entry of ideas.* Individuals can immediately start inputting ideas into the computer without having to wait or having to interrupt others, something that occurs in a traditional brainstorming session (Pinsonneault et al., 1999).

- *Anonymity.* People who are afraid of being criticized by the team in a traditional brainstorming session, and hence are unwilling to contribute their ideas, will find it easier in electronic brainstorming since no one knows whose ideas are whose (Diener, 1979).

- *Better ideas are generated.* Team members find it easier to express unrealistic or unconventional ideas under the cover of anonymity, without having to worry about being criticized by other members (Cooper et al., 1998). Therefore, it is not only the number of ideas that is greater, but also the quality of ideas is often higher in these sessions (Valacich et al., 1994).

- *It can be effectively used with large teams.* Large teams of participants tend to generate more ideas than individuals working on their own, as happens in nominal groups (Dennis and Valacich, 1993). The electronic collection of ideas enables the participants to focus on generating as many ideas as they can without interruption, something that would be hard to achieve in a traditional brainstorming session.

- *It records the ideas for future sessions.* The participants' ideas are stored into a group pool electronically and can form the basis for future electronic brainstorming sessions (Gallupe and Cooper, 1993).

Although electronic brainstorming may prevent certain process losses from occurring, it also has several drawbacks:

- *It is not a panacea for all problems.* As with the traditional brainstorming technique, the use of electronic brainstorming does not guarantee a solution to all problems (Gallupe and Cooper, 1993). This technique is suitable when the outcome is to generate as well as to evaluate ideas.

- *Communication speed.* It requires participants on these sessions to be able, first, to set up the hardware and software required and, second, to have typing skills. The need to type rather than express ideas may inhibit idea generation by slowing down communication (Nunamaker et al., 1991). Moreover, people who prefer talking or do not possess these skills may be reluctant to participate in such sessions or may get frustrated by not being accustomed to typing (Gallupe and Cooper, 1993).

- *Overload of ideas.* Another disadvantage is that too many ideas may be generated, which may result in idea overload. In other words, the amount of cognitive processing necessary goes beyond the abilities of the individual participant to process the multiple, simultaneously generated ideas (Nagasundarum and Dennis, 1993). This problem may get worse when large teams are involved in idea generation.

- *It is relatively expensive.* Electronic brainstorming sessions require computers which are networked and are installed with the brainstorming software. Although the costs are continually falling, small firms still find it comparatively expensive to buy and maintain their own electronic brainstorming facilities (Gallupe and Cooper, 1993).

Brainwriting

Another technique that mobilizes creative problem solving at the team level is called 'brainwriting'. Brainwriting requires the team members who attend a brainstorming session to stop talking and start writing down their own ideas silently (Geschka et al., 1973). It emphasizes the silent generation of ideas in writing. The main logic behind this twist on a brainstorming session is to eliminate the problem of production blocking since team members do not have to wait for their turn in order to contribute their ideas (Thompson, 2003). Aiken et al. (1996) suggest that brainwriting can be categorized as either interactive (face-to-face idea generation) or nominal (non-face-to-face idea generation). Aiken et al. (1996) also suggest that brainwriting is more appropriate when a skilled facilitator or leader is not present, when participants are not experienced or trained in brainstorming, or when there is the possibility for conflict among two or more members.

There are several versions of brainwriting. The first is commonly known as the *individual poolwriting* technique, and uses the following steps (Geschka et al., 1981; VanGundy, 1981). To begin, each team member silently writes ideas on a piece of paper and places the paper in the centre of the table. Each participant then draws one of the sheets from the centre of the table and adds more ideas. This exchange of papers carries on until the end of the session. After several turns, most of the team members have been exposed to most of the ideas and comments.

In the second version of brainwriting, labelled as *'brainwalking'*, sheets of paper are posted on the walls of a room and team members silently walk around the room, read what is on the paper and then add their ideas (Mattimore, 1993). The extra benefit of this technique is that all participants can view all comments at the same time, thereby increasing a feeling of team cohesion. Nevertheless, anonymity may decrease since team members can see other participants' comments (Aiken et al., 1996). According to Wilson and Hanna (1990: 62), four principles need to be followed in order to ensure an effective brainwriting session takes place, namely:

1. Evaluation and criticism of ideas are forbidden.

2. Wild and offbeat ideas are encouraged.

3. Quantity, not quality, of ideas is the goal.

4. New combinations of ideas are sought.

There are several advantages related to the brainwriting process over brainstorming:

-   Many people feel terrified speaking even in front of just a small group. By expressing ideas in writing, people do not need to worry about this (Thompson, 2003).

-   Individuals do not have to wait to speak (team members are encouraged to be writing at the same time). The aim of this technique is to record all ideas and to ensure a high degree of anonymity (Aiken et al., 1996).

-   Brainwriting participants can produce a greater number of ideas since they generate ideas simultaneously (they do not have to take turns in generating ideas).

Although brainwriting may eliminate the problem of production blocking often evident in brainstorming sessions (because there is no need for anyone to wait for their turn to contribute their ideas) and may reduce evaluation apprehension (since there is no need for public speaking) this technique also has several disadvantages. For example, Thompson (2003) found that some brainwriting participants can feel uncomfortable sitting in silence as they think that it interferes with their flow of thinking. She suggests that only individuals who can follow their natural instincts can consistently generate more and better ideas. Some individuals may also feel that they cannot articulate their ideas fully on paper or that their spelling and grammar limits their ability to express ideas through this medium (VanGundy, 1988).

VanGundy notes that whilst this technique may prove useful when used in large groups, when team time is scarce and when verbal communication is not necessary, in the absence of these conditions, brainwriting may prove to be an ineffective technique.

Nominal Group Technique (NGT)

The last main team creativity enhancement technique considered here is the Nominal Group Technique (NGT). NGT was developed by Delbecq and Van de Ven at the University of Wisconsin in 1968 and has been widely used ever since. The difference of this technique compared with brainstorming is that participants within this type of team never interact. The session commences with brainwriting where team members – without any discussion among themselves – write down ideas related to the problem at hand (Summers and White, 1976; Thompson, 2003). Individual lists are then shared by the team in a 'round-robin' fashion and are recorded where all participants can view them: for example, a whiteboard. The team then discusses the generated set of ideas for clarification and evaluation, and finally, each person is asked to vote in order to rank order the ideas.

Brahm and Kleiner (1996) argue that the Nominal Group Technique (NGT) outperforms traditional brainstorming for two main reasons. First, NGT will prevent the development of tension and hostility among team members through securing reasonably equal participation and minimizing potential conflict. For example, employees who are usually reluctant to contribute ideas because they are worried about being criticized, or those who want to maintain a pleasant atmosphere and hence avoid creating any potential conflict within the team, are more likely to participate under NGT. Second, it has proven to be very effective in situations when judgement is important in the decision-making process and it can also be a time-saving technique.

Brahm and Kleiner (1996) also recognize that there are a number of disadvantages associated with NGT. One of the problems with this technique is that it focuses on one issue at a time and therefore lacks flexibility. As such, it often prohibits the cross-fertilization of ideas during the team problem-solving process. Another issue arises from the structured nature of NGT. Individuals that find it difficult to conform to the structure of this process may feel uncomfortable in utilizing the technique. Finally, NGT is not a spontaneous process. It demands a lot of preparation and a clear plan of organization; for example, the facilitator needs to plan ahead with regard to the facilities and equipment that are required in the session.

IN-CLASS EXERCISE

Problem to consider

Your team acts as naming consultants advising a start-up team of a new video game console aiming to sell its first version to a global market. This video game console is characterized by a sleek design and a lot of advanced features, such as wireless connectivity, expandable hard drive, ergonomic controllers, etc. You are required to provide the client with several names for the first version of this video game console. Your team has to complete two tasks:

First, you need to think about and decide on the following issues:

- Which problem-solving technique is more appropriate for this occasion? Defend your position.
- How many people do you think that you need in your team in order to have an effective result? What kind of criteria would you set in order to have a diverse range of viewpoints (e.g., discipline, gender, educational background, etc.)?

Second, you need to spend about 15 minutes to generate 20 different names. Have fun!

Interpersonal processes

Interpersonal processes encompass the relationships among team members working towards achieving their goal (Martins et al., 2004). Although interpersonal negotiations and the reaching of agreements for implementation are inherent in team creativity, studies that have examined the behavioural influence and persuasion patterns at different stages in the creative process are limited. In this realm, several authors have focused on highlighting the different forms of interpersonal interactions in team-based environments (Flores, 1979; Fukuyama, 1995; Sethia, 1995).

Trust

Fukuyama (1995) highlights the importance of people's ability to associate with each other and suggests that this is critical not only to economic life but virtually to every other aspect of social existence. Flores (1979), on the other hand, proposes that dialogue should be the more creative, open-ended activity of a team's thinking. In discussion, people take and hold positions as they do in a debate; in dialogue, people suspend their positions and probe others for reasoning to discover new possibilities. A crucial precondition for effective team working in creative environments is that the team is perceived as interpersonally non-threatening and safe (Kivimäki et al., 1997). In other words, behaviours that are grounded in informal bases of influence, such as friendliness and coalition-building among team members, are more likely to provide the basis for creativity-enhancing team outcomes. Riley (1992) and Schmuck and Runkel (1988) also emphasize the importance of trust in teams as the foundation for taking risks, exploring new and useful ideas, and solving problems. The risk factor is important to the development of creative thinking since fear of criticism is highly detrimental to both individual and group cognitive development (Manley, 1978).

Conflict

Researchers have investigated the impact that conflict has on idea generation and decision making (e.g., Amason, 1996; Amason and Sapienza, 1997). In particular, Jehn and Mannix (2001) found that conflict allows teams to reach better decisions since more alternatives are generated and discussed before a decision is made. Early research in organizational behaviour suggested that interactions designed to minimize conflict will increase consensus and affective relationships among team members (e.g., Janis, 1972). Recent studies have highlighted several benefits of conflict that have not previously been considered (Eisenhardt et al., 1997). For example, because productive questioning of generated ideas and processes can lead to higher-quality decisions, conflict may be useful when creativity is a desired outcome. The evidence supports this argument. Studying three leading professional service firms (branding consultancy, design studio and an architectural practice), Andriopoulos and Lowe (2000) found that rigorous debates of different and opposing viewpoints were often initiated by the senior management team. The intellectual stimulation aims to recognize, extract and synthesize diverse perspectives prior to reaching a decision.

Team cohesiveness

Cohesiveness can be defined as the process that reflects a group's tendency to stick together and remain united in search of a common goal (Carron, 1982). Research has shown that cohesiveness is the principal discriminating variable between high and low innovative teams (Wallace and West, 1988). In his study with scientists, Pelz (1956), for instance, identifies that employees' performance is higher not only when they come into contact with colleagues from different settings, but also when they are close to at least one colleague who 'talks the same language'. Moreover, the lack of an effective 'translator' in the group may lead to conflict since the diverse range of definitions of the problem in hand, as well as the heterogeneous set of viewpoints to be considered, may cause problems in communication and therefore in reaching a shared understanding of what to do and how to proceed (Kirton, 1976; Kurtzberg and Amabile, 2001). Craig and Kelly (1999) suggest that interpersonal cohesiveness can have several positive influences on team interaction and creativity. Teams with increased creative performance tend to be characterized by an interpersonal liking (Hogg, 1992); team members laugh and smile more together (Firestein, 1990) and share increasing feelings of psychological safety and self-actualization (Nyström, 1979). Amabile (1998) also suggests that employees must express a willingness to help their teammates through difficult periods and setbacks. Similarly, Hargadon and Sutton (2000) note that employees of innovative companies should be willing to go out of their way to share their knowledge and help others. In other words, it is not enough to recruit the most creative, diverse and talented people in the industry in order to increase the probability of coming up with a range of different solutions; team leaders also need to instil their group with a belief in the power of spreading information within the workplace. This of course requires every team member to recognize and respect the unique knowledge and perspective of others.

Moderators of team performance

In returning to the Hackman and Morris (1975) inputs–processes–outcomes framework, they identify task type and team leadership as important moderators of team performance. Each of these is briefly discussed below.

Task type

Task type, or even the selection of projects to be pursued, does not only specify the work to be done but also the competencies that need developing for future work (Andriopoulos and Lowe, 2000; Mumford, 2000). It is interesting to note that when team members recognize the need for creativity in order to get the job done more effectively, this increases their willingness to experiment with new ideas, technologies, materials, components, markets or processes (Gilson and Shalley, 2004). In particular, Kahn's (1990) study with designers in an architectural practice found that their motivation to try new things went up when they were encouraged to try innovative design methods. Similarly, Bennis and Biederman's (1997) work in high-performing teams from business, science and politics reinforces the premium put on the task by noting that the job itself becomes the most important reward. This, in return, encourages team members not to view the task as 'work' but as fun. Consequently, team members may become so immersed in the task at hand, that they do not think about anything else and prefer to be around people who feel and act the same way (Lipman-Blumen and Leavitt, 1999).

Team leadership

There is a general consensus among authors in this area that a democratic–participative leadership style facilitates creativity and innovation in teams (e.g., Nyström, 1979; Pelz, 1956; Wallace and West, 1988). Cummings and Oldham (1997), for instance, argue that a 'supportive' supervisory management style is more likely to contribute to creativity than a 'controlling' one, since it enhances individual motivation. Supportive supervisors tend to demonstrate concern for employees' feelings and wants, provide them with positive and constructive feedback and act as facilitators to their professional growth (Deci and Ryan, 1987). In contrast, a controlling style is more likely to decrease individual motivation simply because it does not allow the creative processes to flow (Deci and Ryan, 1987; Deci et al., 1989). In other words, controlling supervisors tend to closely monitor employees' behaviour, are reluctant to involve employees in decision making and force them to think or behave in certain ways (Deci et al., 1989).

Thacker's (1997) study also proposes that team members need to regard the team leader as someone who is trying to be supportive of creativity; otherwise the creative processes of the group may be stifled. Thacker (1997) suggests that the team leader must provide an 'open field' in which members can feel free to roam with new ideas and suggestions, unlike a tightly constructed set of rules and guidelines that is likely to leave team members with little latitude to express new thoughts and ideas.

There are certain elements that team leaders must possess so that they can develop the conditions upon which team creativity can flourish. If we consider the state of complexity within which many organizational functions operate, the task of the team leader is challenging. Nowadays, organizational teams are increasingly faced with complicated issues. This emphasizes the need for specialization and underlines the requirement for teams to have a range of experts that can effectively deal with complex problems. Therefore, the first and most important task that team leaders need to do is to build an effective work team that represents a diversity of skills, is made up of individuals who trust and communicate well with each other, who are willing to challenge each other's ideas in constructive ways, and who are mutually supportive of the work they are doing (Amabile and Gryskiewicz, 1989). Teams need to be formed in a way that supports the shared goals of the team and not the goals of the individual. Similarly, both Anderson et al. (1992) and Jones and McFadzean (1997) argue that team leaders should be competent facilitators in order to assist their teams to reach their objectives. They should also be in a position to balance employees' freedom and responsibility, without domination or control, while at the same time be willing to show concern for employees' feelings and needs, generously recognize creative work by individuals and teams, and encourage them to voice their concerns, provide feedback and facilitate skill development (Amabile, 1998; Pelz, 1956). Taking into consideration the intra-organizational verbal and non-verbal exchanges among team members, supervisors are required to employ conflict management techniques in order to positively influence group outcomes. Team leaders that possess these qualities help employees develop feelings of self-determination and personal initiative at work, while at the same time they encourage team members to consider, develop and ultimately contribute to creative outcomes.

Team outcomes

The main focus in the literature is on performance outcomes, such as the quality and quantity of ideas generated and on team member satisfaction. As we have already indicated, researchers have consistently found that members of electronic brainstorming sessions are more satisfied than their face-to-face participants. This may occur due to the fact that the simultaneous entry of ideas into the system does not allow one team member to dominate the generation process, as may happen in a face-to-face brainstorming session (Gallupe et al., 1992).

With regards to performance outcomes results can, at best, be described as mixed. The effectiveness of the brainstorming technique has puzzled practitioners and academics for many years. Nearly all laboratory studies conducted over the last 40 years have found that brainstorming sessions lead to the generation of fewer ideas than if the brainstormers were left to come up with ideas through working on their own (Diehl and Stroebe, 1987; Mullen et al., 1991; Thompson, 2003). These findings contradict earlier suggestions made by academics and practitioners about the value of brainstorming (e.g., Osborn, 1963). So why is the potential of brainstorming sessions not realized in these studies? Diehl and Stroebe (1987, 1991) and Gallupe and Cooper (1993) suggest that there are three factors that may explain this:

1. *Evaluation apprehension.* Brainstorming participants may be reluctant to contribute their ideas because they worry about what other people would think of them. Productivity loss in the generation of new ideas is noticeably higher when an authority figure attends the brainstorming session (Mullen et al., 1991) and when all or some of the participants experience anxiety about team interaction (Camacho and Paulus, 1995).

2. *Social loafing (or free-riding)*. As we have already explained, individuals working in teams may not feel as accountable as they would if they were working alone, and hence may reduce their efforts. This may also occur because all brainstorming participants contribute their ideas into a collective pool and, therefore, recognition and rewards occur at a team level. Goldenberg and Mazursky (2002) propose that brainstorming participants with a 'free-riding' mentality tend to either keep silent in the session or to repeat ideas that have been already proposed by other members.

3. *Production blocking*. Brainstorming participants may think that their idea generation is blocked because of their inability to express their ideas if they have to wait for their turn to talk. Also, listening to others may impede their own thinking.

Although the literature offers many studies based on similar laboratory experiments, Sutton and Hargadon (1996) are critical of results that suggest that face-to-face groups produce fewer non-overlapping ideas per person when compared to people who generate ideas on their own. Sutton and Hargadon (1996: 688) argue that most of the experiments conducted throughout the last 20 years have used participants

> [w]ho (1) had no past or future task interdependence; (2) had no past or future social relationships; (3) didn't use the ideas generated; (4) lacked pertinent technical expertise; (5) lacked skills that complement other participants; (6) lacked expertise in doing brainstorming; and (7) lacked expertise in leading brainstorming sessions.

They therefore argue that these experiments often overlook the context within which brainstorming sessions occur. Similarly, Hackman (1985) and Mowday and Sutton (1993) note that there is a tendency to generalize oversimplified or incomplete conclusions about team behaviour when significant contextual factors, such as reward schemes or incentives, are not taken into account. What is needed are further fieldwork studies into the dynamics of these creative processes and the factors that impede and promote team creativity at work.

CASE 6.1   THE OTHER HALF (BIL BUNGAY OF TBWA ADVERTISING)

(Source: *Creative Review*, 1 March 2001, www.creative review.co.uk)
http://www.accessmylibrary.com/coms2/summary 0286-10942358 ITM

WHILE TREVOR BEATTIE GETS MOST OF THE HEADLINES, HIS PARTNER'S ROLE IS OFTEN IGNORED. BUT BIL BUNGAY INSISTS IT DOESN'T BOTHER HIM.
I HAVE NEVER INTERVIEWED ANYONE as well organised as Bil Bungay. When I arrived at his office in TBWA's Whitefield Street building, Bungay was prepared. A sheet of transparencies containing the highlights of his advertising career lay

on his desk. He handed me a typewritten CV, annotated with comments on the various stages of his working life and thoughts on various industry issues. A day after the meeting, an email arrived with more thoughts, just in case his "witterings" had "come across as a little vague". As if.

Bungay, like all advertising art directors, has a copywriting partner. Usually the one is never referred to without the other – Tom and Walt, Richard and Andy – but Bungay's partner is Trevor Beattie. With Beattie, the opposite seems to apply: a recent Observer profile referred to him as the man behind a string of campaigns without once mentioning his other half. The anti-Beattie faction would attribute this to rampant egotism by the man himself but Bungay has other ideas.

"His profile has helped develop the reputation of TBWA – it has never been in terms of Trevor Beattie independent of TBWA, it has always been Trevor Beattie at TBWA," he states. "It's important for any business to have a figurehead, having none or more than one simply creates confusion and the company will appear to lack direction. A company and its employees are a reflection of its leader, Virgin for example."

So his own comparatively low profile isn't an issue? "It doesn't bother me in slightest for the simple reason that we are in the business of promoting brands and products," he insists. "The fact that the press are interested in talking to Trevor about anything he is involved with means that the brand or product has an even better chance of becoming famous and our ad along with it, which means that my book is full of ads that got noticed. That's more than enough for me."

Bungay insists that he "absolutely doesn't have a problem" with the suggestion that credit for high-profile work that the pair have done together usually goes to Beattie alone. And it must be said that the suggestion for this feature came from Beattie, who felt it about time that Bungay's contribution was recognised.

So who is Bil Bungay? With parents in the forces, Bungay moved around a lot when young. He was born in the army town of Aldershot, then grew up in Yeovil, attending the local comprehensive and taking a foundation course at Yeovil School Of Art. In 1982, Bungay, like his contemporaries, applied to art schools but failed to get a place—"a terrible time" he says.

Undaunted, he decided not to let such formalities bother him and turned up at St Martins anyway – visiting a friend, he decided to go into college with him one day, sat down in the studio and started working. He stayed two weeks until, one day, he asked to borrow a dictionary and was finally confronted by a mystified tutor.

"I applied there again and when I turned up for the interview they all said 'It's the phantom student'," Bungay recalls. Impressed with his commitment, St Martins offered him a place on the design course. "After six months they got the students together and explained they were going to start an advertising course and asked if anyone wanted to do it. I didn't know what advertising was but I put my hand up. The course was a bit shambolic but there were a lot of good tutors and it gave me the start I needed," he says.

However, there were things about the experience that still rankle: "The thing that troubled me most was their insistence that we finish up every idea to a high

(Continued)

(Continued)

standard for the degree show when in reality it's your ideas that get you a job and not the grade that tutors give you for making things look nice. The last six months of the course were spent visualising – precious time that could have been spent coming up with job-winning ideas instead.

"The reality is that you develop your art directing (and writing) skills on the job, though I'll admit that that isn't ideal," he continues. "It can take years to learn how to work to a brief, construct a layout (one that can be read, preferably), work within a budget, learn how to present your idea, choose the right director for the job – not to mention fathoming out how the flip you get him on the set. And who are all these people? And who the hell are Henry and Harry? I'm sure that if St Martins started a post-job art direction course – distinctly different from the 'learn how to have ideas that'll get you a job' course – it would be very well received. Either that or young creatives should assist senior art directors: that'd benefit both parties."

After graduating, Bungay joined a small agency in Covent Garden, found a partner in Pat Holden (now a director) and moved to TBWA for the first time in 1987. There, he and Holden worked on high-profile accounts including Nissan and Absolut, but it is the work that the pair did for Marlboro that he is most proud of. "It's the one piece of work from the early days that I still think was a good idea," he says.

Presented with the brief "how do we continue to advertise Marlboro after cigarette advertising has been banned?" the pair devised a three-month campaign for Germany in which they would attempt to establish ownership of the colour red for Marlboro, so that anytime a consumer saw the colour they would think of the brand. A pair of Gilbert and George types were employed to hand out cards with cryptic red-related messages on, red limousines were hired – anyone wearing an item of red clothing could stop one and get a free ride to anywhere in Germany – and red theme parties thrown. Despite generating a large amount of PR, TBWA lost the account as a nervous Philip Morris HQ thought the strategy was in danger of killing off its famous cowboy. On the morals of the strategy, Bungay says: "It's not for me to question whether any product should be advertised or not – fact is I have chosen to become an advertising creative in a capitalist country that believes in freedom of speech. It would be hypocritical of me to then take the moral high ground and refuse to work on anything."

In 1994, Bungay left TBWA to start his own new product development company called Ignition. "All I really knew was advertising – Pat and I had been at TBWA for seven years – but I had all these other ideas about various products. It was an opportunity to learn about myself."

Among the things Bungay learned was that it takes a long time to develop a new product. He ended up taking on more and more advertising freelance work to pay the bills until, in 1997, an offer came in that was too good to turn down. Trevor Beattie, then at GGT, needed a partner to help him on a new account – French Connection.

"When I first entered the industry people talked about a Unique Selling Point – find the USP and amplify it – but actually there is a better and more powerful vehicle – ESP, the Emotional Selling Point," Bungay says of the campaign: "It's infinitely more powerful because it taps into the way people feel about a product. FCUK is all about ESP – we never sell it on the quality of the clothing or this season's colours. We only sell FCUK on the emotional connection people might have. We have an FC attitude and we use it."

That attitude has, of course, generated huge amounts of controversy (as well as huge sales). "Yesterday, another FCUK ad was banned by the ASA [Advertising Standards Authority] because of one complaint. That worries me because it means that the world is becoming accustomed to our acronym and can't be bothered to react, and when the punter stops reacting so will the journalists. It's time to turn up the volume – either that or we'll have to start complaining about our own ads," says Bungay, only half joking. "By the way, I love the ASA because at least they give us a run for our money – it's actually been fun jumping through their hoops attempting to appease them. I can understand the need for regulation on posters, everyone sees those, it's the BACC [Broadcast Advertising Clearance Centre] that troubles me the most. I have never been able to understand why this body should want to apply restrictions to ads that will appear after 9pm and more than likely in films filled with sex, violence and swearing.

"I'm sure that a lot of people disagree with the sexual innuendo in some of our ads. The fact is that, like it or not, sex can and does sell but only for a brand or product where it's appropriate – for instance, I can't imagine sex being an effective means of selling the Conservatives to the public at the next general election, can you? I'm not saying the work that Trev and I have done is particularly exceptional, or that we think that we've discovered a new direction. All I'm saying is that we are at least prepared to stick our necks out a little and attempt something noticeable and different in a predictable and ever more restrictive industry. If that somehow encourages others to attempt to do the same (but in their own way!) then that'd be an achievement."

Achievement in advertising is more usually measured by awards won but Bungay, like Beattie, voices some concerns. "By and large formulaic stuff wins awards," he claims. "There should be more recognition of work that is making an effort to push the boundaries. It's a vicious circle – the people who are on the juries are the same people who learned from looking at awards books."

"It sounds like sour grapes but I've won my fair share of awards," Bungay continues. "We should have awards – love them or hate them they are an essential part of the system. Unfortunately they are seen as a way of elevating the status of a team so it's now Catch 22 – if you don't apply the system, you don't win. If you don't win you won't get recognition and you'll fade away. You almost have no choice but to comply."

"It's nice when your associates say something positive about your work, but in truth I only really care about what the punter thinks. If he buys into my idea, I'm happy; if he doesn't, I wonder where I went wrong."

Since their return to TBWA two years ago, Beattie and Bungay have had plenty of punters buying into their ideas: campaigns for PlayStation and Pretty Polly have continued FCUK's high profile success. The pair have just been out to

(Continued)

(Continued)

Mozambique with Hugh Hudson where they were filming Nelson Mandela no less for a forthcoming UNICEF spot.

Last October, Bungay became deputy creative director at the agency, sharing Beattie's workload but, as yet, little of his limelight. "An ad that doesn't get noticed, doesn't exist," he says. Obviously, that doesn't apply to its art director.

Questions

1. Is there evidence in this case that supports the fact that dyads experience a unique and exclusive one-to-one capability to share and exchange ideas?
2. Why do you think that the psychological phenomena discussed in this chapter cannot cause a dyad's performance to deteriorate? Defend your ideas.

Conclusion

This chapter has examined how people work together in teams in attaining something more than the sum of individual achievements. The team is critical to processes of change, creativity and innovation and we have sought to shed light on factors that enable and constrain these processes within work settings. To summarize:

- A group can be defined as two or more individuals, interacting and interdependent, who work together to achieve particular objectives. Groups can be either formal or informal. Formal groups tend to have specific tasks to perform and their responsibilities and behaviours are often set by the organizational goals. In contrast, informal groups are characterized by a lack of formal structure and are generally not organization-led. The key distinguishing factors of teams are team members' complementary skills, their commitment to a common purpose, performance goals and mutual accountability.

- People tend to join teams for a variety of reasons. Belonging or leading a team helps individuals to deal with their own insecurities, get a strong sense of self-worth by voicing their opinions and achieve more than if they were working on their own.

- Team working usually requires the effective management of individuals. Taking into account the challenges posed by team dynamics (e.g., blind conformity, groupthink and social loafing) this is rarely an easy process.

- Inputs to a team's creative process include the size of the team, resources that are made available, team longevity, task, KSAs and team composition. All these inputs can have a direct impact on team performance.

- The literature on creativity proposes several techniques for mobilizing creative problem solving. The most common creativity-enhancement technique is brainstorming. Electronic brainstorming, brainwriting and the Nominal Group Technique (NGT) have recently gained more attention from academics and practitioners. All these team techniques are useful in generating ideas. This process of idea generation needs to be followed by an evaluation process, where team members are asked to talk about, combine or refine the generated ideas and decide on the most appropriate solution to the problem at hand. This challenging process requires each team member to justify his or her preferred idea and then confer with the whole team to identify the most appropriate solution. Although teams in different organizational settings treat this process differently, they are commonly asked to vote for the best solution, in order to ensure that the screening process is democratic and inclusive.

- Contradictory results for creative team working mainly stem from the fact that much of the empirical research has been conducted in laboratory settings. Sutton and Hargadon (1996) suggest that empirical research must move into the field in order to advance our knowledge. In addition to examining the direct effects of team inputs and processes on team performance, researchers have also examined moderating variables, such as task type and team leadership.

RESOURCES, READINGS AND REFLECTIONS

CASE 6.2   DON'T THINK, JUST LEARN – MBA DIARY: STEVEN SONSINO LOSES A STONE AND HIS ILLUSIONS ABOUT TEAM WORKING BY STEVEN SONSINO

(Source: *Financial Times,* 12 January 1998)

I woke with a start sitting in the car. I looked at my watch and saw there were still 20 minutes until the accounting exam. Thankfully I hadn't missed it. In fact, there *was* still time to revise variance analysis before strolling across the road to the exam hall. It was lucky I went over it again – variance analysis did come up, in a question worth 30 per cent of the marks. But whether my cramming was enough to get me through I won't know until the results are issued later in January.

The episode summarised for me the whole of the first term on Cranfield University's full-time MBA programme. There is simply so much material and so many new concepts to take in that you snatch any spare time you can to study. You have to be ready for the next lecture or the next meeting. You sleep only when you drop.

Exams? Whether they are a realistic or relevant test of a manager's abilities I doubt, but I didn't have time to think seriously about that just then. The exams were just another set of hurdles between the Christmas break and me. There had been open days at the university where previous students had warned that the

(Continued)

(Continued)

workload was unbelievably high. But nothing prepared me for the barrage of books, papers and case studies to read, not to mention presentations to prepare and projects to write. I managed only four to five hours sleep a night over the first term. I was exhausted.

The worst part was that I hardly saw my wife Jacqueline in the evenings, except when we ate together, a ritual I tried to keep up, though my promised weekends off failed to materialise. I tried to explain that the work wasn't hard – with some exceptions – it was just that there was so much of it. All Jacqueline could see, six weeks into the course, was that I was losing weight. I didn't believe her until Ananya Sen, a colleague in my learning team, said he thought I'd lost weight, too. When I checked I found I'd lost a stone since coming to Cranfield.

Sen was one of five students I spent roughly half my time with during the day. We, and the other six learning teams in our stream, had been painstakingly mixed and matched by Martyn Jones, director of the full-time MBA programme, on the grounds of personal background and work experience. Given such a degree of diversity perhaps some clashes were inevitable. The teams initially shared the task of reading core textbooks and of preparing notes to summarise key points. No individual could get through the entire reading list, especially not the overseas students for whom English was a second or third language (though some tried). The system generally worked well and was certainly structured more effectively than my undergraduate biochemistry degree. Two days before each lecture we read core texts or cases individually and then, one day before, the team would compare notes or prepare a short presentation in case we were called on in class. We soon learned which courses it was essential to prepare for (accounting, strategy and marketing) and which we could safely ignore (people in organisations, or human resources).

On reflection, the single most important function of the team, it seemed to me, was to broaden our experience of working intimately with very different people. I envisaged us as a board of directors, pooling our experience and offering different degrees of leadership at different times. But we didn't always work well together, struggling with a mixture of personal priorities and commitments. There were other teams, however, that fared far worse. A fundamental problem facing those groups seemed not what to do but how to complete the tasks set. Some people clearly felt uncomfortable in teams, for instance, preferring to work alone and bring to the group complete and non-negotiable solutions to cases or presentations. These colleagues were highly focused on getting the job done, but not at all interested in how we got there. Clashes with co-workers were frequent and occasionally bitter.

The saddest comment I heard came from one individual disillusioned with team working: 'I am not being assessed on how we work together as a team' he said. For me that completely missed the point of the learning team, if not of Cranfield's entire MBA culture. Another character who disappointed me was the anonymous student who scrawled the words 'patronising prat' on a note about report writing I had been asked to prepare and circulate. I found the note in my pigeonhole with another that had been torn to shreds. Dozens of colleagues went out of their way to say how useful the note had proved, but it was the two childish responses that rankled. They were a timely reminder that not everyone sees teamwork the same way.

Outside the learning team, my time was spent in the lecture theatre, where the most valuable courses for me were marketing and strategy. All the elements of relationship marketing and strategic management integrated seamlessly into a powerful and useful whole, easily applicable to the business I've left behind while I attend the programme.

As I bathe my two-year-old son Christopher and put him to sleep before starting work in the evening, I often think of my work colleagues running the business in my absence. I think that although I'm the one attending the MBA programme it is in fact a collaboration with them. First they are collaborating in running the business now to help put me through the programme. And in the future I hope they will collaborate with me to develop the business using ideas and techniques from the MBA. I do feel wary, however, of introducing my colleagues to new ideas too quickly. They haven't seen anything of me for four months and there is bound to be a feeling that the concepts are just 'Steven's new toys'.

I think of my wife as a collaborator, too. Every day throughout the term she has suffered the brunt of my simply not being available to help with Christopher at home. Yet she still makes time to help at Owlets (the MBA partners' toddler group) and to study Spanish on a Monday. She also commutes to her London-based job share for five days every fortnight. I don't know how she does it.

Questions

1. What are the main challenges identified in this case?
2. Have you ever experienced similar problems when working in teams? Did these problems affect your performance? Why or why not? How?
3. What would you do in order to help the team work better? Write some general guidelines, which could be followed by all team members. Be as specific as you can.
4. Do you think that diversity is important in generating new ideas or in identifying new opportunities? How much diversity is good for creativity?

Chapter questions

The questions listed below relate to the chapter as a whole and can be used by individuals to further reflect on the material covered, as well as serving as a source for more open group discussion and debate:

1. How is a working group different from a team? Defend your arguments.

2. What are the main reasons why people join teams? Discuss your answer by using relevant examples.

3. Why do you think that teams may fail?

4. The core idea of this chapter was creative team working. Discuss the variables related to creative team inputs, processes and outcomes as well as the team moderators that may affect team performance.

5. Do you think that brainstorming is a problem-solving technique for all problems? Why or why not?

6. Discuss the advantages and disadvantages of brainstorming.

7. Which are the five stages of the electronic brainstorming process?

8. What is 'brainwriting'? In your opinion, how is it different from brainstorming?

9. Discuss the advantages and disadvantages of the Nominal Group Technique (NGT).

Hands-on exercise

Students are required to find a magazine or newspaper article illustrating a creative team's project and answer the following questions:

1. Is there enough evidence in the article to suggest that this is a team and not a working group? What type of work team is it?

2. Why did team members get together to form this team?

3. What are the most important factors identified in this article related to the team's success?

4. Has the team in the article experienced any challenges? If yes, how did they overcome them? If not, what would you advise them to do (develop a plan with relevant suggestions)?

Team debate exercise

Debate the following statement:

> *Team diversity can only enhance creativity.*

Divide the class into two groups. One should argue as convincingly as possible that team diversity can only enhance creativity. The other should prepare its arguments against this, highlighting that diversity within a team may hinder creativity. Each group should be prepared to defend their ideas against the other group's arguments by using real-life examples.

References

Adams, J.L. (2001) *Conceptual Blockbusting: A Guide to Better Ideas*. Cambridge, MA: Perseus.

Aiken, M., Vanjani, M. and Paolillo, J. (1996) 'A comparison of two electronic idea generation techniques', *Information and Management*, 30: 91–9.

Allen, T. (1977) *Managing the Flow of Technology: Technology Transfer and the Dissemination of Technological Information within the R&D Organization*. Cambridge, MA: MIT Press.

Amabile, T.M. (1983) *The Social Psychology of Creativity*. New York: Springer-Verlag.

Amabile, T. M. (1996) *Creativity in Context*. Boulder, CO: Westview.

Amabile, T.M. (1998) 'How to kill creativity', *Harvard Business Review*, 76 (6): 76–87.

Amabile, T.M. and Glazebrook, A.H. (1982) 'A negativity bias in interpersonal evaluation', *Journal of Experimental Social Psychology*, 18 (January): 1–22.

Amabile, T.M. and Gryskiewicz, S.S. (1989) 'The creative environment scales: the work environment inventory', *Creativity Research Journal*, 2: 231–54.

Amason, A. (1996) 'Distinguishing effects of functional and dysfunctional conflict on strategic decision making: resolving a paradox for top management teams', *Academy of Management Journal*, 39: 123–48.

Amason, A. and Sapienza, H. (1997) 'The effects of top management team size and interaction norms on cognitive and affective conflict', *Journal of Management*, 23: 496–516.

Anderson, N., Hardy, G. and West, M. (1992) 'Management team innovation', *Management Decision*, 30 (2): 17–21.

Andriopoulos, C. and Lowe, A. (2000) 'Enhancing organizational creativity: the process of perpetual challenging', *Management Decision*, 38: 734–42.

Asch, S. (1951) 'Effects of group pressure upon the modification and distortion of judgments', in H. Guetzkow (ed.), *Groups, Leadership and Men*. New York: Carnegie Press.

Bennis, W. and Biederman, P.W. (1997) *Organizing Genius: The Secrets of Creative Collaboration*. London: Nicholas Brealey.

Bouchard, T.J. and Hare, M. (1970) 'Size, performance and potential in brainstorming groups', *Journal of Applied Psychology*, 54: 51–5.

Brahm, C. and Kleiner, B. (1996) 'Advantages and disadvantages of group decision-making approaches', *Team Performance Management*, 2: 30–5.

Brajkovich, L.F. (2003) 'Executive commentary', *Academy of Management Executive*, 17: 110–11.

Buchanan, D. and Huczynski, A. (2003) *Organizational Behaviour: An Introductory Text*, 5th edn. London: Financial Times Prentice Hall.

Camacho, L.M. and Paulus, P.B. (1995) 'The role of social anxiousness in group brainstorming', *Journal of Personality and Social Psychology*, 68: 1071–80.

Carron, A. (1982) 'Cohesiveness in sport groups: interpretations and considerations', *Journal of Sport Psychology*, 4: 123–38.

Cooper, W.H., Gallupe, R.B., Pollard, S. and Cadsby, J. (1998) 'Some liberating effects of anonymous electronic brainstorming', *Small Group Research*, 29: 147–78.

Craig, T.Y. and Kelly, J.R. (1999) 'The effects of task and interpersonal cohesiveness on group creativity', *Group Dynamics: Theory, Research, and Practice*, 3: 243–56.

Cummings, A. and Oldham, G.R. (1997) 'Enhancing creativity: managing work contexts for the high potential employee', *California Management Review*, 40 (1): 22–38.

De Bono, E. (1990) *Lateral Thinking: A Textbook of Creativity*. London: Penguin Group.

Deci, E.L. and Ryan, R.M. (1987) 'The support of autonomy and the control of behavior', *Journal of Personality and Social Psychology*, 53: 1024–37.

Deci, E.L., Connell, J.P. and Ryan, R.M. (1989) 'Self-determination in a work organisation', *Journal of Applied Psychology*, 74: 580–90.

Dennis, A.R. and Valacich, J.S. (1993) 'Computer brainstorms: more heads are better than one', *Journal of Applied Psychology*, 78: 531–7.

Diehl, M. and Stroebe, W. (1987) 'Productivity loss in brainstorming groups: toward the solution of a riddle', *Journal of Personality and Social Psychology*, 53: 497–509.

Diehl, M. and Stroebe, W. (1991) 'Productivity loss in idea-generating groups: tracking down the blocking effect', *Journal of Personality and Social Psychology*, 61: 392–403.

Diener, S.C. (1979) 'Deindividuation, self-awareness, and disinhibition', *Journal of Personality and Social Psychology*, 37: 1160–71.

Eisenhardt, K.M., Kahwajy, J.L. and Bourgeois L.J. III, (1997) 'How management teams have a good fight', *Harvard Business Review*, 75(4): 77–85.

Falk, D.R. and Johnson, D.W. (1977) 'The effects of perspective taking and egocentrism on problem solving in heterogeneous groups', *Journal of Social Psychology*, 10: 63–72.

Firestein, R.L. (1990) 'Effects of creative problem solving training on communication behaviours in small groups', *Small Group Research*, 21: 507–21.

Flores, F. (1979) 'Management and communication in the office of the future'. Unpublished PhD thesis, University of California, Berkeley.

Fukuyama, F. (1995) *Trust: The Social Virtues and the Creation of Prosperity*. New York: The Free Press.

Gallupe, R.B. and Cooper, W.H. (1993) 'Brainstorming electronically', *Sloan Management Review*, 35: 27–36.

Gallupe, R.B., Dennis, A., Cooper, W., Valacich, J. and Nunamaker, J., Jr (1992) 'Electronic brainstorming and group size', *Academy of Management Journal*, 35: 350–69.

Geschka, H., Schaude, G.R. and Schlicksupp, H. (1973) 'Modern techniques for solving problems', *Chemical Engineering*, 80 (August): 91–7.

Geschka, H., von Reibnitz, U. and Storvik, K. (1981) *Idea Generation Methods: Creative Solutions to Business and Technical Problems*. Columbus, OH: Battelle Memorial Institute.

Gilson, L.L. and Shalley, C.E. (2004) 'A little creativity goes a long way: an examination of teams' engagement in creative processes', *Journal of Management*, 30: 453–70.

Goldenberg, J. and Mazursky, D. (2002) *Creativity in Product Innovation*. Cambridge: Cambridge University Press.

Hackman, J.R. (1985) 'Doing research that makes a difference', in E.E. Lawler III, A.M. Mohrman Jr, S.A. Mohrman, G.E. Ledford, Jr. and T.G. Cummings (eds), *Doing Research That Is Useful for Theory and Practice*. San Francisco: Jossey Bass.

Hackman, J.R. and Morris, C.G. (1975) 'Group tasks, group interaction processes and group performance effectiveness: a review and proposed integration', in L. Berkowitz (ed.), *Advances in Experimental Social Psychology*, Vol. 8. San Diego, CA: Academic Press. pp. 45–99.

Hargadon, A.B. and Sutton, R.I. (1997) 'Technology brokering and innovation in a product development firm', *Administrative Science Quarterly*, 42: 716–49.

Hargadon, A.B. and Sutton, R.I. (2000) 'Building the innovation factory', *Harvard Business Review*, 78 (3): 157–66.

Hoegl, M. and Gemuenden, H.G. (2001) 'Teamwork quality and the success of innovative projects: a theoretical concept and empirical evidence', *Organization Science*, 12 (4): 435–49.

Hogg, M.A. (1992) *The Social Psychology of Group Cohesiveness: From Attraction to Social Identity*. London: Harvester Wheatsheaf.

Huczynski, A. and Buchanan, D. (1991) *Organizational Behaviour*. Hemel Hempstead: Prentice Hall.

Isaksen, S.G. and Lauer, K.J. (2002) 'The climate for creativity and change in teams', *Creativity and Innovation Management*, 11: 74–86.

Janis, I.L. (1972) *Victims of Groupthink: A Psychological Study of Foreign Policy Decisions and Fiascoes*, 2nd edn. Boston, MA: Houghton Mifflin.

Jehn, K.A. and Mannix, E.A. (2001) 'The dynamic nature of conflict: a longitudinal study of intragroup conflict and group performance', *Academy of Management Journal*, 44: 238–51.

Jones, G. and McFadzean, E.S. (1997) 'How can Reboredo foster creativity in her current employees and nurture creative individuals who join the company in the future?', *Harvard Business Review*, 75 (5): 50–1.

Kahn, W.A. (1990) 'Psychological conditions of personal engagement and disengagement at work', *Academy of Management Journal*, 33: 692–724.

Katz, R. and Allen, T.J. (1982) 'Investigating the not invented here syndrome: a look at the performance, tenure and communication patterns of 50 R&D project groups', *R&D Management*, 12: 7–19.

Katzenbach, J.R. and Smith, D.K. (1993) 'The discipline of teams', *Harvard Business Review*, 83 (7/8) (March–April): 162–71.

Kelley, T. and Littman, J. (2001) *The Art of Innovation*. London: HarperCollins Business.

Kirton, M.J. (1976) 'Adaptors and innovators: a description of a measure', *Journal of Applied Psychology*, 61: 622–9.

Kivimäki, M., Kuk, G., Elovainio, M., Thomson, L., Kalliomäki-Levanto, T. and Heikkilä, A. (1997) 'The team climate inventory (TCI) – four or five factors? Testing the structure of TCI in samples of low and high complexity jobs', *Journal of Occupational and Organisational Psychology*, 70: 375–89.

Kreitner, R., Kinicki, A. and Buelens, M. (2002) *Organizational Behaviour*. Maidenhead: McGraw-Hill.

Kurtzberg, T.R. and Amabile, T.M. (2001) 'From Guilford to creative synergy: opening the black box of team-level creativity', *Creativity Research Journal*, 13: 285–94.

Lipman-Blumen, J. and Leavitt, H.J. (1999) *Hot Groups: Seeding Them, Feeding Them, and Using Them to Ignite Your Organization*. Oxford: Oxford University Press.

Manley, G.J. (1978) *Readings in Educational Psychology*. New York: Holt, Rinehart & Winston.

Marks, M.A., Mathieu, J.E. and Zaccaro, S.J. (2001) 'A temporally based framework and taxonomy of team processes', *Academy of Management Review*, 26: 356–76.

Martins, L., Gilson, L. and Maynard, M. (2004) 'Virtual teams: what do we know and where do we go from here?', *Journal of Management*, 30: 805–35.

Mattimore, B. (1993) *99% Inspiration: Tips, Tales & Techniques for Liberating Your Business Creativity*. New York: AMACOM.

Menzel, H. (1965) 'Information needs and uses in science and technology', in C. Cuadra (ed.), *Annual Review of Information Science and Technology*. New York: John Wiley. pp. 41–69.

Milliken, F. and Martins, L. (1996) 'Searching for common threads: understanding the multiple effects of diversity in organizational groups', *Academy of Management Review*, 21: 402–33.

Mowday, R.T. and Sutton, R.I. (1993) 'Organizational behavior: linking individuals and groups to organizational contexts', in J.T. Spence, J.M. Darley and D.J. Foss (eds), *Annual Review of Psychology*. Palo Alto, CA: Annual Reviews.

Mullen, B., Johnson, C. and Salas, E. (1991) 'Productivity loss in brainstorming groups: a meta-analytic integration', *Basic and Applied Social Psychology*, 12: 3–23.

Mumford, M.D. (2000) 'Managing creative people: strategies and tactics for innovation', *Human Resource Management Review*, 10: 313–51.

Mumford, M.D. and Gustafson, S.B. (1988) 'Creative syndrome: integration, application and innovation', *Psychological Bulletin*, 103: 27–43.

Mumford, M.D., Whetzel, D.L. and Reiter-Palmon, R. (1997) 'Thinking creatively at work: organizational influences of creative problem-solving', *Journal of Creative Behavior*, 31: 7–17.

Murray, H.A. (1964) 'Dyadic creations', in W.G. Bennis, E.G. Schein and F.I. Steele (eds), *Interpersonal Dynamics*. Homewood, IL: Dorsey Press.

Nagasundarum, M. and Dennis, A.R. (1993) 'When a group is not a group', *Small Group Research*, 24: 463–89.

Nickerson, R.S. (2002) 'Enhancing creativity', in R.J. Sternberg (ed.), *Handbook of Creativity*. Cambridge: Cambridge University Press.

Nunamaker, J.F., Dennis, A.R., Valacich, J.S., Vogel, D.R. and George, J.F. (1991) 'Electronic meeting systems to support group work', *Communications of the ACM*, 34 (7): 41–61.

Nyström, H. (1979) *Creativity and Innovation*. Chichester: John Wiley.

Osborn, A. (1963) *Applied Imagination*, 3rd edn. New York: Charles Scribner's Sons.

Parmerter, S.M. and Gaber, J.D. (1971) 'Creative scientists rate creativity factors', *Research Management*, 14: 65–70.

Parnes, S.J. and Meadow, A. (1959) 'Effects of "brainstorming" instructions on creative problem solving by trained and untrained subjects', *Journal of Educational Psychology*, 50 (4): 171–6.

Payne, R. (1990) 'The effectiveness of research teams: a review', in M.A. West and J.L. Farr (eds), *Innovation and Creativity at Work*. Chichester: John Wiley.

Pelz, D.C. (1956) 'Some social factors related to performance in a research organization', *Administrative Science Quarterly*, 1: 310–25.

Pinsonneault, A., Barki, H., Gallupe, R.B. and Hoppen, N. (1999) 'Electronic brainstorming: the illusion of productivity', *Information Systems Research*, 10: 110–33.

Price, D. (1965) 'Is technology historically independent of science? A study in statistical historiography', *Technology and Culture*, 6: 553–68.

Reich, R. (1987) 'Entrepreneurship reconsidered: the team as hero', *Harvard Business Review*, 65(3) (May–June): 77–83.

Renzulli, J.S., Owen, S.V. and Callahan, C.M. (1974) 'Fluency, flexibility and originality as functions of group size', *Journal of Creative Behavior*, 8: 107–13.

Ricchiuto, J. (1996) *Collaborative Creativity: Unleashing the Power of Shared Thinking*. Greensboro, NC: Oak Hill Press.

Riley, M.N. (1992) 'If it looks like manure ...', *Phi Delta Kappa*, 74: 239–41.

Robbins, S., Waters-Marsh, T., Cacioppe, R. and Millett, B. (1994) *Organisational Behaviour*. Sydney: Prentice Hall of Australia.

Schmuck, R.A. and Runkel, P.J. (1988) *The Handbook of Organizational Development in Schools*. Prospect Heights, IL: Waveland Press.

Sethia, N.K. (1995) 'The role of collaboration in creativity', in C.M. Ford and D.A. Gioia (eds), *Creative Action in Organisations: Ivory Tower Visions & Real World Voices*. Thousand Oaks, CA: Sage.

Sternberg, R.J., O'Hara, L.A. and Lubart, T.I. (1997) 'Creativity as investment', *California Management Review* 40 (1): 8–21.

Summers, I. and White, D.E. (1976) 'Creativity techniques: toward improvement of the decision process', *Academy of Management Review*, 1 (2) (April): 99–107.

Sutton, R. and Hargadon, A. (1996) 'Brainstorming groups in context: effectiveness in a product design firm', *Administrative Science Quarterly*, 41: 685–718.

Thacker, R.A. (1997) 'Team leader style: enhancing the creativity of employees in teams', *Training for Quality*, 5 (4): 146–9.

Thompson, L. (2003) 'Improving the creativity of organisational work groups', *Academy of Management Executive*, 17: 96–109.

Thornburg, T.T. (1991) 'Group size and member diversity influence on creative performance', *Journal of Creative Behavior*, 25: 324–33.

Tuckman, B.W. and Jensen, M.A.C. (1977) 'Stages of small group development revisited', *Group and Organizational Studies*, 2: 419–27.

Valacich, J.S., George, J.F., Nunamaker, J.F. and Vogel, D.R. (1994) 'Physical proximity effects on computer-mediated group idea generation', *Small Group Research*, 23: 83–104.

Van Gundy, A. (1992) *Idea Power: Techniques and Resources for Unleashing the Creativity in Your Organization*. New York: AMACOM.

VanGundy, A.B. (1981) *Techniques of Structured Problem Solving*. New York: Van Nostrand Reinhold.

VanGundy, A.B. (1988) *Techniques of Structured Problem Solving*. New York: Van Nostrand Reinhold.

Wageman, R. (1995) 'Interdependence and group effectiveness', *Administrative Science Quarterly*, 40: 145–80.

Wallace, M. and West, M.A. (1988) 'Innovation in primary health care teams: the effects of role and climate'. Paper presented at the Annual Occupational Psychology Conference of the British Psychological Society, University of Manchester.

Weingart, L.R. (1997) 'How did they do that? The ways and means of studying group process', *Research in Organizational Behavior*, 19: 189–239.

Whitfield, P.R. (1975) *Creativity in Industry*. Harmondsworth: Penguin Books.

Wilson, G.L. and Hanna, M.S. (1990) *Groups in Context: Leadership and Participation in Small Groups*. New York: McGraw-Hill.

Yeung, R. and Bailey, S. (1999) 'Get it together', *Accountancy*, 123 (1270) June, 40.

Recommended reading

- De Bono, E. (1995) *Serious Creativity: Using the Power of Lateral Thinking to Create New Ideas*. London: Profile Business.

- Eisenhardt, K.M., Kahwajy, J.L. and Bourgeois, L.J., III (1997) 'How management teams can have a good fight', *Harvard Business Review*, 75 (4): 77–85.

- Fischer, B. and Boynton, A. (2005) 'Virtuoso teams', *Harvard Business Review*, 83 (7): 117–23.

- Gilson, L.L., Mathieu, J.E., Shalley, C.E. and Ruddy, T.M. (2005) 'Creativity and standardization: complementary or conflicting drivers of team effectiveness?', *Academy of Management Journal*, 48: 521–31.

- Oh, H., Chung, M. and Labianca, G. (2004) 'Group social capital and group effectiveness: the role of informal socializing ties', *Academy of Management Journal*, 47: 860–75.

- Sundstrom, E., DeMeuse, K.P. and Futrell, D. (1990) 'Work teams: applications and effectiveness', *American Psychologist*, 45: 120–33.

Some useful websites

- A wide range of articles, tools and techniques about all aspects of teamwork from the Fast Company website (http://www.fastcompany.com).

- A wide range of articles, tools and techniques about all aspects of brainstorming (http://www.brainstorming.co.uk).

7

The Leader: Promoting New Ideas at Work

Learning objectives

After reading this chapter you will:

1. Know the defining characteristics of leadership.
2. Be able to clarify the differences between a manager and a leader.
3. Understand the trait, behavioural, contingency and contemporary theories of leadership.
4. Be able to explain the leadership approach that is conducive to change, creativity and innovation.
5. Be able to identify the challenges that contemporary leaders face in creating and sustaining these processes in organizations.

Introduction

Although the value of good leadership skills has been recognized since the times of Aristotle and Plato, today's complex business environment continues to spotlight the need for effective leadership in organizations. Trends like shorter product life cycles, the increase in mergers and acquisitions, the issue of global relocation, the increase in outsourcing activities, the constant drive for innovation and the unprecedented pace of change (to name but a few) are challenging leaders perhaps more than ever before. Many commentators stress the importance of leadership in mobilizing creativity and change in organizations. Their vision, their actions and the way that they direct and support 'followers' in their creative endeavours, can suppress or mobilize creative thinking and stifle or activate change processes. Competent contemporary leaders, therefore, often enjoy heroic status; leaders like Bill Gates (Microsoft Corporation), Steve Jobs (Apple Computers), Richard Branson (Virgin Group) and Stelios Haji-Ioannou (EasyGroup) are often treated like celebrities. In examining the key role of business leaders, this chapter is devoted to understanding leadership and its part in encouraging creativity and innovation at work. We start by identifying key ingredients in exploring the concept of leadership. The question of how leaders differ from managers is addressed and the importance of 'followers' is assessed. We then present an historical overview of some of the most influential leadership theories. Theories that focus on personality traits, behaviours, situational variables, as well as the more contemporary approaches on transformational and transactional leadership are all examined. Our main focus is on the relationship between leadership and creativity and change and, as such, we identify its role and discuss leadership styles that are conducive to mobilizing creativity and change within organizations. We conclude by discussing some of the challenges facing creative leaders who seek to mobilize employees' self-determination and personal initiative and encourage employees to consider, develop and ultimately contribute to more creative outcomes. But first, we ask the question 'what is leadership?'

Defining leadership

The topic of leadership has fascinated many researchers in the last century and even though the last 40 years have witnessed a plethora of articles, books and video presentations on the subject of leadership, there remains no generally accepted, unambiguous definition. The ongoing disagreement over definitions of leadership is encapsulated by Stogdill (1974: 259), who concluded that 'there are almost as many definitions of leadership as there are persons who have attempted to define the concept'. This situation is further complicated if one considers that the area of leadership has been researched by several disciplines, including management, psychology, sociology and political science. Definitions of leadership have therefore varied, and four illustrative examples are provided below:

- 'The social influence process in which the leader seeks the voluntary participation of subordinates in an effort to reach organizational goals' (Schriesheim et al., 1978);

- 'The art or process of influencing people so that they will strive willingly and enthusiastically toward the achievement of group goals' (Weihrich and Koontz, 1993);

- 'The ability to influence a group toward the achievement of goals' (Robbins et al., 1994); and

- 'The ability of an individual to influence, motivate and enable others to contribute toward the effectiveness and success of organizations of which they are members' (House et al., 1997).

In each of these definitions, the notion of influencing others in supporting the effective working of organizations is evident. But as we shall see, the extent to which leadership involves more direct autocratic or open participative styles remains an area of debate.

How are managers different from leaders?

Clarifying the difference between managers and leaders is important, since although several authors and practitioners still use the two concepts inter-changeably, they have very different characteristics. First, managers are usually chosen and appointed to their positions, while leaders are more likely to emerge from the work group (Robbins and Coulter, 2002). Second, the central distinction between a manager and a leader is that managers influence and direct others due to their recognized power, which is inherent in their position, while leaders go beyond that, by inspiring employees to work towards a shared goal. Third, although leaders anticipate change whilst setting direction for orga-nizations, managers focus more on generating results than on forecasting and dealing with change (Kotter, 1990). Accordingly, managers are interested in how things are organized and implemented, while leaders are more concerned with what inspires and motivates people, and this requires extensive commu-nication with subordinates (Bennis, 1989; Kotter, 1990; Zaleznik, 1977). Heller and Van Til (1982) point out that effective leaders need a 'followership'. In other words, it is the willingness of people to follow that turns an individual into a leader. However, there is a great difference in the way leaders and managers see their roles. For instance, managers tend to bring people together to imple-ment their plans as effectively as possible, whilst leaders strive to align their subordinates to their vision (Kotter, 1990).

Ingredients of leadership

So what are the key ingredients of leadership? Weihrich and Koontz (1993) argue that leadership consists of four main elements:

- *Power:* leaders have power over their followers.

- *Understanding of people:* leaders understand what motivates people. They are aware of their followers' needs, ambitions and requirements.

- *Ability to inspire:* leaders are able to envision the future of their respective industries and inspire the rest of the organization to follow their vision and achieve common goals.

- *A specific style:* not all leaders share the same style. Some are more directive, others are more participative in their decision making. Some place an emphasis on performance, others focus on motivating followers and creat-ing cult-like environments.

A longstanding question is: what constitutes an effective leader? In order to shed light on this question, the following section offers an historical overview of traditional and contemporary leadership theories. We consider what makes an effective leader and discuss the different styles of leadership that are deemed appropriate to a range of different contexts and situations.

Historical overview of key leadership theories

Leadership has always been an issue of interest since the early days of human civilization. The first writings on leadership date back to the ancient Greeks and Romans who believed that leaders were born and not made. They tried to identify the physical and mental abilities, as well as the personality traits, of various leaders of their times. These early theories often assumed that leaders would be men (the 'great man' theory) and forwarded the notion that certain individuals are endowed with certain personality traits. This focus on traits led to the initiation of studies that identified characteristics that may be used to differentiate leaders from non-leaders. At this time, it was political, religious and military leaders that drew most attention. The two world wars in the 20th century stimulated further interest in leadership. Over the intervening years, leadership theorists have tried: to identify personality traits associated with effective leadership (traits theories); to examine how leaders interact with their group (behavioural theories); to explain how different situations affect the relationship between leaders and their followers (contingency theories); and, more recently, to discuss the characteristics of transformational, charismatic and visionary leaders (contemporary approaches). The following sections briefly present these main schools of thought.

Trait approaches to leadership

Several studies were conducted up to the 1940s with the aim of discovering leaders' proposed extraordinary abilities. These early studies, however, proved unsuccessful and they were criticized for failing to find any traits that predicted leadership achievement or that distinguished a leader from a non-leader (Stogdill, 1974). Nevertheless, the search for leadership traits has continued and some scholars have found a consistent pattern. Kirkpatrick and Locke (1991), for instance, argue that the six common traits associated with effective leadership are:

- *Drive.* Leaders exhibit a relatively high degree of achievement. They are ambitious, they are tirelessly persistent in their actions and display initiative.

- *The desire to lead.* Leaders are willing to influence and lead others and are prepared to take responsibility for their actions.

- *Honesty and integrity.* Effective leaders tend to build trusting relationships with their followers by being truthful and by showing great consistency between their 'words' and their 'actions'.

- *Self-confidence.* Competent leaders have a belief in themselves and this allows them to convince their followers about the suitability and validity of their goals, decisions or actions. Leaders riddled with self-doubt are less likely to gain other people's trust since they may find it hard to take the necessary action.

- *Intelligence.* Effective leaders are intelligent enough to collect, synthesize and interpret large amounts of data. The leader's role demands a sufficient level of intelligence to devise appropriate strategies, solve problems and make correct decisions.

- *Job-relevant knowledge.* Competent leaders also tend to be very knowledge-able about their industry, organization and relevant technical issues. It is the depth of knowledge that they have that allows them to put together well-informed decisions and to recognize their implications.

In general, studies of leadership traits have not been very successful in shedding light into the 'mystery' of effective leadership. The trait theories have been criticized for not providing guidance on how much of any trait a person should have in order to become an effective leader (Weihrich and Koontz, 1993). Furthermore, authors and researchers in the area agree that these traits alone are not sufficient for predicting effective leadership since they ignore the interaction between leaders and their followers as well as other important situational factors (Robbins and Coulter, 2002).

Behavioural theories

In response to the limitations associated with trait theories, the next phase of research aimed to provide more robust answers on the characteristics of an effective leader. The focus of study switched to a concern with the behaviour of leaders rather than their personality traits. These theories assume that a leader's behaviour is likely to directly affect the effectiveness of the work group (Kreitner et al., 2002). Consequently, whilst trait theorists argue that only individuals with the 'right' traits should take over formal leadership, behavioural theorists argue that individuals can be trained to become effective leaders. This led authors and researchers in the area to begin identifying patterns of behaviour (labelled as 'leadership styles') that enabled effective leadership.

The University of Iowa studies

Kurt Lewin with his associates at the University of Iowa identified three styles of leadership (Lewin and Lippitt, 1938; Lewin et al., 1939). They labelled the first one as the *autocratic style* of leadership where the leader tends to consolidate authority, commands, takes decisions and expects compliance. The second style of leadership was classified as *democratic.* Here the leader tends to involve individuals in decision making and goal setting, consults with subordinates and encourages participation. In the last one, the *laissez-faire style*, the leader usually provides the group with a high degree of independence in setting their own goals and how they go about implementing them.

The initial results of Lewin's studies showed that the democratic style of leadership was the most effective, although later studies in democratic and autocratic styles of leadership generated mixed outcomes. For instance, sometimes the democratic style of leadership generated superior performance compared to the autocratic style; whereas sometimes it produced inferior or the same level of performance among subordinates (Robbins and Coulter, 2002). More consistent results were discovered when subordinates' satisfaction levels were examined; for example, researchers found that democratic leadership is usually associated with greater levels of subordinate satisfaction. Consequently, the central contribution of these early studies was the acknowledgement of the dual role of effective leaders. On the one hand, leaders need to be focused on the work and the means of achieving output performance; on the other, they need to concentrate on the people aspects of work group dynamics.

The Ohio State studies

The Ohio State studies aimed to identify independent dimensions of leader behaviour. In the late 1940s, researchers at the Ohio State University began with more than 1,000 behavioural dimensions and managed to narrow them down to just two, which they claim account for most of the leadership behaviour described by group members. They called these two dimensions 'initiating structure' and 'consideration'.

1. *Initiating structure* refers to the extent to which a leader is likely to structure and define their role and the roles of the group members in the accomplishment of set goals. In other words, it consists of behaviour that tries to sort out work, work-related interactions and goals. A leader who is focusing on initiating structure tends to allocate group members to particular tasks and stresses the significance of meeting agreed deadlines.

2. *Consideration* is described as the degree to which a leader develops working relationships that are characterized by mutual trust and the extent to which the leader values followers' views and feelings. Leaders characterized as high in consideration tend to show concern for the well-being, comfort and job satisfaction of their subordinates, and they tend to be friendly and approachable, often willing to assist group members with their personal problems.

Research shows that leaders who have high levels of initiating structure and consideration (*a high–high leader*) achieve high group task performance and satisfaction more frequently than the ones rated low on either one or both dimensions. Leader behaviour characterized as 'high' on initiating structure tended to generate higher levels of grievances, absenteeism and turnover and lower levels of job satisfaction for employees carrying out regular tasks. Thus, although the Ohio State studies showed that the 'high–high' style of leadership typically generates positive outcomes, there were several exceptions to this that suggested that the context or situation may need to be considered as a factor influencing leadership.

The University of Michigan studies

At about the same time as the Ohio State studies, researchers at the University of Michigan were also aiming to identify behavioural differences between effective and ineffective leaders. Their studies identified two dimensions to leadership that reflected whether leaders were more *employee-oriented* or *production-oriented* (Kahn and Katz, 1960). They show how employee-oriented leaders tend to emphasize interpersonal relationships through focusing on the needs of their subordinates, and by acknowledging individual differences between work group members. In contrast, leaders who are production-oriented tend to stress the task aspects of the job, viewing the group as a means to achieving objectives. The Michigan studies illustrate that in cases where leaders were employee-oriented, high levels of production and job satisfaction were evident. On the contrary, production-oriented leaders were associated with low group production and low levels of job satisfaction.

The managerial grid

These studies led to the development of a two-dimensional grid for assessing leadership styles. The behavioural scientists Robert Blake and Jane Mouton developed the leadership grid. The proposed grid is a matrix formed by the intersection of two dimensions of leader behaviour (see Figure 7.1). The horizontal axis is 'concern for production', and the vertical axis is 'concern for people'.

Although the grid has 81 potential positions into which a leader's behavioural style may fall, Blake and Mouton placed an emphasis on five:

1. *Impoverished Management* (position 1,1), which suggests that leaders exhibit little consideration for task completion and little concern for cultivating relationships with subordinates.

2. *Country Club Management* (position 1,9), which indicates attention to the needs of individual employees leading to the development of a friendly and relaxed working atmosphere. However, at the same time there is little or no consideration for the actual job outcome.

3. *Middle-of-the-Road Management* (position 5,5), which puts the same emphasis on both production and on realizing reasonable levels of job satisfaction and morale.

4. *Task Management* (position 9,1), which indicates a high degree of task structuring to develop an efficient operation, while showing little concern for the needs of people.

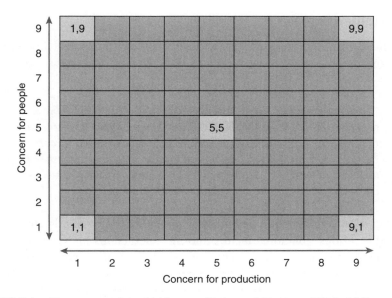

FIGURE 7.1 The managerial grid (*Source*: Blake and Mouton, 1964: 136)

5. *Team Management* (position 9,9), which indicates a high dedication both to the actual job outcome and the relationships between the leader and their subordinates. These interpersonal relationships are mainly based on mutual trust and respect. In other words, they have the ability to align the individuals' needs to the production goals.

This leadership grid can be used to identify and classify leadership styles, although the notion that *Team Management* (position 9,9) is more effective in all situations is not supported by the empirical evidence. Both the trait and behavioural streams of research highlight the difficulties of identifying a simple list of key characteristics (traits or behaviours). Thus, this lack of reliable results in identifying consistent relationships between traits and patterns of leadership behaviour with group performance has encouraged researchers to consider leadership as a more complex phenomenon. What early theorists were neglecting was the range of different situational factors that may potentially influence the success or failure of group performance.

Contingency theories

The quest for identifying the role of situational factors in the study of leadership has led to a stream of studies that are commonly known as 'contingency theories'. The following sections briefly present the most widely recognised contingency theories, namely, the Fiedler, Hersey–Blanchard, leader participation and path–goal models.

The Fiedler model

Fred Fiedler and his associates at the University of Illinois developed the first thorough contingency model for leadership. The Fiedler contingency model proposes that:

> *The performance of a leader depends on two interrelated factors: the degree to which the situation gives the leader control and influence – that is, the likelihood that (the leader) can successfully accomplish the job; and the leader's basic motivation – that is, whether (the leader's) self-esteem depends primarily on accomplishing the task or on having close supportive relations with others.*

In other words, this model assumes that the performance of a leader depends upon the various situational factors and the interactions between leaders and group members, rather than on any personality traits they may possess. It also assumes that different leadership styles may be appropriate in different types of situations. Fiedler proposes two main styles of leadership, namely: task oriented and relationship oriented. Leaders who are task oriented tend to gain satisfaction from seeing tasks being performed. In contrast, achieving good interpersonal relationships mainly motivates leaders who are relationship oriented. To measure the leader's style, Fiedler developed the *least preferred co-worker* (LPC) questionnaire. This questionnaire contains 16 sets of contrasting adjectives (e.g., pleasant–unpleasant, efficient–inefficient, and so forth). The questionnaire asks respondents to think of all the colleagues they have ever worked with and to describe the individual they least liked to work with by rating them on a scale from I to VIII for each of the 16 sets of contrasting adjectives. The central logic behind this questionnaire is that the respondents who mainly derive satisfaction from good relationships with their co-workers will describe the least preferred colleague in relatively positive terms (a high LPC score) and therefore their style would be labelled as *relationship oriented.* In contrast, respondents who mainly derive their satisfaction from the output will describe the least preferred colleague in comparatively adverse terms (low LPC score) and therefore, their style would be labelled as *task oriented.*

After identifying an individual's basic leadership style through the use of the LPC, Fiedler then identifies three contingency dimensions of the leadership situation for determining leadership effectiveness. They comprise:

- *Leader–member relations.* This dimension is regarded as the most important one from a leader's point of view. In a situation where there are good leader–member relations, the leader tends to depend on the group, therefore making sure that they will try to achieve the goals set by the leader.

- *Task structure.* This refers to the degree to which tasks can be formalized and broken down into a series of clearly identifiable procedures. For instance, if tasks are clear and structured, the output can be more easily managed and therefore subordinates can be held more responsible for their performance.

- *Position power.* This refers to the level of influence a leader has on getting group members to comply with his/her vision.

Each leadership situation was evaluated against these three contingency dimensions. More specifically, a leader needs to find out whether they are in a situation where leader–member relations are good or poor; whether task structure is high or low; and whether their position power is strong or weak. By mixing these three dimensions, there are potentially eight different situations that a leader may come across (see Figure 7.2).

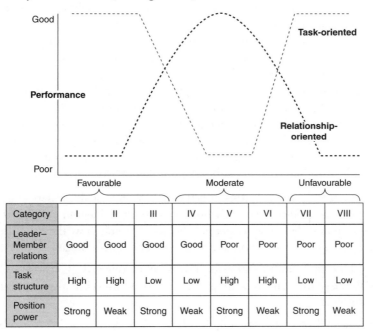

FIGURE 7.2   Findings of the Fiedler model
(*Source*: Robbins and Coulter, 2002: 465 Reprinted by
permission of Pearson Education, Inc., Upper Saddle River, NJ.

Based on Fiedler's study with 1,200 groups in which he compared relationship-oriented against task-oriented leadership styles in each of these eight different situations, he concluded that task-oriented leaders tend to perform better in contexts that are either very favourable to them or very unfavourable. However, relationship-oriented leaders tend to perform better in moderately favourable situations (in the middle of the scale in the figure). Although Fiedler has collected considerable evidence to support his proposed model, several limitations have been identified (Peters et al., 1985). For example, researchers have pointed out the methodological problems in verifying his proposed theories. These include weak measures and questionable analyses, as well as conceptual deficiencies such as the narrow focus on a single leader trait and the absence of explanatory processes (Vecchio, 1983; Yukl, 1989). Despite its limitations, the Fiedler model shows considerable support for the claim that effective leadership style must reflect situational factors (Robbins and Coulter, 2002).

Hersey–Blanchard's situational theory

Hersey and Blanchard's situational theory is one of the most widely acknowl-edged contingency theories. The theory suggests that effective leadership relies on the level of the followers' readiness. Why should we focus on 'followers' and what do we mean by the term 'readiness'? Regardless of a leader's actions, it is the followers who will either accept or reject the leader and, hence, ultimately determine how effective they are (Robbins and Coulter, 2002; Robbins et al., 1994). Followers therefore play a pivotal role in leadership. Moreover, their willingness to take responsibility for directing their own behaviour and accom-plish specific tasks related to their job is often labelled as followers' 'maturity' or 'readiness'. There are two types of maturity: job maturity and psychological maturity (Robbins et al., 1994). Job maturity refers to individuals who have a level of knowledge and experience that allows them to perform their jobs with-out seeking directions from others. On the other hand, psychological maturity refers to individuals who are self-motivated and hence rarely need external encouragement to perform tasks related to their jobs. In this way, Hersey and Blanchard extend Fiedler's *task* and *relationship* leadership styles by considering each of these dimensions as high or low and then combining them to form four distinct leadership behaviours (Robbins and Coulter, 2002). They are:

- *Telling* (high task–low relationship): this behaviour usually reflects directive/autocratic leadership. Leaders who adopt *telling* behaviours define roles in their group and dictate what people should be doing, how they should do it, when it should be completed and where it should take place.

- *Selling* (high task–high relationship): this behaviour reflects leaders who are both directive (in terms of setting tasks and deadlines) but also supportive to their followers.

- *Participating* (low task–high relationship): as opposed to the *telling* behav-iour, leaders that adopt *participating* behaviours share the decision making and task setting with their followers. In this scenario, they often assume the role of a facilitator/communicator.

- *Delegating* (low task–low relationship): this behaviour refers to leaders who are neither directive nor supportive.

Hersey and Blanchard then go on to identify the following four stages of fol-lower readiness:

- *R1:* this is the lowest readiness level; followers are neither able nor willing to take responsibility and actively pursue a task. They are neither compe-tent in their jobs nor confident in their abilities.

- *R2:* followers are unable to complete required tasks, but are willing to take them on. These individuals are self-motivated but often lack the necessary skills and knowledge to complete tasks.

- *R3:* followers are able to complete tasks but they are not willing to follow the leader's requirements.

- *R4:* followers are both able and willing to complete the tasks that the leader assigns.

The leadership behaviours and levels of follower readiness outlined above are integrated into Hersey–Blanchard's Situational Leadership® model. The model recommends appropriate leadership styles by cross-referencing the level of follower readiness with one of the leadership behaviours (see Figure 7.3). The model demonstrates that for followers with low readiness, leaders need to adopt a telling, directive leadership style. When followers' readiness reaches level R2, leaders are then advised to move to a selling style. This should involve a high-task orientation that compensates for the followers' lack of ability to complete the tasks, combined with a high relationship behaviour which encourages followers to 'buy into' the required tasks. At level R3 followers' readiness increases and, hence, a high relationship–low task leadership style is required. In such cases, leaders are therefore advised to adopt a participating style; this requires supportive and non-directive behaviour. Lastly, when followers' readiness is of a high level (R4) leaders are advised to adopt a delegating style. Here,

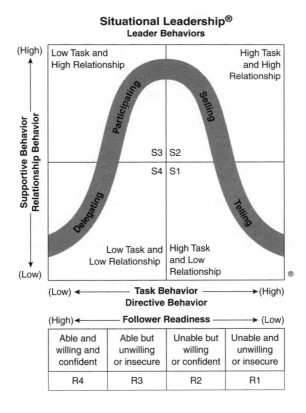

FIGURE 7.3   Hersey and Blanchard's Situational Leadership ® Model
(*Source*: Hersey, 1984, The Center for Leadership Studies)
© Copyright 2006 Reprinted with permission of the Center for Leadership Studies, Inc., Escondido, CA 92025. www.situational.com. All rights reserved.

Situational Leanership ® and Performance Readiness ® are registered trademarks of the Center for Leadership Studies, Inc. www.situational.com

leaders take a back seat, as followers are both able and intrinsically motivated to complete job-related tasks. Although Hersey–Blanchard's situational theory has received little empirical support (Graeff, 1983; Hambleton and Gumpert, 1982; Vecchio, 1987), it is widely used as a training tool both in corporate and military settings. Situational Leadership® is a registered trademark of the Center for Leadership Studies.

Leader participation model

Victor Vroom and Phillip Yetton developed the Leader Participation Model (LPM) in the early 1970s. The model is based on the notion that a leader's behaviour should be related to their participation in decision making. Vroom and Yetton argued that leaders' behaviour must reflect the structure of the tasks, since tasks may sometimes require routine activities and other times may demand nonroutine activities. LPM was originally designed as a complex decision tree, which allowed leaders to identify the different leadership styles that they should adopt in different situations determined by seven variables. Subsequently, Vroom and Yetton revised their original model and now include 12 contingency variables in their decision tree (Vroom and Jago, 1988). Leaders are expected to evaluate the situation that they are experiencing based on these 12 variables:

- *Quality requirement:* how important is the technical quality of this decision?

- *Commitment requirement:* how important is subordinate commitment to the decision?

- *Leader information:* do you have sufficient information to make a high-quality decision?

- *Problem structure:* is the problem well-structured?

- *Commitment probability:* if you were to make the decision by yourself, is it reasonably certain that your subordinates would be committed to the decision?

- *Goal congruence:* do subordinates share the organizational goals to be attained in solving this problem?

- *Subordinate conflict:* is conflict among subordinates over preferred solutions likely?

- *Subordinate information:* do subordinates have sufficient information to make a high-quality decision?

- *Time constraint:* does a critically severe time constraint limit your ability to involve subordinates?

- *Geographical dispersion:* are the costs involved in bringing together geographically dispersed subordinates prohibitive?

- *Motivation time:* how important is it to you to minimize the time it takes to make the decision?

- *Motivation development:* how important is it to you to maximize the opportunities for subordinate development?

Based on the situation at hand, the leadership participation model suggests that any of the following five behaviours may occur in a given situation:

- *Autocratic I:* leaders need to solve the problems themselves; rather than involving subordinates, the leaders should reach a decision based on their knowledge of the situation.

- *Autocratic II:* in certain situations it is appropriate to ask subordinates to provide information that may aid problem solving. However, subordinates do not provide solutions, only information. It is up to the leader to analyse this information and identify a solution for the task.

- *Consultative I:* in some cases, it makes more sense to discuss the problem at hand with each of your subordinates, individually. Once leaders have listened to different views they can then offer a solution, which may or may not reflect subordinates' suggestions.

- *Consultative II:* under some circumstances it may be more appropriate to gather subordinates together as a group, in order to generate a pool of ideas and potential solutions. Again, the leader will then reach a solution, which may or may not reflect subordinates' suggestions.

- *Group II:* in this case a more inclusive approach to decision making may be required based on the leader's diagnosis of the problem at hand. It may therefore be more appropriate to gather subordinates in a group and jointly decide on the most appropriate solution.

LPM is a valuable framework for determining the role of subordinates' participation in decision making and hence, for identifying the different styles that leaders may need to adopt based on the situations that they encounter.

Path–goal theory

The path–goal theory, developed by Robert House, proposes that the main job of the leader is to assist his/her subordinates to achieve their goals (set and agreed by both the leader and the subordinates) by providing the necessary support. The term 'path–goal' is used since the theory suggests that effective leaders tend to clarify the path to help their subordinates to achieve their goals, while at the same time they try to remove obstacles and prevent pitfalls. This theory builds on various leadership writings, such as the Ohio State studies on initiating structure and consideration and motivational theories (House, 1971). Essentially, the theory suggests that there are two factors that contribute to effective leadership that need to be taken into account. The first relates to *subordinates' characteristics,* such as their wants, self-belief and abilities. The second refers to the *working environment,* consisting of

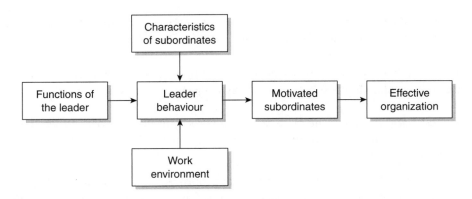

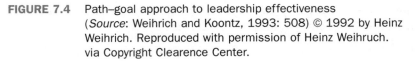

FIGURE 7.4   Path–goal approach to leadership effectiveness
(*Source*: Weihrich and Koontz, 1993: 508) © 1992 by Heinz
Weihrich. Reproduced with permission of Heinz Weihruch.
via Copyright Clearence Center.

elements, such as the task itself, the reward system and the relationship with colleagues (Weihrich and Koontz, 1993). Figure 7.4 summarizes the path–goal theory.

House (1971) identifies four leadership behaviours:

- *Directive leadership:* give subordinates specific direction and make explicit what is expected of them, whilst at the same time the leader focuses on work procedures to be done so that goals are achieved.

- *Supportive leadership:* consider the needs of subordinates and their well-being and create a friendly working environment. This leadership behaviour is particularly effective on the followers' performance when they are demotivated and dissatisfied.

- *Participative leadership:* allow followers to voice their opinions and take them into consideration before reaching a decision (this behaviour typically increases subordinates' motivation).

- *Achievement-oriented leadership:* focus on setting challenging goals and expect subordinates to achieve the set goals as best as they can.

The difference between the 'goal–path' theory and Fiedler's theory is that it suggests that there is no one best way to lead, but that the same leader can exhibit any or all of these behaviours depending on the situation. In the case of an ambiguous or uncertain situation, which may be fairly frustrating for subordinates, a more task-oriented style may be appropriate. In the case of a routine situation with clearly identified tasks, such as those found on a production line, imposing additional structure may be perceived by subordinates as an attempt to exert greater control and may lead them to feelings of dissatisfaction.

The significance of path–goal theory is encapsulated in its two propositions. First, the theory proposes that a leader's behaviour is viewed as acceptable by subordinates to the degree that they view it as an instant basis of satisfaction or as a way to future satisfaction. Second, a leader's behaviour is motivational to the degree that it (a) makes subordinates' needs dependent on effective performance and (b) offers the coaching, direction, assistance and rewards that are essential for effective performance.

Contemporary approaches to leadership

Over the last two decades, we have witnessed the emergence of new perspectives on leadership theory. For instance, scholars are increasingly talking about the difference between transformational and transactional leaders; some researchers are revisiting the early trait theories; and a growing number of studies now focus on the characteristics of charismatic and visionary leaders. In the sections that follow, two key contemporary approaches to leadership – transformational–transactional leadership and charismatic–visionary leadership – are briefly examined.

Transformational and transactional leadership

There is a stream of research in the leadership area that focuses on differentiating transformational from transactional leaders (Bass, 1985a; Bass and Avolio, 1990; Burns, 1978). Most of the traditional leadership theories and models that we have reviewed in this chapter (for instance, the Ohio State studies, Fiedler's model, the path–goal theory and the LPM) focus on transactional leaders. Transactional leaders guide and motivate their subordinates towards the completion of goals by clarifying role descriptions and setting task requirements (Robbins et al., 1994). Transactional leadership has two key characteristics (Kreitner et al., 2002). First, these leaders tend to use rewards to motivate employees. Second, they tend to take corrective action only when followers fail to complete the required task or under-perform. On the other hand, transformational leaders pay attention to the concerns and developmental needs of their subordinates, encourage followers to examine old problems in new ways and, perhaps most importantly, are able to inspire organizational members to go out of their way in order to achieve common goals. Interestingly, transformational leaders are usually portrayed as heroes within and outside of their organizational settings; they seem to have a great effect on their subordinates, often contributing to cult-like organizational cultures.

Although at first glance transactional and transformational leadership appear as opposing approaches, in reality, transformational leadership is built on top of the transactional approach (Bass, 1985b; Seltzer and Bass, 1990). While empirical research increasingly supports the notion that transformational leadership is superior to the transactional approach, especially in organizational and military settings (see Bass and Avolio, 1990; Parry, 1992), the debate on leadership goes on unabated.

Charismatic and visionary leadership

Contemporary leaders like Steve Jobs, the Chief Executive of Apple Computers Inc., and Richard Branson, the British entrepreneur behind the Virgin Group, are often described as charismatic business leaders. Jobs has been repeatedly pictured in the business press as a genius, who, armed with zeal and enthusiasm, keeps his troops fascinated and productive and continuously propels Apple forward, even in difficult times. Branson is also often referred to as the 'dream boss', the leader who inspires his subordinates with great vision and charisma. Such charismatic leaders have the ability to exert great influence on their followers; they inspire people to behave in certain ways. They are generally enthusiastic, self-confident and passionate about their business.

Taking into consideration the growth of hero-leaders in today's competitive business environment and the increasing recognition that charismatic leadership is positively correlated with high follower performance and satisfaction, leadership researchers increasingly seek to identify the main characteristics of these charismatic leaders. Several studies that have been conducted suggest that these charismatic leaders have five key characteristics (see Robbins and Coulter, 2002): they have a vision; they are able to communicate that vision; they are willing to take risks in order to realize their vision; they are sensitive to the opportunities and threats posed by the external environment in achieving their vision and are alert to their followers' needs and requirements; and they behave in ways that are 'extraordinary' compared to non-charismatic leaders. Although a number of studies still claim that charismatic leaders are 'born', research supports the view that leaders can be trained to exhibit charisma in their actions (Caudron, 1998). A number of leadership researchers are therefore moving beyond this notion of charisma and focusing on the concept of what they term 'visionary leadership'. Visionary leaders 'create and articulate a realistic, credible, and attractive vision of the future that improves the present situation' (Robbins and Coulter, 2002: 473). In this sense, we are talking about vision that transforms the way we do business and often changes people's lives. In the post-dot.com-bubble era the examples are numerous. Consider the vision that created the first personal computer, the first online bookstore, the first PC web-retailer that removed the middleman; the list is long. Steve Jobs of Apple, Jeff Bezos of Amazon.com and Michael Dell of Dell Computers are all prominent examples of leaders with clear and compelling visions; visions that inspired enthusiasm and mobilized energy across their organizations. So what are the characteristics of a visionary leader? Research has highlighted three key qualities:

- *Ability to explain vision to subordinates.* Being visionary *per se* is not enough; visionary leaders need to be able to clearly communicate their vision, clarify its requirements and explain what they expect from their followers in order to fulfil this vision.

- *'Walk the talk'.* Visionary leaders need not only talk about their vision but also proselytize by behaving in ways that continually promote and reinforce their vision.

- *Ability to extend or apply the vision to different contexts.* Visionary leaders need to be able to make their vision relevant to different parts of their organization, different stakeholders, employees in different countries, and so forth.

All of these theories of leadership have contributed to our understanding of what makes an effective leader. But how does this relate to our concern with processes of change, creativity and innovation? In exploring this question, the next section examines the importance of leadership as a vehicle for mobilizing these processes in organizational settings.

Leading change, creativity and innovation

Leadership is an organizational factor that significantly influences change, creativity and innovation (Amabile, 1998; Jung, 2001; Palmer et al., 2006). This is true if one considers the role of leaders in managing change (Kotter, 1996) and the way that leaders may shape creative processes and support innovative work practices (Jung et al., 2004). Leaders influence culture, structure and resources that are all likely to affect the generation and implementation of ideas within an organization (Tushman and O'Reilly, 1997), and they are often responsible for developing systems that nurture and reward the creative efforts of employees (Amabile, 1996). Given this significant relationship, what can we draw out of leadership theories that relates specifically to change, creativity and innovation?

Leadership and change

Leadership is one of the most widely researched and debated concepts and the role of leadership in change management is hotly contested. Most commentators agree that leadership is necessary for change, but what style of leadership is required, how this may vary in different contexts and how different types of leaders may be appropriate at different stages in the life cycle of organizations, are all contentious issues. As we have shown, from questions of whether leaders are born or made (traits of leadership) through to the leadership grid (Blake and McCanse, 1991), Fiedler's (1967) contingency model, Hersey and Blanchard's (2001) theory of situational leadership, and House's (1971) path–goal theory, there is a considerable body of literature in this area. One of the main debates centres on whether participative soft approaches to leadership are always or generally the most appropriate or whether there are circumstances when more directive, hard approaches to leadership are required, and whether senior managers can switch between these different styles during major change programmes.

Behind the figurehead of change leadership, there may be a coalition of leadership roles at various organizational levels and these may in turn change and shift over time. As Senior (2002: 258) concludes in her chapter on leadership and change:

> *Leadership theories vary from those which maintain that there are a set of characteristics which leaders must have if they are to gain success in what they do to those which argue that no single leader can be successful regardless of their own preferences and the*

situation they find themselves in. Regardless of which set of theories gain attention at any time, agreement is becoming evident that leading change requires more than the command and control behaviours fashionable in times when organisations operated in stable predictable environments. The replacement of repetitive work with machines, the increasing emphasis on knowledge and the need to innovate to survive and prosper have brought a recognition that, for people to be creative, while working in situations of uncertainty, requires leaders who are able to harness the skills of others through working in collaborative rather than hierarchical ways.

Kotter's (1996) eight-step model on leading change that was first published in the *Harvard Business Review* in 1995 highlights the importance of forming a powerful coalition – a change team – with a mixture of management and leadership skills in order to successfully drive change in organizations.

His well-known model, briefly outlined in Chapter 3, consists of the following elements:

1. *Establishing a sense of urgency:* companies need to examine their market position and make a realistic assessment of their competitive situation. They need to identify and discuss any current problems, looming potential crises and opportunities. This assessment needs to be broadly communicated so that people are motivated to co-operate in taking the company forward, they need to move out of their comfort zones. Unpleasant facts need discussion and the need for major change needs to be established.

2. *Forming a powerful coalition:* it is important to bring together a group of people who have enough power to lead the change effort and sustain the transformation even in the face of resistance. The group needs to work together as a team – a powerful coalition – this group may consist of between five and 50 people who have a shared commitment to bringing about change (in large organizations this group needs to be between 20 and 50 people if they are to be a successful guiding team). The coalition comprises a core of senior managers but also often includes other individuals, such as local managers, trade unionists or key customers.

3. *Creating a vision:* developing a vision and a strategy for achieving that vision is a central element of change management. The vision helps signal the purpose and direction of change and conveys a clear picture of a realizable future that can be easily communicated to all employees and other key stakeholders. Kotter (1996) recognizes that initially this vision may be a little vague but is quick to stress that the coalition needs to further refine and develop a clear and concise vision if they want their transformation effort to succeed. He argues that there are often plenty of plans and directives in failed change initiatives with no clear vision.

4. *Communicating the vision:* communication is a key element mentioned in all the major best-practice guidelines and it is often identified as something that is generally underestimated by change agents (see the discussion in Chapter 9).

5. *Empowering others to act on the vision:* getting employees committed to this vision is not enough by itself as old ways of doing things, structures and, for example, existing performance-appraisal systems, can all inhibit and prevent behavioural change. Consequently, some of the barriers to change need to be dismantled. The guiding coalition needs to encourage employees to try new approaches and they need to ensure that major obstacles are removed. Although some barriers to change will remain, the major systems and structures that undermine achievement of the vision need to be tackled and redesigned to accommodate the change effort.

6. *Planning for and creating short-term wins:* major change takes time and therefore waiting until the end of the programme before rewarding individuals or groups is a mistake. A good change initiative plans for visible performance improvements and creates short-term wins for employees. To sustain employee motivation and commitment it is important to recognize and reward them for improvements at regular stages throughout the longer-term process of organizational transformation. As Kotter (1996: 16) states: 'When it becomes clear to people that major change will take a long time, urgency levels can drop. Commitment to produce short-term wins help keep the urgency level up and force detailed analytical thinking that can clarify or revise visions'.

7. *Consolidating improvements and producing still more change:* as the change progresses and short-term wins are achieved the credibility of the change programme may strengthen. At this stage, structures and systems can be further developed, refined and replaced to ensure movement towards the main vision for change. Employees serving the change initiative may be promoted, new people may be recruited to the organization to take changes forward, and new themes and projects may be instigated to maintain the momentum of change. For Kotter, declaring victory too soon is a major reason why some change initiatives fail. As he explains (1996: 16): 'in the recent past, I have watched a dozen change efforts operate under the reengineering theme. In all but two cases, victory was declared and the expensive consultants were paid and thanked when the first major project was completed after two to three years. Within two more years, the useful change that had been introduced slowly disappeared.'

8. *Institutionalizing new approaches:* embedding the new approaches and behaviours into the culture of the organization. This involves clarifying and highlighting the links between the new ways of doing things and corporate success. It is also important to ensure appropriate succession planning has taken place so that a new chief executive officer or leader of the company does not undo what has taken considerable time and effort to achieve. For Kotter, change needs to be anchored in the corporate culture and the next generation of senior management needs to 'personify the new approach'.

These then are the eight key steps identified by Kotter (1996) that should be followed by companies who seek to successfully transform their organizations.

Although this approach has been criticized for being linear, John Kotter (1996) does recognize that change is often unpredictable, messy and full of surprises, and that there are a host of mistakes that people can make in managing large-scale change projects. In his interactive CD on *Realising Change* (1996), he breaks these change processes down into three stages. *Set-up*, that involves creating a sense of urgency, teamwork and developing a vision. *Roll-out*, where communication and empowering of others are central, together with the creation of short-term wins. *Follow-through*, where any remaining obstacles or pockets of resistance are removed and the new ways of behaving are anchored into the culture of the organization. He argues for the importance of leadership at all levels of an organization in order to overcome the immense barriers to change. For Kotter, it is leadership that creates change whilst management keeps things under control. Thus, whilst there is a need for both in organizations, leadership is the engine for transformational change. As Kotter (1996) explains in a keynote summary on the CD:

> *The change process I showed you earlier, get the urgency up, get a team at the top, get the vision clear, communicate the vision, empower the people, get the short-term wins, take on even bigger projects, connect it to the culture. If I gave you an hour to think about that with the following question in mind: how much of that process is a management and how much of this is a leadership process? ... After thinking about it for a while, do you know what you would conclude, most of you? You would conclude that 75 per cent of the process is leadership and 25 per cent is management.*

Some of these debates on leadership and change are further discussed in Chapter 10 when we examine different frameworks and models for making sense of change.

Ingredients of leadership for creativity and innovation

Leadership is one of the factors that authors agree can considerably enhance or inhibit creativity within the working environment (Mumford et al., 2002; Oldham and Cummings, 1996). But how can leaders do this?

Leaders may influence creativity both directly and indirectly (Zhou and George, 2003). The behaviour of a leader may nurture or stifle employees' creative potential. There is a general consensus supporting a democratic–participative style of leadership as conducive to creativity and innovation (Nyström, 1979; Wallace and West, 1988). Cummings and Oldham (1997) argue that a 'supportive' supervisory management style is more likely to contribute to creativity than a 'controlling' one since it enhances individual motivation. A controlling style is more likely to hinder individual motivation simply because it does not allow the creative processes to flow (Deci and Ryan, 1985; Deci et al., 1989). Thacker's (1997) empirical study found that group members should see the leader as trying to be supportive of creativity; otherwise the creative processes may be stifled. Leaders, it would seem, can either provide an 'open forum' in which members feel free to roam with new ideas and suggestions, or, conversely, they can provide a tightly constructed set of rules and guidelines in which members have little latitude to express fresh thoughts. Leaders can also influence employees' creativity indirectly by creating a working environment conducive to the generation and implementation of novel and useful ideas (Amabile et al., 1996). This can be achieved by concentrating on enhancing the factors that nurture employees' creativity (e.g., supervisory encouragement, stimulating work, autonomy) while at the same time aiming to minimize, or even eliminate, those factors that inhibit creativity within the workplace.

Several authors identify a range of elements that leaders need to possess in order to develop the conditions under which creativity and innovation can flourish (Amabile, 1998; Amabile et al., 1996; Mumford et al., 2002). Eight of these are discussed in more detail below.

Expertise and technical skills: the level of technical and creative problem-solving skills among leaders appears to be a significant predictor of creative performance (Andrews and Farris, 1967; Barnowe, 1975). First, leaders need to act as idea advocates by sensing and moving ideas around the organization so that they can attract resources and gain acceptance (Cook, 1998). Second, they need to evaluate other people's ideas and provide evaluative feedback. Evaluation must be handled as skilfully as possible since its aim is, first, to identify the merit of different ideas and, second, to provide avenues for further development. Leaders' expertise may also become vital under conditions of uncertainty or where problems are ill-defined. A leader's role is therefore critical in creative environments as they need to be competent facilitators assisting their employees in the achievement of organizational objectives (Amabile and Gryskiewicz, 1989; Mumford, 2000a, 2000b).

Creating and articulating a vision: good leaders are characterized by their ability to inspire others to 'buy-in' to their vision. This starts by clearly articulating their vision in a way that is understood by employees at all levels. For instance, leaders in Lunar Design (a leading Silicon Valley-based NPD consultancy) actively articulate their vision to their employees. Lunar's leaders not only communicate their vision effectively through formal communication channels, but also 'walk the talk' in encouraging employees to think and act beyond current wisdom (Andriopoulos and Gotsi, 2002). By so doing, they create a forum where company employees can openly voice their viewpoints and concerns. This creates a sense of empowerment since employees believe that they are part of something 'bigger', which in turn creates a sense of 'ownership' throughout the organization.

Setting the direction: leaders concerned with environmental scanning and who prefer to voice their opinions on what projects should be further exploited, tend to have a positive effect on creative performance (Cardinal and Hatfield, 2000; Cohen and Levinthal, 1990). During the initial stage of idea generation, leaders need to help teams to correctly define the task at hand and then initiate the generation of alternative ideas/concepts. Once different ideas are generated and the organization agrees on the most appropriate ones, leaders then have to identify the requirements for these new ideas to develop and the resources needed for their implementation. Their role is therefore to manage resources and co-ordinate different teams or groups of people to translate these ideas into products/ services. This calls for an in-depth knowledge not only of the area at hand but also a clear understanding of their organization as well as the industry in which they operate (Sharma, 1999).

Powers of persuasion: the persuasive skills of a leader are often vital to mobilizing creative efforts, especially when one considers that creative people are not easily persuaded and tend to act autonomously during much of their working lives (Mumford et al., 2002). Dudeck and Hall (1991), in a study that explored the factors that contributed to the creative success of professional architects in leadership positions, found that persuasive skills were critical. These architects actively generated more new business for their companies, while at the same time persuading clients about the value of their proposals. Some scholars argue that this form of direct persuasion needs to be accompanied by indirect persuasion, where leaders demonstrate social insightfulness, flexibility, wisdom and social assessment skills (Zaccaro et al., 1991).

Communication and information exchange: another effective social skill relates to the encouragement of communication among individuals. In previous chapters we have stressed the importance of the exchange of information as a means of increasing the likelihood of innovation. Communication is vital to the creative process since the cross-fertilization of different ideas/concepts is more likely to lead to more and better ideas. Individuals tend to make more connections when they are exposed to a diverse range of sources and this will eventually lead them to be more creative. For instance, Smart Design, a New York-based design consultancy, promotes the acquisition of both internal and external information. Its employees are not only encouraged to communicate informally through social interaction and during the more formalized weekly staff meetings, but they are also regularly expected to gather information from outside the company. For example, its designers are encouraged to visit and observe how their clients' or their competitors' products are currently used by people in order to identify new opportunities for innovation. At other times, groups of designers may organize trips to exhibitions or several retail stores so that they can gather information related to the latest material and design trends in different industries.

Intellectual stimulation: creative employees are motivated by interesting and complicated problems that require considerable intellectual skills. Leaders must see the need for positive challenges in order to appeal to their employees' need for self-actualization and fulfilment (Mikdashi, 1999). Following the same line of argument, Oldham and Cummings (1996) propose that when the task at hand is complicated and intellectually demanding, creative individuals tend to focus all their energy and time on their jobs. In contrast, tasks that seem more simple or mundane tend not to motivate employees, or allow them to take risks and come up with creative solutions (Shalley and Gibson, 2004). Accordingly, leaders need to pursue projects that encourage intellectual engagement, a sense of personal achievement and a feeling of control over their professional lives.

Involvement: another social aspect that is generally held to be of importance to creativity and innovation is the extent to which leaders encourage employees' involvement in the creative process. Creative people, as we have already explained, tend to be highly motivated when the task at hand is aligned to their passions and/or interests. A good tactic for effective leaders is to allow employees to choose the projects that they wish to work on, or to strive to provide them with projects that they find attractive and challenging (Pelz, 1967). Another common strategy that leaders may follow is to encourage participation in the framing of the problem at hand and how best to approach it (Mumford et al., 2002), as employees tend to show higher levels of satisfaction when they are allowed to participate in such activities (Mossholder and Dewhurst, 1980).

Autonomy: has been suggested as the final variable of effective leadership. Taking into account the character of the creative individual, research has long suggested that creative employees need 'room to manoeuvre'. Autonomy allows creative individuals flexibility to experiment with new ideas/concepts. However, creative leaders need to balance the amount of autonomy that they grant their employees with accountability and this is often tricky, as it must not be perceived by employees as an attempt to control the work process (Mikdashi, 1999). Research in this area has generated some very interesting insights. For instance, regimes that lack control or are very strict tend to hamper innovation, whilst those that can balance autonomy and accountability promote higher levels of motivation and productivity (Pelz and Andrews, 1976). An explanation of this might be that too much control is often perceived by creative employees as a loss of autonomy, whereas too loose controls may allow employees to focus on pursuing their own passions and ignore the directions set by the organization. In other words, it is important to gauge an appropriate level of autonomy for employees in the pursuit of an efficient level of creative performance (Shalley and Gilson, 2004).

Before moving on to our next section, read the case below on creativity and leadership style and consider the questions posed from the story of Niklas Zennstrom and Janus Friis.

CASE 7.1   WEB TELEPHONY'S QUIET DUO
BY SCOTT MORRISON AND CHRIS NUTTALL

(*Source*: *Financial Times*, 17 September 2005)

They are under attack from the world's most powerful entertainment companies, feared by the world's leading telecommunications groups and avoid US soil for fear they will be subject to American law. But that has not stopped Niklas Zennstrom, a 39-year-old Swede, and Janus Friis, a 29-year-old Dane, from becoming Silicon Valley's newest stars.

The duo made their mark in 2001 as the renegade programmers behind Kazaa, the peer-to-peer software that has enabled hundreds of millions of computer users to share copyrighted music tracks illegally over the internet. Mr Zennstrom and Mr Friis are now hailed as the visionaries behind Skype, the internet telephony start-up sold this week to eBay, the internet auction company, for at least $2.6 billion (£1.4 billion). It was not immediately clear how much money each would net from the sale, given that several venture capital groups will share the bounty. But with performance incentives that could boost the overall sale price to $4.1 billion, Mr Zennstrom and Mr Friis are likely to join the exclusive billionaires' club.

(Continued)

(Continued)

The softly-spoken Mr Zennstrom seems to be taking it all in stride. His most vivid memories of the sale are of days spent camped in the office dealing with lawyers and bankers. He says he has not given thought to the idea of celebrating his big payday. 'We had a small office party but I left quite early. I needed some sleep and we had a road show on Tuesday. I was just very happy to be home with my wife', he says.

Timothy Draper, founder of Draper Fisher Jurvetson, a venture capitalist group that invested in Skype, describes Mr Zennstrom as 'exciting, revolutionary, brilliant and heroic'. Others suggest he can be downright dull. Wayne Rosso, the brash music impresario who once ran Kazaa rival Grokster, says talking with Mr Zennstrom is about as exciting as watching paint dry. Jeffrey Gersh, the US attorney who represents Mr Zennstom and Mr Friis in their legal battle against the US entertainment industry, says that is harsh. 'They are fun guys. Are they outgoing and gregarious? Probably not', says Mr Gersh.

But if Mr Zennstrom prefers a low-key approach, it is hard to overstate the challenge that Skype represents for the traditional telecoms industry. With headquarters in Luxembourg, but run out of a backstreet office in London's Soho district, Skype has signed up 55 million registered users in just two years. Its software allows people around the world to talk to each other via their computers for free, circumventing traditional phone circuits. Users can also place calls to regular phones for a small charge. Many analysts believe internet telephony will soon make paid phone calls a thing of the past, a shift that will force large incumbent carriers to make dramatic changes to their business models. 'They deserve to be challenged. They provide bad and expensive service', says Mr Zennstrom of the established telecoms companies. But the goal is not simply to disrupt traditional industries. The aim, he says, is to 'create a very good business based on sustainable competitive advantages'.

With Kazaa and Skype under their belts, the two Scandinavians are now responsible for developing the two most downloaded programmes on the internet. They are at first glance an unlikely duo. Mr Zennstrom has a masters degree in computer engineering, an undergraduate degree in business administration and a wealth of telecoms industry experience. Mr Friis never finished high school because, according to Mr Zennstrom, it was too easy for him. 'I think he benefited from not having formal schooling. His thought process is much freer. He doesn't think conventionally', says Mr Zennstrom.

The two met in 1997, when Mr Zennstrom hired his future partner to manage the help desk at Get2Net, a Danish internet service provider. They shared a similar vision for internet communications and a few years later set off on their own to launch Kazaa. Danny Rimer, a general partner at Index Ventures, an early-stage investor and a Skype board member, says the pair form a complementary team. 'I would say Janus is the vision guy, he comes up with ideas every second. Niklas is good at picking up on which ideas are the great ones and honing them into products. They have full faith in one another and really value one another's skills', he says.

Mr Zennstrom rejects the notion that he has the business brain and his partner is the engineering visionary. 'That is exactly how it is not', he says. 'We are very complementary with each other. It is a very creative process and it's easier to be creative with two people. You need to try things out and challenge each other.'

It remains to be seen how they will fit into eBay's corporate culture. Mr Zennstrom is quick to point out that he spent nine years at Tele2, the European telecoms group. Mr Rimer says the two men are committed to fulfilling Skype's potential and would never have sold the company if Meg Whitman, eBay's chief executive, had not agreed to give them a lot of authority. Mr Zennstrom says he is looking forward to being part of one of Silicon Valley's most successful companies – at least for the foreseeable future. 'I think I can learn a lot of things from Meg. We want to see this thing through but we also have some other ideas', he says.

For the time being at least, the Skype duo will have to do most of their learning from a distance. The entertainment industry's lawsuit against Kazaa still has their names on it, in spite of the fact that they sold Kazaa in 2002. The two Scandinavians have filed a motion to be dropped from the suit, on the grounds that a US court should not have jurisdiction over citizens of another country who do not live or work in the US. Their lawyer has warned that travelling to US at this point could undermine that argument.

Mr Zennstrom believes the Kazaa suit may have worked to their benefit. He suggests Skype might have adopted a more insular perspective had it been based in the US. As it turned out, Skype was forced to focus on markets in Europe and Asia, where the demand for telecoms alternatives is greater. 'Not being in the US was actually pretty good for us', he says. But will his reluctance to travel to the US now prevent him from carrying out his duties as a senior member of eBay's executive team? 'It's probably a bit more of a challenge but we have some great communications technology we can use', he says.

Questions

1. Were Niklas Zennstrom and Janus Friis creative?
2. How would you describe their leadership style? Discuss.
3. Assess the 'for and against' arguments for their decision to sell their company to eBay and eventually become members of its executive team. Be as specific as you can.
4. In your opinion, will Niklas Zennstrom and Janus Friis' leadership style change at eBay? Why or why not?

Challenges

Today, the complexity of creative tasks that organizations face presents a multiplicity of challenges for leaders of innovative and creative companies. This contextual complexity makes it difficult for leaders to possess all the skills necessary to provide both direction and feedback to their employees. They often have to rely on additional experts and use the problem-solving skills of others in order to achieve their objectives (Baumgartel, 1957). In the companies that we have researched effective leadership of creativity often follows a twofold process (Andriopoulos and Lowe, 2000). First, leaders try to actively combine the personal aspirations of employees with emerging commercial trends and hence stimulate consideration of new projects that need to be explored. It is not unusual for creative companies to initiate their own internal projects (also known as 'blue-sky projects') and then try to identify potential clients who will be interested in funding their ideas/concepts. In other words, effective leaders are aware of the importance of speculative projects and actively support them by providing the required resources. Companies that adopt this strategy often create another source of income by selling their ideas to potential clients. They may also provide key stakeholders with an opportunity to learn about intriguing and interesting ideas that the company is thinking about. Blue-sky projects are therefore not only important for 'keeping the spark alive' within the working environment, but also in providing companies with excellent opportunities to demonstrate to potential clients, or even prospective employees, that the company's leadership encourages intellectual stimulation and cutting-edge work.

Second, effective leaders are often very skilful in evaluating which projects are suitable for the company's portfolio. Leaders assess the potential of projects with the opportunities they afford for the intellectual engagement of employees. An interesting observation that has emerged from our research is that effective creative leaders tend to maintain very detailed databases, which describe the nature and the duration of the projects that their employees have been involved with in the past. By so doing, they can allocate potential projects that not only develop creative people's existing skills, but also motivate them by giving them the opportunity to be involved in something new and interesting.

Conclusion

The chapter has examined a range of approaches to leadership and how these relate to processes of change, creativity and innovation. Leadership is critical to managing change, to creating and sustaining environments conducive to creativity and in supporting the translation of new ideas into commercial products and services. To summarize:

- A key element of leadership is getting employees to turn their creative ideas into tangible products/services that can better serve the needs of their customers. Accordingly, leaders need to understand the context within which their employees work and manage their human resources in order to support change, creativity and innovation. One of the biggest challenges that leaders face is to create an environment where everyone feels empowered to take action that seeks to achieve a common target. Imposing strict regimes to ensure that people behave in predefined ways in order to complete tasks successfully does not lead to the generation and implementation of novel and useful ideas. Conversely, if leaders allow their employees to only go after interesting problems and encourage them to ignore the company's rules, or to constantly challenge the established norms, opportunities for creative solutions to company problems may also be lost.

- Effective leaders have to be able to balance autonomy and control, direction and space, through integrating and aligning a range of organizational variables. Although leadership is a critical influence, it is not the only factor that steers change and enhances creativity and innovation within the workplace. Culture, structure, systems and resources are all factors that can be developed and used in providing an environment that promotes rather than stifles change, creativity and innovation.

- Leading change, creativity and innovation involves more than a single leader or style of leadership; it involves a range of people and approaches that need to adapt and change over time to meet different contextual requirements and changing expectations and needs of all those involved in these complex dynamic processes. This is perhaps one of the reasons why there may never be an all-embracing theory of leadership.

RESOURCES, READINGS AND REFLECTIONS

CASE 7.2   FALL OF A MOVIE MOGUL: DISNEY AND THE BEAST
BY KATHERINE GRIFFITHS

(*Source*: The Independent, 10 August 2005)
http://findarticles.com/p/articles/mi_qn4158/is_20050810/ai_n14857294

When Disney celebrated the fiftieth birthday of its iconic theme park in California this summer, it was hard to resist the impression that all was well in the enchanted kingdom of America's best-loved institution. Art Linkletter, the veteran TV broadcaster who emceed when Disneyland opened on 17 July 1955, said he had told Walt the idea was not a goer. California's governor, Arnold Schwarzenegger, also attended and was given a gold-coloured motorbike.

At the centre of the affectionate celebrations was Michael Eisner, Disney's chairman and chief executive for the past 21 years, who took a faltering company in 1984 and restored its image as one of the most recognised and well-loved brands in the world.

But, as he delivered his final set of financial results yesterday, before finally stepping down on 30 September, Mr Eisner, must have been wondering where all the enchantment had gone.

His departure from the Magic Kingdom is marred by a backdrop of rising criticism of the 63-year-old media mogul, damaging lawsuits and high-profile rows with some of Hollywood's most powerful insiders, including the Weinstein brothers, who founded Miramax film studio, and Jeffrey Katzenberg, who set up DreamWorks.

Indeed, such was Mr Katzenberg's animosity towards the man he worked with for almost two decades that he is widely rumoured to have modelled the

(Continued)

(Continued)

evil Lord Farquaard in Shrek on his former boss. This year, a book called Disney War, by Pulitzer prize-winning writer Jim Stewart, added to Mr Eisner's woes with a colourful insider's account of his eccentricities and volatility, which left people wondering whether the Disney boss was living in an unreal world.

Mr Stewart, who spent many hours with Mr Eisner, shadowing him as he went about the business of running Disney, said: 'He was enormously creative, enormously successful, highly intelligent, witty, charming, and wickedly funny. But there were bad qualities as well. Impulsiveness, hastiness, a paranoia about people around him, an inability to choose a successor.'

It would seem Mr Eisner's less good qualities have come to dominate his reputation. Even his long-standing friend, Barry Diller, another powerful businessman whose empire includes the travel website Expedia and the search engine Ask Jeeves, said recently: 'His is a truly great career. The downslopes, the ends of careers, are usually never pretty for anybody.'

Such has become Mr Eisner's lack of popularity that corporate America last year did an almost unprecedented thing. Some 45 per cent of Disney's shareholders at the company's 2004 annual meeting did not back his re-election as chief executive. So he was pressured into promising to hand over to his deputy, Bob Iger, on 1 October.

Yesterday, a jury was to vote on whether Mr Eisner and the rest of Disney's board was lax in handing $140m to Michael Ovitz, who was president of the company for just 14 months before he was summarily fired in 1996.

Mr Eisner has even managed to fall out with the only person bearing the Disney name on his board. Roy Disney, a nephew of Walt, led the campaign last year to oust Mr Eisner, saying he had mismanaged the company and has been too autocratic a manager. For some, such an account of Mr Eisner seems overly harsh. Friends and foes say he has built the company from being an old-fashioned owner of theme parks and a movie studio into an international conglomerate, which ranges from the TV networks ABC and the sports-focused channel ESPN to EuroDisney.

In addition, they say, Mr Eisner has been dedicated to the iconic company. A famous story about the company's larger-than-life boss goes that just as he was about to undergo quadruple bypass surgery in July 1994, Mr Eisner used time talking to his wife and sons to discuss who would be CEO if something went wrong. He later mused in a memo that it was a 'sad truth' that no one from Disney was on the list, (though Mr Diller and Mr Ovitz were).

On Wall Street at least, Mr Eisner has enjoyed considerable popularity. When he joined from Paramount Pictures in 1984, Mr Eisner rescued Disney from nearcollapse, saving it from corporate raiders who were circling the financially weakened company and wanted to break it up.

He made bold decisions, including taking Disney into television with the acquisition of ABC in 1995. He paid $19bn for the network, at the time the largest in the US. Weeks later the surprises continued when Mr Eisner announced that Michael Ovitz, head of the Creative Artists Agency and often called the most powerful man in Hollywood, was joining as Disney's president. The pairing did not last long. Just

14 months later, Mr Eisner told his old friend he had to go, leading to the controversial $140m pay-off which shareholders are now suing Disney over.

Mr Eisner, who was forced to testify in a shareholder class-action lawsuit this year, tried to distance himself from Mr Ovitz, whom he had once portrayed as one of his closest friends and had shared holidays with. On the stand, Mr Eisner said Mr Ovitz had visited him once during his heart surgery, and he was only one of many visitors. 'I was a good friend. I was a reasonable friend. I liked his wife. I was amused by him. He was one of my friends.'

The pattern was similar to other long-standing professional relationships, which Mr Eisner abruptly ended. Despite having a successful 19-year working relationship with Mr Katzenberg at Paramount and at Disney, Mr Eisner sacked him in 1994.

Observers have said the unexpected move was partly because he was irritated that his protagonist had done too good a job bringing back Disney's animation studio from near death with the hits The Little Mermaid and The Lion King, and was attracting too much publicity for himself.

Allegedly out of pique, Mr Eisner reportedly refused to negotiate a settlement with Mr Katzenberg, whose payoff ballooned from $60m to $280m. He left to found DreamWorks, a rival studio, with the director Steven Spielberg and music supremo David Geffen. DreamWorks' animation arm has long since overtaken that of Disney. While his colourful behaviour has added to Hollywood lore, Mr Eisner's high-handed and sometimes bizarre way of treating senior executives has won him no favours in the company. One such example came when he rounded on Andrea Van de Kamp, a board member who was critical of Mr Eisner's management and supported the campaign to oust him led by Mr Disney and another director, Stanley Gold.

In a meeting in his office, Mr Eisner scolded Ms Van de Kamp, who was the head of Sotheby's on west coast of the US, saying: 'You are a terrible director. You're so loyal to Stanley. It's like you've carried his babies.'

Mr Eisner's business decisions have also not been foolproof. Some on Wall Street believe he overpaid for ABC, whose long-established brand rivalled Disney's, but whose network was being encroached on by competitors. ABC has had mixed success in the Disney stable, though it did score a big hit with Desperate Housewives last year.

Mr Eisner's hankering to expand into Europe has also not impressed investors. He reportedly wanted to set up EuroDisney just outside Paris because he had fallen in love with it when he was at college. Unfortunately, the French did not feel the same way. Public resistance and lagging attendance drove EuroDisney almost to the point of bankruptcy.

Mr Eisner, who has described wanting to have a 'third act' in his life, is rumoured to be keen to try another profession when he leaves: acting. It might be a precious chance to put the pizzazz back into his Hollywood legacy, if he can get a studio to take him on.

(Continued)

(Continued)

Questions

1. How would you describe Michael Eisner's leadership style?
2. Do you think that Michael Eisner should have retired? Why or why not?
3. What do you think is the new CEO's biggest challenge in sustaining and igniting creativity at Disney at this point? Be as specific as possible.
4. What should the new CEO do to meet this challenge? Devise an action plan.

Chapter questions

The questions listed below relate to the chapter as a whole and can be used by individuals to further reflect on the material covered, as well as serving as a source for more open group discussion and debate.

1. In your opinion, how are managers different from leaders? Be as specific as you can and support your arguments.

2. Which are the key ingredients of leadership?

3. What are the main differences between the trait and behavioural theories?

4. What is the main contribution of the contingency theories?

5. Which of the discussed theories has the greatest practical application? Please use examples of business leaders to illustrate your points.

6. Identify the key elements that leaders need to possess in order to develop the conditions under which creativity and innovation can flourish.

7. What kind of challenges do leaders in creative/innovative companies have to address in order to be efficient in their roles? Please discuss.

Hands-on exercise

Students are required to find an article (magazine, newspaper or internet) where an individual from any part of life (business, politics, sports, arts, etc.) has demonstrated leadership qualities. Each student is expected to bring this article to the class for discussion and also describe the leadership style that the individual of their choice is exhibiting by using one of the theories discussed in this chapter.

Team debate exercise

Debate the following statement:

The leadership style is undoubtedly more important than the situation.

Divide the class into two groups. One should argue as convincingly as possible that the leader's behaviour is the main factor that affects the effectiveness of the work group. The other should prepare its arguments against this, highlighting that the situation is more important in determining the effectiveness of the work group. Each group should be prepared to defend their ideas against the other group's arguments by using real-life examples.

References

Amabile, T.M. (1996) *Creativity in Context*. Boulder, CO: Westview Press.

Amabile, T.M. (1998) 'How to kill creativity', *Harvard Business Review*, 76 (6): 76–87.

Amabile, T.M. and Gryskiewicz, S.S. (1989) 'The creative environment scales: the work environment inventory', *Creativity Research Journal*, 2: 231–54.

Amabile, T.M., Conti, R., Coon, H., Lazenby, J. and Herron, M. (1996) 'Assessing the work environment for creativity', *Academy of Management Journal*, 39: 1154–84.

Andrews, F.M. and Farris, G.F. (1967) 'Supervisory practices and innovation in scientific teams', *Personnel Psychology*, 20: 497–515.

Andriopoulos, C. and Gotsi, M. (2002) 'Creativity requires a culture of trust: lessons from Lunar Design Inc.', *Design Management Journal*, 13 (Spring): 57–63.

Andriopoulos, C. and Lowe, A. (2000) 'Enhancing organizational creativity: the process of perpetual challenging', *Management Decision*, 38: 734–42.

Barnowe, J.T. (1975) 'Leadership and performance outcomes in research organizations: the supervisor of scientists as a source of assistance', *Organizational Behavior and Human Performance*, 14: 264–80.

Bass, B.M. (1985a) *Leadership and Performance beyond Expectations*. New York: The Free Press.

Bass, B.M. (1985b) 'Leadership: good, better, best', *Organizational Dynamics*, 13 (3) (Winter): 26–40.

Bass, B.M. and Avolio, B.J. (1990) 'Transformational leadership, charisma and beyond', Working Paper, School of Management, State University of New York, Binghamton. p. 14.

Baumgartel, H. (1957) 'Leadership motivation, and attitudes in research laboratories', *Journal of Social Issues*, 12: 24–31.

Bennis, W. (1989) *On Becoming a Leader*. Reading, MA: Addison-Wesley.

Blake, R.R., Mouton, J.S., Barnes, L.B. and Greiner, L.E. (1964) 'Breakthrough in organizational development', *Harvard Business Review*, 42 (6): 133–55.

Blake, R. and Mouton, J. (1964) *The Managerial Grid: The Key to Leadership Excellence*. Houston: Gulf Publishing Co.

Burns, J.M. (1978) *Leadership*. New York: Harper & Row.

Cardinal, L.B. and Hatfield, D.E. (2000) 'Internal knowledge generation: the research laboratory and innovative productivity in the pharmaceutical industry', *Journal of Engineering and Technology Management*, 17: 247–71.

Caudron, S. (1998) 'Growing charisma', *Industry Week*, 4 May: 54–5.

Cohen, W.M. and Levinthal, D.A. (1990) 'Absorptive capacity: a new perspective on learning and innovation', *Administrative Science Quarterly*, 35: 128–52.

Cook, P. (1998) 'The creativity advantage – is your organisation the leader of the pack?', *Industrial and Commercial Training*, 30 (5): 179–84.

Cummings, A. and Oldham, G.R. (1997) 'Enhancing creativity: managing work contexts for the high potential employee', *California Management Review*, 40 (1): 22–38.

Deci, E.L. and Ryan, R.M. (1985) *Intrinsic Motivation and Self-Determination in Human Behavior*. New York: Plenum Press.

Deci, E.L., Connell, J.P. and Ryan, R.M. (1989) 'Self-determination in a work organisation', *Journal of Applied Psychology*, 74: 580–90.

Dudeck, S.Z. and Hall, W.B. (1991) 'Personality consistency: eminent architects 25 years later', *Creativity Research Journal*, 4: 213–31.

Graeff, C.L. (1983) 'The situational leadership theory: a critical view', *Academy of Management Review*, 8 (2) (April): 285–91.

Hambleton, R.K. and Gumpert, R. (1982) 'The validity of Hersey and Blanchard's theory of leader effectiveness', *Group and Organization Studies*, 7 (June): 242–52.

Heller, T. and Van Til, J. (1982) 'Leadership and followership: some summary propositions', *Journal of Applied Behavioral Science*, 18: 405–14.

Hersey, P. and Blanchard, K. (1982) *The Management of Organization Behavior: Utilizing Human Resources*. Englewood Cliffs, NJ: Prentice Hall.

House, R.J. (1971) 'A path–goal theory of leader effectiveness', *Administrative Science Quarterly*, 16: 321–39.

House, R.J., Wright, N.S. and Aditiya, R.N. (1997) 'Cross-cultural research on organizational leadership: a critical analysis and a proposed theory', in P.C. Earley and M. Erez (eds), *New Perspectives in International Industrial Organizational Psychology*. San Francisco: New Lexington.

Jung, D.I. (2001) 'Transformational and transactional leadership and their effects on creativity in groups', *Creativity Research Journal*, 13: 185–97.

Jung, D.I., Chow, C. and Wu, A. (2004) 'The role of transformational leadership in enhancing organizational innovation: hypotheses and some preliminary findings'. CIBER Working Paper Series, San Diego State University.

Kahn, R. and Katz, D. (1960) 'Leadership practices in relation to productivity and morale', in D. Cartwright and A. Zander (eds), *Group Dynamics: Research and Theory*, 2nd edn. Elmsford, NY: Row, Paterson.

Kirkpatrick, S.A. and Locke, E.A. (1991) 'Leadership: do traits really matter?', *Academy of Management Executive*, 5 (2) (May): 48–60.

Kotter, J.P. (1990) 'What leaders really do', *Harvard Business Review*, 68 (3) (May–June): 103–11.

Kotter, J. (1996) *Leading Change*. Harvard: Harvard Business School Press.

Kotter, J. (1996) *Realising Change*. Interactive CD produced by Harvard Business School.

Kreitner, R., Kinicki, A. and Buelens, M. (2002) *Organizational Behaviour*, 2nd edn. London: McGraw-Hill.

Lewin, K. and Lippitt, R. (1938) 'An experimental approach to the study of autocracy and democracy: a preliminary note', *Sociometry*, 1: 292–300.

Lewin, K., Lippitt, R. and White, R.K. (1939) 'Patterns of aggressive behavior in experimentally created social climates', *Journal of Social Psychology*, 10: 271–301.

Mikdashi, T. (1999) 'Constitutive meaning and aspects of working environment affecting creativity in Lebanon', *Participation and Empowerment: An International Journal*, 7 (3): 47–55.

Mossholder, K.W. and Dewhurst, H.D. (1980) 'The appropriateness of management by objectives for development and research personnel', *Journal of Management*, 6: 145–56.

Mumford, M.D. (2000a) 'Managing creative people: strategies and tactics for innovation', *Human Resource Management Review*, 10 (1): 1–29.

Mumford, M.D. (2000b) 'Managing creative people: strategies and tactics for innovation', *Human Resource Management Review*, 10: 313–51.

Mumford, M.D., Scott, G.M., Gaddis, B. and Strange, J.M. (2002) 'Leading creative people: orchestrating expertise and relationships', *Leadership Quarterly*, 13: 705–50.

Nyström, H. (1979) *Creativity and Innovation*. Chichester: John Wiley.

Oldham, G.R. and Cummings, A. (1996) 'Employee creativity: personal and contextual factors at work', *Academy of Management Journal*, 39: 607–34.

Palmer, I., Dunford, R. and Akin, G. (2006) *Managing Organizational Change: A Multiple Perspectives Approach*. Boston, MA: McGraw-Hill.

Parry, K.W. (1992) 'Transformational leadership: an Australian investigation of leadership behaviour', in A. Kouzmin, L. Still and P. Clarke (eds), *Directions in Management 1992: The Best Management Research in Australasia*. Sydney: McGraw-Hill.

Pelz, D.C. (1967) 'Creative tensions in the research and development climate', *Science*, 157: 160–5.

Pelz, D.C. and Andrews, F.M. (1976) *Scientists in Organizations. Productive Climates for Research and Development*, revd edn. Ann Arbor, MI: Institute for Social Research, University of Michigan.

Peters, L.H., Hartke, D.D. and Pohlmann, J.T. (1985) 'Fiedler's contingency theory of leadership: an application of the meta-analysis procedure of Schmidt and Hunter', *Psychological Bulletin*, 97: 274–85.

Robbins, S. and Coulter, M. (2002) *Management*. Englewood Cliffs, NJ: Prentice Hall.

Robbins, S.P., Waters-Marsh, T., Cacioppe, R. and Millett, B. (1994) *Organisational Behaviour: Concepts, Controversies and Applications*. Sydney: Prentice Hall.

Schriesheim, C.A., Tolliver, J.M. and Behling, O.C. (1978) 'Leadership theory: some implications for managers', *MSU Business Topics*, (Summer): 35.

Seltzer, J. and Bass, B.M. (1990) 'Transformational leadership: beyond initiation and consideration', *Journal of Management*, 16 (4) (December): 693–703.

Senior, B. (2002) *Organizational Change*. (2nd edn) London: Pitman Publishing.

Shalley, C.E. and Gilson, L.L. (2004) 'What leaders need to know: a review of social and contextual factors that can foster or hinder creativity', *Leadership Quarterly*, 15: 33–53.

Sharma, A. (1999) 'Central dilemmas of managing innovation in large firms', *California Management Review*, 41: 146–64.

Stogdill, R.M. (1974) *Handbook of Leadership*. New York: The Free Press.

Thacker, R.A. (1997) 'Team leader style: enhancing the creativity of employees in teams', *Training for Quality*, 5 (4): 146–9.

Tushman, M. and O'Reilly, C. (1997) *Winning through Innovation: A Practical Guide to Leading Organizational Change and Renewal*. Boston, MA: Harvard Business School Press.

Vecchio, R.P. (1983) 'Assessing the validity of Fiedler's contingency model of leadership effectiveness: a closer look at Strube and Garcia (1981)', *Psychological Bulletin*, 93: 404–8.

Vecchio, R.P. (1987) 'Situational leadership theory: an examination of a prescriptive theory', *Journal of Applied Psychology*, 72 (3) (August): 444–51.

Vroom, V.H. and Jago, A.G. (1988) *The New Leadership: Managing Participation in Organizations*. Englewood Cliffs, NJ: Prentice Hall.

Wallace, M. and West, M.A. (1988) 'Innovation in primary health care teams: the effects of role and climate'. Paper presented at the Annual Occupational Psychology Conference of the British Psychological Society, University of Manchester, January.

Weihrich, H. and Koontz, H. (1993) *Management: A Global Perspective*, 10th edn. London: McGraw-Hill.

Yukl, G. (1989) *Leadership in Organizations*, 2nd edn. Englewood Cliffs, NJ: Prentice Hall.

Zaccaro, S.J., Gilbert, J.A., Thor, K.K. and Mumford, M.D. (1991) 'Leadership and social intelligence: linking social perceptiveness and behavioral flexibility to leader effectiveness', *Leadership Quarterly*, 2: 317–42.

Zaleznik, A. (1977) 'Managers and leaders: are they different?', *Harvard Business Review*, 55 (3) (May–June): 67–78.

Zhou, J. and George, J.M. (2003) 'Awakening employee creativity: the role of leader emotional intelligence', *Leadership Quarterly*, 14: 545–68.

Recommended reading

- Bennis, W. and Nanus, B. (2003) *Leaders.* New York: HarperCollins.
- Heenan, D.A. and Bennis, W. (1999) *Co-leaders: The Power of Great Partnerships.* New York: John Wiley.
- Kanter, R.M. (1983) *The Change Masters.* New York: Simon & Schuster.
- Kotter, J. (1999) *John P. Kotter on What Leaders Really Do.* Boston, MA: Harvard Business School Press.

Some useful websites

- The Center for Creative Leadership's website has many articles, book suggestions and other information on networking events and programmes related to leadership (http://www.ccl.org).
- This is the website of the Leader to Leader Institute, which provides insight and information on leadership (http://www.pfdf.org).

8

The Internal Environment: Orchestrating Structure, Systems and Resources

Learning objectives

After reading this chapter you will:

1. Understand how structure, systems and resources can support organizational change, creativity and innovation.
2. Be able to define the concept of structure and outline the six key elements that managers need to consider when they design their organization.
3. Be able to explain the difference between mechanistic and organic structures and critically evaluate their influence.
4. Understand the effects of goal setting, rewards and evaluation on creativity in the work setting.
5. Be aware of the different types of resources that are essential to mobilizing creativity.
6. Be able to explain the notion of 'sufficient resourcing' and the importance of organizing resources around the 'threshold of sufficiency'.
7. Be able to identify the benefits of effective project selection.

Introduction

Novel and useful ideas are generated when the whole organization is designed in a way that supports them. Leaders and managers within innovative environments need to decide upon the most appropriate organizational structure and systems that are conducive to the creation of innovative work environments; they also need to ensure that employees are adequately resourced for the generation of new ideas, their development and eventual implementation in the form of new products or services. The management of these interrelated organizational variables is important to the effective management of creative teams.

The balanced scorecard: value creation and performance management

The *balanced scorecard* is an approach to strategic management and performance measurement that has generated substantial interest among academics and practitioners. Kaplan and Norton (1992) argue that managers should not only focus on financial measures but also on non-financial criteria when making decisions. The concept of the 'scorecard' aims to provide managers with clear measures that may track and also drive performance. The balanced scorecard allows managers to look at the business from four critical indicators of current and future performance: the financial perspective; the customer perspective; the internal business perspective; and the learning and growth perspective (see Figure 8.1). These perspectives represent three major stakeholders of any business (shareholders, customers and employees), thereby ensuring that a holistic view of the organization are used for strategic reflection and implementation.

- *Financial perspective: how do we look to shareholders?* The financial performance measures define the long-term objectives of an organization. Managers have to answer the question: is the company's strategy and their implementation and execution of plans contributing to bottom-line improvements? They need to investigate whether improvements in manufacturing capabilities is leading to an increase in profitability, as there can be a disparity between improved operational performance and financial results. In this unlikely situation, managers may have to acknowledge that they have not followed up their operational improvements with additional actions. For instance, managers should not only collect regular feedback on different areas of improvement in the different stages of the production process, they also need to empower and motivate staff to act upon this knowledge in allowing them to continually improve operations.

- *Customer perspective: how do customers see us?* Managers must identify the customer and market segments in which the company competes and clarify the appropriate measures of performance in these targeted segments. Outcome measures, such as customer satisfaction, customer retention, new customer acquisition, customer profitability and market share, must be linked to the targeted customer segments in which the business anticipates its greatest potential for growth and profitability (Kaplan and Norton, 1996).

- *Internal business perspective: what must we excel at?* Excellent customer performance may be derived from processes occurring throughout the organization (Kaplan and Norton, 1992). It is important for organizations to

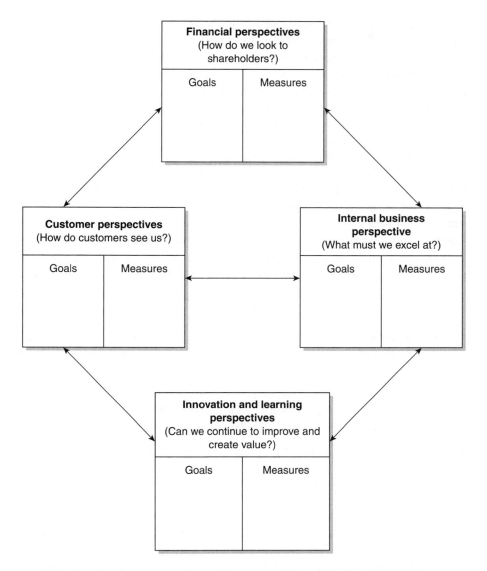

FIGURE 8.1 The balanced scorecard (*Source*: Kaplan and Norton, 1992: 72)

decide the processes and competencies they must excel at and to provide measures for each.

- *Innovation and learning perspective: can we continue to improve and create value?* The identified parameters that the company considers critical to success will keep changing and, hence, continuous improvements to existing products and/or processes as well as the introduction of entirely new products is an ongoing activity essential to company performance.

Kaplan and Norton (1996) stress the importance of aligning this scorecard information with business strategy. They argue that this concept gives managers a better understanding of how their companies are really doing and how their current actions may influence tomorrow's goals. It enables companies to track financial results while simultaneously monitoring progress in the building of capabilities and the acquisition of intangible assets that they will need for future growth. To translate strategic goals into tangible objectives and measures they suggest four interrelated management processes. These comprise: clarifying and translating the vision and strategy; communicating and linking strategic objectives with appropriate measures; business planning and target setting; and enhancing strategic feedback and learning. In their book *The Strategy Focused Organization*, Kaplan and Norton (2001) introduce five principles to keep strategy the focus of organizational management processes, namely: translate the strategy into operational terms, align the organization to the strategy, make strategy everyone's everyday job, make strategy a continual process, and mobilize change through executive leadership. Kaplan and Norton's balanced scorecard has evolved from a performance measurement tool to a framework for determining the alignment of strategy with an organization's human, information and resource capital (Kaplan and Norton, 2004). Their framework is central to creative/innovative companies where:

- good collaboration within and among departments within an organization will aid the translation of vision and strategy into operational measures and relevant action;

- continuous adaptation and use of internal processes and systems to respond rapidly to the changing customer needs and turbulent external environment are of critical importance (see also Braam and Nijssen, 2004);

- getting support from the top management in terms of the necessary resources to launch new products, creates more value for customers and improves operating efficiencies.

In their extensive research within leading organizations across a range of sectors they note how performance is not only driven by an emphasis on bottom-line improvement, excellent customer performance and the company's ability to innovate, but also by the internal environment. The internal environment is viewed as critical to enhancing creativity and innovation in organizations. The sections that follow examine the organizational structure, systems and resources that drive creativity and innovation in the workplace.

What is organizational structure?

When founders or managers of firms develop organizational structures in order to enable growth or to seize opportunities, they have to deal with the challenges involved in organizational design, a course of action that involves decisions about six key elements: work specialization, departmentalization, chain of command, span of control, centralization/decentralization, and formalization (Daft, 1998). Let's now look at these six elements in more detail.

Work specialization

Work specialization has been identified as a critical factor in determining employees' productivity. Henry Ford, in the beginning of the 20th century, was one of the first to adopt this idea in his factories, where jobs were broken down into their component parts and then allocated to workers who were required to perform specific and repetitive tasks that were clearly defined. For example, McDonald's, although praised as one of the most creative applications of production standardization to a service industry, base their operations on a high division of labour and work specialization in an attempt to increase efficiency and maximize profits (Levitt, 1972). Unlike employees in creative industries, people working on assembly lines or in fast-food chains often find that they are required to perform tasks that are relatively unskilled and repetitive. This contrasts, for example, to work specialization in a medical research department where tasks often require a high level of expertise. As such, the level of skill required in carrying out specialist tasks is highly pertinent; for example, highly specialized unskilled tasks have been associated with low employee morale and high levels of industrial conflict (or what Braverman, 1974, refers to as the *dehumanization* of work). Conversely, studies on skilled employees highlight how a wide variety of specialists often offer a wider knowledge base that can be used to enhance the cross-fertilization of ideas in organizations (Aiken and Hage, 1971; Kimberley and Evanisko, 1981). Not surprisingly, the majority of creative companies that we have studied often try to broaden their employees' scope by involving them in different activities throughout the creative process. We found that during the initial stage of idea generation, employees from different departments are often invited to participate in brainstorming sessions in order to contribute their viewpoints and that this, in turn, can enrich the pool of ideas from which suggestions can be drawn and potentially broaden employees' skills in various specialities.

Departmentalization

Work specialization creates job activities, which must be grouped together so that common tasks can be co-ordinated. Typically, medium to large-sized organizations group employees together who are working on similar activities, who are associated with particular products or services, or who are based in a particular location. We are all familiar with the grouping of people into functional departments, such as marketing, research and development, production, HRM and finance. However, departmentalization can also take place according to:

- *Product*: where jobs are grouped around a particular product or service. Individuals from different areas are assigned to a specific product or service. Department stores are examples of companies that use product departmentalization. Their structures are based on their varied product lines which include men's clothing, women's clothing, children's clothing, home accessories, electrical appliances, and so forth.

- *Geography:* where jobs are brought together around geographic location. For example, Coca-Cola's organization structure reflects the company's operation in two broad geographic areas – the North American sector and the international sector (for example, European Community, Africa and Latin America).

- *Process:* where jobs are grouped based on process or customer flow. A patient preparing for an operation would go through some diagnostic tests and then be admitted, undergo surgery, receive post-operative care and then be discharged. All these services in the patient process are managed by different departments.

Chain of command

The third element that influences decisions about organizational design is the chain of command. This refers to formal lines of authority which span different hierarchical levels, from top management to workplace employees, and aims to clarify who reports to whom in the work setting. This monitoring and control mechanism aims to ensure that the right people are doing the right tasks at the right time (Kreitner et al., 2002). The logic behind this system of control is that organizations need to maintain a hierarchy of authority to prevent conflicting demands from different departments or divisions that might disrupt operations and create inefficiencies (Finkelstein and D'Aveni, 1994).

Span of control

Van Fleet and Bedeian (1977) define span of control as the number of people reporting directly to a manager. In other words, in designing organizations there is a choice on whether to adopt a flat structure with few hierarchical levels or a tall structure with many levels. Flat structures are usually characterized by a wide span of control, they emphasize work autonomy and empowerment and seek to minimize costs (since administrative costs tend to be relatively low) (see Figure 8.2). In contrast, tall structures are characterized by a relatively narrow span of control, which means that the manager-to-employee ratio is higher. This increases the costs associated with the supervision and management of operations (see Figure 8.3).

Over the last two decades, companies have adopted flatter structures in order to avoid some of the more common problems associated with tall structures, including the following (Hill and Jones, 1995):

- *Problems of co-ordination.* Communication across different levels takes longer, since the chain of command is larger. This often causes a degree of inflexibility where valuable time may be lost in generating and implementing ideas or products across the organization. Poor communication may also result in a failure to capitalize on changes in the external environment (Gupta and Govindarajan, 1984).

- *Distortion of information.* Employees across different levels may either misunderstand information due to mixed messages or misinterpret information

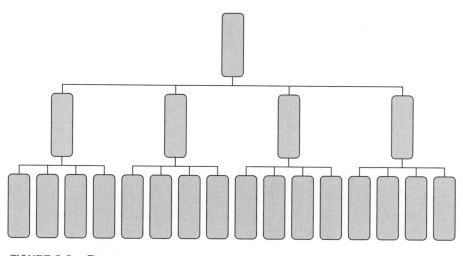

FIGURE 8.2   Flat structure

(sometimes to suit their own personal agendas). The important implication of this problem is that information transmitted up and down the hierarchy does not reach its receiver(s) intact, which may in turn affect co-ordination.

- *Problems of motivation.* Increasing the number of hierarchical levels in an organization reduces the span of control and authority exercised by managers and supervisors. In other words, under tall structures managers have less authority and are likely to find their decisions constantly scrutinized by their superiors. As a result, managers' performance in tall structures is often hindered as they cannot take responsibility for the organization's performance and this in turn can de-motivate staff.

Centralization and decentralization

The processes by which decisions are made within an organization influence the degree to which an organization is centralized or decentralized. For instance, centralization refers to the extent to which decisions are made at a single point in the organization (Robbins and Coulter 2002: 617). Zaltman et al. (1973) propose that high centralization inhibits the initiation of innovations because it restricts channels of communication and reduces available information (Burns and Stalker, 1961; Hage and Aiken, 1967). Conversely, decentralization occurs in firms where decision making is devolved and where lower levels of the hierarchy are encouraged to provide input. The recent emphasis on business flexibility and responsiveness to changing consumer markets spotlights the significance of decentralized decision making in contemporary work settings. Let's take, for example, a service organization like a bank. Frontline employees are often closer to the customer and have a greater awareness of problems that arise from a change in customer expectations. This knowledge gives them the ability to identify solutions in a much more direct and informed way than those generated by top management. The greater participation that results from a decentralized

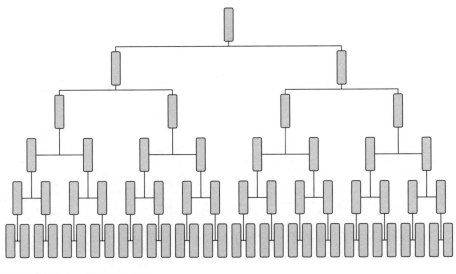

FIGURE 8.3   Tall structure

structure allows more viewpoints to be brought into consideration and this in turn is likely to produce a greater diversity of ideas and solutions.

Formalization

Job formalization is the last key element to consider when determining the organizational design of a work setting. This term refers to the degree to which jobs within a firm are standardized through formal job descriptions, and the degree of discretion available to employees in pursuing activities and tasks (Cohn and Turyn, 1980; Kaluzny et al., 1974). For instance, a job that is highly formalized is characterized by little discretion over how and when job tasks are done. Employees in formalized jobs are expected to abide by the rules and procedures found in employees' handbooks, specified in job descriptions, or learnt through induction. In contrast, when job formalization is low, employees are given relatively high discretion on how and when they may do their work. Rogers (1983) and Zaltman et al. (1973) note that excessive formalization constrains creativity and innovation because rigid rules and procedures inhibit organizational decision makers from discovering new sources of information.

Not surprisingly, many creative companies in the design industry (such as branding consultancies and graphic design studios) encourage low formalization to promote openness in the generation of new ideas; for example, in allowing employees to experiment with different colours, materials or visual expressions, or in encouraging employees to look for cases relevant to their clients that can contribute to the final product (Andriopoulos, 2003). Within such environments, the objective is not to create a strict process that employees have to blindly follow, but to allow space for freedom and flexibility where employees may find new areas of inspiration and knowledge. Within a single firm, however, the degree of formalization may vary. For example, in graphic design, some groups of employees may have comparatively low levels of discretion, such as those who take ideas generated from others and reproduce them in a digital format for clients (for example, CAD specialists, 3D image engineers, and the like); often these people are also constrained by time limitations that necessitate some standardization on how they perform their tasks.

The decisions that companies make in relation to these six determinants of organizational design will ultimately affect the specific structure that managers adopt for their work setting. It should be noted that a structure that is successful in one firm may not necessarily work in another. Deciding on an appropriate structure therefore requires careful consideration, and the following situational factors are often found to play an important role.

Situational factors

The common factors that managers should consider in order to select the most appropriate and effective structure for their firms comprise: corporate strategy, size and the degree of environmental uncertainty.

Corporate strategy

Alfred Chandler (1962) conducted pioneering research into the relationship between strategy and structure. In his study of several large US firms over a period of 50 years, he concluded that changes in strategy result in changes in structure. In the majority of firms that he studied he found that organizations usually begin by producing a product or a product line that demands a simple or loose form of organization but, as organizations grow, their strategies tend to become much more elaborate.

Organizational size

Organizations, which grow and become increasingly complex, tend to adopt structures that encourage effective co-ordination and control of a diverse range of operations and people. They are often characterized by high degrees of specialization, a large number of departmental groupings, and formalized rules and procedures. This contrasts with their smaller counterparts who may adopt more informal systems of operation and low levels of specialization.

Environmental uncertainty

The pressures of change and the speed at which an organization must act are influenced by the dynamism and complexity of the external environment. External uncertainty tends to threaten the well-being of an organization. This is why organizations that operate in highly uncertain, high-velocity industries tend to adopt structures that accept and endorse changes within the work setting (Yasai-Ardekani, 1986).

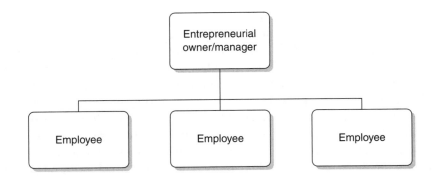

FIGURE 8.4   The entrepreneurial structure

Structural forms

Organizations may adopt several alternative structural forms to accommodate these situational variables. In the following sections, we present some of the key options, beginning with some traditional forms and then focusing on new structures which are becoming increasingly common in the contemporary business landscape.

Traditional structures

Traditionally, the most common types of organizational structure have been the entrepreneurial structure, the functional structure and the divisional structure. Most organizations start as entrepreneurial ventures in the early stages of their development. The *entrepreneurial structure* is very simple and is built around the founder/manager, who acts as an authority figure in making most of the decisions (see Figure 8.4). Mintzberg (1983) notes that this type of structure is characterized by low departmentalization and control spans with little formalization. If the demand for products or services increases then the company may recruit more employees in order to expand operations and accommodate growth. Their initial entrepreneurial structure will at some point be replaced by a more formalized and centralized structure. This often results in the introduction of rules and procedures, the specialization of work and the creation of departments, all of which will make the organization increasingly bureaucratic. At this point, managers have the option to choose between organizing their firms around a functional or divisional structure.

A *functional structure* groups similar or related tasks into functional areas (see Figure 8.5). For example, a cosmetics company may be organized around the functions of operations, finance, marketing and sales, human resources, and research and development. Efficiency is achieved through specialization, but the organization may risk losing sight of its overarching strategic direction as different departments pursue their own goals.

A *divisional structure* is, on the other hand, made up of several units or divisions, such as product groups or geographic regions (Thompson, 1993). This

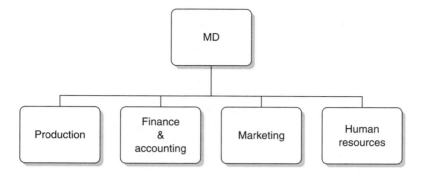

FIGURE 8.5   The functional structure

form divides the firm into relevant divisions that are managed by a divisional manager who has authority over his/her unit (see Figure 8.6). The company as a whole co-ordinates and controls various units and offers support services to its divisions (Kreitner et al., 2002).

Contemporary organizational structures

Companies today face several challenges that relate to the volatility of business markets and the unprecedented pace of change. For example, globalization, changing customer expectations and the constant evolution of technologies used in the production and delivery of goods and services, all call for new ways of organizing and working. As firms embrace new organizational structures there has, among other changes, been a move towards more *team-based structures* (Katzenbach and Smith, 1993). Under these new arrangements, the entire team is responsible for the performance results of their designated area of operation, and employees are often empowered to design the work flow as they think best.

Another popular type of organizational structure is the *matrix structure*. This form of structure emphasizes the co-ordination of specialists into project-oriented teams. Under these arrangements, people with individual accountability work on one or a number of projects and are usually led by project managers (Torrington et al., 2002). Lastly, the *boundaryless organization* is characterized by an organizational structure which is not limited by boundaries between tasks and departments (Dess et al., 1995). This results in greater collaboration across levels and departments in order to achieve the goals of an organization.

Organizing for change, creativity and innovation

In having introduced the key structural forms, we now turn our attention to answering the following question: which form(s) of organizational structure facilitate the generation and implementation of new and useful ideas? The desired structure should aim to unleash employees' creativity by creating an

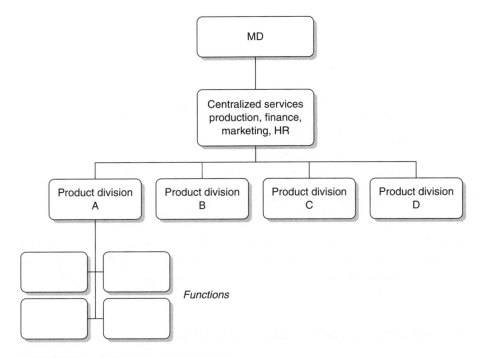

FIGURE 8.6   The divisional structure

internal environment where a large pool of ideas will become the basis for new products or services.

Burns and Stalker (1961) were the first to study how organizational structures might be effective in this respect. As explained in Chapter 2, their research in the electronics industry on technological innovation identified two ideal types of organizational structure that tend to characterize these firms, namely mechanistic and organic structures. Mechanistic structures tend to be evident in environments which are stable, while organic structures usually exist under more turbulent conditions. Mechanistic structures are characterized by formal relationships and communication channels that operate on a hierarchical basis (Heap, 1989). Research indicates that mechanistic structures characterized by rigid rules and procedures with a formal and clear chain of command, where decisions are made by the top management and employee involvement is relatively limited, often inhibit creativity (Kopnowski, 1972). Such structures are also characterized by limited top-down information networks, with a strong emphasis on following rules (Kimberley, 1981). Although mechanistic structures can aid the effectiveness and performance of firms by enforcing rules, regulations and common systems of control, studies also highlight how they should not be adopted by organizations where high levels of change and creative thinking are needed (Kreitner et al., 2002; Shalley et al., 2000).

In contrast, organic structures are better suited to rapidly changing external environments where innovation is perceived as an important factor in maintaining a firm's competitive advantage (Zaltman et al., 1973). Contrary to the mechanistic form, organic structures endorse more informal and participative interaction and communication. A study with scientists by Andrews and Farris (1967), for instance, shows how creativity levels were higher when managers paid attention to their employees' worries and allowed them to offer input into the decision-making process. Employees operating in such organic structures are given autonomy and discretion over how and when their tasks were performed, and their extensive training enabled them to deal with a variety of problems without the need for extensive controls. Hatcher et al.'s (1989) study also found a positive relationship between autonomy and creativity. Their research supported the notion that the more discretion one has over his/her work the more likely it is for ideas to be generated in the work setting. As Lovelace (1986: 165) noted: 'an organic, decentralised structure will provide the creative individual with freedom sufficient to be creative'. Similarly, Arad et al. (1997) suggest that a flat structure that encourages autonomy and team work tends to enhance creativity. This flexibility makes the organic type of organizational structure better equipped to adapt to a changing external environment in promoting processes of change, creativity and innovation.

The main implication of these findings is that the type of organizational structure that a firm adopts will be a critical factor for endorsing or inhibiting individual and team creativity in the work setting. Structural forms affect many of the variables discussed above, such as discretion over task, freedom and autonomy. For example, mechanistic structures tend to emphasize a unidirectional top-down flow of information along hierarchical lines where employees are told what to do by their line managers (Affuah, 2003; Porter and Roberts, 1976). In contrast, structures in creative organizations need to be flexible, with few rules and regulations, loose job descriptions and high autonomy. Brand (1998) therefore notes that creative organizations should adopt flat structures since these allow for important decisions to be made at all levels.

Systems

Organizational structures often dictate what employees should do, but do not tell us what managers need to do in order to keep their employees motivated and passionate in their tasks (Hill and Jones, 1995). What we need to look into are the specific organizational systems that support and promote creativity at work (Shalley et al., 2000). These often relate to the careful planning and management of goal setting, and the appropriate use of reward and recognition systems.

Goal setting and reward systems

A number of studies have examined the effects of rewards and goals on creativity. In the 1990s, Locke and Latham (1990) noted the significance of goal setting as a means of enhancing employees' performance and increasing business productivity. Since then, Mumford (2000) has argued that organizations managing creative people should:

- Define goals and objectives in broad terms, focusing more on the generation of ideas rather than their implementation. By doing this, employees are given the opportunity to approach the problem at hand as they deem best (Tesluk et al., 1997).

- Focus on how the work is carried out rather than on its outcomes (Zhou, 1998). They should concentrate on the strategies that are adopted by creative individuals, while at the same time they should provide support so that problems can be resolved.

The notion of reward is widely used in organizations to compensate employees' contribution; it is defined by Maund (2001: 431) as: 'something which is given or received for behaviour that is commendable and valuable'. Rewards can range from monetary (financial rewards) to non-monetary rewards (recognition or praise). Recognition programmes may, for instance, entail managers making sure that inventors are known and recognized across the company through relevant articles and presentations (Brand, 1998). For example, 3M (the company behind Post-it Notes) recognizes its innovators by organizing an Oscar night once a year to celebrate their successes (Affuah, 2003). However, Zell (2001) highlights that the extent to which organizations should praise or recognize creative effort is critical and warns that too much glorification and exposure of 'successful' projects may cause resentment among employees and lead to resistance to new ideas. Bouwen and Fry (1988: 13), for example, argue that 'part of managing novelty is therefore concerned with how the enterprise allows and rewards such courageous persons to emerge and attract others' attention'. Interestingly, Sternberg et al. (1997) highlight how employees' thinking-style preferences follow the reward structure of their environment. In other words, goals and rewards should be as informative as possible and should not be considered as a fixed evaluative mechanism. Employees should be rewarded both for their overall behaviour and the generation of new processes and practices that improve current thinking (Shalley and Gilson, 2004).

A series of studies by Amabile (1979, 1983, 1990) suggest that the use of extrinsic rewards can suppress creativity. Amabile (1998) proposes that organizations aiming to enhance the generation and implementation of new ideas should consistently reward creativity up to the point that money is not perceived as a 'bribe'. Edwards (1989) also highlights that rewarding for creativity within the working environment means that some employees will inevitably receive higher rewards than their counterparts whose contribution is limited. Therefore, companies adopting such a policy are more likely to focus on the performance and creativity measurement procedures rather than the creative process *per se* (Edwards and Sproull, 1984).

Conversely, several authors suggest that 'bribing' may be conducive to creativity if a 'bonus' reflects a confirmation of one's competence, or is used as a means of enabling one to do better, more interesting, work in the future (Abbey and Dickson, 1983; Cummings, 1965). Such 'bonus' systems may take the form of financial rewards or non-monetary praise. Quinn's (1985) empirical study identifies the importance of achievement for the innovator and observes that this sense of achievement can provide these individuals with clear satisfiers of economic, psychological and career goals. In the same line of argument, Eisenberger and Armeli (1997) argue that rewards are not always bad for creativity. However, they suggest that two factors need to be considered:

- What types of behaviours are being rewarded? Rewards may be used to offer important information to employees about the thinking styles that get rewarded.

- How are the rewards being distributed? Rewards should be associated and linked to the creative process as well as the actual creative output.

In sum, while the content of reward packages may include monetary rewards, they should also consider non-monetary rewards, such as: providing employees the freedom to work in areas that interest them; encouraging risk taking; praising employees on an informal or formal basis; and providing intellectual stimulation that is valued by creative individuals (Adair, 1990).

Evaluation

Closely linked to rewards is the important element of evaluating employees' creative contribution and output. In this respect, one stream of research proposes that evaluation can have a negative effect on creativity (Amabile, 1979, 1990); whilst another stream suggests that evaluation may have a positive effect on intrinsic motivation and creativity (Shalley, 1995). Amabile (1998), for instance, stresses the notion of 'negativity bias' as a severe consequence when evaluating employees for their creative output. She argues that a culture of evaluation encourages staff to concentrate their time and effort on external rewards (extrinsic motivation) that may have negative effects on intrinsic motivation. She also notes how a culture of evaluation is more likely to create a climate of fear and how feelings of negativity may arise in response to the way managers treat people whose ideas are not implemented. Nevertheless, a number of field experiments have demonstrated that supportive, informative evaluations can enhance an intrinsically motivated state that is conducive to creativity (Cummings, 1965; Deci and Ryan, 1985). In this respect, Shalley (1995) has undertaken two studies to assess the effect of evaluation on creativity. Although the first study revealed that there is no significant relationship, the second study identified that creative individuals working on their own with clear creative goals and assessment procedures, demonstrated high levels of creativity.

Although these two schools of thought propose opposing views on the importance of evaluation for assessing individual creativity, research increasingly suggests that organizations should focus on performance feedback rather than evaluation *per se*. This research also spotlights how creative individuals are often sensitive to negative feedback (Andrews and Gordon, 1970). Shalley and Perry-Smith (2001), for example, argue that creativity is enhanced when creative individuals expect and get constructive feedback on how their performance can be improved. Similarly, Zhou (2003) adds that feedback that focuses on providing information to learn from, to enhance future performance, leads to higher levels of creativity. In analysing employee evaluation, Shalley and Gilson (2004) conclude that there are two elements that managers of creative organizations should focus on. First, on how feedback is communicated to creative individuals and, second, to provide constructive and developmental feedback that aims to improve creative outcomes.

Resources

Once an organization's strategy is established and a corporate structure is in place, the focus turns to the necessary 'means' to achieve corporate goals. Proponents of the resource-based view (RBV) argue that the firm develops competitive advantage through its resource base (Grant, 1991; Wernerfelt, 1984). In other words, emphasis is placed on the role of managers in the acquisition, development and effective deployment of its physical, human and organizational resources in ways that add inimitable value (that is, value that cannot be easily replicated by competitors), and not only on selecting areas of competitive advantage in the operating environment (Barney, 1991; Colbert, 2004). Grant (1991) also refers to the importance of developing sustainable competitive advantage which cannot be easily eroded or replicated by competitors. He points out four characteristics of resources that are important determinants in sustaining competitive advantage:

- *Durability:* this represents the rate at which resources depreciate or become obsolete over time. One may argue that increased technological change and shorter product life cycles will contribute to physical resources being less durable than intangible assets such as reputation (brand and corporate image).

- *Transparency:* this reflects the degree of difficulty others experience in determining the source of competitive advantage. The less transparent an advantage the more difficult it is to imitate.

- *Transferability:* this relates to the ability to acquire a source of advantage once it has been identified. This ability may be hampered by: geographic immobility (for example, the cost of relocating equipment and hiring highly specialized staff may put the company in a disadvantaged position against existing companies which already own them); imperfect information (for example, knowledge built up over time about the productivity of resources is hard to assess externally); firm-specific resources (for example, an employee's performance may be affected by situational and motivational factors which are firm-specific); and the immobility of capabilities. On this latter point, Grant (1991: 127) notes that even, 'if the resources that constitute the team are transferred, the nature of organizational routines – in particular the role of tacit knowledge and unconscious coordination – make the recreation of capabilities within a new corporate environment uncertain'.

- *Replicability:* this refers to the extent to which a competitor can reproduce the source of advantage.

This approach demonstrates how organizational resources that are valuable (contribute to a firm's efficiency), rare (are not widely held) and non-substitutable (where different resources cannot perform the same task) can yield sustained competitive advantage (Dierickx and Cool, 1989; Meyer, 1991). Managers need to recognize that this bundle of assets is central to an organization's competitive position (Dierickx and Cool, 1989). As such, organizations need to supply employees with sufficient resources, establish effective communication systems and, most importantly, provide staff with challenging work in order to increase their creative/innovative output. We now look at each of these in more detail.

Sufficient resourcing

The generation of new and useful ideas often necessitates access to a diverse range of resources. But what do we mean by 'resources'? Chatterjee and Wernerfelt (1991) classify resources into three main categories, namely: physical, intangible and financial. Physical resources in general are fixed in nature and include a company's buildings as well as its raw materials and equipment. Intangible assets, on the other hand, include brand names, patents, reputation, trademarks and the firm's innovative capability (for example, the knowledge, skills and competencies of people). Financial resources refer to the financial holdings of a company (equity, debt, cash flow, etc.) and these can provide some resource flexibility in enabling the acquisition (purchase) of other types of productive resources.

Damanpour (1991) argues that the most important determinant of success in any creative endeavour is the acquisition of the necessary resources. Especially in the formative stages of development, acquiring resources is a key activity of entrepreneurial ventures. Interestingly, research has indicated that firms which tend to strongly focus on financial resources are more inclined to restrain the development of new products (Hitt et al., 1994, 1996). In contrast, companies that focus on strategic rather than financial controls tend to thrive in the development and commercialization of new products (Mumford, 2000). Studies also show how initiating and sustaining seed money throughout an organization provides employees with ample opportunities to develop their ideas and that this is conducive to organizational creativity (for example, Jelinek and Schoonhoven, 1990).

Apart from the financial funds necessary to pursue ideas that seem noteworthy, Amabile (1998) adds that time is also a very vital resource in enhancing or (if managed poorly) hindering creativity. Several authors argue that central to individual creativity is the provision of adequate time to experiment with different ideas/concepts in order to discover and develop new and useful solutions to problems at hand (Amabile, 1998; Ford, 1995; Mumford, 2002). Thus, when supervisors do not allow the time for proper experimentation in the initial phase of idea generation, they are in fact standing in the way of the creative process (Andriopoulos, 2001). Experimenting and trying new approaches rather than relying on tried and accepted routines requires time (Shalley and Gilson, 2004). Although time is a valuable resource, commercial pressures often further constrain this resource when one considers that companies today are often racing against time to bring new ideas to the marketplace. Undeniably, the business pressures for change and innovation have forced employees to put in longer hours than expected in the continuous drive for new ideas or creative improvements on existing innovations (Florida, 2002).

Empirical studies have also demonstrated that creative individuals working in project-based environments tend to adjust both their pace of work and their style of interaction according to the time they have on their hands (Frye and Stritch, 1964; Isenberg, 1981; McGrath and Kelly, 1986). Studies reveal that unlimited time may not always have positive outcomes as time enhances creativity only up to a point (Nohria and Gulati, 1996). This is because creative individuals may lose focus when they have a lot of time on their hands (since their activities or tasks are often ambiguous in nature) and may pursue activities that are irrelevant to the problem at hand (Fiest, 1997). In fact, many scholars in the creativity literature claim that tight deadlines spark creative thinking. For instance, McGrath and Kelly (1986) discovered that when individuals are brought together under high time pressure, they manage to solve problems at a higher rate. Isenberg's (1981) laboratory experiments generated similar results where work teams under strict time constraints tended to communicate at a faster pace and used autocratic decision-making processes in order to solve the problem at hand.

Amabile and her colleagues, who argue that creativity is hindered by tight constraints, have challenged the notion that breakthrough ideas thrive under pressure. Their research with 177 employees from seven companies in the USA concludes that the more time pressure employees experience on a given day, the less likely they are to think creatively (Amabile et al., 2002: 57). However, their article in the *Harvard Business Review* identifies one exception to this rule: namely, that certain individuals *do* show high levels of creative thinking under time pressure, but that these individuals are able to come up with creative ideas because of specific working conditions. The most important of these are the following:

- They tend to focus on a single work activity for a considerable part of the day.

- Concentration on one task entails some level of isolation from external interruptions and collaboration.

- Individuals with high creative output tend to perceive the tight deadlines as 'meaningful energy'. They believe that completing the job at hand is critical to the success of the overall project and, hence, they feel that they are 'on a mission'.

Amabile et al. (2002) conclude their article by suggesting that firms that aim to protect and support creativity in their working environment need to reduce time pressure. But if the circumstances do not allow firms the ability to reduce commercial time constraints, developing one's mindset towards the idea that the work at hand is critical and the time pressure justifiable, may go some way to counterbalancing these negative effects.

Apart from adequate financial resources and sufficient time, colleagues are another important resource for sparking creativity and innovation in the work setting. One often needs to have access to expertise that spans different knowledge fields in order to gain the information needed to tackle challenging problems or capitalize on promising opportunities. In this respect, Mumford et al. (2002) identify the substantial impact of colleagues in the development and implementation of novel and useful ideas, while Zhou (2003) notes how the presence of creative role models influence how people behave. Interestingly, Bandura (1986) also identifies how individuals tend to display similar types of behaviours to those they observe. But is this true for individuals within innovative environments? If so, does it make sense to assume that employees who observe others being creative are also encouraged to be creative?

The presence of creative role models at work has generated mixed results with regard to their effect on individual creativity (Amabile et al., 1996). One stream of studies supports the notion that the presence of creative role models encourages observers to display relatively high levels of creativity (Bloom and Sosniak, 1981; Mueller, 1978); but another stream of research suggests that the presence of creative role models causes observers to display relatively low levels of creativity (Zimmerman and Dialessi, 1973). Why do these findings conflict? Research highlights how creativity is hampered in situations where people work in front of their bosses, clients or colleagues who are likely to evaluate their performance (Sutton and Kelley, 1997). In such circumstances, employees tend to adopt tried and trusted approaches that can enhance their reputation or will be easy to justify later (the *social facilitation effect*) rather than trying new methods that require learning or involve tasks that are novel to them (otherwise called the *social inhibition effect*) (see Sutton and Galunic, 1996; Tetlock, 1991; Zajonc, 1965). The inconclusive nature of these results suggests that the relationship between the presence of creative role models and creativity is very complicated (Amabile et al., 1996; Halpin et al., 1979).

In situations where information exchange and collaboration must be preserved, founders or managers need to ensure that political problems are kept to a minimum. Amabile (1998), for instance, suggests that infighting, politicking and gossiping are detrimental to creativity since they can divert people's attention away from the task/problem at hand. Martins and Terblanche (2003) also note that employees should be taught that differences of opinion must be tolerated, since this gives them the opportunity to be exposed to dilemmas or conflicts that promote openness in communication. In short, individuals are more likely to feel intrinsically motivated to solve problems when they see their colleagues similarly energized by their jobs, rather than in situations where competitive cliques are seen to be in competition with one another.

Interestingly, Amabile (1998) introduces the notion of the 'threshold of sufficiency' with regard to all the necessary resources for sustaining creativity in the workplace. She argues that when resources are added above a certain threshold,

creativity and innovation are not enhanced. However, Rosner (1968) emphasizes the importance of slack resources and highlights how slack allows a firm to
acquire innovations, absorb failure and explore new ideas in advance of an
actual need. Conversely, when resources are below the desired threshold, creativity is likely to be hindered because creative individuals focus on the problem
of finding additional resources rather than concentrating on generating new
ideas/concepts. In addition, Amabile et al. (1996) suggest that employees' perceptions of the adequacy of resources may affect them psychologically by leading to beliefs about the intrinsic value of the projects that they have undertaken.

In summary, research in this area has identified the need for: sufficient funds,
adequate time for developing new products and new ideas, relevant information, and sufficient material resources in order to fully support creativity and
innovation in the workplace (Amabile and Gryskiewicz, 1989).

Systems of communication

The relationship between creativity and communication has long been recognized by scholars in this area, to the extent that creativity itself has even been
defined as: 'making and communicating meaningful connections' (Isaksen and
Treffinger, 1985: 13).

Communication is an active, dynamic process that aims to facilitate understanding (Hyatt, 1992). Numerous studies recognize that internal communication within work groups, as well as regular contact with external groups, all
need to be carefully managed when aiming to mobilize organizational creativity and innovation (Dougherty and Hardy, 1996; Keller, 2001). Research has
highlighted how managers of creative firms need to find ways to promote both
group communication and the acquisition of external information (Mumford
et al., 2002). Internally, knowledge can be exchanged across divisions by forming
and capitalizing on personal relationships (Zell, 2001). Osborn (1963) as well as
Parnes and Noller (1972), argue that the probability of creative idea generation
increases as exposure to other potentially relevant ideas extends. Basadur
(2004) suggests that one of the most effective ways to encourage employees to
think creatively is to introduce an 'employee suggestion' system. By so doing,
employees openly discuss feedback on problems faced and solutions implemented. Likewise, Martins and Terblanche (2003) show how an 'open-door'
policy between individuals and groups enables a more open exchange of information that supports the development and implementation of new products or
ideas. Moreover, Stringer (2000) proposes that organizations that want to stimulate
innovation in their workplace must first establish autonomous teams, otherwise
called 'idea markets' or 'knowledge markets', and that these teams should
consist of internal entrepreneurs with a remit to identify and commercialize radical innovations. However, this may only occur when sanctioned by corporate
strategy and consistent with a balanced, properly resourced project portfolio.
Nowadays, the evolution of information technology has given rise to management software packages that allow these 'idea markets' to operate electronically
across geographical and functional boundaries.

Ruef's (2003) research spotlights how networking with acquaintances and strangers outside the organization is critical to creativity and innovation in organizational settings. The study of alumni entrepreneurs from Stanford Business School challenges the popular belief that networking with like-minded colleagues creates new information; Ruef concludes that acquaintances or colleagues who are not friends are more likely to serve as a bridge between disconnected social groups. In other words, these 'external' interactions allow for experimentation in bringing together ideas from disparate sources. More specifically, Ruef's study suggests that entrepreneurs who interact with a diverse range of groups (ranging from family members and business colleagues to acquaintances and complete strangers) are three times more likely to innovate than their counterparts, who limit themselves to a stable social network. Similarly, Zhou and George (2003) propose that the generation of new ideas is enhanced when creative individuals are exposed to novel information that they might not usually come across. For example, a creative employee attending a training or conference session may encounter information that is not directly related to his/her area of expertise and, in so doing, broaden their point of view (George and Jones, 2001). Building on the notion that it may be easier to make novel connections between apparently disparate ideas, Hallmark Cards developed an online community where the connection between the company and the marketplace is used to produce a rich dialogue of perspectives and experiences (Brailsford, 2001). This web-based collaborative environment includes a bulletin board, an on-line chat room and a resource centre where community members can post articles or suggest websites that may be of interest to others in the community. Its central objective is to encourage community members to contribute topics, which in turn will provide the basis for useful learning and product development in Hallmark Cards. An important aspect of this effort has been the connection to external audiences which gives the company an opportunity to gain insights that are 'out there' which may potentially contribute to new business opportunities (Brailsford, 2001).

The research within IDEO by Sutton and Kelley (1997), illustrates some of the benefits of bringing outsiders into creative environments, namely:

- *Bringing new knowledge.* The continuous flow of clients keeps the company up to date with the latest developments from a diverse range of industries.

- *Teaching creative individuals to interact with outsiders.* The constant influx of visitors, whether these are students, researchers, journalists, suppliers or even job candidates, provides employees with the opportunity to build their interpersonal skills and not just their technical expertise.

- *Breaking-down stereotypes.* Individuals in general fear change and, despite the fact that many people claim to value novel ideas, there is strong evidence that they do not like them. More specifically, Zajonc (1968) states that one of the most solid findings in psychology is the 'mere-exposure effect': people like most what is familiar to them. The more they hear or study something, the more comfortable they become and the more they like it. This is also true for interpersonal relationships. For instance, by working with outsiders,

IDEO's employees are not overly influenced by negative stereotypes when they collaborate with others on projects. Individuals get better information about one another through open communication and interaction, and this makes them more able to appreciate each other's viewpoints and strengths (Sutton and Kelley, 1997).

Project selection

As we have already mentioned, employees within creative and innovative environments are motivated when the tasks at hand are complex and intellectually challenging (Amabile, 1988; Hackman and Oldham, 1980). Managers of creative organizations have an important role in selecting work that is commercially or creatively interesting, and which offers ample opportunities for exploration (Andriopoulos, 2003; Andriopoulos and Lowe, 2000). Usually, companies select projects because they offer opportunities which can aid the firm in the generation of income or valuable publicity. However, when firms select projects because of their innovative nature (or requirements) they often stimulate the creative environment and raise employee interest. Not surprisingly, studies in the creativity literature have shown that complex and challenging projects are more likely to get people excited about their work, which in turn usually provides them with the motivation to complete the projects on time (Oldham and Cummings, 1996). Cummings and Oldham (1997) identify the following benefits when employees are involved in highly complex jobs:

- They are able to perceive the significance of, and exercise responsibility for, the whole of their work.

- They have the discretion to assess options about how and when the work gets done using a variety of skills.

- They are more open to receive enough feedback from the work itself to monitor their progress.

Stringer (2000) also highlights the importance of freeing-up employees' time so that they can experiment with wild ideas. Similarly, Peters and Waterman (1982) argue that the initiation and existence of informal project laboratories in 3M were behind the radical new products introduced by the company. From our own research, we have found that the selection of suitable work happens in two ways. First, the managers of the companies that we have studied consciously and actively try to attract or generate projects which are relevant to their services or their employees' interests or hobbies (Andriopoulos, 2003). Second, projects, which come as a result of existing clients or through word of mouth, are evaluated against the company's current portfolio of projects, as well as against the opportunity to creatively experiment or innovate. Both these elements are carefully considered before they are included in the company's portfolio.

Several authors (Amabile, 1998; Amabile and Gryskiewicz, 1989; Paolillo and Brown, 1978; Siegel and Kaemmerer, 1978) also emphasize the importance of appropriately matching individuals to work assignments (on the basis of both skills and interests), to maximize a sense of positive challenge in the work that in turn enhances employees' creative abilities. Amabile (1997), for instance, suggests that employees are more likely to be creative in pursuits that they enjoy. If employees do not enjoy an activity, they will not invest the substantial amounts of time and energy necessary to succeed in it. Managers should therefore try to match people with jobs that are related to their expertise and their skills in creative thinking and thereby ignite intrinsic motivation. Interestingly, Pfeffer (1998) in his article in the *Harvard Business Review* entitled: 'Six dangerous myths about pay', highlights how people work harder when they find meaning in their work and when the work is considered to be fun. He also warns that companies, which do not pay enough attention to this parameter and instead prefer to 'bribe' their employees, will have to face the consequences of disloyalty and lack of employee commitment. Amabile (1998) also stresses the importance of the amount of stretch in project selection. She argues that employees should not be stretched either too little, since they will feel bored, or too much, since this is likely to make them feel overwhelmed and threatened by a loss of control. Ensuring a good match between projects and project members requires that managers possess rich and detailed information about their employees and available assignments. In practice, such information is often difficult and time consuming to gather.

Conclusion

In attempting to create an environment conducive to creativity and innovation, several variables need to be taken into consideration. This chapter has shown how the generation of new ideas or products can only flourish under the right conditions. To summarize, we have shown:

- The need to translate strategic goals into tangible objectives and measures, and the importance of the internal environment to enhancing creativity and innovation.

- How organic structures are better suited to rapidly changing external environments where innovation is perceived as an important factor in maintaining a firm's competitive advantage.

- That there are two elements that managers of creative organizations should focus on when evaluating their employees. First, on how feedback is communicated to creative individuals and, second, to provide constructive and developmental feedback in order to improve creative outcomes.

- How the generation of new ideas is enhanced when creative individuals interact with a diverse range of groups (ranging from family members and business colleagues to acquaintances and complete strangers). Such employees are three times more likely to innovate than their counterparts, who limit themselves to a stable social network.

- That complex and challenging projects are more likely to get people excited about their work, which in turn usually inspires them to complete the projects on time.

- The complex nature of these variables and the key role of managers in balancing the needs of employees and their business.

- The need to adopt a holistic approach in organizing structures, systems and resources.

RESOURCES, READINGS AND REFLECTIONS

CASE 8.1   FLOODGATES OPEN UP TO A SEA OF IDEAS
BY SIMON LONDON

(Source: *Financial Times,* 7 June 2005)

Procter & Gamble (P&G) is an unlikely poster child for innovation. The 170-year-old maker of wet wipes and shampoo is based in Cincinnati, Ohio, far from the technology hotbeds of California or Massachusetts. Since 2000, the group has cut research and development spending as a percentage of sales and focused resources on a handful of big brands. Yet what looks at first glance like retrenchment is actually far more interesting. The company, once renowned for its inward looking culture, these days gets about one-third of its product ideas from outside. AG Lafley, chairman and chief executive, has set a target of 50 per cent under an initiative dubbed *Connect and Develop.*

'P&G is one of the most aggressive adopters of the open innovation model,' says Henry Chesbrough, professor of management at the University of California, Berkeley. The open approach stems from a realisation that corporate labs can no longer be expected to carry the full burden of innovation. Knowledge is so widely distributed and, thanks to the internet, travels so fast that great ideas can come from rank and file employees, customers, suppliers, competitors, universities or lone inventors. Yet the pressure on companies to innovate has never been greater. Yesterday's market leaders can easily become tomorrow's has-beens. Just think of Kodak, which failed to move fast enough to embrace the digital photography revolution, or General Motors' tumbling US market share. 'There are all kinds of alternatives to innovation. In the short term you can cut costs, you can make acquisitions; you can buy back your own shares. But in the medium to long term there is no alternative,' says Gary Hamel, visiting professor at the London Business School.

Yet P&G's focus on its core brands is a reminder that great ideas from whatever source must be turned into hard cash. The company learned the hard way that internet incubators, corporate venture capital funds and other artefacts of the dotcom era under most circumstances destroy more value than they create. Enlightened pragmatism is now the order of the day.

Thus P&G's Crest brand has been revitalised by the launch of Crest Whitestrips, a tooth whitening product, and the Crest Spinbrush line of inexpensive, battery powered toothbrushes. The former was developed by internal R&D, the latter acquired from the company that pioneered the category. Launching both under the Crest name has transformed the brand from mere toothpaste into an oral care franchise.

This blend of openness, discipline and focus on the core business captures the innovation zeitgeist. The resurgence of Apple Computer, maker of the iconic iPod digital music player, is built on similar foundations. While Steve Jobs, co-founder and CEO, presents the facade of lone, maverick genius the reality is different. Apple has long been happy to embrace ideas from the outside. Thus the electronic guts of the iPod were engineered by PortalPlayer, a small company headquartered not far from Apple in Silicon Valley.

Similarly, Apple's much praised OS-X operating system, which powers the company's resurgent personal computers, is based on Unix, the operating system that runs many of the world's big corporate data centres. None of this is to deny Apple's talent for product design, user interface and marketing. But its willingness to embrace ideas from outside has leveraged these talents into a remarkable corporate renewal.

Another lesson from the iPod's success is that innovation is about more than just products. To be sure, the iPod is a neat consumer gadget. But Mr Jobs' real breakthrough was persuading record companies to make their music available at 99 cents per download via iTunes, Apple's online music store. Yes, iTunes without iPod might have succeeded. The iPod without iTunes probably would have sold by the lorry load. But it is the combination of hardware, software and business model that produced a cultural phenomenon.

For innovation junkies this is old news. Business model innovation was one of the hot topics of the 1990s. The most successful US companies of the decade – think of Dell or Southwest Airlines – offered not breakthrough products but breakthrough ways to deliver familiar products. Yet all too often we think of innovation as something practised by engineers rather than the unsung heroes of sales, marketing, finance or administration. This is a costly mistake according to proponents of 'business process' innovation. Here, the emphasis is on finding new ways of working that cut costs or add value for customers. Whereas business model innovations tend to be grand in conception, business process innovations are more often incremental, cumulative and, frankly, mundane to all but industry insiders.

P&G's Connect and Develop programme is an example. The company's business model selling branded consumer products through third party retailers is the same as ever. But the process by which ideas are identified and developed is being transformed. It is innovating in innovation. The competitive advantage of some companies rests squarely on their ability to improve continually on established

(Continued)

(Continued)

ways of working. Wal-Mart, the world's largest retailer, has pioneered a range of process innovations that, taken together, have changed the face of retailing. For example, the Arkansas based company was a pioneer of 'cross docking' in which consumer goods companies deliver products direct from the factory to stores.

For the next wave of process innovation, look to China. In *The Only Sustainable Edge*, published earlier this year, authors John Hagel and John Seely Brown argue that the success of China's low cost manufacturers stems not only from cheap labour but also from the finely honed ability to orchestrate specialist suppliers. Combined with modular product designs, this enables them to deliver a huge variety of products at implausibly low prices. Write Messrs Hagel and Seely Brown: 'these models of innovation spell out a clear message for many companies in the developed world: if you are not participating in the mass market segment of emerging economies, you're not developing the capabilities you will need to compete back home.'

Facing low cost competitors is bad enough. But how do you compete against products that are free? This is the dilemma confronting companies such as Microsoft, Oracle and Sun Microsystems as they try to combat software developed by the open source community of programmers. If you picture the open source movement as a small collection of bearded idealists, think again. Thousands – perhaps tens of thousands – of programmers are collaborating to build operating systems, databases and other software that rival huge civil engineering projects in terms of scale and complexity. So far, the economic impact is restricted mainly to software. But companies in other knowledge-based industries cannot afford to relax. Already reference book publishers find themselves competing against free online products such as Wikipedia, the 'open source' encyclopedia. Open source textbooks may be not far behind. Blogs and other forms of 'participatory journalism' are challenging the hegemony of traditional media over news and views.

The common thread is that open innovation starts to dissolve the distinction between producers and consumers, between 'us' and 'them'. This challenges companies to change not only innovation processes but also corporate mindsets. Eric von Hippel, professor at Massachusetts Institute of Technology, argues that demanding consumers have long been customising mass produced products to fit their exacting needs. In adventure sports technical innovations often originate with elite practitioners. Similarly, Linux, the open source computer operating system, had its genesis when Linus Torvalds, then a computer science student in his native Finland, was trying to find a way to run Unix on his personal computer. Since no suitable software was then available, he decided to build his own. The lesson, argues Prof von Hippel, is that companies should stay in close touch with their most demanding and sophisticated customers.

One company moving in this direction is Intel, the largest semiconductor company. In a spirit of open innovation, Intel has over the last five years built a network of small 'lablets' based on university campuses to supplement its conventional R&D operation. Through the resulting contacts, it hopes to stay in touch with emerging technologies. The next step: put lablet researchers in direct contact with companies that could benefit from immediate application of far out technologies. The hope is that this combination of lead users and open innovators will yield new insights. 'Researchers are always accused of technology push,' says David Tennenhouse, Intel's director of research, 'now we are trying to create customer pull.'

Another sign of changing times is the emergence of a breed of innovation intermediaries. Innocentive, a spin off from Eli Lilly, the pharmaceuticals company, uses an international network of scientists and engineers to solve problems brought to it by corporate clients. Cash rewards are offered for successful solutions. Innocentive takes a cut. Many of Innocentive's problem solvers are freelance – university professors supplementing their income – or retired industrial researchers. Others are established research labs with spare capacity. Whether Innocentive's innovative business model is robust remains to be seen. But its very existence underlines that there is a worldwide well of inventiveness and knowledge waiting to be tapped.

To be sure, the open innovation model raises tricky management questions:

- What degree of openness is appropriate for any particular project?
- How will intellectual property rights be protected?
- What skills are required to co-ordinate an extended network of collaborators?

Don't expect old style corporate research labs to disappear in the near future. There will always be value in patented products developed in private. But there is much more to the management of innovation in an educated, networked world.

Questions

1. What are the new challenges for creative/innovative companies?
2. Can firms maintain their competitive advantage by not taking into consideration these changes? Why or why not?
3. Based on this case, which structure has the greatest practical application from those discussed in this chapter? Explain your rationale.
4. This case undoubtedly stresses the importance of a firm's structure, systems and resources. Which do you think will be the most important in the future?

Chapter questions

The questions listed below relate to the chapter as a whole and can be used by individuals to further reflect on the material covered, as well as serving as a source for more open group discussion and debate.

1. Which are the key elements of an organizational structure?

2. What are the main problems associated with tall structures?

3. In your opinion, what are the most common factors that managers need to consider in order to select the most appropriate and effective structure? Be as specific as you can and support your arguments.

4. Which are the most popular traditional structures?

5. What do managers need to do in order to keep their employees motivated and passionate in their tasks?

6. What does Amabile mean by the notion of the 'threshold of sufficiency'?

7. Why is project selection important in enhancing creativity and innovation in the workplace? Please discuss.

Hands-on exercise

Students are allocated to small groups and are required to undertake a study by researching 3M's informal laboratories. They should collect articles through the company's website, magazines or newspapers, which explain the process, its pros and cons. Student groups are expected to make a brief presentation based on their findings.

Team debate exercise

Debate the following statement:

> *An 'open-door' policy is conducive to the generation and implementation of new and useful ideas.*

Divide the class into two groups. One should argue as convincingly as possible that the open exchange of knowledge is imperative to the company's success and the well-being of its employees. The other group should prepare arguments highlighting the problems that may arise from having such a policy for increasing organizational effectiveness. Each group should be prepared to defend their ideas against the other group's arguments by using real-life examples.

References

Abbey, A. and Dickson, J.W. (1983) 'R&D work climate and innovation in semiconductors', *Academy of Management Journal*, 26: 362–8.

Adair, J. (1990) *The Challenge of Innovation*. London: Kogan Page.

Affuah, A. (2003) *Innovation Management*. Oxford: Oxford University Press.

Aiken, M. and Hage, J. (1971) 'The organic organization and innovation', *Sociology*, 5: 63–82.

Amabile, T.M. (1979) 'Effects of external evaluation on artistic creativity', *Journal of Personality and Social Psychology*, 37: 221–33.

Amabile, T.M. (1983) *The Social Psychology of Creativity*. New York: Springer-Verlag.

Amabile, T.M. (1988) 'A model of creativity and innovation in organizations', in B.M. Staw and L.L. Cummings (eds), *Research in Organizational Behaviour*, Vol. 10. Stamford, CT: JAI Press.

Amabile, T.M. (1990) 'Within you, without you: the social psychology of creativity and beyond', in M.A. Runco and R.S. Albert (eds), *Theories in Creativity*. Thousand Oaks, CA: Sage.

Amabile, T.M. (1997) 'Motivating creativity in organizations: on doing what you love and loving what you do', *California Management Review*, 40 (1): 39–58.

Amabile, T.M. (1998) 'How to kill creativity', *Harvard Business Review*, 76 (6): 76–87.

Amabile, T.M. and Gryskiewicz, S.S. (1989) 'The creative environment scales: the work environment inventory', *Creativity Research Journal*, 2: 231–54.

Amabile, T.M., Conti, R., Coon, H., Lazenby, J. and Herron, M. (1996) 'Assessing the work environment for creativity', *Academy of Management Journal*, 39: 1154–84.

Amabile, T.M., Hadley, C.N. and Kramer, S.J. (2002) 'Creativity under the gun', *Harvard Business Review*, 80 (8): 52–61.

Andrews, F.M. and Farris, G.F. (1967) 'Supervisory practices and innovation in scientific teams', *Personnel Psychology*, 20: 497–515.

Andrews, F.M. and Gordon, G. (1970) 'Social and organizational factors affecting innovation research', *Proceedings for the American Psychological Association*, 78: 570–89.

Andriopoulos, C. (2001) 'Determinants of organizational creativity: a literature review', *Management Decision*, 39: 834–40.

Andriopoulos, C. (2003) 'Six paradoxes in managing creativity: an embracing act', *Long Range Planning*, 36: 375–88.

Andriopoulos, C. and Lowe, A. (2000) 'Enhancing organizational creativity: the process of perpetual challenging', *Management Decision*, 38: 734–42.

Arad, S., Hanson, M.A. and Schneider, R.J. (1997) 'A framework for the study of relationships between organizational characteristics and organizational innovation', *Journal of Creative Behavior*, 31: 42–58.

Bandura, A. (1986) *Social Foundations of Thought and Action: A Social Cognitive Theory*. Englewood Cliffs, NJ: Prentice Hall.

Barney, J.B. (1991) 'Firm resources and sustained competitive advantage', *Journal of Management*, 17: 99–120.

Basadur, M. (2004) 'Leading others to think innovatively together: creative leadership', *Leadership Quarterly*, 15: 103–21.

Bloom, B.S. and Sosniak, L.A. (1981) 'Talent development vs. schooling', *Educational Leadership*, 39 (2): 86–94.

Bouwen, R. and Fry, R. (1988) 'An agenda for managing organizational innovation and development in the 1990s', in M. Lambrecht (ed.), *Corporate Revival*. Leuven: Catholic University Press.

Braam, G.J.M. and Nijssen, E.J. (2004) 'Performance effects of using the balanced scorecard: a note on the Dutch experience', *Long Range Planning*, 37: 335–49.

Brailsford, T.W. (2001) 'Building a knowledge economy at Hallmark Cards', *Research Technology Management*, 44 (5): 18–25.

Brand, A. (1998) 'Knowledge management and innovation at 3M', *Journal of Knowledge Management*, 2: 17–22.

Braverman, H. (1974) *Labor and Monopoly Capital. The Degradation of Work in the Twentieth Century*. New York: Monthly Review Press.

Burns, T. and Stalker, G.M. (1961) *The Management of Innovation*. London: Tavistock.

Chandler, A. (1962) *Strategy and Structure: Chapters in the History of the American Industrial Enterprise*. Cambridge, MA: MIT Press.

Chatterjee, S. and Wernerfelt, B. (1991) 'The link between resources and type of diversification: theory and evidence', *Strategic Management Journal*, 12: 33–48.

Cohn, S.F. and Turyn, R.M. (1980) 'The structure of the firm and the adoption of process innovations', *IEEE Transactions on Engineering Management*, 27: 98–102.

Colbert, B.A. (2004) 'The complex resource-based view: implications for theory and practice in strategic human resource management', *Academy of Management Review*, 29 (3): 341–58.

Cummings, A. and Oldham, G.R. (1997) 'Enhancing creativity: managing work contexts for the high potential employee', *California Management Review*, 40 (1): 22–38.

Cummings, L.L. (1965) 'Organizational climates for creativity', *Academy of Management Journal*, 3: 220–7.

Daft, R.L. (1998) *Organization Theory and Design*. St Paul, MN: West.

Damanpour, F. (1991) 'Organizational innovation: a meta-analysis of effects of determinants and moderators', *Academy of Management Journal*, 34: 555–90.

Deci, E.L. and Ryan, R.M. (1985) *Intrinsic Motivation and Self-Determination in Human Behaviour*. New York: Plenum Press.

Dess, G.G., Rasheed, A., McLaughlin, K.J. and Priem, R.L. (1995) 'The new corporate architecture', *Academy of Management Executive*, 9 (3): 7–20.

Dierickx, L. and Cool, K. (1989) 'Asset stock accumulation and sustainability of competitive advantage', *Management Science*, 35: 1504–11.

Dougherty, D. and Hardy, C. (1996) 'Sustained product innovation in large, mature organizations: overcoming innovation-to-organization problems', *Academy of Management Journal*, 39: 1120–53.

Edwards, M.R. (1989) 'Measuring creativity at work: developing a reward-for-creativity policy', *Journal of Creative Behavior*, 23: 26–37.

Edwards, M.R. and Sproull, J.R. (1984) 'Creativity: productivity gold mine?', *Journal of Creative Behavior*, 18: 175–84.

Eisenberger, R. and Armeli, S. (1997) 'Can salient reward increase creative performance without reducing intrinsic creative interest?', *Journal of Personality and Social Psychology*, 72: 652–63.

Fiest, G.J. (1997) 'Quantity, quality, and depth of research as influences on scientific eminence: is quantity most important?', *Creativity Research Journal*, 10: 325–36.

Finkelstein, S. and D'Aveni, R.A. (1994) 'CEO duality as a double-edged sword: how boards of directors balance entrenchment avoidance and unity of command', *Academy of Management Journal*, 37 (5): 1079–108.

Florida, R. (2002) *The Rise of the Creative Class: And How It's Transforming Work, Leisure, Community and Everyday Life*. New York: Basic Books.

Ford, C.M. (1995) 'Creativity is a mystery', in C. M. Ford and D.A. Gioia (eds), *Creativity in Organizations: Ivory Tower Visions and Real World Voices*. Thousand Oaks, CA: Sage.

Frye, R. and Stritch, T. (1964) 'Effect of timed vs. non-timed discussion upon measures of influence and change in small groups', *Journal of Social Psychology*, 63: 139–43.

George, J.M. and Jones, G.R. (2001) 'Toward a process model of individual change in organizations', *Human Relations*, 54: 419–44.

Grant, R.M. (1991) 'The resource-based theory of competitive advantage', *California Management Review*, 33 (3): 114–35.

Gupta, A.K. and Govindarajan, V. (1984) 'Business unit strategy, managerial characteristics, and business unit effectiveness at strategy implementation', *Academy of Management Journal*, 27: 25–41.

Hackman, J.R. and Oldham, G.R. (1980) *Work Redesign*. Reading, MA: Addison-Wesley.

Hage, J. and Aiken, M. (1967) 'Program change and organizational properties, a comparative analysis', *American Journal of Sociology*, 72: 503–19.

Hatcher, L., Ross, T.L. and Collins, D. (1989) 'Prosocial behavior, job complexity, and suggestion contribution under gainsharing plans', *Journal of Applied Behavioral Science*, 25: 231–48.

Heap, J.P. (1989) *The Management of Innovation and Design*. London: Cassell.

Hill, C.W.L. and Jones, G.R. (1995) *Strategic Management: An Integrated Approach*, 3rd edn. Boston, MA: Houghton Mifflin.

Hitt, M.A., Hoskisson, R.E. and Ireland, R.D. (1994) 'A mid-range theory of the interactive effects of international and product diversification on innovation and performance', *Journal of Management*, 20: 297–326.

Hitt, M.A., Hoskisson, R.E., Johnson, R.A. and Moesel, D.D. (1996) 'The market for corporate control and firm innovation', *Academy of Management Journal*, 39: 1084–196.

Hyatt, K. (1992) 'Creativity through interpersonal community dialog', *Journal of Creative Behavior*, 26: 65–71.

Isaksen, S. and Treffinger, D. (1985) *Creative Problem Solving: The Basic Course*. Buffalo, NY: Bearly.

Isenberg, D.J. (1981) 'Some effects of time pressure on vertical structure and decision-making accuracy in small groups', *Organizational Behavior and Human Performance*, 27: 119–34.

Jelinek, M. and Schoonhoven, C.B. (1990) *The Innovation Marathon: Lessons Learned from High Technology Firms*. Oxford: Blackwell.

Kaluzny, A.D., Veney, J.E. and Gentry, J.T. (1974) 'Innovation of health services: a comparative study of hospitals and health departments', *Health and Society*, 52: 51–82.

Kaplan, R.S. and Norton, D.P. (1992) 'The balanced scorecard – measures that drive performance', *Harvard Business Review*, 70 (1): 71–9.

Kaplan, R.S. and Norton, D.P. (1996) *The Balanced Scorecard: Translating Strategy into Action*. Boston, MA: Harvard Business School Press.

Kaplan, R.S. and Norton, D.P. (2001) *The Strategy Focused Organization*. Boston, MA: Harvard Business School Press.

Kaplan, R.S. and Norton, D.P. (2004) 'Measuring the strategic readiness of intangible assets', *Harvard Business Review*, 82 (2): 52–63.

Katzenbach, J.R. and Smith, D.K. (1993) 'The discipline of teams', *Harvard Business Review*, 71 (March–April): 111–20.

Keller, R.T. (2001) 'Cross-functional project groups in research and new product development: diversity, communications, job stress, and outcomes', *Academy of Management Journal*, 44: 546–55.

Kimberley, J.R. (1981) 'Managerial innovation', in P.C. Nyström and W. H. Starbuck (eds), *Handbook of Organizational Design*. Oxford: Oxford University Press.

Kimberley, J.R. and Evanisko, M.J. (1981) 'Organizational innovation: the influence of individual, organizational and contextual factors on hospital adoption of technological and administrative innovations', *Academy of Management Journal*, 24: 689–713.

Kopnowski, E.J. (1972) 'Creativity, man, and organizations', *Journal of Creative Behavior*, 1: 49–54.

Kreitner, R., Kinicki, A. and Buelens, M. (2002) *Organizational Behaviour*. London: McGraw-Hill.

Levitt, T. (1972) 'Production-line approach to service', *Harvard Business Review*, 50 (4) (September–October): 41–52.

Locke, E.A. and Latham, O.P. (1990) 'Work motivation: the high performance cycle', in U. Kleinbeck, H.H. Quast, H. Thierry and H. Häcker (eds), *Work Motivation*. Hillsdale, NJ: Lawrence Erlbaum.

Lovelace, R.F. (1986) 'Stimulating creativity through managerial intervention', *R&D Management*, 16: 161–74.

Martins, E.C. and Terblanche, F. (2003) 'Building organizational culture that simulates creativity and innovation', *European Journal of Innovation Management*, 6: 64–74.

Maund, L. (2001) *An Introduction to Human Resource Management*. Basingstoke: Palgrave.

McGrath, J.E. and Kelly, J.R. (1986) *Time and Human Interaction: Toward a Social Psychology of Time*. New York: Guilford Press.

Meyer, A.D. (1991) 'What is strategy's distinctive competence?', *Journal of Management*, 17: 821–33

Mintzberg, H. (1983) *Structure in Fives: Designing Effective Organizations*. Englewood Cliffs, NJ: Prentice Hall.

Mueller, L.K. (1978) 'Beneficial and detrimental modeling effects on creative response production', *Journal of Psychology*, 98: 253–60.

Mumford, M.D. (2000) 'Managing creative people: strategies and tactics for innovation', *Human Resources Management Review*, 10: 313–51.

Mumford, M.D. (2002) 'Social innovation: ten cases from Benjamin Franklin', *Creativity Research Journal*, 14: 253–66.

Mumford, M.D., Scott, G.M., Gaddis, B. and Strange, J.M. (2002) 'Leading creative people: orchestrating expertise and relationships', *Leadership Quarterly*, 13: 705–50.

Nohria, K. and Gulati, S. (1996) 'Is slack good or bad for innovation?', *Academy of Management Journal*, 39: 799–825.

Oldham, G.R. and Cummings, A. (1996) 'Employee creativity: personal and contextual factors at work', *Academy of Management Journal*, 39: 607–34.

Osborn, A. (1963) *Applied Imagination*, 3rd edn. New York: Charles Scribner's Sons.

Paolillo, J.G. and Brown, W.B. (1978) 'How organizational factors affect R&D innovation', *Research Management*, 7 (March): 12–15.

Parnes, S.J. and Noller, R.B. (1972) 'Applied creativity: the creative studies project part II: results of the two year program', *Journal of Creative Behavior*, 6: 164–86.

Peters, T. and Waterman, R.H., Jr (1982) *In Search of Excellence*. New York: Harper & Row.

Pfeffer, J. (1998) 'Six dangerous myths about pay', *Harvard Business Review*, 76 (3): 108–19.

Porter, L.W. and Roberts, K.H. (1976) 'Communication in organizations', in M.D. Dunnette (ed.), *Handbook of Industrial and Organizational Psychology*. Chicago: Rand McNally.

Quinn, J.B. (1985) 'Managing innovation: controlled chaos', *Harvard Business Review*, 63 (3): 73–84.

Robbins, S.P. and Coulter, M. (2002) *Management*, 7th edn. Englewood Cliffs, NJ: Prentice Hall.

Rogers, E.M. (1983) *Diffusion of Innovations*. New York: The Free Press.

Rosner, M.M. (1968) 'Economic determinants of organizational innovation', *Administrative Science Quarterly*, 12: 614–25.

Ruef, M. (2003) 'Innovators navigate around cliques', *Stanford Business Magazine*. Retrieved 20 December 2004, from http://www.gsb.stanford.edu/news/bmag/sbsm 0305/ideas_ruef_networking.shtml.

Shalley, C.E. (1995) 'Effects of coaction, expected evaluation, and goal setting on creativity and productivity', *Academy of Management Journal*, 38: 483–503.

Shalley, C.E. and Gilson, L.L. (2004) 'What leaders need to know: a review of social and contextual factors that can foster or hinder creativity', *Leadership Quarterly*, 15: 33–53.

Shalley, C.E. and Perry-Smith, J.E. (2001) 'Effects of social–psychological factors on creative performance: the role of informational and controlling expected evaluation and modeling experience', *Organizational Behavior and Human Decision Processes*, 84: 1–22.

Shalley, C.E., Gilson, L.L. and Blum, T.C. (2000) 'Matching creativity requirements and the work environment: effects on satisfaction and intention to leave', *Academy of Management Journal*, 43: 215–23.

Siegel, S.M. and Kaemmerer, W.F. (1978) 'Measuring the perceived support for innovation in organizations', *Journal of Applied Psychology*, 63: 553–62.

Sternberg, R.J., O'Hara, L.A. and Lubart, T.I. (1997) 'Creativity as investment', *California Management Review*, 40 (1): 8–21.

Stringer, R. (2000) 'How to manage radical innovation', *California Management Review*, 40 (4): 70–88.

Sutton, R.I. and Galunic, D.C. (1996) 'Consequences of public scrutiny for leaders and their organizations', in B.M. Staw and L.L Cummings (eds), *Research in Organizational Behavior*, Vol. 18. Greenwich, CT: JAI Press.

Sutton, R.I. and Kelley, T. (1997) 'Creativity doesn't require isolation: why product designers bring visitors "backstage"', *California Management Review*, 40 (1): 75–91.

Tesluk, P.E., Farr, J.L. and Klein, S.R. (1997) 'Influences of organizational culture and climate on individual creativity', *Journal of Creative Behavior*, 31: 27–41.

Tetlock, P.E. (1991) 'The impact of accountability on judgment and choice: toward a social contingency model', *Advances in Experimental Social Psychology*, 25: 331–76.

Thompson, J. (1993) *Strategic Management: Awareness & Change*. London: Chapman & Hall.

Torrington, D., Hall, L. and Taylor, S. (2002) *Human Resource Management*. Harlow: Financial Times Prentice Hall.

Van Fleet, D.D. and Bedeian, A.G. (1977) 'A history of the span of management', *Academy of Management Review*, 2 (3): 356–72.

Wernerfelt, B. (1984) 'A resource-based view of the firm', *Strategic Management Journal*, 5: 171–80.

Yasai-Ardekani, M. (1986) 'Structural adaptations of environments', *Academy of Management Review*, 11 (1): 9–21.

Zajonc, R.B. (1965) 'Social facilitation', *Science*, 149: 269–74.

Zajonc, R.B. (1968) 'Attitudinal effects of mere exposure', *Journal of Personality and Social Psychology – Monograph Supplement*, 9: 1–27.

Zaltman, G., Duncan, R. and Holbek, J. (1973) *Innovations and Organizations*. New York: John Wiley.

Zell, D. (2001) 'Overcoming barriers to work: lessons learned at Hewlett-Packard', *Organizational Dynamics*, 30 (1): 77–86.

Zhou, J. (1998) 'Feedback valence, feedback style, task autonomy, and achievement orientation: interactive effects on creative performance', *Journal of Applied Psychology*, 83: 261–76.

Zhou, J. (2003) 'When the presence of creative coworkers is related to creativity: role of supervisor close monitoring, developmental feedback, and creative personality', *Journal of Applied Psychology*, 88: 413–22.

Zhou, J. and George, J.M. (2003) 'Awakening employee creativity: the role of leader emotional intelligence', *Leadership Quarterly*, 14: 545–68.

Zimmerman, B.J. and Dialessi, F. (1973) 'Modeling influences on children's creative behavior', *Journal of Educational Psychology*, 65: 127–35.

Recommended reading

- Christensen, C.M., Overdorf, M., Macmillan, I., McGrath, R. and Thomke, S. (2001) *Harvard Business Review on Innovation.* Boston, MA: Harvard Business School Publishing Corporation.

- Hesselbein, F. and Johnston, R. (2002) *On Creativity, Innovation and Renewal.* San Francisco: Jossey-Bass.

Some useful websites

- This Gary Hamel consultancy website provides insights into some interesting findings as well as other information relevant to innovation (http://www.strategos.com).

- This website has been set up by the MIT Institute, Cambridge, MA. It provides insights, articles and event information on competitiveness and innovation (http://www-innovation.jbs.cam.ac.uk/index.html).

9

Culture: Enabling and Constraining Creative Processes at Work

Learning objectives

This chapter has seven key learning objectives:

1. To explore how the concept of organizational culture has evolved.
2. To provide a working definition of organizational culture.
3. To outline different perspectives on organizational culture.
4. To explain why culture is an important shaper of organizational creativity, innovation and change.
5. To identify norms that mobilize creativity and innovation at work.
6. To present key principles for promoting 'cultures' conducive to change and creative processes.
7. To discuss whether strong, cohesive culture hinders change, constrains creativity and stifles innovation or supports the development of new ideas.

Introduction

Encouraging and sustaining an organization-wide culture that promotes the generation and implementation of new ideas among organizational members is considered central to nurturing 'cultures of change' in the development of creative and innovative work settings (Cooper, Cartwright and Earley, 2001). Firms like 3M, Apple, Lunar Design and Smart Design (two leading new product design consultancies), which are constantly praised in the business press for their 'creative' organizational DNA – a metaphor for those hidden characteristics that can define the culture of an organization (see http://www.orgdna.com) – generally pride themselves on sustaining an intra-organizational value and behavioural norm system that enables the perpetual development and introduction of original and useful products (see Neilson et al., 2005). Academic scholars and management consultants continue to search for the key elements of organizational culture that support dynamic innovative companies that embrace creativity and change in sustaining their competitive advantage in the face of fierce competition (an early example of this is provided by Peters and Waterman, 1982).

This chapter identifies the cultural characteristics that promote organizational creativity. An historical overview of the concept of 'culture' is presented through reviewing definitional developments, comparing and contrasting key perspectives, and evaluating whether organizational culture can indeed be managed and changed. We then focus on contemporary writings that highlight the elements of creative and innovative cultures. The chapter concludes by critically discussing recent views that consider strong cultures as an anathema to creativity, change and innovation.

The evolution of the concept

The concept of culture has its roots in the disciplines of anthropology and sociology (Hatch, 1993). The term 'culture' was first used in an anthropological context at the end of the 19th century to refer to 'civilisation' and 'social heritage' (Morgan, 1986). Numerous anthropological studies have focused on the subject, contributing no less than 164 meanings to the concept of culture (Kroeber and Kluckhohn, 1952). Anthropologists have argued that culture 'is a product; is historical; includes ideas, patterns and values; is selective; is learned; is based upon symbols; and is an abstraction from behaviour and the products of behaviour' (Kroeber and Kluckhohn, 1952: 157). Scholars of sociology later paralleled anthropologists' interest in the concept of culture. Jacques (1951: 251), for instance, wrote about 'the culture of the factory', which he defined as 'its customary and traditional way of thinking and doing things, which is shared to a greater or lesser degree by all its members, and which new members must learn, and at least partially accept, in order to be accepted into service in the firm'.

However, it was not until the mid-1970s that the concept of culture was popularized in organizational texts. Organizational sociologists realized that traditional models of organizations did not always provide an adequate framework for understanding observed disparities between organizational goals (strategy) and actual outcomes (implementation) and this led to the development of interest in the concept of organizational culture (Ouchi and Wilkins, 1985). At this time, researchers largely used the concept as a metaphor to study organizations as forums where meanings were constructed and expressed through social interactions (Wilson, 1996). Organizational sociologists viewed companies as mini-societies that collectively expressed their personalities through distinct cultural traits. Culture was therefore perceived as something an organization 'was', rather than as a variable, something an organization 'had'.

In the beginning of the 1980s, the concept of culture caught the interest of management researchers and practitioners. Management authors initially examined culture as an external independent variable embedded in geographic, linguistic or ethnic groups that was imported into organizations through their members (Smirich, 1983). As different societies presumably have different cultures, researchers explored the notion whether organizations within these different cultures also exhibit different structures, practices and management styles. Writings from this period mainly focused on: the applicability of American management practices to other cultures; analyses of managerial and organizational practices within specific cultures; and comparisons of managerial and organizational practices across different cultures (see, for example, Hofstede, 1980; Ouchi, 1981; Pascale and Athos, 1981). While these studies on culture were widely read and generated considerable debate, their focus was rather ethnocentric, emphasizing societies' culture as the catalyst for differences across organizations rather than viewing culture as an integral part of organizations. During this period, culture started to become part of the common vocabulary of management, and academic researchers began to explore differences in cultures *within* organizations. For some writers, these differences offered a possible explanation of why some firms were more competitively effective than others (Ouchi and Wilkins, 1985). Organizational culture was increasingly seen as an element which, if effectively managed, could provide companies with managerial effectiveness, superior performance and internal integration (see, for example, Deal and Kennedy, 1982; Peters and Waterman, 1982; Wilkins and Ouchi, 1983). In conjunction with this line of thinking, more and more researchers supported the notion that culture should be viewed as an organizational variable rather than as a 'metaphor' for the organization itself (Smirich, 1983); something an organization 'has' rather than something an organization 'is'.

So what is organizational culture?

Within the 'culture' literature, numerous definitions have been proposed for the concept of organizational culture. Some authors define organizational culture simply as 'the rules of the game' (van Maanen, 1976, 1977), or 'the way we do things around here' (Deal and Kennedy, 1982), while others propose more all-encompassing definitions (see, for example, Denison, 1990; Kotter and Heskett, 1992; Schein, 1984; Schneider, 1988; Schwartz and Davis, 1981; Wilson, 1996). Schneider (1988: 353), for instance, defines culture as 'the values that lie beneath what the organization rewards, supports and expects; the norms that surround and/or underpin the policies, practices and procedures of organizations; the meaning incumbents share about what the norms and values of the organization are'. Focusing on the deeper, 'less visible' level, Schein (1984: 3) views culture as something an organization 'is' and defines culture as 'the pattern of basic assumptions that a given group has invented, discovered or developed in learning to cope with its problems of external adaptation and internal integration and that have worked well enough to be considered valid and, therefore, to be taught to new members as the correct way to perceive, think, and feel in relation to those problems'. Moreover, acknowledging both the 'visible' and 'less visible' layers of culture, Kotter and Heskett (1992: 4) argue that 'at the deeper and less visible level, culture refers to values that are shared by the people in a group and that tend to persist over time even when group membership changes. At the more visible level, culture represents the behaviour patterns or style of an organization that new employees are automatically encouraged to follow by their fellow employees'. Each level of culture has a tendency to influence the other.

Reviewing the plethora of definitions of organizational culture three dominant characteristics can be assigned to the concept (Wilson, 1996). First, culture is a *shared phenomenon*. Culture is viewed as a kind of social or normative binding that is shared by a given group and holds together potentially diverse members (Schein, 1985). In a corporate setting, the group may be the whole organization or one of a number of subgroups. Researchers like Bloor and Dawson (1994), Gregory (1983), Kotter and Heskett (1992), Louis (1983), Martin and Siehl (1983), Schein (1991a) and Wilson (1996), for instance, illustrate how companies often have multiple subcultures associated with functional or geographical groups within the organization.

Second, culture exists at two levels, namely: the surface (visible) level and deeper (less visible) level. The surface level includes elements such as audible and visible patterns of behaviour exhibited by the group and physical artefacts, such as buildings or décor. The deeper level of culture relates to the values that the group shares and the norms that establish the kind of behaviours members of the group should expect from one another (Wiener, 1988). In a corporate setting, these values may be shared across the organization (they may be explicitly stated in the company's mission statement) but these broader company values are usually what are termed 'espoused values' (Martin and Meyerson, 1988; Schein, 1984; Siehl and Martin, 1988). Espoused values are the desired corporate values put forward by senior management that are often out of line with the 'values-in-use', that is, the values that are actually enacted through formal practices and other, more indirect processes, such as jargon, humour, organizational stories or ceremonies and rituals (see, for example, Siehl and Martin, 1988). Scholars argue that the degree to which 'values-in-use' reflect 'espoused' values often determines the strength of culture in corporate settings (Martin and Meyerson, 1988; Sathe, 1985; Wiener, 1988). Once values have been established within the group, norms then allow members to understand the types of behaviours that are expected of them in different situations. Schein (1985) adds that values and norms are underlined by a deeper level of what he calls 'basic assumptions', that is, assumed ideas or concepts that guide the group in coping with its environment and yet lies at the preconscious level of the human mind.

Third, culture is *learned*. Within a corporate setting, new members learn about the culture that prevails within their group through formal and informal, explicit and implicit cultural socialization processes (Schein, 1991a, 1991b). Moreover, as cultures are learned, they are also *relatively stable and change slowly over time*; as such, they serve the human need for order and consistency (Schein, 1984). When a group is forming and growing, culture often serves as the 'glue' that binds people together in providing a sense of identity and belonging. According to Schein (1991b), a culture provides

> *... group members with a way of giving meaning to their daily lives, setting guidelines and rules for how to behave, and most important reducing and containing the anxiety of dealing with an unpredictable and uncertain environment. Culture stabilizes and normalizes events and thus makes day-to-day functioning possible.*

Different perspectives on organizational culture

The range of definitions that exist for the concept of organizational culture mirrors the different approaches that management authors have developed. Frost et al. (1991) and Martin and Meyerson (1988) identified three key perspectives in the study of organizational culture, comprising the integration, differentiation and fragmentation perspectives. Scholars adopting the integration perspective examine shared values (for example, Badovick and Beatty, 1987), focus on elements of 'cultural strength' (for example, Sathe, 1985) and/or explore the cultural manifestations necessary for corporate success (for example, Peters and Waterman, 1982). Martin (1992: 12) contends that the integration perspective is adopted by studies that possess

> *... three defining characteristics: all cultural manifestations mentioned are interpreted as consistently reinforcing the same themes, all members of the organization are said to share in an organization-wide consensus and the culture is described as a realm where all is clear. Ambiguity is excluded.*

Frost et al. (1991) explain that within these studies 'espoused' values are regarded as consistent with formal policies, which are consistent with informal norms, stories, rituals and so forth. Cultural members share the same values and understandings and, hence, loyalty and commitment are promoted within the organization. There is therefore unanimous agreement on what people within the organization are meant to do and why it is worthwhile exhibiting relevant behaviours. In this realm of clarity, there is no room for ambiguity. Therefore, when inconsistencies, conflict or even subcultural differentiation are identified in studies adopting this perspective, then these factors are seen to indicate either the absence of a 'corporate culture' (Frost et al., 1991) or as evidence of a weak or negative culture (Wilson, 1996).

Studies adopting a differentiation perspective are more attentive to alternative points of view within organizations. Researchers within the differentiation perspective suggest that cultural manifestations within organizations are predominantly inconsistent (Frost et al., 1991) and, as such, organizational cultures are sometimes portrayed as 'mosaics of inconsistencies' (Martin and Meyerson, 1988). The defining characteristics of the differentiation perspective comprise: 'inconsistency, subcultural consensus and the relegation of ambiguity to the periphery of subcultures' (Martin, 1992: 83). Studies within the differentiation perspective argue that formal corporate policies are in reality often undermined by contradictory informal norms and hence cultural consensus only emerges at the boundaries of subcultures. Subcultures within organizations may co-exist in harmony, may operate in conflict with each other or with indifference to each other (Martin and Meyerson, 1988). Bloor and Dawson (1994) demonstrate how subcultures can relate both to different levels of organizational status and to different professions that may combine or overlap in providing certain types of healthcare (see also, for example, Sackman, 1992; van Maanen, 1991); to different teams of people working together across the organization (see Wilson, 1996); or to gender differences (see Rosen, 1985). While the differentiation perspective recognizes the inevitability of conflict within organizations, some suggest that it nevertheless fails to account for the *ambiguities* of organizational existence (Harris and Ogbonna, 1997).

This concern with ambiguity is central to the fragmentation perspective on organizational culture. Studies adopting a fragmentation perspective regard ambiguity as a hallmark of corporate life (Martin and Meyerson, 1988) and acknowledge the 'uncontrollable uncertainties that provide the texture of contemporary life' (Martin, 1992: 354). They mainly focus on events that illustrate ambiguity and the constant state of flux within corporations. According to this viewpoint, clear consistencies or clear inconsistencies are rare in corporate settings; there is rather a constantly fluctuating pattern influenced by changes in events, attention, salience or cognitive overload (Frost et al., 1991). Relationships among 'espoused' values, formal practices and informal processes within the organization are seen as blurred. Consensus is neither organization-wide nor on a subcultural basis; it is rather issue-specific. Scholars adopting this perspective study specific incidents such as the decision making at Tenerife airport (Weick, 1991), social workers' experiences of ambiguity (Meyerson, 1991) and policy analysts' reactions to the uncontrollable ambiguity involved in their work (Feldman, 1991).

Can we manage organizational culture?

The multiplicity of definitions offered on the concept of culture in corporate settings, with some authors regarding culture as something an organization 'is' and others as something an organization 'has', has led to an ongoing debate as to whether culture can actually be managed and therefore changed. Researchers who consider culture as something an organization 'is', view the concept as inseparable from organizations and hence argue that there is very little point in trying to control a phenomenon which is embedded in the very roots of organizational existence (Ogbonna, 1993). Siehl (1985: 125), for instance, notes that 'organizations do not have cultures, they are cultures, and this is why cultures are so difficult to change'. Similarly Fombrun (1983: 151) argues that 'managing corporate culture is … an awesome if not impossible task'. Other researchers, such as Martin and Siehl (1983), go a step further and argue that corporate culture simply cannot be managed because it exists within the subconscious assumptions and values that guide people's behaviour. From this perspective, a deep-rooted, permanent change of corporate culture would therefore require changing the deeper beliefs and basic underlying assumptions that, without their awareness, guide people's behaviour; a task that is awfully difficult if not impossible to complete.

Robbins (1987: 368) argues that if one accepts that 'managers cannot guide their organizations through planned cultural change, the subject [culture] has limited practical utility'. For those researchers that view culture as something an organization 'has', culture can be managed (for example, Chapman, 1988; Graves, 1986; Kilmann, 1982; Ogbonna, 1993; O'Reilly, 1989; Sathe, 1985; Silverzwieg and Allen, 1976; Sparrow and Pettigrew, 1988), and managers can encourage desired behaviours and provide organizational members with a sense of identity. The task is, however, still difficult taking into account the possible existence of subcultures within the work setting. The perspective that corporate culture can be managed is built around the notion that although there are a set of underlying norms and expectations, which whilst not written constitute a major influence on the behaviour of organizational members, individuals are not merely shaped by their cultures but also influence and shape the culture of which they are a part (Ogbonna, 1993). Proponents of this viewpoint argue that the management of culture does not have to focus at the level of changing the subconscious beliefs and underlying assumptions of organizational members but, rather, may concentrate on changing the more visible, behavioural patterns in evidence in organizations (for example, Deal and Kennedy, 1982; Ogbonna, 1993; Peters and Waterman, 1982).

Why is culture an important determinant of organizational creativity and innovation?

Scholars argue that culture lies at the heart of organizational creativity and innovation (Tushman and O'Reilly, 2002). If sustained creativity and innovation is to occur in organizations, it has to happen at the cultural level (Flynn and Chatman, 2004); quick fixes and short-term changes rarely lead to sustained innovative outputs. The components of organizational culture (shared values, beliefs and behavioural norms) are key in promoting the generation and implementation of novel and useful ideas. For instance, through formal and informal socialization processes, employees gradually learn which behaviours are acceptable and what activities are valued within their organizations. In accordance with shared norms, staff will make assumptions about and decide on whether creative and innovative behaviours are part of the way in which their organization operates (Tesluk et al., 1997). Moreover, the dominant values, assumptions and beliefs within the work setting will be mirrored by the structure and management practices of the organization and these, again, may directly or indirectly support or hinder creativity and innovation in the workplace. For example, as we have discussed in the previous chapter, providing resource support to pursue the development of new ideas is often critical for organizational innovation; this attitude, however, requires an organizational culture that promotes experimentation, inquisitiveness and flexibility.

Innovative companies therefore tend to have cultures, which emphasize and reward values and norms that support the generation and implementation of new ideas. Their value systems encourage everyone across the organization to develop original and useful products (Peters and Waterman, 1982). They promote innovative ways of representing problems and finding solutions, they consider creative and innovative outputs as both desirable and normal, and they regard creative and innovative employees as role models (Locke and Kirkpatrick, 1995). Innovative companies value flexibility, mobilize freedom within the work setting and encourage co-operative team work. These are important in setting the tone about the value that the company places on creativity, change and innovation.

Norms that promote creativity and innovation

It is because innovation usually involves (and often requires) risk taking, non-standard solutions and unconventional teamwork practices (elements that are not easily managed by formal control systems), that the effective management of culture is critical in mobilizing organizational creativity and innovation (Tushman and O'Reilly, 2002). Pivotal in these efforts is the establishment and continuous encouragement of behavioural norms that promote the generation and implementation of novel solutions. These norms refer to the socially created expectations that guide the acceptable attitudes and behaviour in the work setting. Over the years, scholars have documented a variety of norms that tend to consistently promote creativity and innovation in organizational settings. Six of these are discussed in more detail below.

A focus on idea generation. It may sound obvious, but promoting idea-generating behaviours is a key for mobilizing creativity in the workplace. In 3M for instance, a company often quoted as a prototype for its innovative outputs, employees are required to follow the so-called '15 per cent rule'. Staff are expected to devote up to 15 per cent of their working time in order to generate and pursue ideas that may prove to be valuable for 3M developments. To encourage and sustain this norm, Martins and Terblanche (2003) emphasize that managers of creative environments need to promote open communication and forums of intra- and extra-organizational debate. Sustaining such an information flow is pivotal. Kanter (2002) notes that lack of information hinders creativity in organizational settings and that culture needs to encourage open discussions, constructive conflict, fair evaluation of ideas and fast approvals (Amabile, 1998; Kanter, 2002). All this, of course, needs to happen in a positive co-operative atmosphere, as conflict across internal units is likely to bring the opposite results (Kanter, 2002). Lastly, Tushman and O'Reilly (2002) highlight that an important way of signalling the value of idea-generating behaviours is by rewarding them.

Supporting a continuous learning culture. Creativity is also mobilized in environments where continuous learning is a company-wide expectation (Martins and Terblanche, 2003). Arad et al. (1997) note that employees should have a continuously curious attitude; this will allow them to discover and explore 'wild' or groundbreaking ideas and potentially identify novel and valuable solutions. Keeping staff's knowledge and thinking skills up to date is key in this respect. New product design consultancies like Astro Studios, Design Continuum and Frog Design pride themselves on regularly sending their staff to skill-development seminars, local exhibitions, even local supermarkets and toy stores; all in an effort to support continuous learning and widen their creative horizons.

Risk taking. As we have highlighted at several points in this book, the creative process often involves risky endeavours. The generation of ideas requires experimentation and, as such, taking risks is usually unavoidable (and often necessary). Encouraging risk-taking behaviours therefore needs to be part of the creative culture (Martins and Terblanche, 2003). To mobilize and encourage risk taking managers need to avoid applying too many controls in the creative process, as this is likely to inhibit experimentation and impede 'creative flow'. However, creative organizations also have to face a commercial reality and, hence, excessive risk taking may lead to costly results on the profit and loss account. Rather than discouraging excessive risk taking, the creative companies that we have studied encourage employees to take risks as long as they follow the established processes that should guide them through the creative process. This is supported by well-crafted mentoring systems where more senior colleagues take on monitoring responsibilities, help junior colleagues during their creative endeavours, and create a risk-tolerant atmosphere in viewing mistakes as learning experiences.

Tolerance of mistakes. Experimentation and risk taking is likely to lead to mistakes. Mistakes are therefore an everyday practice in creative environments. Martins and Terblanche (2003) argue that supporting a culture that tolerates mistakes and handles them effectively is central to encouraging staff to think and act creatively. Creative organizations need to have faith in their employees to try new things, even if this leads to failure or disappointing results. Organizations that punish employee mistakes discourage creativity, inhibit change and stifle innovation (Kanter, 2002). Creative organizations therefore need to acknowledge (and on some occasions even celebrate) failure and constantly create opportunities to openly discuss mistakes and learn from the pitfalls of the creative process. The successful management of mistakes often also relies on managers' skill to clarify which mistakes are acceptable and which are not. Tushman and O'Reilly (2002) refer to the case of Johnson & Johnson to illustrate this point. Although Johnson & Johnson's motto: 'Failure is our most important product' remains at the heart of the company's culture, managers clearly differentiate between mistakes that are considered acceptable and those that are not. In Johnson & Johnson's case, mistakes are reasonable 'if they are based on analysis, foster learning and are modest in impact' (Tushman and O'Reilly, 2002: 115). The same applies to many organizations that are known for their creative cultures; in DuPont, for example, failures are often labelled as 'good tries'.

Supporting change. Arad et al. (1997) emphasize that behaviours that promote change in the work setting are likely to positively influence organizational creativity and innovation. To support creativity the culture must tolerate uncertainty (Kanter, 2002), promote and reward positive attitudes towards change and encourage employees to constantly challenge the status quo and explore novel ways of finding creative solutions (Tushman and O'Reilly, 2002).

Conflict handling. Change and constant experimentation are likely to lead to conflict in the workplace; conflict between colleagues, conflict between departments, conflict between individuals' creative freedom and the constraints set by the client's commercial reality. Managers in creative organizations, for instance, often complain about conflict between the 'creatives' (designers, architects, etc.) and the 'non-creatives' (consultants, project managers, etc.). This is why many creative organizations try to employ managers with design and business experience; that is, to bridge the gap between the two disciplines and the stereotypes that go with them. The literature suggests that companies need to expect and tolerate conflict and handle it effectively in order to support creative behaviours in the work setting (Judge et al., 1997). As the starting point of creativity often stems from individual expression, it is important to acknowledge and to be sensitive to different styles of working. At the same time, managers need to train employees in the process of constructive confrontation in order to promote constructive feedback and an open, supportive culture in the workplace (Martins and Terblanche, 2003).

Norms that promote implementation

Although creativity is important, commercial reality requires implementation; ideas need to be turned into innovations that will positively influence the corporate profit and loss account. In order to encourage action, Tushman and O'Reilly (2002) argue that several norms are important: an emphasis on team work and effective group functioning, a focus on speed and urgency, a need for flexibility and adaptability, and a sense of autonomy.

Team work and effective group functioning. The need to work together in project teams is common in creative environments. Depending on the company, teams may be fixed for each and every project or staff may join different teams depending on the nature of the project, their expertise, the challenge that senior colleagues aim to set to junior staff, and so forth. Staff may join different teams in order to promote a fresh perspective and encourage employees to stretch their work capabilities and interpersonal skills. Tushman and O'Reilly (2002) note that employees need to be encouraged to work and communicate effectively, and that implementation is enhanced when teams work harmoniously, communicate well and have common goals.

Speed and urgency. Promoting behaviours that support speed and urgency is also important for translating ideas into innovations. After the initial experimentation stage, which is key in generating creative outputs, decisions need to be made quickly. Norms like speed, a sense of urgency and commitment to meeting deadlines (even if teams need to work long hours to achieve their goals) are important (Tushman and O'Reilly, 2002). Although issues of work–life balance are receiving greater attention in creative environments, it is not uncommon for designers to work long hours. The designers that we have interviewed usually talk about this with enthusiasm rather than disappointment. It seems that the creative hype and the magic of discovering and delivering something new and novel drives people to excel and redefines 'acceptable' working hours.

Flexibility and adaptability. Promoting flexibility and adaptability in the workplace is also a key factor in supporting implementation (Tushman and O'Reilly, 2002). Effective team work requires team co-operation as quick decisions and tight deadlines mean that staff are often required to work on others' ideas, build on their strengths and deal with their weaknesses. The constructive confrontation required in the creative process demands staff to be open-minded and flexible in their thinking. The team also needs to agree on the potential value of the idea for the company or its clients. Constantly challenging the status quo and the way things can or cannot be done is important for generating novel solutions. Employees need to be perpetually challenged and this therefore requires strong characters that can constantly deal with change and cope with the inevitable conflict.

A sense of autonomy. Sustaining a sense of autonomy in the workplace is also important in promoting implementation in the work setting (Tushman and O'Reilly, 2002). Innovation has no room for a 'taking a back seat' attitude. Individuals need to be autonomous, self-starters and take action without necessarily being asked to do so. This does not only promote the perpetual generation of new ideas but also the quick filtering and implementation of valuable concepts. In the new product design consultancies that we have studied, staff are allowed as much freedom as required to work on projects and find novel solutions; senior colleagues set the objectives and the project constraints and employees then bring their thoughts and ideas to the table to reach the best solution to the issue at hand. Encouraging and sustaining these behavioural norms in the workplace is, however, seldom an easy process. Developing a culture for creativity and innovation requires managers to carefully mobilize the generation and implementation of ideas in the workplace. According to Pfeffer (2002) and Pfeffer and Sutton (2002), this demands that managers avoid the following five pitfalls:

1. *Overemphasizing individual accountability.* Despite the fact that innovation requires autonomy and personal initiative, overemphasizing individual accountability can be detrimental to the creative process. Although staff need to be given individual targets and be evaluated against their achieved outcomes, Pfeffer (2002) notes that over-relying on individual accountability can lead to finger-pointing, is likely to create a climate of fear and may discourage employees from taking the risks that are so important in the early stages of the creative process. Evidently, these go against the requirement for open communication, constructive feedback and the necessity of an open-learning culture. Moreover, although individual performance appraisals serve an essential human resource management tool they need

to be carefully crafted so that they do not substitute regular and informal feedback and they do not promote a controlling and risk-averse culture.

2. *Overemphasizing quantitative goals and budgets.* Although for-profit organizations need to focus on the bottom line and consider financial constraints, Pfeffer (2002) argues that overemphasizing quantitative goals and financial budgets rarely promotes a culture of perpetual discovery and innovation. Objectives and financial constraints will certainly set the frame upon which the creative process will be initiated, but employees also need to be encouraged to think outside the box and, if necessary, negotiate with the client or their company for extra resources. Evidently, the external environment affects an organization's approach to this issue. From our research, it appears that prior to the dot.com bust, design consultancies were much more flexible in stretching budgets and providing 'extra' resources; in contrast, library budgets, field trips and 'blue-sky' projects all suffer during times of economic uncertainty.

3. *Punishing mistakes.* As we have already mentioned, the way that companies handle the inevitable mistakes of creative discovery can enhance or constrain creative processes at work. Pfeffer (2002) argues that punishing mistakes is a common pitfall in corporate environments; it creates a culture of fear and hinders organizational creativity. Pfeffer and Sutton (2002) note that managers need to acknowledge mistakes as part of the learning experience. Creative endeavours inevitably involve (often long) trial-and-error processes and treating mistakes harshly can be detrimental to the generation of new ideas. Companies that are innovation-driven tend to promote a 'forgiveness' culture, a culture of empowerment and not punishment. Such a managerial attitude mobilizes an action orientation across the organization, where people focus on doing things rather than on hesitating through fear of the career consequences of failure.

4. *Promoting internal competition.* Promoting internal competition is often used as a means for mobilizing initiative within work settings. However, innovation usually entails collaboration across intra- or extra-organizational boundaries. Designers and engineers co-operate to achieve feasible results, clients and project teams cross-fertilize ideas to generate novel outcomes, even competitors sometimes work together to ensure that the required expertise and resources are obtained. Consequently, promoting internal competition may hinder effective team working and stimulate organizational politicking that may prove to be detrimental to the creative process (Pfeffer and Sutton, 2002).

5. *Striving to be the same.* Although managers increasingly acknowledge the value of creativity and innovation as a means of developing and sustaining competitive advantage, paradoxically, many companies strive to be the same as their competitors. They use similar processes, generate similar products and avoid the implementation of 'risky' novel ideas and practices. Pfeffer (2002), on the contrary, argues that innovation requires managers to dare to be different, as the returns on successful innovations are generally far greater than those achieved through imitation.

Principles of creativity and innovation

Taking into consideration the increasing interest in organizational culture as an important shaper of organizational change, creativity and innovation, several authors have proposed 'principles' that companies should follow in order to build and sustain a culture that promotes the generation and implementation of new ideas and novel outcomes. Zien and Buckler (2004), for instance, propose the following seven principles:

1. *Sustain faith and treasure identity as an innovative company.* Zien and Buckler (2004: 483) argue that 'the crafting of an innovative culture requires creating an environment of faith and trust that good ideas have a likely chance to become great products'. In good and bad times, truly innovative companies maintain creativity and innovation as a key corporate priority. Rather than focusing on 'safe', ready-made, uninspired solutions, visionary managers 'see' and continuously evangelize the value of discovery and the fact that innovation propels profitability. Successful design consultancies dare to be different; they continuously experiment with untried concepts, bring in people with fresh perspectives, try new ventures, question conventional thinking, and have faith that new ideas will eventually turn into profits.

2. *Be truly experimental in all functions, especially at the front end.* Experimentation is a critical part of the creative process. Especially in the early stages of creative discovery, encouraging employees to 'go wild' in their creative endeavours is essential; and, thereafter, taking 'sensible risks' is equally important (Sternberg and Lubart, 1995). Creative employees need to be constantly challenged and highly experimental work can help in this respect. As we have previously noted, 'blue-sky' projects outwith client-commissioned work can also help to achieve this. Innovative companies also keep the 'fruits of discovery' alive. The best design consultancies maintain active computerized databases of previous work (ideas, concepts, prototypes and finished products) that serve as the organization's memory and aids experimentation in future projects.

3. *Structure 'real' relationships between marketing and technical people.* Promoting close and meaningful relationships between the technical innovators and the market-driven business minds is another essential principle for promoting a culture of creativity and change (Mohr et al., 2005). Although such arrangements may create some initial conflict, open communication and constructive criticism between the two functions is critical. Zien and Buckler (2004) encourage companies to bring together the two functions formally and informally, as such a relationship does not only serve to resolve the traditional tensions between cost control and experimentation, but also helps to provide a balance between the wild ideas of creative discovery and the concept of feasibility; the project and market constraints that the company needs to consider.

4. *Generate customer intimacy.* Creativity and innovation in corporate settings is not about fulfilling artistic individual needs. The commercial reality requires creative organizations to anticipate and meet market-driven requirements. This is why the barriers between creative experimentation and established exploratory market research methods are becoming increasingly blurred in creative corporate environments (Mohr et al., 2005). Innovative organizations achieve the much needed customer intimacy by observing potential users, videotaping their actions, interviewing key stakeholders and studying customers' lifestyles and product decisions. They also increasingly employ staff with skills outwith the traditional design disciplines. Sociologists, anthropologists and MBAs are becoming part of the creative process; larger companies increasingly employ them as full-time staff, whilst smaller organizations often subcontract their services to cross-fertilize ideas and bring in market-driven perspectives.

5. *Engage the whole organization.* Being creative in organizations should not be a privilege of the select few. Visionary leaders realize that they need to engage the whole organization in the 'hype' of generating and implementing novel solutions. Creating a sense of community where everyone works towards a common goal and believes in the value of discovery and innovation is critical. This needs to happen both formally and informally. Formally, through planned communication activities: regular meetings that motivate staff and provide opportunities for feedback, e-mails that celebrate achievements, intranets that bring the company together and reinforce visions. Informally, by 'leading by example', initiating social 'get togethers', engaging staff in impromptu discussions, and so forth.

6. *Never forget the individual.* Sternberg and Lubart (1995) and Zien and Buckler (2004) note how innovative organizations should not forget the individual. Acknowledging and celebrating individual idiosyncrasies, providing ample opportunities for personal expression and encouraging employees to follow their passions and work on challenging projects, are all important in mobilizing cultures of change, creativity and innovation. Innovative companies create a fun working environment and actively assist employees in achieving their ambitions and career aspirations. Some of the design consultancies that we have studied even encourage employees to start up their own companies and maintain working relationships with them even after their departure from the organization.

7. *Tell and embody powerful and purposeful stories.* The role of hero/heroine stories and the efforts in keeping the company's innovative vision and history alive, also reinforce creative processes. This is all part of 'thinking for the long term' (Sternberg and Lubart, 1995). In the new product design consultancies that we have studied, designers often idolize colleagues that have created breakthrough concepts, recall the professionalism and ethos of certain senior members of staff and discuss myths about the first days of the company and the creative activities that led to its success. Zien and Buckler (2004) argue that keeping these stories alive is critical in sustaining creative cultures.

Similarly, Andriopoulos and Gotsi (2002) in their study of Lunar Design – a leading new product development consultancy in the Silicon Valley – identify four principles that promote creative cultures, namely:

1. *Start with a collaborative approach to management.* A collaborative approach to management, whereby employees are constantly aware of the company's actions and able to voice their views and opinions in numerous formal and informal occasions, is a key principle for fostering a creative culture.

2. *Create a 'no fear' climate.* As we have mentioned several times in this chapter, the fear of failure can be detrimental to organizational creativity. Creating a culture that supports perpetual experimentation is therefore essential in mobilizing innovation-enhancing behaviours. Regarding ideas as the company's most valuable assets, initiating 'blue-sky', internally driven projects and creating a mentoring system that supports individuals in their creative endeavours, are some of the things that Lunar does to foster a 'no fear' climate in the workplace.

3. *Encourage stretching beyond the comfort zone.* A 'stretching beyond the comfort zone' mentality is also essential when it comes to energizing staff with challenging projects. This involves asking employees from the day that they join the organization to work on projects that do not necessarily reflect their expertise and to get them involved in different projects. This not only brings fresh perspectives to the creative process, but also enhances the learning experience of creative employees.

4. *Celebrate individuality and encourage uncertainty.* Creative employees need to have autonomy over their work and be able to express themselves and their passions in their working environment. This includes the personalization of their own offices, the usual lack of dress code and even bringing in their passions (musical instruments, jewellery designs, and so forth) to the working environment. Diversity in the workplace is also essential, as it encourages employees to break down stereotypes and enhances the creative process, and this is why companies like Lunar Design strive to recruit people from different countries, educational backgrounds and work experiences.

Can strong, cohesive cultures hinder innovation?

Creative individuals are usually characterized by personality traits such as the need for independence, a preference for non-conformity, a requirement for challenging work and complexity, and a playful, sometimes even childlike, attitude (Nemeth, 1997). Highly creative employees are also often stereotyped as *prima donnas*, characters that force their views and seek to dominate discussions, and are commonly portrayed as 'lone riders', distant from close interpersonal work relations. One would expect that such individuals would not want to belong to highly cohesive, strong organizational cultures. At first glance, strong cultures that demand employees to conform to and continuously follow established norms would seem to be an anathema to creative employees. One might conclude that despite the benefits of the cultural norms that we have outlined in this chapter, innovative companies: 'require a culture that is diametrically opposed to that which encourages cohesion, loyalty and clear norms of appropriate attitudes and behaviour' (Nemeth, 1997). However, there is considerable debate on this issue.

Those that agree with this notion argue that strong cultures are likely to induce uniformity (Nemeth and Staw, 1989) and hence hinder the ambiguity and divergence needed in creative environments. Culture is a system of social control that influences the attitudes and behaviours of organizational members (Tushman and O'Reilly, 2002) and strong cultures tend to exhibit cohesion around acceptable values and behavioural norms (for example, O'Reilly and Chatman, 1996). Some authors therefore argue that companies that exhibit strong cultures tend to limit their creative and innovative potential through selection processes that promote uniformity in the workplace (Flynn and Chatman, 2004). The resulting homogeneity goes against the diversity that is so essential for encouraging dialogue between different perspectives that ultimately promotes new combinations of ideas in the creative process (Hoffman, 1959).

Despite these arguments, many innovative companies are known for their strong, cohesive cultures. For instance, 3M's product development teams pride themselves on their cohesion, which they see as essential in translating interesting concepts into profitable product launches (Flynn and Chatman, 2004). Apple is also known for its strong culture and community feeling. From this perspective, the scholars that view such cultures as an essential component of organizational innovation argue that creativity is better directed in strong cultures that emphasize these innovation-enhancing norms.

Flynn and Chatman (2004) argue that although the existence of behavioural norms requires members to conform to certain behavioural requirements, this does not necessarily translate into uniformity in the work setting. Conformity is about agreement and harmony in the workplace; uniformity is about lack of variation, identical attitudes and behaviours. Strong cultures may therefore promote conformity but not uniformity. Organizational members, for instance, may be encouraged to 'agree to disagree'. In the new product design consultancies that we have studied, diversity, individuality, divergent thinking and constructive criticism are some of the prominent behavioural norms. Sutton and Hargadon's (1996) study in IDEO, a world leading product design consultancy, revealed that although they have a strong culture, their brainstorming sessions promoted conformity not uniformity. In the brainstorming sessions, 'facilitators and participants discourage criticism, even negative facial expression, but often nod, smile and say "wow", and "cool" in response to an idea' (Sutton and Hargadon, 1996). In this environment new ideas are positively encouraged and members are expected to conform to this expectation.

Scholars following this school of thought argue that one should not confuse cultural strength with cultural content. However, this confusion often exists because many organizations that are known for their strong cultures are regularly portrayed as controlling and manipulative (O'Reilly and Chatman, 1996). Although authors like Nemeth and Staw (1989) propose that the mere presence of shared norms hinders, by default, creativity and innovation in the workplace, others argue that this depends on the nature of the behavioural norms that prevail within the organization. Flynn and Chatman (2004) refer to many companies that have strong cultures that are in the form of innovation-enhancing behavioural norms. Employees at 3M, for instance, are encouraged to take risks and make mistakes and consider this process as part of their learning experience, rather than as incidents to be ashamed of (Nicholson, 1998). Similarly at Hewlett-Packard, employees are required to conform to norms that promote individuality and autonomy in the workplace (Cole, 1999). The culture does not promote uniformity; it promotes a sense of urgency and encourages individual expression that is so important in the idea-generating phase of the creative process. In the case of Disney, a company well-known for its strong culture, behavioural norms that promote supportive conflict are evident (Wetlaufer, 2000). It is therefore naïve to automatically assume that strong cultures encourage conformity and hinder creativity and innovation in the workplace.

Several authors argue that social cohesion is necessary in order to implement creative ideas and to translate creativity into innovation (Caldwell and O'Reilly, 1995). Keller's (1986) study of research and development teams, for instance, confirmed that cohesion among team members influenced their performance. Moreover, Anderson and West (1998) found that the team's cohesiveness affected the quantity and quality of innovations produced. This raises the question of whether cohesive cultures can actually hinder innovation. Potentially, yes, they can prove problematic, but only if the prevailing behavioural norms discourage organizational members to exhibit behaviours that enhance creativity and innovation. Innovative companies, on the contrary, manage to foster behavioural norms that promote diversity and innovative thinking and at the same time maintain the cohesion and social control required to translate creative ideas into innovative, money-generating outcomes (Flynn and Chatman, 2004).

Conclusion

This chapter has examined the role of culture in encouraging and sustaining creativity, innovation and change in organizational settings. The concept of organizational culture has been one of the most widely researched management topics, and in overviewing this large topic we have presented some of the prevailing perspectives on organizational culture and discussed current debates on whether culture can be managed and changed. To summarize:

- Culture is considered as a form of social control that is characterized as: a shared phenomenon, which exists in both visible artefacts and mission statements as well as in less visible and deeper subconscious levels; is learned by organizational members through a process of socialization; and is enduring and relatively stable.

- Culture plays an important role in shaping the creative process as it can promote or hinder innovation-enhancing behavioural norms. Norms like risk taking, a tolerance of mistakes, and continuous support for change, are just some of the attitudes and behaviours that innovative companies strive to promote in their culture.

- Strong cultures *per se* are not necessarily conducive to generating and implementing ideas in organizations; rather, what is required is strong cultures that foster innovation-enhancing norms and at the same time promote the social cohesion necessary for turning ideas into product innovations.

- In examining cultures that nurture creativity and innovation, and environments that promote creative thinking and innovation-enhancing behavioural norms, we examined how to create 'cultures of change' in which the novel, the revised, the redesigned and alternative 'ways of doing things', are all part of ongoing internal change processes. When these change processes become integral to the culture of an organization then change becomes routinized and a part of normal behaviour. Within such organizations a failure to change, to examine and implement new ways of doing things – to be creative and innovative – is far more threatening than regular small-scale change initiatives.

In the next chapter, we identify and define different types of change and turn our attention to both changes associated with everyday internal activities in sustaining creative and innovative organizations, as well as the more radical and large-scale change initiatives that can transform organizations. Whilst ongoing change can be the norm in many creative industries, radical divergence from these norms represents significant departures from the known and, as such, will often be resisted by employees. In fact, managing the people aspects of change is seen by many as the most critical factor, often being cited as a primary cause for failed change initiatives.

CASE 9.1   CULTURES AT WORK: THE CASE OF HOME CARE SERVICE
BY GEOFFREY BLOOR AND PATRICK DAWSON

The case of a Home Care Service (HCS) in Australia provides a practical illustration of the increasing importance of professional subcultures in a growing number of organizations. The case of HCS is particularly illuminating as it provides an empirical example of the coexistence of a number of different 'cultures' (referred to as subcultures) within a single organization.

Home Care Service (HCS) was established in the early 1970s as a result of societal and particularly hospital staff concerns about the care of the elderly. Its history, the vision of its founder and early members, professional expectations and its link with the central metropolitan hospital, all serve to influence local attitudes and perceptions. Certain patterns of behaviour and operational practice combine with prescriptive regulatory rules and legitimated authority relationships in shaping cultural change at work. These patterns create and sustain an ideational cultural system that places a high premium on the provision of professional services to geriatric clients. Currently, the primary cultural system supports a medically dominated operating system which is integrated with general medical services provided at the major metropolitan hospital.

An examination of the values held by HCS staff reveals the existence of a number of subcultures. The dominant subcultural value system is that of the medical staff who hold a particularly influential position within the organization's power structure. For example, although allied health professionals are nominally case managers, geriatricians who work part time at HCS and at the major metropolitan hospital randomly review their decisions. This practice was established early in the history of the organization by the founding Medical Director and was justified on the basis of the need to maintain high standards of services that do not promote client dependency. This is an example of a founder/leader's values being translated into practices for organizational members who might not hold the same values (Hofstede, Nueijen, Ohayv and Sanders, 1990). A major part of the ideology of the medical authority is the need to maintain high standards of professional practice and in particular, to make accurate professional assessments and diagnoses of patients' conditions before deciding what services to provide to meet their needs. In practice this usually results in the provision of services which support the care plans of general medical practitioners and hospital medical staff. Medical dominance is further reinforced by the provision of private offices for geriatricians, while other professionals (with the exception of senior staff), have their desks grouped in local government teams in a large open office. The geriatricians also speak of 'my team' (much to the annoyance of other staff), and insist that team meetings are held on days when they are available even if some part-time allied health professionals are not.

Despite some resentment of the working practices associated with the 'enhancing subculture' of geriatricians (in amplifying the assumptions, values and beliefs of the primary hospital culture), staff do not challenge the status quo. Junior staff rarely speak at meetings and allied health chiefs will frequently defer to the wishes of the geriatricians despite inconsistency in decision making. Although the medical staff dispute claims that they dominate, they place great emphasis on maintaining work practices which support medical authority. Furthermore, one of the reasons given for a recent increase in the number of geriatricians was the need to review more of the allied health staff's work.

The physiotherapists and occupational therapists form what Martin and Siehl (1983) call 'orthogonal subcultures'; that is, they accept the basic assumptions of the primary cultural system regarding the need for high standards of professional practice but also hold some that are unique and in conflict with those of the dominant medical subculture (see also, Ott, 1989: 46). This group are the most concerned of all the allied health professions with the image of their profession. They are also relatively young professions and place their major emphasis on developing and maintaining 'hands-on' skills. However, much of the therapeutic work done in HCS is routine (that is, once

(Continued)

(Continued)

assessments are completed and programmes established the work is generally done by paramedical aides) and hence, therapists typically regard HCS as a stepping stone to other positions (usually in hospitals) which results in a relatively high turnover of staff. Consequently, whilst many therapists are not happy with their relative powerlessness, they are disinclined to speak out against the dominant subculture as they generally do not see themselves staying in HCS very long.

In contrast, social workers are more outspoken. Whilst they also value high professional standards and have a commitment to client rehabilitation (and in this sense share the core values of the organization), they interpret these concepts in different ways to the other professional groups. For example, their code of ethics includes a strong commitment to client self-determination and they are therefore more inclined to accept clients' own assessments of their needs. Moreover, this group tends to encourage clients to be assertive about what they want (although they may over time attempt to get clients to gain a more realistic perspective if necessary). As such, they generally advocate on behalf of clients even in the face of medical authority dissension. They also serve as an important source of innovative proposals and are often willing to deal with complex situations that other professionals do not wish to tackle. In this way, social workers can be seen to lie somewhere between an orthogonal and counter-culture and represent a type of 'dissenting subculture' within the existing service philosophy for home care provision (see Bloor and Dawson, 1994). In other words, while they are not directly opposed to a culture of health care, their philosophy of home care service provision is often at odds with other professional groups and the dominant medical subculture. They therefore represent a dissenting professional subculture in holding an alternative pattern of shared values and practices which have the potential to replace the current medical service philosophy and become the new dominant (and enhancing) subculture. However while this illustrates the possibility of shifting subcultural positioning within the primary cultural system, this is unlikely to occur in practice as there is minimal subcultural conflict because clients will generally request the treatment that doctors recommend.

Members of these various professional groups seek to control their organizational destinies. They can do this by drawing upon their particular skills and codes to demonstrate that they have particular areas of knowledge and expertise which the others lack, thus legitimating their domination over certain aspects of the organization's work. Hence, codes of ethics, the belief in the client's right to self-determination, knowledge of how to perform particular therapies, can all assume an ideological significance in arguments aimed at controlling the organisational destinies of different individuals and groups. Rawson, Hinings and Greenwood (1980: 6) have similarly noted that professions frequently articulate and draw upon discrete elements of their professional mantle to justify their areas of control. In the case of HCS, the fact that clients must have chronic diseases or physical disabilities to be eligible for assistance is one of the major factors in legitimating the dominance of the medical profession over the other health professionals.

In addition to these three professional subcultures, there exist two other major organizational subcultures or 'occupational communities' (Van Maanen and Barley, 1984: 287). These comprise: the administrative staff, who form an orthogonal subculture in supporting the core values of the dominant culture; and the paramedical aides (PMAs), who form a 'deferential subculture' in deferring to health professionals, especially the medical profession (see Bloor and Dawson, 1994). The organizational culture serves to reinforce this position through the maintenance of a mythology that professional staff' 'put PMA's down', which has served to make PMAs more remote and further reinforces the belief that they are 'lesser' team members. On the other hand, paramedical aides often resort to 'atrocity stories' (Dingwall, 1977; Stimson and Webb, 1975) as a means of defending their group against what they perceive to be excessive claims of superiority by others in the organization.

Counter-culture and enhancing and orthogonal subcultures have been identified elsewhere (Rose, 1988; Siehl and Martin, 1984); whereas the other two types of subcultures: dissenting and deferential, represent Bloor and Dawson's (1994) identification of further subcultural groupings (as illustrated in the case of HCS). Each of these subcultures shape the primary organizational culture in a number of different ways. The enhancing and deferential subcultures are both compatible with the organizational culture. With the latter it is through deference, and with the former it is through unquestioning support and advocacy of the 'rightness' of the core assumptions, values and beliefs. In the case of dissenting subcultures, these were shown to challenge the existing dominant subculture and offer an alternative set of operating practices and values within the primary cultural system of home care provision. Finally, the more common orthogonal subculture was shown to act as a midway point between the enhancing and dissenting subcultures, and facilitate the development of new proposals and the redefinition of common elements without radically questioning the dominance of the medical subculture.

The case of HCS demonstrates how there are often a number of 'cultures' that co-exist in large organizations and that these interact and influence each other in shaping a more general 'culture' of the organization. We refer to these as subcultures and in this case, as these are also influenced by external professional affiliation of the various groups that constitute HCS, we refer to them as professional subcultures. HCS usefully illustrates how the element of professional culture is central to understanding why certain subcultures can sustain themselves in potentially alien cultural environments. At its simplest, professional subcultures are often stronger than other groupings within an organisation in the sense of having extra-organisational associations and peers to aid them in shaping new cultures and codes of conduct, and resisting the imposition of other cultural values and practices. In other words, professional cultures that reside outside of organisations are central to sustaining professional subcultures within organisations. Thus, whilst professional subcultures conflict, coincide and interlock with each other, they each

(Continued)

(Continued)

have the potential to redirect and shape organisations (see Alvesson and Sveningsson, 2008).

Questions

1. How many subcultures co-exist within Home Care Service and how do they compare and contrast?
2. How useful is Bloor and Dawson's characterization of the different types of subcultures?
3. Is there an organizational culture? What is it and how does it differ from the professional subcultures that exist within HCS?
4. How is it possible to manage cultural change in such an organization? What are the problems and issues that you are likely to encounter?
5. Consider Alvesson and Sveningsson's (2008: 39) claim that 'the concept of culture is often used to refer to top management beliefs of organizational culture (ideas of a specific culture can often be seen as a senior management subculture) that marginalize the (sometimes contrasting) meaning creation of other groups in an organization.'

Chapter questions

The questions listed below relate to the chapter as a whole and can be used by individuals to further reflect on the material covered, as well as serving as a source for more open group discussion and debate.

1. Which are the key characteristics of organizational culture?
2. Which are the three key perspectives in the study of organizational culture?
3. Discuss the difference between espoused and enacted values.
4. Summarize the key 'principles' that companies should follow in order to build and sustain a culture that promotes the generation and implementation of new ideas and novel outcomes.
5. In your opinion, are strong, cohesive cultures conducive or detrimental to creativity and innovation? Illustrate your points by using real-life examples.
6. How important is it to understand the influence of subcultures in managing change, creativity and innovation?

Hands-on exercise

Students are allocated to small groups and are required to undertake a study focusing on uncovering the corporate values being promoted by Yahoo and Google. Both companies are excellent examples of companies which operate in very dynamic external environments. Students should search the web and collect articles related to these companies' cultures and are expected to make a brief presentation based on their findings uncovering the similarities and differences in the corporate values being promoted by these companies.

Team debate exercise

Debate the following statement:

> *Strong, cohesive cultures are an anathema to organizational creativity and innovation.*

Divide the class into two groups. One should argue as convincingly as possible that creativity is better directed in strong cultures that emphasize innovation-enhancing norms. The other group should prepare its arguments against this, highlighting that uniformity discourages individual expression and, hence, creativity and innovation. Each group should be prepared to defend their ideas against the other group's arguments by using real-life examples.

References

Amabile, T.M. (1998) 'How to kill creativity', *Harvard Business Review*, 76 (6): 76–87.

Anderson, N.R. and West, M.A. (1998) 'Measuring climate for work group innovation: development and validation of the team climate inventory', *Journal of Organizational Behavior*, 19: 235–58.

Andriopoulos, C. and Gotsi, M. (2002) 'Creativity requires a culture of trust: lessons from Lunar Design Inc.', *Design Management Journal*, Spring: 57–63.

Arad, S., Hanson, M.A. and Schneider, R.J. (1997) 'A framework for the study of relationships between organizational characteristics and organizational innovation', *Journal of Creative Behavior*, 31: 42–58.

Badovick, G.J. and Beatty, S.E. (1987) 'Shared organizational values: measurement and impact upon strategic marketing implementation', *Journal of the Academy of Marketing Science*, 15 (Spring): 19–26.

Bloor, G. and Dawson, P. (1994) 'Understanding professional culture in organizational context', *Organization Studies*, 15: 275–95.

Burnes, B. (2000) *Managing Change: A Strategic Approach to Organational Dynamics*, 3rd edn. London: Pitman.

Caldwell, D. and O'Reilly, C. (1995) 'Promoting team-based innovation in organizations: the role of normative influence'. Paper presented at the Fifty-Fourth Annual Meetings of the Academy of Management. Vancouver, BC Canada.

Chapman, P. (1988) 'Changing the culture at Rank Xerox', *Long Range Planning*, 21 (2): 23–8.

Cole, R.E. (1999) *Managing Quality Fads: How American Business Learned to Play the Quality Game*. New York: Oxford University Press.

Cooper, C.A., Cartwright, S. and Earley, P.C. (2001) *Handbook of Organizational Culture*. Oxford: Blackwell.

Deal, T.E. and Kennedy, A.A. (1982) *Corporate Cultures*. Reading, MA: Addison-Wesley.

Denison, D. (1990) *Corporate Culture and Organizational Effectiveness*. Chichester: John Wiley.

Feldman, M.S. (1991) 'The meanings of ambiguity: learning from stories and metaphors', in P.J. Frost, L.F. Moore, M.R. Louis, C.C. Lundberg and J. Martin (eds), *Reframing Organizational Culture*. Thousand Oaks, CA: Sage.

Flynn, F.J. and Chatman, J.A. (2004) 'Strong cultures and innovation: oxymoron or opportunity?', in M.L. Tushman and P. Anderson (eds), *Managing Strategic Innovation and Change: A Collection of Readings*, 2nd edn. Oxford: Oxford University Press.

Fombrun, C.J. (1983) 'Corporate culture, environment and strategy', *Human Resource Management,* 22 (1/2): 139–52.

Frost, P.J., Moore, L.F., Louis, M.R., Lundberg, C.C. and Martin, J. (1991) *Reframing Organizational Culture.* Thousand Oaks, CA: Sage.

Graves, D. (1986) *Corporate Culture*. London: Frances Pinter.

Gregory, K. (1983) 'Native-view paradigms: multiple cultures and culture conflicts in organisations', *Administrative Science Quarterly*, 28: 359–76.

Harris, L.C. and Ogbonna, E. (1997) 'A three-perspective approach to understanding culture in retail organizations', *Personnel Review*, 27 (2): 104–23.

Hatch, M.J. (1993) 'The dynamics of organizational culture', *Academy of Management Review*, 18: 657–93.

Hoffman, L.R. (1959) 'Homogeneity of member personality and its effect on group problem-solving', *Journal of Abnormal and Social Psychology*, 58: 27–32.

Hofstede, G. (1980) *Culture's Consequences*. Thousand Oaks, CA: Sage.

Jacques, E. (1951) *The Changing Culture of a Factory*. London: Tavistock Institute.

Judge, T., Locke, E. and Durham, C. (1997) 'The dispositional causes of job satisfaction: A core evaluations approach', *Research in Organizational Behavior*, 19: 151–88.

Kanter, R.M. (2002), 'Creating the culture for innovation', in F. Hesselbein, M. Goldsmith and I. Somerville (eds), *Leading for Innovation and Organizing for Results*. San Francisco: Jossey-Bass.

Keller, R.T. (1986) 'Predictors of the performance of project groups in R&D organizations', *Academy of Management Journal*, 29: 715–26.

Kilmann, R.W. (1982) 'Getting control of the corporate culture', *Managing* (USA), 2: 11–17.

Kotter, J.P. and Heskett, J.L. (1992) *Corporate Culture and Performance*. New York: The Free Press.

Kroeber, A.L. and Kluckhohn, C. (1952) 'Culture: a critical review of concepts and definitions', *Papers of the Peabody Museum*, 47 (1a).

Locke, E.A. and Kirkpatrick, S.A. (1995) 'Promoting creativity in organisations', in C.M. Ford and D.A. Gioia (eds), *Creative Action in Organisations: Ivory Tower Visions & Real World Voices*. Thousand Oaks, CA: Sage.

Martin, J. (1992) *Cultures in Organizations: Three Perspectives*. New York: Oxford University Press.

Martin, J. and Meyerson, D. (1988) 'Organizational culture and the denial, channelling and acknowledgement of ambiguity', in L.R. Pondy, R.J. Boland and H. Thomas (eds), *Managing Ambiguity and Change*. Chichester: John Wiley.

Martin, J. and Siehl, C. (1983) 'Organizational culture and counter-culture: an uneasy symbiosis', *Organizational Dynamics*, 12 (2): 52–64.

Martins, E.C. and Terblanche, F. (2003) 'Building organizational culture that simulates creativity and innovation', *European Journal of Innovation Management*, 6 (1): 64–74.

Meyerson, D. (1991) 'Normal ambiguity? A glimpse of an occupational culture', in P.J. Frost, L.F. Moore, M.R. Louis, C.C. Lundberg and J. Martin (eds), *Reframing Organizational Culture*. Thousand Oaks, CA: Sage.

Mohr, J., Sengupta, S. and Slater, S. (2005) *Marketing of High-Technology Products and Innovations*, 2nd edn. Englewood Cliffs, NJ: Pearson Prentice Hall.

Morgan, G. (1986) *Images of Organization.* Thousand Oaks, CA: Sage.

Neilson, G., Paternack, B. and Van Nuys, K. (2005) 'The passive–aggressive organization', *Harvard Business Review*, 83 (10) (October): 1–11.

Nemeth, C.J. (1997) 'Managing innovation: when less is more', *California Management Review*, 40 (1): 59–74.

Nemeth, C.J. and Staw, B.M. (1989) 'The tradeoffs of social control and innovation within groups and organizations', in L. Berkowitz (ed.), *Advances in Experimental Social Psychology.* New York: Academic Press.

Nicholson, G.C. (1998) 'Keeping innovation alive', *Research Technology Management*, 41 (3): 34–40.

Ogbonna, E. (1993) 'Managing organizational culture: fantasy or reality?', *Human Resource Management Journal*, 3 (2): 42–54.

O'Reilly, C. (1989) 'Corporations, culture and commitment: motivational and social control in organizations', *California Management Review*, 31 (4): 9–25.

O'Reilly, C. and Chatman, J. (1996) 'Culture as social control: corporations, cults and commitment', in B. Staw and L.L. Cummings (eds), *Research in Organizational Behavior.* Stamford, CT: JAI Press.

Ouchi, W.G. (1981) *Theory Z.* Reading, MA: Addison-Wesley.

Ouchi, W.G. and Wilkins, A.L. (1985) 'Organizational culture', *Annual Review of Sociology*, 11: 457–83.

Pascale, R.T. and Athos, A.G. (1981) *The Art of Japanese Management.* New York: Warner Books.

Peters, T. and Waterman, R.H., Jr (1982) *In Search of Excellence.* New York: Harper & Row.

Pfeffer, J. (2002) 'To build a culture of innovation, avoid conventional management wisdom', in F. Hesselbein, M. Goldsmith and I. Somerville (eds), *Leading for Innovation and Organizing for Results.* San Francisco: Jossey-Bass.

Pfeffer, J. and Sutton, R. (2002) 'Snapping managerial inertia', in *Business: The Ultimate Resource.* London: Bloomsbury.

Robbins, S.P. (1987) *Organization Theory: Structure, Design and Application.* Englewood Cliffs, NJ: Prentice Hall.

Rosen, M. (1985) 'Breakfast at Spiro's: dramaturgy and dominance', *Journal of Management*, 11 (2): 31–48.

Sackman, S.A. (1992) 'Culture and subcultures: an analysis of organizational knowledge', *Administrative Science Quarterly*, 37 (1): 140–61.

Sathe, V.J. (1985) *Culture and Related Corporate Realities.* Homewood, IL: Irwin.

Schein, E.H. (1984) 'Coming to a new awareness of organizational culture', *Sloan Management Review*, 12: 3–16.

Schein, E.H. (1985) *Organizational Culture and Leadership.* San Francisco: Jossey-Bass.

Schein, E.H. (1991a) *Organizational Culture and Leadership*, 2nd edn. San Francisco: Jossey-Bass.

Schein, E.H. (1991b) 'What is culture?', in P. Frost, L. Moore, M. Louis, C. Lundberg and J. Martin (eds), *Reframing Organizational Culture.* Thousand Oaks, CA: Sage.

Schneider, B. (1988) 'Notes on climate and culture', in C. Lovelock (ed.), *Managing Services.* Englewood Cliffs, NJ: Prentice Hall.

Schwartz, H. and Davis, S.M. (1981) 'Matching corporate culture and business strategy', *Organizational Dynamics*, 10: 30–48.

Siehl, C. (1985) 'After the founder: an opportunity to manage culture', in P.J. Frost, L.F. Moore, M.R. Louis, C.C. Lundberg and J. Martin (eds), *Organizational Culture.* Thosand Oaks, CA: Sage.

Siehl, C. and Martin, J. (1988) 'Measuring organizational culture: mixing qualitative and quantitative methods', in M. Owen Jones, M. Dane Moore and R.C. Snyder (eds), *Inside Organizations: Understanding the Human Dimension*. Thousand Oaks, CA: Sage.

Silverzweig, S. and Allen, R.F. (1976) 'Changing the corporate culture', *Sloan Management Review*, 17 (3): 33–49.

Smirich, L. (1983) 'Concepts of culture and organizational analysis', *Administrative Science Quarterly*, 28: 339–58.

Sparrow, P.R. and Pettigrew, A.M. (1988) 'Strategic human resource management in the UK computer supplier industry', *Journal of Occupational Psychology*, 61: 25–42.

Sternberg, R.G. and Lubart, T.I. (1995) 'Ten tips toward creativity in the workplace', in C.M. Ford and D.A. Gioia (eds), *Creative Action in Organisations: Ivory Tower Visions & Real World Voices*. Thousand Oaks, CA: Sage.

Sutton, R. and Hargadon, A. (1996) 'Brainstorming groups in context: effectiveness in a product design firm', *Administrative Science Quarterly*, 41: 685–718.

Tesluk, P.E., Farr, J.L. and Klein, S.R. (1997) 'Influences of organizational culture and climate on individual creativity', *Journal of Creative Behavior*, 31: 27–41.

Tsoukas, H. and Chia, R. (2002) 'On organizational becoming: Rethinking organizational change', *Organization Science* 13/5: 567–82.

Tushman, M.L. and O'Reilly, C. (2002) *Winning through Innovation: A Practical Guide to Leading Organizational Change and Renewal*. Boston, MA: Harvard Business School Press.

van Maanen, J. (1976) 'Breaking in: socialisation to work', in R. Dubin (ed.), *Handbook of Work, Organization and Society*. Chicago: Rand McNally.

van Maanen, J. (1977) *Organizational Careers: Some New Perspectives*. New York: John Wiley.

van Maanen, J. (1991) 'The smile factory: work at Disneyland', in P.J. Frost, L.F. Moore, M.R. Louis, C.C. Lundberg and J. Martin (eds), *Reframing Organizational Culture*. Thousand Oaks, CA: Sage.

Weick, K.E. (1991) 'The vulnerable system: an analysis of the Tenerife air disaster', in P.J. Frost, L.F. Moore, M.R. Louis, C.C. Lundberg and J. Martin (eds), *Reframing Organizational Culture*. Thousand Oaks, CA: Sage.

Wetlaufer, S. (2000) 'Common sense and conflict: an interview with Disney's Michael Eisner', *Harvard Business Review*, 78 (1): 114–24.

Wiener, Y. (1988) 'Forms of value systems: a focus on organizational effectiveness and cultural change maintenance', *Academy of Management Review*, 13: 534–45.

Wilkins, A.L. and Ouchi, W.G. (1983) 'Efficient cultures: exploring the relationship between culture and organizational performance', *Administrative Science Quarterly*, 28: 468–81.

Wilson, A.M. (1996) 'The role and importance of corporate culture in the delivery of a service'. PhD thesis, Department of Marketing, University of Strathclyde, Glasgow.

Zien, K.A. and Buckler, S.A. (2004) 'Dreams to market: crafting a culture of innovation', in R. Katz (ed.), *The Human Side of Managing Technological Innovation*. New York: Oxford University Press.

Recommended reading

- Poole, M.S. and Van de Ven, A. (2004) *Handbook of Organizational Change and Innovation*. New York: Oxford University Press.

- Schein, E. (1999) *The Corporate Culture Survival Guide*. San Francisco: Jossey-Bass.

- Schein, E. (2004) *Organizational Culture and Leadership*, 3rd edn. New York: John Wiley.

- Westwood, R. and Clegg, S.R. (2003) *Debating Organization: Point–Counterpoint in Organization Studies.* Oxford: Blackwell.

Some useful websites

- This is the website of Professor Edgar Schein, which provides information on his papers, books, presentations and events on organizational culture (http://web.mit.edu/scheine/www/home.html).

- From the Department for Business Enterprise and Regulatory Reform (BERR, UK) you can find many reports, articles and practical guidelines on improving organizational innovation (http://www.berr.gov.uk/index.html).

10

The Organization: Managing Processes of Change

Learning objectives

This chapter has 10 learning objectives:

1. To provide an explanation of what we mean by 'organizational change' and to categorize different types of change.
2. To identify the main drivers for change and to clarify the context of managing change in business organizations.
3. To outline the main reasons why people resist change and to consider the implications of viewing resistance as a 'problem' to be overcome.
4. To consider the role of communication in managing the process of organizational change.
5. To provide an accessible summary on the main theoretical frameworks and conceptual models for understanding change.
6. To outline the essential elements of an organizational development perspective to managing planned change.
7. To examine the contribution of contingency theory through the discussion of a situational model for leading change.
8. To summarize the key components of a political perspective on managing change.
9. To clarify the central dimensions of a processual framework for understanding change.
10. To provide a case study that illustrates some of the issues raised in this chapter.

Introduction

No organization in the twenty-first century would boast about its constancy, sameness, or status quo compared to ten years ago. Stability is interpreted more often as stagnation than steadiness, and organizations that are not in the business of change and transition are generally viewed as recalcitrant. The frightening uncertainty that traditionally accompanies major organizational change has been superseded by the frightening uncertainty now associated with staying the same. (Cameron and Quinn, 2006: 1)

Change is integral to all our lives and an essential feature of work environments. In the case of business organizations, theories have developed that chart the life cycles of organizations demonstrating how certain groups or populations of companies follow certain patterns and trajectories. For example, there has been an increase in the number of low-cost airlines with the growth in demand for fast travel between cities. This growth in demand would suggest a vibrant industry and yet external forces and events can radically change the fortunes of airlines. Critical world events often arrive unannounced and unexpected – stimulating a radical rethink or a change in the way that business is done. Some changes may be reactive to unanticipated changes in external market conditions; others may reflect a proactive strategy to reposition or change corporate operations; and yet others may be stimulated by a change in key personnel as new staff seek to make their imprint on the organization. Change, it would seem, is more complex than any simple definition might suggest and therefore it is clarifying this concept and making sense of processes of change that is the focus of this chapter.

In seeking to understand change, a number of studies have been carried out and theories developed (see, for example, Carnall, 2007; Hayes, 2007; Senior and Fleming, 2005). This body of knowledge draws on research on the introduction of change initiatives that move an organization from a current method of working to a new form of operating arrangement. As already mentioned, such change initiatives may centre on *proactive* programmes in the uptake of, for example, new technologies, re-engineering programmes and quality schemes, or be more *reactive* in response to unanticipated shifts in business market activities. Although, theoretically, this knowledge base has not generally attended to issues of creativity and innovation, if following Peters and Waterman (1982) we broaden our definition of innovation to include 'creative people developing marketable new products and services' and innovative companies 'continually responding to change of any sort in their environment', then the conceptual boundaries between change, creativity and innovation become blurred. This point is well made by Knights and McCabe (2003: 39) who note that:

One of the problems within the literature is that universal definitions are commonly adopted, which then legislate as to what is to count as innovation independently of the specific conditions of its development and reproduction. Following the view that knowledge

is always contingent on the conditions of its genesis and applica-
tion, we take innovation simply to mean organizational change or the
transformation of established practices.

Although our focus in this chapter is on the change management literature and the associated models for understanding organizational change, we are also concerned with change as innovation and the creative ways in which people steer, resist and make sense of their change experience. Whilst we recognize that the search for a theory that fully explains change, creativity and innovation may not be feasible, there is value in considering frameworks that have been developed to further our understanding of these processes. In the case of organizational change, there remains considerable debate over the speed, direction and effects of change and on the most appropriate methods and concepts for understanding and explaining change. There are a large number of change models that could be categorized and examined, such as Tichy's (1983) Technical, Political, Cultural (TPC) framework; Paton and McCalman's (2000) Intervention Strategy Model (ISM); and the Burke–Litwin Open Systems Model (see Burke, 2002: 195–238); but we have selected four main approaches for more detailed examination. These comprise:

- Organizational Development Approach
- Situational (Contingency) Model
- Political Process Framework
- Processual Perspective

We have included organizational development (Gallos, 2006) and contingency approaches (Donaldson, 2001), as these have been particularly influential in terms of research and teaching (see, for example, Cummings, 2008; French et al., 2004); whereas, the political process (Buchanan and Badham, 2008; Knights and McCabe, 2003) and processual frameworks (Dawson, 2003b; Pettigrew, 1985) are gaining in credibility with growing theoretical and empirical support of these more fluid and dynamic perspectives on change (Tsoukas and Chia, 2002).

Change and organizations

Change is endemic to all organizations operating in business markets. Although all organizations are in the process of *changing*, the nature of these changes can vary enormously and so we need a way to differentiate between the scale and scope of change experienced across different organizations, and within the same organization, over time. Evaluating the extent and depth of company change allows us to classify change from small developmental activities and routine modifications through to large-scale transformational initiatives. The former can involve improvements on current ways of doing things, of fine-tuning operations and implementing incremental changes on standard operating procedures. These changes typically work within the domain of the known, and often form an integral part of in-house monitoring and evaluation activities. Within universities, course and programme evaluations may be used to further refine and develop curriculum design and teaching delivery methods as part of ongoing and regular operating procedures.

At the other end of the spectrum lie the more radical transformational change initiatives that are generally large-scale and strategic in nature. A company may radically rethink their core activities, markets and purpose. The change may be proactive and involve considerable planning and adjustment over a number of years, or it may be in response to a sudden shift in world economies and business market activities. The growth, development and change in the telecommunications and computer industries over the last two decades provide us with a number of examples of radical change – and the concomitant rise and fall of the associated dot.com companies. Within the oil and gas sector, major multinational companies like Shell and BP are repositioning themselves as *energy* companies in a long-term strategy for corporate renewal.

Between large-scale transformational and small-scale developmental change programmes lie a raft of other change initiatives, including branch and divisional restructuring, the reconfiguration of operations in the production of a given good or service, and the transition from some current state to a well-defined new state over a planned timeframe. Within these distinctions, the notion of the known and unknowable arises, especially with respect to the vulnerability and scope of the change in question. Much of the change management literature has focused on large-scale transitions and transformational change initiatives that are also referred to as 'first-order change'. The velocity and vulnerability of such change initiatives draw them to the attention of academic researchers, the media and the business community. And yet, many of these change initiatives do not succeed in practice:

> Internet companies such as eBay, Amazon.com, and American Online recognize that they need to manage the changes associated with rapid entrepreneurial growth. Despite some individual successes, however, change remains difficult to pull off, and few companies manage the process as well as they would like. More of their initiatives – installing new technology, downsizing, restructuring, or trying to change corporate culture – have had low success rates. The brutal fact is that about 70 percent of all change initiatives fail. In our experience, the reason for most of those failures is that in their rush to change their organizations, managers end up immersing themselves in an alphabet soup of initiatives. They lose focus and become mesmerized by all the advice available in print and on-line about why companies should change, what they should try to accomplish, and how they should do it. This proliferation of recommendations often leads to muddle when change is attempted. The result is that most change efforts exert a heavy toll, both human and economic. To improve the odds of success, and to reduce the human carnage, it is imperative that executives understand the nature and process of corporate change much better. (Beer and Nohria, 1998)

Dimensions of change	'Hard' focused theories	'Soft' focused theories	Combinational theories
Goals	Maximize shareholder value	Develop organizational capabilities	Explicitly embrace the paradox between economic value and organizational capability
Leadership	Manage change from the top down	Encourage participation from the bottom up	Set direction from the top and engage the people below
Focus	Emphasize structure and systems	Build up corporate culture: employees' behaviour and attitudes	Focus simultaneously on the hard (structures and systems) and the soft (corporate culture)
Process	Plan and establish programmes	Experiment and evolve	Plan for spontaneity
Reward system	Motivate through financial incentives	Motivate through commitment – use pay as fair exchange	Use incentives to reinforce change but not to drive it
Use of consultants	Consultants analyse problems and shape solutions	Consultant support management in shaping their own solutions	Consultants are expert resources who empower employees

FIGURE 10.1   Comparing Theories of Change (adapted from Beer and Nohria, 1998)

Beer and Nohria (1998) argue that all corporate transformations can be located along six dimensions and that most theories either focus on top-down management approaches or bottom-up approaches (our case study at the end of this chapter provides a good illustration of both top-down and bottom-up approaches). The change model developed by Beer and Nohria (see Figure 10.1) provides a useful categorization in highlighting the tendency within the literature to focus on one element (for example, structure and systems) over another (for example, people and culture). Although the majority of models follow one or other of these two routes, there are some who attempt to combine elements of both approaches (see the combinational column in Figure 10.1), whereas in practice it is not uncommon for companies to adopt different change strategies (models of change) over time (see Case Study 10.1).

According to Beer and Nohria (1998), approaches that are able to combine the best of the 'hard' and 'soft' models (our third column) are generally the most fruitful. As such, their characterization provides a useful starting point in spotlighting the need to balance what is often presented as two opposing idealized types and yet there are some key political process issues that are absent in their analysis. As we shall see later, they fail to accommodate the full range of drivers that stimulate and shape change processes. For example, the maximization of shareholder value or the development of organizational capabilities may not be at the forefront of change initiatives that are in response to critical and unforeseen junctures in the world economy. This may be in terms of the collapse of

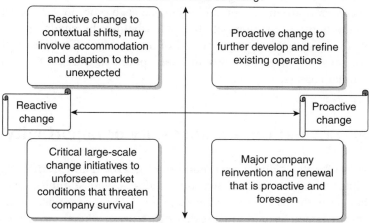

Second-order small-scale change

Reactive change to contextual shifts, may involve accommodation and adaption to the unexpected

Proactive change to further develop and refine existing operations

Reactive change

Proactive change

Critical large-scale change initiatives to unforseen market conditions that threaten company survival

Major company reinvention and renewal that is proactive and foreseen

Transformational large-scale change

FIGURE 10.2 Different types of company change

certain financial markets, world conflicts, terrorist attacks or dubious management practices that undermine the standing of major business corporations. Company decisions to relocate to other parts of the world can leave a significant void in regional business markets and necessitate major change initiatives among network firms.

Whether change is reactive, in response to certain unforeseen events or a proactive decision, can all influence the nature, direction and shape of change. In classifying types of change, Jick and Peiperl (2003: xvii) make a distinction between: improvements to an existing state (developmental change); implementation of a new known state (transitional change); and the emergence of a radical new state that is unknown until it takes final shape (transformational change). In combining these two continua of small-scale to large-scale change, and reactive to proactive initiatives, we can categorize four different types of change. First, *reactive small-scale change* initiatives that seek to accommodate and adapt to unforeseen changes resulting from, for example, problems in launching a new revised product model or business operating procedure. The unexpected problems that arose at Heathrow Airport's Terminal 5 are is a good example of this. Second, *proactive developmental change* programmes that seek to improve on current ways of doing things over a planned period of time. Third, *reactive radical change* initiatives in response to, for example, unexpected world events that necessitates a major repositioning of a company. Fourth, *proactive radical change* projects in the reinvention of company strategy and major transformation of business operations. These four types of organizational change are illustrated in Figure 10.2.

As well as the dimensions of the scale and depth of change, and whether change is reactive or proactive, we can also consider a number of other elements, such as the essential nature and content of change, timeframes of change, and the effects of change on job structures and authority relationships. All these elements are important and influence each other in various ways, for example, the temporal element of change – whether the change promoted is to occur quickly or over a longer period of time – often combines with other factors, such as employee attitudes and perceptions in shaping the process of organizational change.

Change drivers: threat, necessity or opportunity?

As noted in Chapter 2, there are a number of internal and external triggers to change. Internal factors include structural redesign and administrative adjustment, changes in the nature of products and the delivery of services, technology and initiatives aimed at the human side of enterprise, whereas external drivers include changes in business market activity, world events, legislation, trade regulations and advances in technology. For some commentators, the new global business environment represents a radical shift from the mass-production age of the 20th century to the post-industrial (or information/knowledge) age of the 21st century. Under these new conditions, change is characterized as discontinuous, revolutionary, traumatic and fast:

> *Technological advances in tandem with rising consumer expectations and access to global markets have contributed to shorter product life cycles and led to the need for go-to-market speed and flexibility ... In many industries, technological advances also have eroded the traditional barriers to entry, such as high start-up costs and the need for economies of scale. As a result, many new smaller, nimbler companies are entering markets that traditionally have been the sanctum of industry behemoths. To compete against these new entrants, which think global and are untrammelled by the trappings of bureaucracy and tradition, established industry giants must reinvent themselves. (Graetz et al., 2002: 16)*

In considering environmental triggers to change, Senior (2002: 15) argues that the mnemonic PETS is useful for categorizing Political, Economic, Technological and Socio-cultural factors. *Political factors* range from international law and government legislation to trade union activity and local regulations; *economic factors* include financial regulations and exchange rates; changes in transport technology is included under *technological factors*; and lifestyle change and attitudes to work are examples of *socio-cultural factors* (Senior, 2002: 16). She argues that whilst it is possible to identify internal triggers to change, such as the purchase of new IT equipment, these triggers generally occur in response to external influences and hence, in practice, it is often impossible to separate the internal from external drivers of change (see also Senior and Fleming, 2005). As Jick and Peiperl (2003: xix) note:

An organization can encounter a problem, not necessarily life-threatening but one deserving attention, and, thus, can feel the need to introduce change. It might, for example, consider a reorganization in response to a competitor's new product introduction; it might consider creating a quality program after receiving disturbing results about its own product or service quality. Alternatively, an organization faced with a definite threat – most probably will institute change, acutely recognizing the need to do so.

These various internal and external drivers are part of an ongoing flow of forces that continuously shape strategies, implementation plans and the decisions of business leaders. As indicated in our earlier chapters, we support the more process-based accounts that conceptualize change as a fluid and dynamic process. However, there is an alternative position that readers should be aware of. This view advocates that stability and not change is the norm for business organizations. In contrast to theories that view change as an ongoing continuous process, the punctuated equilibrium paradigm argues that relatively long periods of stability (equilibrium) are punctuated by short periods of more radical, revolutionary change (Romanelli and Tushman, 1994). Hayes (2007: 5) usefully captures the key elements of this approach when he states that:

The essence of the punctuated equilibrium paradigm is that systems (organisations) evolve through the alternation of periods of equilibrium, in which persistent deep structures permit only limited incremental change, and periods of revolution, in which these deep structures are fundamentally altered. This is in stark contrast to the traditional gradualist paradigm which suggests that (a) an organisation (or an organisational sub-system) can accommodate any change at any time so long as it is a relatively small change, and (b) that a stream of incremental changes can, over a period of time, fundamentally transform the organisation's deep structure.

The punctuated equilibrium model recognizes how operating practices can become embedded in organizations and how this can stifle creativity and innovation (Tushman and Romanelli, 1985). This type of stagnation in the repression of new ideas creates misalignment with the external environment and necessitate the need for more radical change – what Tushman and Romanelli refer to as 'punctuated equilibrium' – that drives the organization to changes that seek to realign structure, culture and practices with external environmental factors. This process of radical change results in a new period of stability as the organization once again reaches a state of equilibrium. In contrast to process-based theories, where organizations are viewed as being in a state of continual change pocketed by temporary periods of perceived stability (Tsoukas and Chia, 2002), punctuated equilibrium theory posits that stability is the norm and that failures to adjust ultimately result in the need for revolutionary change in the transformation of organizations to a new state of equilibrium (see Hayes, 2007: 4–11; Romanelli and Tushman, 1994; Tushman and Romanelli, 1985).

This debate between stability and ongoing change is taken up later in Chapter 11; from either perspective the urgency for change can be stimulated by change triggers that highlight the need to realign, innovate or radically transform in order to maintain or regain a competitive business market position. Moreover, companies are often involved in more than one change project at any one time and this can further complicate an assessment of business needs and trajectories. As Dawson (2003a: 41–2) explains:

> *Companies continuously move in and out of many different states, often concurrently, during the history of one or a number of organizational change initiatives ... The initial awareness of a need for change may be either in response to external or internal pressures for change (reactive), or through a belief in the need for change to meet future competitive demands (proactive).*

These drivers and triggers for change can be important, not only to business leaders but to the way others may respond to the need and urgency for change. For example, employee attitudes will be shaped by their understanding of whether the change is necessary and central to the corporation's competitive survival or whether it is merely a management fad that is likely to boost the careers of a few whilst threatening existing arrangements and authority relationships of employees in general. Whether change is accepted or resisted by employees is an important factor that will not only influence the potential pace and direction of change, but also strategies adopted in the management of change.

People and change: the 'problem' of resistance?

> *Perhaps the greatest challenge of all comes with the awareness that managing change includes managing the reactions to that change. Unfortunately, change frequently is introduced without considering its psychological effect on others in the organization – particularly those who have not been part of the decision to make the change: those who arrive on Monday only to learn 'from now on, it's all different'. Further, when reactions are taken into account, they often are lumped under 'resistance' to change, a pejorative phrase that conjures up stubbornness, obduracy, traditionalism, 'just saying no'. It seems fair to state, however, that, if the reactions to change are not anticipated – and managed – the change process will be needlessly painful and perhaps unsuccessful. (Jick and Peiperl, 2003: xxi)*

Managing the human aspects of change is frequently cited as one of the most significant factors to the 'success' or 'failure' of major change initiatives (Pendlebury et al., 1998). As we shall see, the importance of communication, employee involvement and ensuring that behavioural change is rooted within the culture of an organization has a longstanding history in the field of Organizational Development (OD). Democratic and participative strategies are viewed as ways to ensure that employees buy into and commit to change, and yet Kotter (1996) maintains that more company transformations 'fail' than 'succeed'. Why is this?

We would argue that in a context where there is continual pressure to change, it is as important to know when not to change as it is to know when to change. It is ironic, given the number of failed change initiatives, that those that question the need for change are often cast as the villains of the piece, 'unable' to adapt to changing conditions. The time, energy, resources and money that can be wasted through persisting with an ill-thought-out change, even in the face of strong employee resistance and articulate employee critiques, perhaps goes some way to explain the high level of failure among company transformation efforts. Although most change management writers recognize that employee resistance is to be expected in any major company change programme (Strebel, 1998), employee resistance should not simply be treated as an obstacle to be overcome, but as a valuable source of knowledge and critique of change programmes. As Collins (1998: 92) notes:

> *Workers who 'resist' change tend to be cast as lacking the psychological make-up to deal with change, and so, are said to be weak and fearful of change, whereas, those who support or manage change are regarded as 'go-ahead' chaps who have the 'right-stuff' for career success.*

Why do people resist change?

One of the main reasons why people resist change is that the proposed change may break the continuity of a working environment and create a climate of uncertainty and ambiguity. Following company change initiatives, it is not uncommon for old-established relationships to be redefined, for familiar structures to be redesigned and modified, and for traditional methods of work to be replaced and/or modified. Understandably, some employees may seek to maintain the status quo and resist these types of changes. Typically, resistance has been identified as resulting from one, or a combination, of the following factors:

- substantive change in job (change in skill requirements);
- reduction in economic security or job displacement (threat to employment);
- psychological threats (whether perceived or actual);
- disruption of social arrangements (new work arrangements); and
- lowering of status (redefinition of authority relationships).

A substantive change in the nature of work and the skills required to perform certain functions is likely to engender distrust and resistance, particularly in situations where employees are not informed of the change prior to implementation. Even if these threats reflect an individual's perception of change rather than an actual threat, employee resistance to change is likely to result. Bedeian (1984) suggests that parochial self-interest, misunderstanding and lack of trust are common causes of resistance to organizational change. Paton and McCalman (2000: 48) identify six main reasons why people fear change and these are outlined in Figure 10.3. For them, effective communication is often the key to overcoming the 'problem' of change resistance and they conclude that, 'the effective change agent must be capable of orchestrating events; socializing within the network of stakeholders; and managing the communication process' (2000: 51).

Managing the communication process

Communication is generally recognized as one of the most important factors that influence change outcomes (Jackson and Callon, 2001). For example, Hayes (2007) argues that the features of communication networks and the effects of interpersonal relations can have a major influence on the process and outcomes of organizational change. Particular attention is given to the notion of 'effective communication' that informs employees, enables feedback and promotes wide-scale consultation. Many writers in this area assume that such action will overcome resistance to change (resistance is often seen to stem from natural anxiety, ignorance and misunderstanding) by stimulating interest and commitment and thereby reducing opposition (e.g., Paton and McCalman, 2000).

Hersey and Blanchard (1988) argue that communication is a key process skill required of change agents to get others to understand and accept change. Drawing on the work of Bennis (1984), Carnall (2003) views this as involving an ability to communicate clear objectives, to be consistent and to ensure that others understand and are aware of the reasons and intentions of change. These three competencies Carnall labels as: the management of attention, the management of trust, and the management of meaning (see also Carnall, 2007). Paton and McCalman (2000) also identify a number of guidelines on effective communication and change, namely:

- To customize the message to ensure that it is set at an appropriate level to be understood by the intended audience.

- To set the tone of the message so it does not offend or seem patronizing.

- To recognize that communication is a two-way process and that feedback is essential.

- To do as you say (to practise what you preach).

- To use the appropriate medium to ensure penetration, so that the message reaches those it is intended to reach in the time required.

Why employees fear change	Explanation of employee fears and anxieties: individual and group
It challenges old ideas	By their very nature organizations have traditionally encouraged stability, continuity and the pursuit of security. Continuity of procedures, services, products and staff leads to a stable operating environment. Remember that the basis of today's success lies in the past and this encourages management to reinforce the lessons of the past. For example, senior management do not retire, they take up non-executive positions on the board; non-executive directors are recruited for their past knowledge of the business environment; organizational design attempts to reflect the perception of historical success; recruitment policies endeavour to reinforce old beliefs by ensuring the appointment of like-minded personnel. Success in the future will depend upon a management understanding the lessons of the past, but if too much emphasis is placed upon this 'history' then these lessons will simply reinforce old ideas.
It confronts apathy	A great many employees grow apathetic in their approach to working life. Careers falter, positions of apparent security and ease are achieved, competencies are developed and the employee becomes apathetic to their working environment. They do what they do well, or have convinced their peers and manager that they do, and deep down they would prefer the status quo. Change may have the audacity to wake them up from their slumbers!
It creates new technological challenges	New techniques, procedures and skills acquisition can bring out, no matter how briefly, the 'Luddite' that lurks just beneath our outer veneer of confidence. Never underestimate the 'power' of technological change. No matter how insignificant the change looks to the well informed it can have far-reaching effects and consequences.
It permeates throughout the supply chain	Change for change's sake is both foolish and potentially expensive. The effective and efficient management of the supply chain ensures that the final consumer is delivered a product or service that meets their expectations. Stakeholders within the supply chain, including the final consumer, tend to be sceptical of any change that results in the 'equilibrium' being disturbed. Management must be careful to ensure that the effects of a change, although beneficial to a particular member, do not cascade through the chain causing negative results further down stream.
It can result in organizational redesign	Tampering with the design will modify, at least in the short term, existing power bases, reporting structures and communications networks. In extreme cases issues regarding security of employment will be raised and undoubtedly questions concerning redeployment and training emerge.
It encourages debate	Debate is healthy when well managed, but it does tend to identify those lacking in understanding or knowledge. Once again, the assumptions of the past and those who promote them will be challenged.

FIGURE 10.3   Employee resistance to change (the text in this figure is sourced from Paton and McCalman, 2000: 48)

Within the popular management literature, John Kotter's (1996) eight-stage model on how to successfully manage change emphasizes the importance of communication. For Kotter (1996) communicating the vision is viewed as a critical stage in leading change (see also Kotter and Cohen, 2002). He argues that change leaders should communicate their vision in many different forums over and over again if they wish to develop an effective implementation strategy. He notes that:

> *Communication comes in both words and deeds. The latter is generally the most powerful form. Nothing undermines change more than behavior by important individuals that is inconsistent with the verbal communication. And yet this happens all the time, even in some well-regarded companies. (Kotter, 1996: 10)*

On the flip side, he claims that a major reason why change initiatives fail is because of ineffective communication. This takes three main forms:

1. Communication is limited to only a few memos.

2. The head of the company makes many speeches but everybody else remains silent.

3. There is effort in communicating the vision but the behaviour of some highly visible individuals conflicts with the message communicated, and employee cynicism results.

For many commentators, resistance and conflict are seen to result from poor communication, the spreading of rumours and misinformation, and an inability to allay the natural fears and anxieties of employees awaiting the unknown (Paton and McCalman, 2000). These writers contend that by providing clear communication through appropriate mediums at a tone and pitch suitable to the audience, and in practising what is preached, a programme of effective communication in the 'successful' management of change can be put into place (Carnall, 2007; Kotter, 1996). In contrast, Buchanan and Badham (2008) question this apolitical approach and argue that change agents simply use communication as another political tool in the tough contact sport of 'winning the turf game'. The politics of change is viewed as a part of organizational life (Dawson, 1994; Senior, 2002) in which power plays and the management of meaning is critical to the way others view and experience change (Collins, 1998; Itzin and Newman, 1995; Pettigrew, 1985).

Under this more critical perspective, communication and change are part of a political process in steering an organization from one configuration to another. To paraphrase Pfeffer, the use of power is about changing the course of events in getting people to change in ways that they would otherwise not do (Pfeffer, 1981). Politics as 'power in action' (Robbins, 1996) is thereby evident within communication processes that seek to influence the views and behaviours of others, especially in change agent engagement, or what Buchanan and Badham (2008) refer to as 'power-assisted steering'. Whichever stance one takes, the experience of communicating a change strategy in a context where change is generally viewed as important and necessary to company survival is going to be markedly different to a context where the strategy is highly contested and questioned.

Assessing the speed and context of change

The context of change and the speed within which change occurs can all influence employee experience and reaction to change initiatives. In an attempt to address issues of context and the speed and direction of change, Balogun and Hailey (1999) have developed a diagnostic tool known as the *change kaleidoscope*. They highlight the importance of context in deciding on an appropriate implementation strategy (or 'change path') and the need to take into account potential 'enablers' and 'blockers' to change. A change agent needs to examine change through a contextual lens in order to make the right decisions over: the starting point for change; the implementation strategy or change path; change style; change target; change levers; and the change roles. In considering each of these decisions the change agent should carefully evaluate eight contextual features. These comprise: the time available for change (how quickly is change needed); the scope or scale of change (is there a need for some radical transformation or simply incremental realignment); the need to preserve what currently exists (in terms of staffing, ways of working and specific organizational competencies); levels of diversity within the organization (in terms of employee groups, taking into account the norms and values held by members of the organization); staff capability (for example, what is the level of expertise and availability of skill sets to successfully implement change); resource availability (what is the organizational capacity for change); readiness for change (are people generally motivated and supportive of the need for change); and power support (that is, whether those responsible for bringing about change hold enough power to impose the changes required).

Through assessing these contextual elements change agents can make a judgement on whether a programme for organizational change is likely to succeed, have significant difficulties or is likely to fail (Balogun and Hailey, 1999). They argue that the four main strategic options that organizations face centre on whether change is incremental, which they term 'incremental realignment: adaption strategy' and 'incremental transformation: evolution strategy', or more radical in the form of 'big bang realignment: re-construction strategy' and 'big bang transformation: revolution strategy'. The former are likely to be planned, take place over a series of stages and be proactive, whereas the latter are often forced and reactive. They point out that companies seeking to reconstruct will need to devote considerable resources to the change initiative and to match these with strong leadership, stressing how changing the way people think and behave is going to take time (Balogun and Hailey, 1999; Balogun and Johnson, 2004). Often companies may embark on such transformational change strategies and follow these up with a more planned evolutionary strategy for change. In this way, the focus of the change strategy may need to change over time (see also Hayes, 2002: 163–5) and, as Balogun notes, local interpretations and responses are in turn likely to influence the speed and direction of change. She contends that we should 'move away from reifying change as something done to and placed on individuals, and instead acknowledge the role that change recipients play in creating and shaping change outcomes' (Balogun, 2006: 43).

Communicating change, taking account of the scale, context and the speed of change, recognizing the political nature of managing change and being aware of the need for flexibility in being able to adapt to the unexpected and unforeseen, are all in differing measures part of a number of academic perspectives that we are going to compare and contrast in the sections that follow. As we shall see, some of these approaches offer normative prescriptions on how to plan for effective change, whilst others are highly critical of any best-practice approach to change management.

The organizational development approach to change management

Within North America, the Organizational Development (OD) approach to change management has dominated discussion over the last 50 years (Cummings, 2008). This dominant textbook approach to organizational change – which developed from the pioneering work of Kurt Lewin (1947) – spotlights the importance of participation and employee involvement (Huse, 1982). The approach is historically rooted in the human relations perspective that emphasizes the importance of people and collaboration through a two-way process of communication (French and Bell, 1983; French et al., 2004). Although the origination of the term remains a little uncertain, it became established in the 1960s with the notion of organizational development perhaps being coined by Richard Beckhard (as part of the consultancy work he was engaged in with Douglas McGregor). As a label, OD suggests something broader than Management Development (MD) by involving the whole organization, as well as encompassing a wider remit than conventional human relations training (see Beckhard, 1969). One of the leading founders of the approach, Warren Bennis (1969), defined OD as follows:

> *A response to change, a complex educational strategy intended to change the beliefs, attitudes, values and structure of organizations so that they can better adapt to new technologies, markets, and challenges, and the dizzying rate of change itself.*

According to Beckhard (1969) the approach attempts to include all employees, is planned, seeks to improve both working conditions and organizational effectiveness, and is supported by top management. This attention to the place of people in change, the importance of individual dignity and the need to hear the voices of all and not just the powerful, stems from the founding influence of Kurt Lewin (see Marrow, 1969). As a German Jew, Lewin was forced to leave Germany in 1933 and this early experience of anti-Semitism is shown in his concern for democracy and participation at the workplace (De Board, 1978).

His work on inter-group dynamics and leadership has proven to be particularly influential on those practising within the field of OD, and many theories of organizational change originate from his landmark work on planned change (Kreitner and Kinicki, 1992).

Lewin's model of change

Lewin (1947, 1951) argued that in order for change to be successfully managed it is necessary to follow three general steps, comprising: unfreezing, changing and refreezing. Unfreezing is the stage in which there is a recognized need for change and action is taken to unfreeze existing attitudes and behaviour. This initial phase is seen to be critical in gaining employee support. For example, in his pioneering research (some of which was published after his death in 1947), Lewin found that in order to minimize worker resistance, employees should be brought in to participate in the process of planning proposed change programmes. Managing change through reducing the forces that prevent change, rather than through increasing the forces which are pushing for change, is central to Lewin's approach and his technique of force-field analysis. He maintained that within any social system there are driving and restraining forces which serve to maintain the status quo, and that organizations generally exist

> *[i]n a state of equilibrium which is not itself conducive to change ... The opposing pressures of driving and restraining forces will combine to produce a quasi-stationary equilibrium – a kind of temporary state of balance. In order to promote the right conditions for change, individuals have to identify driving and restraining forces. Then there has to be an unfreezing of the quasi-stationary equilibrium. This means creating an imbalance between the driving and restraining forces. (Wilson, 1992: 29–30)*

The example of drink-driving illustrates this where, although there may be strong driving forces to stop drinking and driving, such as public condemnation, fear of losing driving licence, cost, new laws, publicity campaigns, disapproval of spouse, the concern of harming others, and so forth, the restraining forces of habit, camaraderie, relief of tension, friends drinking, social pressure and the dislike of coercive methods may act to maintain the status quo. If these two opposing forces are equal in strength, then a state of equilibrium is said to exist. Consequently, to bring about change you either need to increase the strength of the driving forces or decrease the strength of the resisting forces. For example, publicity campaigns and television advertisements that stress the anti-social and irresponsible behaviour of drink-drivers can have a major influence on public behaviour and attitudes. Communicating a message not only about the illegality of such behaviours but also about the dangers and dire effects on other people's lives can bring about significant changes in public values and beliefs.

In the management of organizational change, the focus of OD specialists has been on communicating information that will serve to unfreeze the system through reducing the restraining forces rather than increasing the driving forces

(Gray and Starke, 1988; Weisbord, 1988). Once an imbalance has been created the system can be altered and a new set of driving and restraining forces put into place. A planned change programme is implemented, and only when the desired state has been achieved will the change agent set about 'refreezing' the organization. The new state of balance is then appraised and, where appropriate, methods of positive reinforcement are used to ensure employees 'internalize' attitudes and behaviours consistent with new work regimes.

The sub-discipline of organizational development

Over the years, OD has developed into a sub-discipline with its own literature base and fieldwork studies that support specialized OD courses, higher degrees and OD textbooks. The approach assumes that conflict between individuals and groups in an organization can be reconciled and, generally, OD programmes have common objectives; namely:

- To improve an organization's health and effectiveness through whole system change.

- To systematically introduce planned interventions.

- To apply top-down strategies and get all employees committed to change.

- To introduce change incrementally and to base planned change on empirical data.

- To use a specialist change agent to manage change.

- To achieve lasting rather than temporary change within an organization.

Underlining OD programmes are a core set of values that emphasize the importance of people and the need for individuals to be treated with dignity (French and Bell, 1983). Although resistance to change is expected, it is also expected that all individuals are treated with respect and that solutions to people issues are identified through a process of open communication and collaboration (see Cummings, 2008). Employee involvement is therefore key, as is the development of a climate of trust and openness (French et al., 2004). Control through hierarchy and formal command is seen as ineffective and any problems or conflicts that arise from the change programme should be confronted and reconciled (Robbins, 1986: 461). These core values that underpin OD interventions are viewed as central and run through the series of steps of an OD programme that typically commences with the appointment of a change agent. Once a change agent is appointed, information is then gathered from the client system in order to identify the major areas in need of change and, following feedback to the client, appropriate plans are formulated and action taken. Planning is generally viewed as a collaborative process based on valid information. Following implementation, changes are evaluated and action taken to ensure the 'institutionalization' of change occurs. In this action-research model of OD (that entails cycles of data gathering, diagnosis and feedback), political process is downplayed in the search for a common consensual view on change. As such, OD programmes can be seen to adopt a normative framework that promotes a one best way to manage change that will increase both organizational effectiveness and employee well-being. The professional consultants engaged in OD are therefore not concerned with the development of theory, or with the design of systematic programmes of research but, rather, with a set of normative prescriptions that guide their practice in managing change (Aldag and Stearns, 1991; Ledford et al., 1990).

Implementation remains a key phase under the OD approach and it is at this stage that employee resistance and conflict may be an issue that needs resolving. The approach recognizes that such problems may arise at different levels within the organization. For example, problems at the individual level may arise through personality clashes, task allocations, skill development and training issues. At the group level, conflicts may occur both within and between groups, over issues such as: leadership, resources and areas of responsibility, or through an unwillingness to co-operate or perhaps as a result of competing group priorities. At the organizational level, a lack of vision or clear direction of change may generate concerns over change and lower staff morale. The OD change agent plans for such eventualities and they would usually have their own preferred stage model of change, such as:

- *Scouting:* consultant and client discuss information and ideas about change.

- *Entry:* consultant relationship established.

- *Diagnosis:* information gathered to identify causes and define problem.

- *Planning:* goals established for OD intervention.

- *Action:* intervention strategies implemented.

- *Evaluation:* outcomes evaluated and assessed.

- *Termination:* consultant withdraws.

A matrix model of OD interventions

Pugh has developed a matrix model that accommodates OD interventions at different levels (see Senior, 2002: 322–40). It enables the OD consultant to assess the situation and determine the appropriate level and type of intervention required. For example, is it a question of changing people's behaviour? Of restructuring the organization? Or carrying out a major repositioning of the company through a strategic change initiative? As with different levels of intervention there are different types of change, as illustrated earlier in Figure 10.2 (such as, small group behavioural programmes to major transformational change initiatives). In adopting a matrix OD approach, it is recommended that change agents commence from the left column of the matrix (see Figures 10.4, 10.5, 10.6 and 10.7), then move to the right only when appropriate.

Behaviour What is happening?	Structure What is the system?	Context What is the setting?
• Individual needs not met with few learning and development opportunities • People resist change	• Poor job definition, ambiguity and confusion • Tasks too easy or too difficult	• Poor reward systems and individual job fit • Promotion limited, training and selection poor
Change agent choice	**Change agent choice**	**Change agent choice**
• Job analysis • Career planning • Individual counselling	• Job restructuring or redesign • Setting clear objectives • Job enrichment	• Improve recognition systems and align individuals to jobs • Improve HRM systems

FIGURE 10.4   Individual-level matrix

Behaviour What is happening?	Structure What is the system?	Context What is the setting?
• Poor leadership, low trust relations and conflict with peers and superiors • Atmosphere bad • Goals disputed	• Tasks poorly defined and role relations unclear • Leader overloaded • Inappropriate reporting structures	• Lack of resources • Poor group composition • Inadequate physical facilities • Personality clashes
Change agent choice	**Change agent choice**	**Change agent choice**
• Team building • Process consultation	• Redesign roles and reporting structures • Consider autonomous work groups	• Improve layout • Change the technology • Change group membership

FIGURE 10.5   Group-level matrix

Behaviour What is happening?	Structure What is the system?	Context What is the setting?
• Sub-units not co-operating • Conflict, competition and failure to confront differences	• No common perspective on tasks • Difficulty achieving required interaction	• Difference in sub-unit value and lifestyles • Physical barriers
Change agent choice	**Change agent choice**	**Change agent choice**
• Inter-group consultation • Role negotiation	• Redefine responsibilities • Change reporting relations • Improve liaison • Mechanisms	• Reduce psychological and physical distance • Exchange roles • Arrange cross-functional attachments

FIGURE 10.6   Inter-group-level matrix

Behaviour What is happening?	Structure What is the system?	Context What is the setting?
• Poor morale • Pressure, anxiety, suspicion and weak response to environmental changes	• Poorly defined goals • Strategy unclear • Inappropriate structure • Inadequate environmental scanning	• Geography • Product markets • Labour market • Technology • Physical working conditions
Change agent choice	**Change agent choice**	**Change agent choice**
• Survey employees and provide feedback	• Reappraisal of structure and systems prior to structural change initiative	• Change strategy • Change location • Change conditions • Change culture

FIGURE 10.7   Organizational-level matrix

Although this matrix does provide an interesting diagnostic guide for planning change, it can lead to a rather mechanistic approach to change management. Understanding and knowledge of the context of change (both internal to the organization and the external context) are critical to making judgements on when and how best to manage change.

Criticisms of the planned approach

The linearity of the OD model has been criticized and is not supported by longitudinal empirical studies of change (Clark et al., 1988; Pettigrew, 1985). As Kanter and colleagues indicated: 'organizations are never frozen, much less refrozen, but are fluid entities' (Kanter et al., 1992: 10). In part, the persistence of the OD approach may reflect its historical antecedents; it may also be due to the symbolic and legitimating function it affords the change agent. As Buchanan and Boddy (1992: 24) state:

> *Before dismissing rational-linear models of change, it is necessary to consider the symbolic function of such processes in sustaining the 'myth of organizational rationality' and, by implication, sustaining the legitimacy of the change agent. Such linear models may have a poor relationship with the actual unfolding of organizational changes, while in practice playing a significant symbolic and legitimating function in scripting the ritual that the change agent is required and expected to follow to gain organizational acceptance.*

The strength of the OD/Lewinian model also lies in its simple representation (which makes it easy to use and understand), although this is also perhaps its major weakness as it presents a unidirectional model of change. In other words, by creating an image of a need to design in stability (refreezing), the model has a tendency to solidify what is a dynamic and complex process. It may also result in the creation of cultures and structures not conducive to continuous change. On this point, Marvin Weisbord (1988) has argued that Lewin's concept begins to fall apart as the rate of market and technological change enters a state of continual transition, rather than the 'quasi-stationary equilibrium' that is at the centre of this approach. The OD camp has also been criticized for failing to account for the increasing incidence of revolutionary change that, according to Dunphy and Stace (1990), may more effectively be achieved by coercive rather than collaborative top-down strategies for change. For example, they point out that OD practitioners have tended to focus on collaborative models, whereas corporate strategy consultants have tended to select dictatorial transformation as the appropriate strategy for managing large-scale discontinuous change. Dunphy and Stace argue that whilst there is a place for each strategy, selection should be made on the basis of dominant contingencies rather than assuming that there is a one best way to fit all occasions. This alternative situational model to change management is outlined and discussed below.

A situational approach to change management

Dexter Dunphy (1981), who has a background in the OD area, has developed a model for identifying key contingencies that can be used by managers to determine the most appropriate change strategy given the prevailing circumstances (Dunphy and Stace, 1990: 81–92). The two dimensions of this model are, first, the scale of change and, second, the style of leadership required to bring about change. With regards to the former, the authors identify four types. 'Fine-tuning' and 'incremental adjustment' refer to small-scale changes ranging from the refining and clarification of existing procedures through to the actual adjustment of organizational structures. 'Modular transformation' and 'corporate transformation' refer to large-scale changes from divisional restructuring to revolutionary changes throughout the whole organization. On the second dimension, the appropriate style of leadership is seen to range along a continuum from participative to autocratic, namely: 'collaborative', 'consultative', 'directive' and 'coercive'. By using these dimensions, Dunphy and Stace identify four types of change strategies. *Participative evolution* and *forced evolution* refer to incremental change through collaborating and directive change, respectively. *Charismatic transformation* is described as large-scale discontinuous change achieved by collaborating means; and, finally, *dictatorial transformation* is used to describe major coercive change programmes (see Figure 10.8).

Dunphy and Stace argue that the model provides a framework for planned change strategies which challenges the personal value preference of managers and consultants. They suggest that 'appropriate' change strategies are generally determined by the change agent and not by the needs of the organization. For example, they point out that OD practitioners have tended to focus on collaborative models, whereas corporate strategy consultants have tended to select dictatorial transformation as the appropriate strategy for managing large-scale

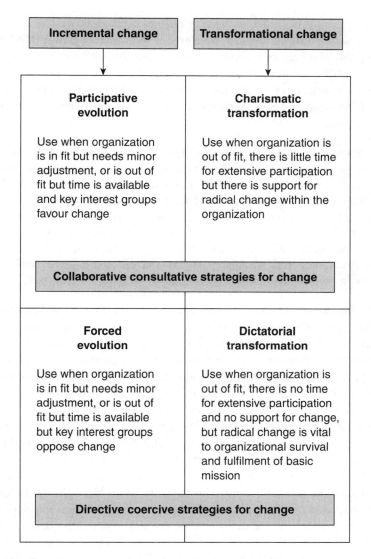

FIGURE 10.8 A typology of change strategies and conditions for use
(adapted from Dunphy and Stace, 1990: 90)

discontinuous change. The authors argue that, whilst there is a place for each strategy, selection should be made on the basis of dominant contingencies.

An appraisal of the Dunphy/Stace model

The model developed by Dunphy and Stace is clearly influenced by Lewin's work, and whilst it attempts to tackle some of the problems associated with the universality of OD, as David Wilson (1992: 31) notes, 'the addition of an extra variable – whether or not the organization is out of fit with its environment – merely adds to the list of driving and restraining forces'. Perhaps one of the major failings of this model, is the way change is characterized as an apolitical process. There is a surprising lack of reference to notions of power (Pfeffer, 1981) and the political nature of workplace change (see, for example, Mangham, 1979; Pettigrew, 1973). As Dunford (1990) points out, 'managers are portrayed as neutral conduits' who ignore their own self-interests in making rational decisions that seek to promote organizational effectiveness and survival. As Dunford (1990: 133) states:

> *This perspective ... seems curiously at odds with a growing literature on organizations as political arenas within which management constitute one or more interest groups ... Kanter (1983: 281) for example, notes that managers 'sometimes make strategic choices based on their own areas of competence and career pay off'. A model of change strategies that seeks to develop our understanding of change processes is unfortunately restricted if it excludes considerations of anything other than management as some sort of 'black box' wherein environmental fit is sought.*

As such, their notion of the environment as 'an entity out there that imposes its will' (Dunford, 1990: 132), discards the importance of perceptions in shaping organizational decision-making and the way that members of organizations may exert their own influence on the environment through various activities, such as lobbying, holding positions on pertinent committees, and social involvement with key politicians. In addition, no attempt is made to provide a typology of change strategies and conditions for their use under different periods during the process of change. In short, the models suggest that there is an appropriate strategy, given that you can identify the context and purpose of change, and that this strategy will see you through the entire process of regaining internal fit with the external environment. This contrasts with the findings of Balogun (2006), Balogun and Johnson (2004) and Hayes (2007), who highlight the influence of change recipients on shaping change outcomes and the need to adapt change strategies over time. In this, the model sidesteps key issues that arise during the dynamic and unpredictable process of large-scale workplace change.

In their follow-up book *Beyond the Boundaries*, Stace and Dunphy further develop their model using the same leadership and scale of change dimensions (1994: 94). Apart from the additional category of Taylorism (which is used to refer to change avoidance) they have renamed three of their change strategies in accepting less clear divisions between various approaches to change. 'Participative evolution' has become 'developmental transitions', and 'forced evolution' has become 'task-focused transition'; both refer to incremental change (with partial overlap with modular transformation) through largely consultative and directive change, respectively. 'Charismatic transformation' continues to refer to inspirational change achieved through consultation, whilst 'dictatorial transformation' has been redefined as 'turnarounds' to account for major coercive change programmes (overlapping with the more modular-directive type). This refined model is an improvement on their previous categorization and they do appropriately advocate the benefits of a more eclectic approach. However, their situational strategies for change continue to ignore critical aspects associated with power relationships and organizational politics. In evaluating the appropriateness of particular strategies to contingent conditions the focus is on the strategic fit between a company and the business environment. Whilst the external environment is a central contextual condition (situation), it is not the only contextual factor (take, for example, the contextual influence of the history and culture of an organization), nor should it be used to avoid analyses of political considerations in understanding the management of change.

The apolitical character of their proposed situational model for managing change is surprising given their discussion of the BHP change programme where they show how David Rice (senior executive) encountered major resistance from the unions to his directive change strategies and, following early retirement, was replaced by John Prescott who developed a participative approach to change that involved union representatives (Stace and Dunphy, 1994: 126–9). Although many studies would support the claim by Stace and Dunphy that: 'there is no single path to successful change implementation that holds in all situations' (1994: 93), their situational model remains limited through neglecting political determinants as shapers of the process of organizational change. Perhaps in part, this reflects the tendency for contingency theorists to impose rational unidirectional models on what is a complex and dynamic process. Developing a framework that is accessible, of practical worth and analytically robust, is not an easy task, and yet apolitical accounts simply sidestep key areas integral to change management programmes. In a further discussion of this issue, the political framework of Buchanan and Badham (1999, 2008) is described below.

A political process approach to change management

Within organization studies, power and politics has been a longstanding area of academic interest. Mainstream texts on management and organizational behaviour frequently use the classic work of French and Raven (1993) that was first articulated in the 1950s and sets out to clarify processes of power. Essentially, they identify five major types of power which they define in terms of influence. They argue that the process of influencing the behaviour of another may be overt, in the form of *reward power* and *coercive power*, or more covert, in, for example, the way that cultural values may support the *legitimate power* of one individual over another. Similarly, *referent power* (the strong identification and need for togetherness/solidarity with one another) often remains unseen or hidden. Expertise is the final basis of power identified by French and Raven, and in explaining *expert power* they argue that it is (1993: 315): 'necessary both for "P" to think that "O" knows and for "P" to trust that "O" is telling the truth (rather than trying to deceive him)'. This notion of deception or manipulation is often associated with organizational politics and, in particular, Machiavellian behaviour in which treachery may be necessary to achieve desired ends in the face of resistance and competition (see Skinner and Price, 1988). In drawing on the work of Machiavelli, Skinner (2000) sets out Machiavelli's advice on power to new rulers:

> *A wise prince will be guided above all by the dictates of necessity: if he 'wishes to maintain his power' he must always 'be prepared to act immorally when this becomes necessary.' Three chapters later, this basic doctrine is repeated. A wise prince does good when he can, but 'if it becomes necessary to refrain' he 'must be prepared to act in the opposite way and be capable of doing it.' Moreover, he must reconcile himself to the fact that, 'in order to maintain power,' he will often be forced by necessity 'to act treacherously, ruthlessly or inhumanely.' (Skinner, 2000: 43)*

This 'power in action' is often used to differentiate 'power' (influence which may lie dormant) from the active use of power in political action. Change as a political process involves decision making and these decisions involve the mobilization of organizational power. As such, outcomes do not reflect a process of rational analysis but a political process arising from power struggles from different vested interest groups (Buchanan and Badham, 2008; Robbins, 1986). This concern with the political aspects of change and the importance of local decision making is highlighted in Wilkinson's (1983) book *The Shopfloor Politics of New Technology*. In reporting on a series of case studies, Wilkinson (1983: 98) concludes that, 'the assumptions and interests of the various parties to the changes, and their particular positions of power within the organizations, were shown to determine outcomes, but rarely was this process of bargaining and accommodation made explicit'. In other words, whilst the outcomes of change are negotiated and socially mediated, these political processes often lie hidden behind explanations of rational behaviour in the so-called logical pursuit of strategic objectives.

The importance of political behaviour

The importance of politics in determining workplace arrangements was spotlighted in the early critical work of Harry Braverman (1974) and the resultant studies that set out to support or dispute the deskilling thesis of labour process theory (Wilkinson, 1983; Zimbalist, 1979). Within this theoretical frame, managerial initiatives that seek to restructure work are cast as attempts by management to enhance management control through strategies that deskill and intensify work. No longer are Taylorized forms of work organization limited to manual work, but with the use of technology it becomes possible to degrade and fragment white-collar work (Braverman, 1974). Typically, labour process theorists view the transformation of work as a political process reflecting broader conflicts of class interest under advanced capitalist society (see Wood, 1989). In an insightful analysis of automatically controlled machine tools, David Noble draws attention to the importance of social choice in machine design (Noble,

1979). For example, in discussing computer-integrated production systems, Noble (1979: 49) states that:

> *How this technology will actually be employed in a plant depends less upon any inherent nature of the technology than upon the particular manufacturing processes involved, the political and economic setting, and the relative power and sophistication of the parties engaged in the struggle over control of production.*

Similarly, studies on gender and change, especially within public sector organizations, also demonstrate the importance of power and control in making sense of change (Itzin and Newman, 1995). This more critical work not only introduces the notion of patterns of power and authority in shaping the experience of change at work (French, 1995; Harlow et al., 1995), but it also illustrates how the need for well-developed communication and collaborative skills in managing change could provide opportunities for women to be more active agents in steering change (Newman, 1995). These studies note how the realizations of such opportunities are often prevented by political process and the gendered relations of power in organizations (Williams and MacAlpine, 1995).

From a different theoretical frame, Pettigrew (1973) also identifies the importance of political behaviour in legitimating a particular position and in de-legitimizing the demands and values of other competing individuals or groups. In the case of change management, meanings are managed by the astute change agent in order to minimize resistance to proposed programmes (Pettigrew, 1985, 1987). However, this view of politics has been criticized by Alvesson and Willmott (1996: 31) as a soft-pedalling approach under which 'established priorities and values are assumed to be legitimate', and thereby supports the status quo and avoids any real critical scrutiny of workplace change. They suggest that whilst this work does provide a useful counterbalance to OD change models, unlike critical theory, it does little to challenge conventional wisdom.

So where does this leave us? It leaves us with the recognition that political process is important to understanding change. However, how we view political process and power (our theoretical lens) will influence our assessment of the place of political process in programmes of organizational change. For example, do we view conflict and resistance as an element that is disruptive to the smooth and rational management of an organization and therefore a 'problem' to be tackled? Or do we see conflict as being endemic to organizations and therefore neither intrinsically good nor bad?

Power, politics and organizational change

In their book *Power, Politics, and Organizational Change,* Buchanan and Badham (2008) focus on the place of political behaviour in organizational life (engagement in techniques and practices in the pursuit of preferred outcomes) and, in particular, on the way a 'cast of characters' shape organizational outcomes. They see an inextricable link between the creation of uncertain and ambiguous situations and the mobilization of power (the capacity of individual managers to exert their will over others) in the form of political behaviour. They claim that 'the political dimension is probably a perennial feature on the terrain of the change driver', and that whilst political processes may not have received so much attention in earlier studies, there is nothing new in politics, only in our 'heightened awareness of political agendas'. In recognizing the centrality of politics, they set out to identify practical guidance on the 'appropriate use of power and political strategies and tactics' in what they term 'power-assisted steering'. As Buchanan and Badham note (1999: 18, 157):

> *The central proposition of this book is that the change agent who is not politically skilled will fail. This implies that it is necessary to be able and willing to intervene in the political processes of the organization, to push particular agendas, to influence decisions and decision makers, to deal with (and potentially silence) criticism and challenge, and to cope with resistance ... This typically involves ensuring that changes do not threaten vested interests and privileges. Major changes rely on the contribution, compliance and co-operation of a range of groups and departments with different values, perceptions and goals.*

They argue that the degree of political intensity varies between different change contexts and that this will in turn influence the effectiveness of a range of strategies for managing change. Whilst in one context a more open and communicative approach may be appropriate, under different conditions there may be less time and reason to engage employees in change strategies which may require power-coercive solutions. As they explain:

> *Change which is more marginal to the success of the business and which can be implemented at a more relaxed pace allows for extensive participation ... Change proposals which are critical and challenged may have to be driven using power-coercive solutions. (Buchanan and Badham, 1999: 181)*

Buchanan and Badham (2008), argue that radical change programmes, which are critical to the survival of the company and yet are highly politicized and contested, will need to be forcefully driven. They note that any form of contested change will necessitate political activity in dealing with opponents and building support for the initiative (Buchanan and Badham, 2008: 249–52). For them, the politically skilled change agent is not a Machiavellian-type manager but rather a political entrepreneur. These types of managers have good diagnostic and judgemental skills; they are creative, self-critical and able to improvise (2008: 308). They do not follow simple recipes for success, as they are aware of the difficult and political nature of change management. As Buchanan and Badham state, the 'political entrepreneur adopts a creative, committed, reflective, risk-taking

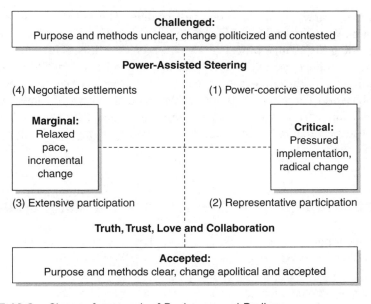
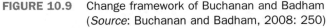

FIGURE 10.9 Change framework of Buchanan and Badham
(*Source*: Buchanan and Badham, 2008: 250)

approach, balancing conventional methods with political tactics when the circumstances render this necessary, appropriate, and defensible' (2008: 307).

Through incorporating this political dimension of change, the authors forward a model that suggests that the degree of political intensity will vary under different settings and with different types of change initiatives. In their framework reproduced in Figure 10.9, they argue that managing change in quadrant (1) (where change is critical to survival but challenged) is likely to require power-coercive solutions. This form of radical change – which has wide implications and has to be managed fairly swiftly – is contrasted with marginal incremental change where there is time to negotiate over disagreements and concerns (quadrant (4)). In both cases the authors identify the need for what they term: 'power-assisted steering'. They further claim that change which is broadly accepted (whether radical or incremental) can be introduced in a more participative manner. If change is marginal then extensive participation is possible whereas, if change is critical, then a strategy of representative participation may prove more appropriate. In these two quadrants ((2) and (3)) they suggest what they term, 'truth, trust, love and collaboration' types of approach (Buchanan and Badham, 2008: 250).

This model is similar to the one advocated by Dunphy and Stace (1990), although in this case political process is included as a central element. Under this framework, the management of change is seen to necessitate strategic choices (Child, 1972) that are modified and challenged collectively by the workforce, or by individuals and groups of managers who are responsible for the implementation of change. These political processes include elements of conflict and resistance, decision- and non-decision-making activities, processes of negotiation and consultation, and the multi-level and external individual and group influence on the content, transition and outcomes of change. They draw attention to the ongoing power plays and political activity, as well as the management of meaning in guiding the change process in certain preferred directions.

These elements of political process (Buchanan and Badham, 1999, 2008), of the importance of the context in which change takes place (Dunphy and Stace, 1990; Stace and Dunphy, 1994), and of the dynamic forces of change in moving from some current state to some future state (Lewin, 1951) are taken up in the final section that debates and outlines a processual perspective for making sense of change.

A processual perspective for understanding change

A processual perspective views change as a dynamic fluid process that continues *ad infinitum*. As Alvesson and Sveningsson (2008: 28) state:

> *Organizational change seen as processual involves applying an understanding of a complex and chaotic organizational reality. Unforeseen consequences of planned organizational change, resistance, political processes, negotiations, ambiguities, diverse interpretations and misunderstandings are part of this (Balogun, 2006; Dawson, 2003a; Pettigrew et al., 2001). Consequently, organizational change is not mainly a matter of carrying out a sequential list of steps.*

The approach of Pettigrew: the awakening giant

In drawing on longitudinal contextual data Pettigrew examines the interplay between internal contextual variables of culture, history and political process with external business conditions that maintain continuity or bring about change. In providing what he terms as a 'holistic, contextualist analysis', the approach provides both multi-level (or vertical) analysis, such as external socio-economic influences on internal group behaviour; and processual (or horizontal) analysis, for example, in studying organizations 'in flight' with a past, present and future. In multi-level theory construction attention is given to the way contextual variables in the vertical analysis link to those examined in horizontal analysis and how, 'processes are both constrained by structures and shape structures ... both in catching reality in flight and in embeddedness' (Pettigrew, 1985: 37).

In his longitudinal study of the unfolding and non-linear aspects of change at Imperial Chemical Industries (ICI), Pettigrew criticizes the aprocessual character of a lot of the material on change management in advocating the need for the adoption of a particular type of research strategy and methodology (Pettigrew, 1990). In contrast to the dominant approach in organization theory that emphasizes the importance of sophisticated quantitative analyses (Ledford et al., 1990: 6–8), the processual approach is concerned with the collection of longitudinal qualitative data which facilitates a more detailed understanding of the complex and dynamic processes of change (Dawson, 1994). Pettigrew (1985: 438–76) demonstrates how strategic change is a continuous process with no clear beginning or end point, and how it often emerges with deep-seated cultural and political roots that support the establishment of a dominant ideology. As such, he usefully illustrates how these strategic change processes are best understood in context and over time, as continuity is often 'a good deal easier to see than change' (Pettigrew, 1985: 439). For example, insufficient commercial pressure, satisfaction with the status quo, lack of vision and the absence of leadership, are all identified as contextual factors constraining change. Drawing on the work of Kanter (1983) he supports the view that integrative structures and cultures are broadly facilitative of 'the processes of vision-building, problem-identifying and acknowledging, information-sharing, attention-directing, problem-solving, and commitment-building which seem to be necessary to create change' (Pettigrew, 1985: 456), whereas segmentalist structures and cultures with clearly defined levels and functions are viewed as inhibitative of change. In conclusion to all five ICI cases, Pettigrew stresses the importance of leadership in initiating strategic change and facilitating a movement from segmentalist to integrative structures and cultures (Pettigrew, 1985: 457).

This foundation work of Pettigrew has been widely referenced and discussed in the organizational change literature (see Burnes, 2004; Collins, 1998; Preece et al., 1999). However, in a critique of the work, Buchanan and Boddy (1992) argue that the richness and complexity of a multi-level analysis does little to simplify or clarify processes of change and thereby renders the research as largely impenetrable for the organizational practitioner. In other words, whilst the research findings adequately convey the complexity of organizational change, they have also tended to mask, mystify and create barriers of interpretation to a non-academic audience who may seek practical tools for action. Although they point out that it was not Pettigrew's intention to offer practical advice, they remain critical of this approach, both as a method for analysing data on change and as a perspective which serves to disable attempts to develop practical managerial advice (Buchanan and Boddy, 1992). Dawson (1994) has attempted to tackle this issue in his development and use of the processual approach in studying change in a number of organizations in the UK and Australia.

Dawson's processual perspective

Accessibility and the practical dimension to understanding change are elements that have informed the processual approach developed by Dawson (1994). Accessibility is sought through the presentation of readable case analyses of change from longitudinal fieldwork on company transition. Companies such as, Hewlett-Packard, General Motors, Pirelli Cables, Faulding, Boeing and Shell (Dawson, 1994, 1996, 2003a, 2003b), are presented in a narrative form that includes original data and quotations from interview transcripts that allows the reader to not only follow the story of change but also to form their own views and interpretations from their reading of primary data (see Dawson, 2003b). The material has also been used to identify lessons on change in setting forward a series of practical guidelines, as Dawson (1994: 173) explains:

> *The guidelines presented are located within and derive from a processual framework which emphasizes the importance of ongoing timeframes and the interconnected dynamics between the substance, context and politics of change. Unlike contingency models, this processual perspective does not advocate or identify a single emergent homogenous structure which can be prescribed as an appropriate design for a 'changed' organization. Change is viewed as an ongoing process which is both progressive and regressive, is planned and unplanned, and incorporates intended and unintended innovations from the initial conception of the need to change through to the emergence of new work arrangements. Furthermore, unlike situational (or contingency) approaches which (whilst recognizing the importance of context) tend to use snapshot models and assume that context is singular and unproblematic, the processual perspective sensitizes the researcher and practitioner to the importance of the interplay between organizational governance and politics, and the history and culture of organizations and change programmes. For example, processual research is able to identify competing histories of change and show how organizational stories may be rewritten to lend support to the claims of differing vested interest groups and thereby, reflect the political agendas of powerful decision-makers rather than representing some 'objective' reconstruction of past events.*

The approach also advocates that the different views and experiences of individuals and groups at all levels within organizations need to be captured and analysed. The framework is able to highlight discrepancy and conflicting views between and within individuals and groups occupying different hierarchical positions. The experiences of shopfloor employees are often markedly different from the senior executive group and, as such, competing stories and accounts of change are not uncommon (see Dawson, 2003b: 99–141). As Dawson (2003b: 110–11) indicates:

> *In the context of change, clarifying the status of these various statements is often a central analytical task in making sense of interview data. Discrepancy between the views of different groups is not problematic, but part of the rich data which is accessible through processual research. Unlike studies that seek to construct a single account of change, the co-existence of competing histories and views can be accommodated under processual research. In the same automotive component company, another senior management member later recast the charismatic champion of change as a dishonest and underhand management fiend after his replacement. Thus, the longitudinal data was able to capture this movement from hero to villain, and make sense of the political motives of rewriting company history to fit current commercial objectives and the required public performance of the senior management group.*

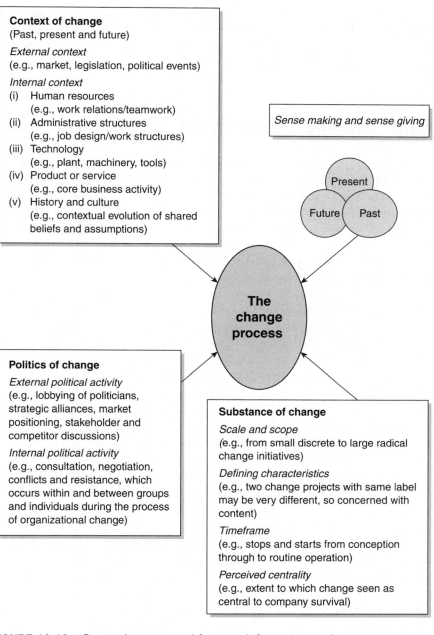

Context of change
(Past, present and future)

External context
(e.g., market, legislation, political events)

Internal context
(i)   Human resources
      (e.g., work relations/teamwork)
(ii) Administrative structures
      (e.g., job design/work structures)
(iii) Technology
      (e.g., plant, machinery, tools)
(iv) Product or service
      (e.g., core business activity)
(v)   History and culture
      (e.g., contextual evolution of shared
      beliefs and assumptions)

Sense making and sense giving

Present
Future   Past

The change process

Politics of change

External political activity
(e.g., lobbying of politicians,
strategic alliances, market
positioning, stakeholder and
competitor discussions)

Internal political activity
(e.g., consultation, negotiation,
conflicts and resistance, which
occurs within and between groups
and individuals during the process
of organizational change)

Substance of change

Scale and scope
(e.g., from small discrete to large radical
change initiatives)

Defining characteristics
(e.g., two change projects with same label
may be very different, so concerned with
content)

Timeframe
(e.g., stops and starts from conception
through to routine operation)

Perceived centrality
(e.g., extent to which change seen as
central to company survival)

FIGURE 10.10   Dawson's processual framework for understanding change
(*Source*: adapted from Dawson, 1996: 27)

The processual perspective proposed by Dawson (2003a, 2003b) aims to make complex change data accessible to the reader, to use the material to identify practical lessons from the research, and to ensure that the views and voices of those who experience change are heard from the shopfloor employee through to middle management and the chief executive officer of an organization. As such, the framework seeks to enable a critical analysis of change which captures competing views, conflicting priorities and the process by which certain accounts of change become legitimized.

Factors shaping the process of change

The processual perspective aims to examine change as-it-happens and is concerned with three groups of determinants that shape this process, namely: the politics, substance and context of change (see Figure 10.10). The **politics** of change is taken to refer to the political activity of consultation, negotiation, conflict and resistance, which occurs at various levels within and outside an organization during the process of managing change. Examples of political activity outside of an organization would be governmental pressure, competitor alliances or the influence of overseas divisions of large corporations. Internal political activity can be in the form of shopfloor negotiations between trade union representatives and management, between consultants (working within the organization) and various organizational groups, and between and within managerial, supervisory and operative personnel. These individuals or groups can influence decision making and the setting of agendas at critical junctures during the process of organizational change.

The **context** of change refers to factors that reside within the organization as well as those within the wider business market environment. External contextual factors are taken to include: changes in competitors' strategies; level of international competition; government legislation; changing social expectations; technological innovations; and changes in the level of business activity. Whereas internal contextual factors are taken to include Leavitt's (1964) fourfold classification of human resources, administrative structures, technology, and product or service, as well as an additional category labelled the history and culture of an organization. This latter category is used to incorporate both an historical perspective that can take account of multiple histories of the context in which change is taking place, and an understanding of organizational culture. By so doing, the framework is able to accommodate the existence of a number of competing change histories (these organizational histories may be further refined, replaced and developed over time) and recognizes that the dominant or 'official version' of change may often reflect the political positioning of certain key individuals or groups within an organization, rather than serving as a true representation of the actual process of change (these change stories may in turn shape, constrain and promote the direction and content of future change programmes).

The **substance** of change (what Pettigrew refers to as content) is seen to consist of a number of interlocking factors. First, the *scale and scope of change*, which may range along a continuum from small-scale discrete change to a more 'radical' large-scale transformation. A distinction can also be made between change at the level of the unit, plant/branch, division and corporation. Second, the *defining characteristics of the change programme*: which refers both to the labels attached to change projects and the actual content of the change in question. In other words, content is never assumed on the basis of the label attached to a particular change programme. Third, the *timeframe of change*: at it simplest this refers to the period over which change occurs from the conception of the need to change through to routine operation. It is also concerned with the starting and stopping of change, and the way certain tasks and decision-making activities may overlap and interlock. Some programmes evolve incrementally over a number of years only to be followed by a fairly rapid and specified period of implementation, whilst others may be triggered by a sudden shift in business market activity or unexpected world events. Fourth, the *perceived centrality of the change*: this refers to whether or not change is seen to be critical to the survival of the organization. For example, if change is viewed as central to the competitive position of the company, then it can have major implications for the timescale, resource support and overall employee commitment to change. Finally, it should be noted that the substance of change is not static but is itself open to change. In other words, the substance of change both influences and is influenced by contextual and political elements. For example, it is not uncommon for definitional confusion to surround the introduction of new management techniques and for the content of change to be redefined during the process of implementation. Moreover, knowledge of the substance of change and clarification of what the change means for a particular organization can in itself become a political process, influenced by external contextual views and the setting of internal agendas around the management of change. In this sense, there is a continual interplay between these three groups of determinants during the ongoing process of change.

Studying change over time: from present to future state

The temporal dimension of Dawson's framework recognizes that for analytical purposes it may prove useful to categorize data collecting during the early periods of change, during the process of moving from a present state to a future state, and at some stage after the changes have been introduced and day-to-day activities are approached in more routine ways. The three general timeframes advocated comprise:

- The initial conception of a need to change.

- The process of organizational change.

- Operation of new work practices and procedures.

The initial awareness of a need to change may either be in response to external or internal pressures for change (reactive), or through a belief in the need for change to meet future competitive demands (proactive). The latter has stimulated a wealth of research into the organizational adoption of management fads (Abrahamson, 1991, 1996; Collins, 2000, 2001; Jackson, 2001) that promise painless solutions to heightened international competitiveness (Mitroff and Mohrman, 1987: 69) through easy-to-follow guides (for a fuller discussion of celebrity professors and management fashions see the latter part of Chapter 3). The increased complexity and uncertainty of international business markets has led some organizations to base change on imitation (which organizations are successful and what changes have they introduced), rather than on any conception of a need to adopt untried technologies or techniques (see, for example, DiMaggio and Powell, 1991; Thompson, 1967). This initial conception of a need to change can be influenced by factors residing within the organization such as operational inefficiencies or employee disputes, or by factors which emanate from outside of an organization, for example, through business press and media reports on the success of other organizations and the direct or indirect promotion of various management fashions (see Jackson, 2001).

Once a need for change has been identified, then the complex non-linear and 'black-box' process of organizational change commences. This period will comprise a number of different tasks, activities and decisions for individuals and groups both within and outside of the organization. Once a decision to change has been made, senior management usually decide upon the type of change they wish to introduce. Their own understanding of the business market, what competitors are doing, and what is generally available often influences their choice. This decision-making period is often marked by stops and starts, revisions to set plans and adjustments as new information and unforeseen events are taken into account. During the planning and implementation of a major change programme, project management, authority relationships, training, timescale, budgets, and so forth, will be the main focus of attention. Once implementation is under way, then factors such as business market considerations are likely to decline in significance, whereas occupational and employee concerns are likely to increase in importance and influence management's change strategy. As Allan (1995: 136) concludes in his case analysis (see also the case illustration in the section that follows by Allan and Dawson), managing change is not a neat linear process:

> *As successive difficulties arose, the organization evaluated and reappraised the progress to date, assessed new options and implemented new strategies to overcome resistance and implement organizational change. This cycle of experimentation and revision demonstrates that the pathway to organizational change cannot be represented by a straight line or Roman road but rather, is a complex, temporal and iterative process. The outcomes of and the barriers to change are never fully known at the outset. The change process will always involve the unanticipated.*

The final general timeframe (operation of new work practices and procedures) is taken to refer to the period when, following the implementation of change, new organizational arrangements and systems of operation begin to emerge.

During this period, a number of novel developments or contingencies may arise which may compromise the change outcomes. For example, unanticipated technical or social problems may undermine the usefulness of the system in its replacement of traditional methods. As a result, this may cause conflict and confusion among staff and management, and threaten the establishment of new working relationships. Thus, the early stages of operating under new systems may be characterized by uncertainty, conflict and misunderstanding among employees, who may variously adapt, modify, reassert and/or redefine their positions under new operating procedures and working relationships set up during the implementation of change. This is also the period in which a relatively stabilized system of operation may emerge comprising new patterns of relationships and new forms of working practices. It is during this timeframe, therefore, that the outcomes of change can be examined and contrasted with the operating system prior to change. Although in reality it is unrealistic to talk of an 'endpoint' of change (as the process continues *ad infinitum*) it does make sense to talk of the 'effects' of a particular type of change. In the case of large-scale or radical change initiatives, it is possible to identify a period after implementation when the daily work routines of employees become part of the operating system (which is no longer regarded as 'new'). Whilst the ongoing process of change will continue, this is the period that can be used to identify the outcomes of change on organizational structures and traditional operating practices.

These three general timeframes provide a useful framework from which to begin a detailed examination of change. Although every major change programme will have an organizationally defined beginning, middle and end, in practice it is not only difficult to identify the start and completion of change programmes (for example, there is often more than one organizational history of change and these may be reconstructed over time), but also to explain the complex pathways and routes to establishing new operational processes. Therefore, in examining the complex and 'black-box' process of organizational change there are considerable returns to be gained from developing a framework for data analysis. It is argued here that a useful way of tackling the problem of analysing complex change data is to construct data categories either around themes or around the various activities and tasks associated with change. For example, data categories for the activities associated with the establishment of new organizational arrangements may comprise: system selection, identification of type of change, implementation, preparation and planning, and search and assessment. These tasks are unlikely to occur in a tidy linear fashion throughout the process of change, but will normally overlap, occur simultaneously, stop and start, and be part of the initial and later phases of major change programmes. Nevertheless, they are useful for locating and sorting data on change that might otherwise be too complex to deal with systematically. Although at a more general level there can be no definitive list of appropriate data categories, as these should be modified or revised to fit particular case examples and/or the characteristics of different change programmes, task-oriented or thematic categories can provide a useful starting point for locating and analysing change data.

Criticisms of Dawson's processual approach

The processual approach advocated by Dawson (1994, 1996, 2003a, 2003b) provides a framework for studying processes of change as they occur in organizations and enables contextual explanations of the non-linear dynamics of change; it does not, however, present a model of how to best manage change. Although the approach offers a series of general guidelines that should be considered in managing change (see Dawson, 1994: 172–80; 2003a: 173–7), Burnes (2000) doubts the use of guidelines that do not give clear advice, as he explains:

> *Dawson puts forward 15 major practical guidelines which can be drawn from a processual analysis of managing organizational transitions. These guidelines range from the need to maintain an overview of the dynamics and long-term process of change, to the need to take a total organizational approach to managing transitions. On the way, he makes the case for understanding and communicating the context and objectives of change, and ensuring managerial and employee commitment ... Unfortunately, the problem with much of the advice ... is that it tends to be relatively cursory or abstract in nature and difficult to apply on a day-to-day basis. (Burnes, 2000: 294–5)*

In an approach that recognizes: that there can never be any universal prescriptions or simple recipes for competitive success; that contextual conditions need to be continually monitored and appraised; that change agents need to be politically astute and sensitive to variations in individual and group experiences of change; and that managing change is often about managing contradictory processes; it is perhaps not surprising that any attempt to offer guidelines is limited. However, Collins (1998), in giving credit to the emphasis in the guidelines on contextual dimensions, states that:

> *To be fair, Dawson does at least draw attention to the importance of contextual factors, and to the role which trade unions play in the management of UK industries. Yet Dawson's willingness to translate and to codify these notions for practitioners does little to communicate the complexity inherent in these matters ... We have to wonder if this really represents such a huge leap forward from, say, Kanter's (1989) advice that corporations should be fast, flexible, focused and friendly! (Collins, 1998: 75)*

Perhaps any attempt to detail practical lessons will prove theoretically contentious, but should this prevent us from drawing lessons from research on organizational change? In our view, there should be a continual dialogue between theory and practice as the two inform each other, and whilst there are no universal recipes for the 'successful' management of change, this should not stop us from identifying practical 'rules of thumb' or further refining change management concepts (see also the section in Chapter 3, *Theory and practice: a reappraisal,* pp. 60–62). Although the practical lessons that we learn from such research are not the sort that enable us to predict all the issues that will arise (in stressing the contextual and unforeseen nature of change), they draw attention to the importance of knowledge and understanding, and to the need for continual analysis and critical reflection.

Conclusion

In this chapter we have examined a number of different models and frameworks for understanding change. Drawing on human relations theory, the OD model set out to prescribe the best way to manage change that will ensure the participation and involvement of all staff. According to this approach, change should be managed in a way that embraces employees at all levels; it should not be rushed nor forcefully imposed (French et al., 2004). In contrast, the situational model of Dunphy and Stace (1990) was developed to explain the rapid and more autocratic approaches to change management that were occurring in many business organizations during the 1980s and 1990s. Empirical data collected from case study fieldwork were used to support their claim that whilst participative approaches may be appropriate in certain circumstances, there are situations when the need for rapid transformation overrides considerations for a participative strategy for change. Following this approach, organizations need to assess their contingent circumstances and then choose the most appropriate change strategy that fits their situation. Buchanan and Badham (2008) develop a similar model in arguing that when employees generally accept change then more collaborative and participative strategies can be used, whereas, when change is contested, politicized and challenged, then more forceful and even manipulative strategies may be called for through what they term as 'power-assisted steering'. In drawing on the work of Machiavelli, they liken contested change to a blood sport, especially in cases where the change is critical to company survival (Buchanan and Badham, 1999). For them, change agents or managers need to take off their gloves and learn to play the political game required if they wish to manage change successfully. This terrain is not for the lighthearted, nor is it a world where the meek will inherit the earth; it is likened to a hard-hitting contact sport where everything and anything should be used in order to outplay those who may seek to block change objectives. In their more recent book, they advocate that the way forward is not Machiavellian management but political entrepreneurship in which the change agent is not only politically skilled but 'trigger sensitive' and 'intellectually equipped' (Buchanan and Badham, 2008: 308).

In building on these approaches, the processual perspective recognizes the political nature of change and the importance of power: the need to orchestrate and steer change, to engage people and overcome obstacles, to respond to the unforeseen and be proactive in circumventing potential barriers and to gaining the support of significant stakeholders (Dawson, 1994, 2003a).

Although it does not prescribe a best way for business practitioners in providing a framework to study and explain complex change processes, it does encourage an examination of multiple voices, of hearing the stories of the powerful and the disenfranchised, of capturing the telling, retelling and rewriting of change histories, in making sense of processes of change (Dawson, 2003b).

In sum, there are strengths and weaknesses to all models that seek to explain change or prescribe change management strategies. As we experience new changes so we will continue to draw on our social science knowledge in further refining and developing approaches to change. What this chapter has attempted to do is to describe and discuss some of the main debates and frameworks on organizational change. But as our next chapter will highlight, as new problems and issues emerge so new theories are developed to try and explain what is happening. This is perhaps what makes the area interesting, as there can never be closure on studies that seek to examine the ongoing processes of change, creativity and innovation.

RESOURCES, READINGS AND REFLECTIONS

CASE STUDY 10.1   MYBANK: A CASE STUDY OF ORGANIZATIONAL CHANGE BY CAMERON ALLAN AND PATRICK DAWSON

Our illustrative case examines an attempt to implement a new managerial approach to the practice of Human Resource Management (HRM) that required a re-organization of work in the development of collaborative employee relations. The case demonstrates how the commitment of middle management to strategy implementation cannot be taken for granted and can significantly influence the successful management of change, particularly in cases where differing vested interests between management levels and functions do not align with strategic objectives. The case study of a medium-sized bank (referred to as Mybank), identifies and analyses the range of choices that were open to managers in developing implementation strategies, and how these were modified over time. In particular, attention is given to a change in management strategy from bottom-up implementation to a top-down approach.

The bottom-up approach to change
During the 1990s, one of the senior executives of Mybank became convinced of the benefits of a quality improvement programme for reducing costs in forming quality improvement teams to identify and rectify inefficient work systems through the elimination of waste and rework. The attraction of such an initiative also stemmed from its potential to achieve cost reduction in-house, using existing staff to improve quality and customer service as well as offering the organization an ongoing methodology for continuous improvement.

In embarking on change the implementation strategy adopted was as follows: an outside consultant was used to introduce the philosophy and tools of the change programme to senior and middle managers in a series of workshops. Once familiar with the concepts and principles, these managers were then expected to encourage their staff to form quality improvement teams to solve specific work problems identified by either the general staff or managers. The involvement of general staff was seen as a crucial issue: operational staff were seen to be intimately acquainted with their own work processes and thus ideally placed to recognize existing inefficiencies and to make recommendations to rectify them. To assist in the implementation process, a quality support group of two people was established to provide training and facilitation for general staff involved in quality improvement projects. In time, it was hoped, the philosophy and methodology of continuous improvement would become an integral part of everybody's job. This model relied on a bottom-up approach based on operative staff involvement with support from management. As one manager expressed it: 'Management's role was to support it and to encourage it rather than be involved in it'. As it turned out, this initiative was only fully implemented and operationalized in a limited number of areas (mainly in departments with routinized administrative tasks).

Participation in quality improvement teams was voluntary and comprised five to 10 intra-department general staff and a quality co-ordinator from the quality support department. The role of the quality co-ordinator was to act as a facilitator, mediator and trainer for the team. Once a problem had been identified, the team would consult with any persons or departments that either use the output to the work system or supplied input into the system. The team would then identify possible inefficiencies, analyse why these may occur and then make recommendations to management as to how the system could be improved. Interestingly, the views of general staff about the new initiative were polarized: they either hated it or loved it. Those that hated it, either didn't want to be involved, didn't understand it, or were simply happy to just get on with their own work. As a supervisor put it: 'They don't want to get involved. They just want to do their 40 hours'.

Employees who embraced the initiative were particularly excited about being given the opportunity to contribute to the construction of their own work organization, as one staff member recalled: 'I have never worked in an organization [until this one] that wanted to hear the input of ... those down the bottom'. Other staff expressed initial trepidation but once involved became active supporters: 'It was absolutely terrific, it improved our system there, 100 per cent, 150 per cent. It's great!' In part, the enthusiasm of some employees can be explained by the material improvement in their working lives:

> *I was working overtime, at times, back until 7.30, 8.00 o'clock at night and he [the manager] told me I had to take three days off all my work, forget about it totally and go into this room and do this thing. Oh my God, I going to be here till doomsday, trying to fix this thing up. It took three days, and it was great. It made such a difference that we stopped doing overtime. It was amazing. Helped us out tremendously.*

(Continued)

(Continued)

Indeed, so successful were some projects, that operations or procedures that had taken weeks were reduced to a matter of days. However, even among the most ardent supporters, enthusiasm soon waned. This was due to two factors. First, employees were still expected to complete all their other tasks in addition to the work required by the change projects. Consequently, improvement meetings that lasted one or two hours could result in quantitative work overload. Even managers who were supportive recognized this problem, as one stated: 'The resistance you get is "Hey! When do I have to do this by, I am flat strapped now!" '

The second factor that caused disillusionment among employees was that management rarely accepted their recommendations for improvements. This was seen to be particularly frustrating given the time, effort and enthusiasm many staff had put into projects. As one employee explained:

> *I was leading a project ... looking at our relationship with builders and under-construction loans in general. We saw it through to completion; we had some recommendations that we thought were good ones. Some of them were put in place but the major ones weren't. Upper levels of senior management in the bank decided that it wasn't the way to go, and we weren't going to do that. That was really running into a brick wall.*

The non-linear process of change

The failure for the change initiative to be adopted in many areas of the organization was due to a number of reasons. The most important was the reluctance of senior and middle managers to actively support the change. They were sceptical about the initiative and felt that it was better suited to the manufacturing sector rather than financial service operations (one more 'open-minded' manager did concede that the initiative could have some use in administrative areas of the organization). As one manager expressed: 'We are more administrative than a lot of other areas and therefore responded to it a little bit better than other parts of the branch'. Many managers were of the opinion that their departments were already over-worked and simply could not afford to allow their staff to take time off to become involved in this change initiative. For some, the acceptance of change implied, implicitly at least, that managers recognized that their departments were currently inefficient and improvements were possible. Interestingly, one of the most common reasons expressed for the lack of adoption was the lack of commitment from top management. As one person put it:

> *They [management] agree that they understand the concept, that they felt it is necessary and they see the advantages, but when it comes to the role-modelling or leading or doing, they back away at a million miles an hour. Maybe they have got too much real work to do, maybe they don't really understand anyway ... I don't believe that we have still passed the first step. That is, have a common understanding at the top and a total commitment.*

The Managing Director also played a part in influencing the process of change. He had a relaxed management style and assumed that departments would become involved in quality improvement projects on their own accord. Participation was not mandatory. Although this 'friendly' and open management style imbued the organization with a strong culture of family values based on respect for the individual, many people also interpreted it as a lack for support from the Managing Director for the initiative. By 2001, the twin effects of limited senior management support and middle management resistance meant that the initiative had slowed to a halt.

The top-down approach to change
In 2003, senior management decided to once again review the company's cost structure. Mybank had committed themselves to building a new corporate head-quarters and the prospect of this major financial outlay plus the firm's continuing high level of operating expenses stimulated the firm to seek cost savings. The firm brought in a large accounting firm to examine the company's operations and to make recommendations on how best to reduce costs and improve performance. In an almost identical fashion to events previously, the firm elected to use an employee involvement initiative to achieve the potential cost savings identified by the consultant group. However, on this occasion the bank adopted a top-down rather than the bottom-up approach to the implementation of change. A consultant was brought in from America to help the organization with their implementation strategy. The consultant recommended that senior managers play a major role in the change initiative. Their role was to identify organizational problems and the likely causes; specify how improvements in performance were to be measured and what the acceptable level of performance would be; nominate individuals to analyse and rectify the problems; and specify timeframes. This implementation strategy was expected to motivate middle managers through highlighting the commitment of senior management. In practice, however, this top-down approach also had its difficulties.

The General Manager of Retail Banking illustrates an example of some of these problems in using a top-down approach to amalgamate two of his lending sections. The bank had two personal lending sections: a housing loans section; and a consumer loans section for credit cards, overdrafts and personal loans. Within the established banks, there would normally only be one lending section which would process both types of loans. The disadvantages of having two separate sections were that many personal clients would often have both types of loans. Thus, having their records spread across two separate sections led to duplication and created administrative problems for the management of clients' accounts.

In addition to the integration of two departments, the General Manager also elected to introduce a new management layer that had experience with both forms of lending. Traditionally, staff in the housing loans section knew little or nothing about personal lending and vice versa. Consequently, managers experienced in

(Continued)

(Continued)

both forms of lending were recruited and located between supervisory staffs and the Departmental Manager, with the title of Regional Lending Managers. However, rather than physically combine the two areas in one location and develop training systems to allow multi-skilling of staff over time, the task of integration was seen to provide the bank with an ideal opportunity to critically examine the whole structure of work systems in order to eliminate unproductive tasks and perhaps reduce staff levels. As such, the integration of the two departments became a major change project.

Four newly appointed Regional Lending Managers were given the task by the General Manager of amalgamating the departments to ensure that the new process became operational within a six-month timeframe. This group discussed and formulated an implementation strategy through consultation with employees in both departments to establish the timing and range of functions and tasks performed. Each task was then scrutinized to determine whether it was 'value adding', 'rework' or 'non-valuing'. Where possible, tasks that were classified as 'rework' or 'non-value adding' were eliminated. The remaining work tasks were then flow-charted and bunches of related tasks lumped together to form new jobs. Staff were then allocated to these new jobs. The redesigned process reduced staff numbers by eight. The bank had a policy of not retrenching people, and those personally eliminated from the new system either found alternative positions within the bank or they were kept on as 'floating' staff until they were able to find positions elsewhere.

Although the project was given total support from the General Manager, the new Regional Lending Managers experienced a lot of middle management resistance. For example, some of the Departmental Managers immediately superior to the Regional Lending Managers strongly resisted their proposed redesign of work organization. These managers were intimately acquainted with the old processes and felt that the new design was at best unrealistic and at worst unworkable. This middle managerial resistance slowed down the progress of the change and acted as a major barrier to securing outcomes within the six-month timeframe. In the case of two managers their obstruction was so harmful to the project that they were relieved of their posts. The effect on staff morale was quite devastating. Both managers were liked and respected by their staff. One, in particular, had spent almost his entire working life with the organization and the way he was treated was highly disturbing for other staff. As one employee put it: 'You know, even us, we're sort of thinking "Well, I've been with the bank for 15 years ... and look what they did to Garry. They weren't very kind to him. How are they going to be with me?" '

Staff morale had also deteriorated because of the way in which general staff and supervisors were consulted about the design of the new system. As one change agent pointed out:

> *We simply could not have involved everyone in the re-organization of retail lending. No one could think of a way to do that because everyone would have a different idea of the way it should be. It would have got too big. So we decided to use a small team.*

This top-down approach to change offended many of the general staff, especially those who had previously been actively involved in the earlier 'bottom-up' change projects. Once again, the implementation of change did not prove successful, only this time the strategy adopted by senior management had failed in its intentions to mobilize middle management commitment and local staff enthusiasm. In the words of one general staff member who had been a very active participator in the bottom-up approach:

> *Whereas before people used to be involved and we were having hassles trying to convince the people that were up there [management] to get involved. Now it seems to be them, up there, just telling, like a Hitler type of situation, telling these people down here 'This is what you are to do!'*

Questions

1. Compare and contrast the case from the perspective of an OD, contingency, political process and processual framework. In so doing, consider whether any of these frameworks are more useful than others in making sense of change.
2. With reference to the case study, outline the advantages and disadvantages of a bottom-up and top-down approach to change implementation.
3. How important is employee commitment to the successful management of change?
4. List the major reasons for employee resistance to change and suggest ways in which these 'obstacles' to change can best be tackled.
5. Discuss whether the Managing Director served as an 'inhibitor' or 'facilitator' of change and evaluate the effects that this may have had on the introduction of the various change initiatives.
6. Is change a non-linear political process? Explain your answer on the basis of the case material, the literature and your own experiences at work.

Chapter questions

The questions listed below relate to the chapter as a whole and can be used by individuals to further reflect on the material covered, as well as serving as a source for more open group discussion and debate.

1. 'The Organizational Development approach to change continues to dominate the literature because the value of this approach has been proven in practice'. Discuss this statement.

2. Discuss the pros and cons of a processual approach for understanding change.

Hands-on exercise

Research a change model or theory of your choice and identify:

1. The major work/studies from which the theory developed (be aware of the context and time of these developments).

2. The main elements of the proposed framework and how they relate to each other.

3. Who are the major supporters of this approach and how far do they differ in their use and adaptation of this model?

4. What are the key criticisms that have been levelled at this perspective?

Team debate exercise

Debate the following two statements:

> 1. *Organizations generally reach a state of equilibrium that is not conducive to change but supports the status quo.*
>
> 2. *Organizations are always in the process of becoming, of changing, they are fluid entities that never come to rest.*

Divide the class into two groups, with one arguing as convincingly as possible for the notion that organizations need to be driven for change to occur otherwise they will maintain existing ways of doing things. The other group will prepare an argument proposing that change is the norm and is a continual dynamic that is part of organizations (an ongoing process).

References

Abrahamson, E. (1991) 'Managerial fads and fashions: the diffusion and rejection of innovations', *Academy Management Review*, 16: 586–612.

Abrahamson, E. (1996) 'Management fashion', *Academy of Management Review*, 21: 254–85.

Aldag, R.J. and Stearns, T.M. (1991) *Management*. Cincinnati, OH: South–Western College Publishing.

Allan, C. (1995) 'The process and politics of change at Vicbank', in P. Dawson, and G. G. Palmer (eds), *Quality Management*. Melbourne: Longman.

Alvesson, M. and Sveningsson, S. (2008) *Changing Organizational Culture: Cultural Change Work in Progress*. London: Routledge.

Alvesson, M. and Willmott, H. (1996) *Making Sense of Management: A Critical Introduction*. London: Sage.

Balogun, J. (2006) 'Managing change: steering a course between intended strategies and unanticipated outcomes', *Long Range Planning*, 39: 29–49.

Balogun, J. and Hailey, V. (1999) *Exploring Strategic Change*. London: Prentice Hall.

Balogun, J. and Johnson, J. (2004) 'Organizational restructuring and middle manager sensemaking', *Academy of Management Journal*, 47 (4): 523–49.

Beckhard, R. (1969) *Organizational Development: Strategies and Models*. Reading, MA: Addison-Wesley.

Bedeian, A. (1984) *Organizations: Theory and Analysis*, 2nd edn. New York: Dryden Press.

Beer, M. and Nohria, N. (1998) 'Cracking the code of change', *Harvard Business Review*, 78 (3): 133–41.

Bennis, W. (1969) *Organization Development: Its Nature, Origins, and Prospects*. Reading. MA: Addison-Wesley.

Bennis, W. (1984) 'The 4 competencies of leadership', *Training and Development Journal*, 38: 15.

Braverman, H. (1974) *Labor and Monopoly Capital. The Degradation of Work in the Twentieth Century*. New York: Monthly Review Press.

Buchanan, D. and Badham, R. (1999) *Power, Politics, and Organizational Change. Winning the Turf Game*. London: Sage.

Buchanan, D. and Badham, R. (2008) *Power, Politics, and Organizational Change: Winning the Turf Game*, 2nd edn. London: Sage.

Buchanan, D. and Boddy, D. (1992) *The Expertise of the Change Agent: Public Performance and Backstage Activity*. London: Prentice Hall.

Burke, W. (2002) *Organization Change: Theory and Practice*. London: Sage.

Burnes, B. (2000) *Managing Change: A Strategic Approach to Organizational Dynamics*, 3rd edn. London: Pitman.

Burnes, B. (2004) *Managing Change: A Strategic Approach to Organizational Dynamics*, 4th edn. Harlow: Financial Times Prentice Hall.

Cameron, K. and Quinn, R. (2006) *Diagnosing and Changing Organizational Culture: Based on the Competing Values Framework*, revd edn. San Francisco: Jossey-Bass.

Carnall, C. (2003) *Managing Change in Organizations*, 4th edn. London: Prentice Hall.

Carnall, C. (2007) *Managing Change in Organizations*, 5th edn. Harlow: Financial Times Prentice Hall.

Child, J. (1972) 'Organization structure, environment and performance: the role of strategic choice', *Sociology*, 6 (1): 1–22.

Clark, J., McLoughlin, I., Rose, H. and King, R. (1988) *The Process of Technological Change: New Technology and Social Choice in the Workplace*. Cambridge: Cambridge University Press.

Collins, D. (1998) *Organizational Change: Sociological Perspectives*. London: Routledge.

Collins, D. (2000) *Management Fads and Buzzwords: Critical–Practical Perspectives*. London: Routledge.

Collins, D. (2001) 'The fad motif in management scholarship', *Employee Relations*, 23: 26–37.

Cummings, T. (2008) *Handbook of Organization Development*. Thousand Oaks, CA: Sage.

Dawson, P. (1994) *Organizational Change: A Processual Approach*. London: Paul Chapman.

Dawson, P. (1996) *Technology and Quality: Change in the Workplace*. London: International Thomson Business Press.

Dawson, P. (2003a) *Understanding Organizational Change: The Contemporary Experience of People at Work*. London: Sage.

Dawson, P. (2003b) *Reshaping Change: A Processual Perspective*. London: Routledge.

De Board, R. (1978) *The Psychoanalysis of Organizations. A Psychoanalytic Approach to Behaviour in Groups and Organizations*. London: Tavistock.

DiMaggio, P. and Powell, W. (eds) (1991) *The New Institutionalism in Organizational Analysis*. Chicago: University of Chicago Press.

Donaldson, L. (2001) *The Contingency Theory of Organizations*. London: Sage.

Dunford, R.W. (1990) 'A reply to Dunphy and Stace', *Organization Studies*, 11: 131–4.

Dunphy, D. (1981) *Organizational Change by Choice*. Sydney: McGraw-Hill.

Dunphy, D. and Stace, D. (1990) *Under New Management: Australian Organizations in Transition*. Sydney: McGraw-Hill.

French, K. (1995) 'Men and locations of power: why move over?' in C. Itzin and J. Newman (eds), *Gender, Culture and Organizational Change: Putting Theory into Practice*. London: Routledge.

French, W. and Bell, C. (1983) *Organization Development: Behavioral Science Interventions for Organization Improvement*. Englewood Cliffs, NJ: Prentice Hall.

French, J. and Raven, B. (1993) 'The basis of social power', in M. Metteson and J. Ivancevich (eds), *Management and Organizational Behavior Classics*, 5th edn. Boston, MA: Irwin.

French, W., Bell, C. and Zawacki, A. (2004) *Organization Development and Transformation: Managing Effective Change*, 6th edn. New York: McGraw-Hill Education.

Gallos, J. (ed.) (2006) *Organization Development*. San Francisco: Jossey-Bass.

Graetz, F., Rimmer, M., Lawrence, A. and Smith, A. (2002) *Managing Organizational Change*. Queensland: John Wiley & Sons Australia.

Gray, J.L. and Starke, F.A. (1988) *Organizational Behavior: Concepts and Applications*. Columbus, OH: Merrill.

Harlow, E., Hearn, J. and Parkin, W. (1995) 'Gendered noise: organizations and the silence and din of domination', in C. Itzin and J. Newman (eds), *Gender, Culture and Organizational Change: Putting Theory into Practice*. London: Routledge.

Hayes, J. (2002) *The Theory and Practice of Change Management*. Basingstoke: Palgrave.

Hayes, J. (2007) *The Theory and Practice of Change Management*, 2nd edn. Basingstoke: Palgrave.

Hersey, P. and Blanchard, K. (1988) *Organizational Behavior*. New York: Prentice Hall.

Huse, E. (1982) *Management*. New York: West.

Itzin, C. and J. Newman (eds) (1995) *Gender, Culture and Organizational Change: Putting Theory into Practice*. London: Routledge.

Jackson, B. (2001) *Management Gurus and Management Fashions*. London: Routledge.

Jackson, R. and Callon, V. (2001) 'Managing and Leading Organizational Change', in K. Parry (ed.), *Leadership in the Antipodes: Findings, Implications and a Leader Profile*. Wellington: Institute of Policy Studies and Centre for the Study of Leadership.

Jick, T. and Peiperl, M. (2003) *Managing Change: Cases and Concepts*, 2nd edn. Boston, MA: McGraw-Hill.

Kanter, R.M. (1983) *The Change Masters: Corporate Entrepreneurs at Work*. London: Allen & Unwin.

Kanter, R.M. (1989) *When Giants Learn to Dance: Mastering the Challenges of Strategy, Management, and Careers in the 1990s*. London: Unwin Hyman.

Kanter, R.M., Stein, B.A. and Jick, T.D. (1992) *The Challenge of Organizational Change: How Companies Experience It and Leaders Guide It*. New York: The Free Press.

Knights, D. and McCabe, D. (2003) *Organization and Innovation: Guru Schemes and American Dreams*. Maidenhead: Open University Press.

Kotter, J. (1996) *Leading Change*. Boston, MA: Harvard Business School Press.

Kotter, J.P. and Cohen, D.S. (2002) *The Heart of Change*. Boston, MA: Harvard Business School Press.

Kreitner, R. and Kinicki, A. (1992) *Organizational Behaviour*, 2nd edn. Homewood, IL: Irwin.

Leavitt, H.J. (1964) 'Applied organizational change in industry: structural, technical and human approaches', in W.W. Cooper, H.J. Leavitt and M.W. Shelly (eds), *New Perspectives in Organizations Research*. New York: John Wiley.

Ledford, G.E., Mohram, S.A., Mohrman, A.M. and Lawler, E.E. (1990) 'The phenomenon of large-scale organizational change', in A.M. Mohrman, S.A. Mohram,

G.E. Ledford, T.G. Cummings and E.E. Lawler, *Large-Scale Organizational Change*. San Francisco: Jossey-Bass.

Lewin, K. (1947) 'Frontiers in group dynamics', *Human Relations*, 1 (1): 5–42.

Lewin, K. (1951) *Field Theory in Social Science*. New York: Harper & Row.

Mangham, I. (1979) *The Politics of Organizational Change*. Westport, CT: Greenwood Press.

Marrow, A. (1969) *The Practical Theorist. The Life and Work of Kurt Lewin*. New York: Basic Books.

Mitroff, I. and Mohrman, S. (1987) 'The slack is gone: how the United States lost its competitive edge in the world economy', *Academy of Management Executive*, 1: 65–70.

Newman, J. (1995) 'Gender and cultural change', in C. Itzin and J. Newman (eds), *Gender, Culture and Organizational Change: Putting Theory into Practice*. London: Routledge.

Noble, D. (1979) 'Social choice in machine design: the case of automatically controlled machine tools', in A. Zimbalist (ed.), *Case Studies in the Labor Process*. New York: Monthly Review Press.

Paton, R. and McCalman, J. (2000) *Change Management. A Guide to Effective Implementation*, 2nd edn. London: Sage.

Pendlebury, J., Grouard, B. and Meston, F. (1998) *The Ten Keys to Successful Change Management*. New York: John Wiley.

Peters, T. and Waterman, R. (1982) *In Search of Excellence: Lessons from America's Best-Run Companies*. New York: Harper & Row.

Pettigrew, A. (1973) *The Politics of Organizational Decision-Making*. London: Tavistock.

Pettigrew, A.M. (1985) *The Awakening Giant: Continuity and Change in Imperial Chemical Industries*. Oxford: Blackwell.

Pettigrew, A. (ed.) (1987) *The Management of Strategic Change*. Oxford: Blackwell.

Pettigrew, A. (1990) 'Longitudinal field research on change: theory and practice', *Organization Science*, 1: 267–92.

Pettigrew, A., Woodman, R. and Cameron, K. (2001) 'Studying organizational change and development: challenges for future research', *Academy of Management Journal*, 44: 697–713.

Pfeffer, J. (1981) *Power in Organizations*. Boston, MA: Pitman.

Preece, D., Steven, G. and Steven, V. (1999) *Work, Change and Competition. Managing for Bass*. London: Routledge.

Robbins, S.P. (1986) *Management: Concepts and Applications*. Englewood Cliffs, NJ: Prentice Hall.

Robbins, S.P. (1996) *Organizational Behavior: Concepts, Controversies, Applications*, 7th edn. Englewood Cliffs, NJ: Prentice Hall.

Romanelli, E. and Tushman, M. (1994) 'Organizational transformation as punctuated equilibrium: an empirical test', *Academy of Management Journal*, 37: 1141–66.

Senior, B. (2002) *Organizational Change*, 2nd edn. London: Pitman.

Senior, B. and Fleming, J. (2005) *Organizational Change*, 3rd edn. London: Financial Times Prentice Hall.

Skinner, Q. (2000) *Machiavelli: A Very Short Introduction*. Oxford: Oxford University Press.

Skinner, Q. and Price, R. (eds) (1988) *Machiavelli: The Prince*. Cambridge: Cambridge University Press.

Stace, D. and Dunphy, D. (1994) *Beyond the Boundaries: Leading and Re-Creating the Successful Enterprise*. Sydney: McGraw-Hill.

Strebel, P. (1998) 'Why do employees resist change?', *Harvard Business Review on Change*, Boston, MA: Harvard Business School Press. pp. 139–57.

Thompson, J.D. (1967) *Organizations in Action*. New York: McGraw-Hill.

Tichy, N. (1983) *Managing Strategic Change: Technical, Political and Cultural Dynamics*. New York: John Wiley.

Tsoukas, H. and Chia, R. (2002) 'On organizational becoming: rethinking organizational change', *Organization Science*, 13: 567–82.

Tushman, M. and Romanelli, E. (1985) 'Organizational evolution: a metamorphosis model of convergence and reorientation', in L. Cummins and B. Staw (eds), *Research in Organizational Behavior*, Vol. 7. Greenwich, CT: JAI Press. pp. 171–222.

Weisbord, M.R. (1988) *Productive Workplaces: Organizing and Managing for Dignity, Meaning and Community*. San Francisco: Jossey-Bass.

Wilkinson, B. (1983) *The Shopfloor Politics of New Technology*. London: Heinemann.

Williams, G. and MacAlpine, M. (1995) 'The gender lens: management development for women in "developing countries" ', in C. Itzin and J. Newman (eds), *Gender, Culture and Organizational Change: Putting Theory into Practice*. London: Routledge.

Wilson, D.C. (1992) *A Strategy of Change. Concepts and Controversies in the Management of Change*. London: Routledge.

Wood, S. (ed.) (1989) *The Transformation of Work?* London: Unwin Hyman.

Zimbalist, A. (ed.) (1979) *Case Studies in the Labor Process*. New York: Monthly Review Press.

Recommended reading

- Buchanan, D. and Badham, R. (2008) *Power, Politics, and Organizational Change: Winning the Turf Game*, 2nd edn. London: Sage.

- Carnall, C. (2007) *Managing Change in Organizations*, 5th edn. Harlow: Financial Times Prentice Hall.

- Dawson, P. (2003) *Understanding Organizational Change: The Contemporary Experience of People at Work*. London: Sage.

- Hayes, J. (2007) *The Theory and Practice of Change Management*, 2nd edn. Basingstoke: Palgrave.

- Senior, B. and Fleming, J. (2005) *Organizational Change*, 3rd edn. London: Financial Times Prentice Hall.

Some useful websites

- The Organization Development Institute has a website that provides links to conferences and developments in the field of Organizational Development. Their aim is to promote a wider understanding of the field of OD (http://www.odinstitute.org).

- There are also a number of websites at universities that are of interest and it is worth checking out websites at leading research institutions. Three suggested here as a starting point are:

1. University of Bath: Andrew Pettigrew has long been involved in change projects and is currently located at the University of Bath (previously at Warwick Business School). Go to: http://www.bath.ac.uk/management/research/ to look at research being conducted by staff.

2. Harvard Business School is always worth visiting as it has a number of professors with an interest in change management (http://www.hbs.edu/research/faculty.html). (For example, click *topics* and then click *leading change*.)

3. In Australia, the Centre for Corporate Change at the AGSM has been involved in studying change for a number of years and they have good links with business and academic staff around the world. Go to: http://www.ccc.agsm.edu.au/web/index.php.

Part 3

CRITICAL REFLECTIONS ON THEORY AND PRACTICE

11

Theoretical Debates and Practical Issues: Some Reflections

Learning objectives

This chapter reflects on theoretical and practical concerns around debates on change, creativity and innovation. It has seven learning objectives:

1. To identify and summarize key links between historical and contextual concerns and the formulation of new theories and concepts. Our intention is to reflect on how these relate to our thinking about creativity, innovation and change.
2. To consider two contrasting philosophies on the fixity and fluidity of organizations and how these can influence the development of theoretical models.
3. To evaluate recent debates on agency and structure and, in particular, the concept of dualities and the theory of structuration.
4. To analyse the complementarities of change in summarizing a major collaborative study on innovative forms of organizing.
5. To examine some of the practical challenges in managing creative individuals and sustaining innovative environments.
6. To outline some practical guidelines on the management change, creativity and innovation.
7. To reflect on the juxtaposition between the narratives of what is happening and the lived experience, and to compare and contrast this with ongoing debates over theory and practice.

Introduction

Processes of change, creativity and innovation are central to organizations that operate in competitive business markets yet each area has developed separate and distinct bodies of knowledge. The change management literature examines the triggers of change and the way change is managed, examining the role of individuals (change agents and leaders), groups (guiding coalitions, management, workers and unions) and various cultural, structural and political elements. The individual, the group and the organization, are all open to analysis and consideration in the movement from a current position 'A' to a preferred future position 'B'. Much of the focus rests on how to move the organization forward and to overcome obstacles that may prevent the organization achieving planned objectives. In the area of creativity, the emphasis has been on the generation of new ideas and how these originate and can be encouraged at the individual and group level. Once again, there is concern with structural characteristics that may promote creative environments and how to create cultures of creativity. In addition to these individual and group processes, there is interest in the growth in creative industries and the way in which these types of organizations are managed. In the field of innovation, the literature is concerned with identifying long-wave business cycles that promote clusters of innovations that diffuse into the economy and stimulate economic growth, as well as processes of innovation at the individual and group level. Some commentators are concerned with innovative forms of organizing (Pettigrew et al., 2003), others with the organizational conditions under which innovation occurs (Burns and Stalker, 1961) and others on the nature of innovation within organizations and how new ideas are translated into commercial products and services (Bessant and Tidd, 2007). In all these, there is a concern with the wider environment that promotes change, creativity and innovation; as well as the processes that occur within organizations. For analytical purposes, it is often easier to delimit an area of study and this is usually achieved through a clear demarcation of areas by definitional means. For example, if we define the creative process as involving the generation of new ideas, innovation as the translation of new ideas into commercial projects, and change as involving the movement of an organization from some current position to a future state, then we clearly demarcate our separate areas of concern. From our perspective, this separation of bodies of thought is limited but understandable, as in practice these elements overlap and interlock.

Fixity and flux: organization or organizing?

There has been a longstanding debate over whether we view organizations as generally stable entities consisting of identifiable objects, resources and structures of control and co-ordination or whether we view organizations as fluid entities in a constant state of flux, as consisting of processes of becoming (Tsoukas and Chia, 2002). Under the latter view, it is sometimes argued that the terms *organizing* and *strategizing* (verbs) are preferable to the terms organization and strategy (nouns) as they more usefully capture the dynamic processes of change (see Pettigrew et al., 2003). Thus, theories of change often take as their starting point a notion of fluidity or stability and then develop a focus of interest in developing a particular theoretical explanation of change. For example, *punctuated equilibrium theory* (Anderson and Tushman, 1990; Romanelli and Tushman, 1994) views stability as the normal state of play but recognizes that industries and organizations can experience major shocks within their business environments that necessitates major change, whereas *chaos theory* assumes a continuous dynamic interplay between forces that create a constant state of flux within which organizations achieve temporary periods of stability (Dubinskas, 1994; Stacey, 1992). Taken from the physical sciences, the basic argument (outlined in Chapter 10) is that disequilibrium is an essential condition in the development of dynamic systems as it promotes an internal resilience to self-renewal (see also Burnes, 2000: 206–7; Hayes, 2007: 4–11). These, and other theories of change, often disagree on the basis of different ontological views about the nature of organizations and, consequently, the appropriate methods for studying change in organizations.

Van de Ven and Poole (2005) examine alternative approaches for studying organizational change and argue that many of these disagreements can be traced back to the differing philosophies of Heraclitus and Democritus. Process was central to Heraclitus's view of the world and was later taken up by the processual philosophers such as Alfred North Whitehead and John Dewey. As Van de Ven and Poole (2005: 1378) note: 'They viewed reality as a process and regarded time, change, and creativity as representing the most fundamental facts for understanding the world'. In contrast, Democritus 'pictured all of nature as composed of stable material substance or things that changed only in their positioning in space and time' (Van de Ven and Poole, 2005: 1377–8). In support of this view, Whetten (2006) argues that the study of organizations should focus on entities, such as structure and culture, rather than on social processes. This distinction between an emphasis on organizing as a process (or verb) and organization as a thing (or noun) has generated considerable debate within the academic literature (see Van de Ven and Poole, 2005). As two alternative and competing views of the world, these debates and issues can never be fully resolved, but perhaps each may serve to address different questions. The quantitative researcher is likely to take a more static-world view in studies on the relationships between variables, whereas the qualitative researcher is more likely to be oriented to a process-world view in studying the processes of change in context and over time. That both approaches can contribute to knowledge on change is not in doubt, but whether the two can ever be fully combined into an holistic approach is questionable, whilst Van de Ven and Poole (2005: 1395–6) conclude that:

> *In our view, the blindness is to regard one form of representation as superior to all others, and thereby deprive ourselves of insights that other forms of research can yield [p. 1395] ... the relevant question is: how might they be combined to yield a more holistic appreciation of complex organizational dynamics? One strategy is to conduct*

> *both variance and process studies of the same organizational*
> *phenomenon viewed as both a noun and a verb ... Even better ...*
> *would be to find a way to combine elements of the ...*
> *approaches in a single analysis ... The best approach for a par-*
> *ticular study depends on the type of questions addressed, the*
> *researchers' assumptions about the nature of organizations and*
> *methodological predispositions, as well as the data they have*
> *access to. Nevertheless, a thorough understanding of the buzzing,*
> *blooming and confusing dynamics often observed in organizational*
> *changes probably requires the use of multiple approaches for under-*
> *standing organizational change.*

We both support and question this position, claiming that whilst there is value in both approaches, attempts to combine the best of the two competing world views into one holistic approach produces something less than what these perspectives offer as standalone approaches. We argue for a more purist approach that enables researchers from competing perspectives with different methodological traditions to continue their studies each offering and contributing to our stock of knowledge. From our own background and preferences, we forward a more processual view of change, creativity and, innovation and, in the next section, briefly consider some of the other debates that have arisen within these areas of study.

Outside the straitjacket of contingent thinking: the world of dualities

Current thinking is moving away from contingency models of innovation and change to a concern with a world of dualities in which the complexity and dynamics of process is recognised (Pettigrew et al., 2003). As Whittington and Melin (2003: 45–6) note:

> *Duality is a theme throughout this book, and the structurationist*
> *duality of action and structure has special resonance here.*
> *Structure enables as well as constrains. By implication, organiza-*
> *tional structures too are not so much passive drags on strategic*
> *action, necessary evils to be regretted and minimized; they are*
> *central resources upon which action must draw, demanding equal*
> *attention alongside strategy and initiative. Action is not simply fet-*
> *tered by structure, it positively relies on it. This duality has impor-*
> *tant implications for our view of business leaders, essential to*
> *action yet dependent on structure. The model of leaders as heroic*
> *individuals downplays – to their own disadvantage – the structural*
> *rules and resources on which they must draw for their empower-*
> *ment. Here, structuration theory points to a delicate reciprocity*
> *between those who will lead and those who follow. Even as they*
> *play creatively on them, still leaders must subscribe to the struc-*
> *tural limits and expectations embodied in their organizations. For*
> *leaders, action and structure are tied together.*

Change, creativity and innovation are enabled and constrained not by structures *per se*, but by our understanding of structure and our interpretation of the limits and possibilities of action through structure that can be used to support certain preferred outcomes. As such, structures and the environment are not set as some objective force that organizations must gain fit with (as often promoted through the lens of the contingency theorist) but, following on from more postmodern constructivist accounts (Hatch and Cunliffe, 2006), it is the meaning and interpretations given to structure that shapes and influences decisions and actions. In adopting Giddens's structuration theory, Orlikowski (1992) illustrates this in her attempt to combine agency and structure in analysing technology. She attempts to embrace both the subjective and objective elements of technology (the duality of technology) through recognizing that technology is physically built by humans but that interpretations and meanings are also given to the technology during this process (that is, technology is also socially constructed within a social context). When the technology is used it is often seen as part of the objective structural properties of an organization (institutionalized and reified) and yet it is, at the same time, open to modification. The concept of *interpretative flexibility* is used to capture this notion of ongoing reconfiguration. Orlikowski (1992) argues that technology that is used is likely to be reshaped over time and that this is influenced both by the characteristics of the material artefact and the social process of change and the meanings that actors attach to the technology.

The four types of relationships identified by Orlikowski (1992) in her structuration model are:

1. Technology is a product of human action; that is, technology is both designed by humans and given meaning through adoption and use.

2. Technology is a medium of human action; that is, our understanding of technology can constrain and enable human action, although it does not determine social practice.

3. Technology is shaped by humans in organizational context, or, to put it another way, human action is shaped by organizational context which may influence their understanding of technology; for example, human action may reinforce a conception of technical constraints.

4. Technology may be used by human agents to reinforce institutional structures.

This concern with dualities has emerged and been developed in a number of different fields of study. As such, it is worth spending a little more time examining the concepts of *dualities* and *structuration*, as these studies highlight the importance of choice and context whilst also demonstrating the problems with approaches that polarize options. From this perspective, the choice is not between A or B (dualism), but in understanding the dynamic relationship between A and B (dualities). A useful starting point for this discussion is the work of John Child (1972), whose landmark paper on strategic choice argued against determinist positions that downplayed the element of choice in decision making.

A reappraisal of John Child's concept of strategic choice

For Child (1972), whatever the constraints or pressures, there is always space for choice. As such, external environmental forces never fully determine the outcomes of change as these are ultimately shaped through a process of choice and decision making. Rapid changes in business market conditions can often be a significant driver for company change; however, there remains 'strategic choice' in how to respond to, accommodate or make the most of these potential threats or opportunities. Child develops the concept of *strategic choice* and points out how choices made by power-holding groups or a dominant coalition (that is, key decision makers) shape, through an essentially political process, change. He notes how more than one dominant coalition may exist and that conflict between different management groups is not unusual. The choices made by senior management can be further modified during the implementation of change, either through middle managers responsible for managing planned change, or through trade union and employee responses to change. In promoting the concept of strategic choice, Child (1972) draws attention away from the determinist arguments in which technology, the environment or size are seen to be the key determining factors of strategy and structure, and refocuses attention on political process, social choice and negotiation in the mutual shaping of work and organization. In a later reappraisal of the strategic choice perspective, Child notes that:

> *Strategic choice articulates a political process, which brings agency and structure into tension and locates them within a significant context. It regards both the relation of agency to structure and to environment as dynamic in nature. In so doing, the strategic choice approach not only bridges a number of competing perspectives but also adopts a non-deterministic and potentially evolutionary position. Strategic choice, when considered as a process, points to the possibility of continuing adaptive learning cycles, but within a theoretical framework that locates 'organizational learning' within the context of organizations as socio-political systems. (Child, 1997: 44)*

In this later paper, Child's main concern is with the way subjective constructions have objective consequences and the way these may in turn influence future actions and interpretations. In drawing on the work of Giddens (1984) and the concept of structuration (see also DeSanctis and Poole, 1994; MacIntosh and Scapens, 1990), Child (1997) forwards what he terms as a 'double structuration' process. He explains how within organizations actors may seek to influence organizational design and in the process be informed or constrained by the existing structures and routines that they may wish to change. In addition to the cycle of 'inner structuration', Child (1997) also forwards the notion of 'outer structuration' where actors may seek to influence and interact with environmental elements, in which they are 'simultaneously informed of the opportunities for action which environmental conditions present and of the constraints which external circumstances place upon their room for action'. As we shall see in a moment, this concept of dualities has been taken up in a number of areas and is a key theme running through Pettigrew et al.'s (2003) research on changing organizations.

Andrew Pettigrew and colleagues: innovative forms of organizing

In their book on *Innovative Forms of Organizing*, Pettigrew et al. (2003) call for a more processual understanding of the dynamic relationship between strategy and organization. As Pettigrew et al. (2003: 345) state:

> *Living with constant change (organizing/strategizing and not organization and strategy) means there are always multiple loose ends. A core driver of this experience of wrestling with order and disorder is the challenge of managing multiple dualities in the modernizing organization.*

In a collaborative study on the development of innovative forms of organizing, Pettigrew and colleagues (Pettigrew et al., 2003) highlight the contextual nature of change and, in so doing, question the value of prescriptive recipes and formulaic solutions (see also Pettigrew, 1985). The authors argue that accommodation and adaptation to local conditions requires customized solutions. Their studies demonstrate how it is possible to identify common international company trajectories and how new innovations overlay and interlock rather than replace current modes of organizing. Patterns emerge from the data and are brought out in their theme of complementarities, change and performance. This concern was built into their research at the outset and follows on from contingency theory with an emphasis on finding an appropriate 'fit' between a range of variables (size, technology, environment) and organization structure. Through broadening this concern and taking a more holistic approach, their attention is on whole types of configurations. As such, they are interested in the complementarities of change where a standalone change, such as just-in-time management systems, may be limited if not accompanied by other complementary changes in management information systems, design for manufacture, quality management, and so forth. They also draw attention not only to the need for a comparison of configurations, but also to disaggregating configurations to identify and analyse individual effects. In so doing, they argue that it is possible to move from the specific change to the overall full-system effects on organizational performance (Pettigrew and Massini, 2003: 16–18).

In studying European, US and Japanese organizations their findings confirm that innovative forms of organizing are in evidence across these three regions, but that radical change is far more common in Europe and the US when compared with Japan. Although change initiatives are seen to be following a common trajectory with a significant correlation between development of strategic alliances and the internationalization of organizations;

their findings do not support the convergence thesis and highlight how there is far greater boundary and process change occurring as opposed to structural change. In other words, the common direction of change and innovation is played out in different ways in different contexts and localities (Pettigrew et al., 2003: 31).

The dualities of change and continuity, innovation and convention, centralization and decentralization, and organizing and strategizing, question neat sequential models or simple continua that contrast and compare two dimensions. In searching for a division between dual factors, they argue that past studies have focused on definitional and conceptual issues in drawing boundaries and clarifying the terrain (as in the example of technology where the division between the social and technical has generated heated debate and discussion). However, longitudinal qualitative and quantitative research data are increasingly calling into question these simple divisions in demonstrating the unending process of organizing. Renewal, change, closure, reconfiguration, constancy and transition all draw attention to temporality in the process of managing dualities over time. As Pettigrew (2003: 347) concludes:

> *Although our research findings raised the significance of the management of dualities as an issue, and have documented the rise of sets of dualities in the modernizing firm, there is a big research agenda here for other scholars to build upon. We need more research on the varieties of management strategy in use in different localities to sense, accommodate, and lead organizations through further cycles of innovation.*

This of course leaves open the need for further research and debate and perhaps raises as many questions as answers. Nevertheless, it does raise interesting material for critical reflection on the separation and links between change, creativity and innovation. As with the work of Knights and McCabe (2003), the suggestion is that we are often too quick to separate and distinguish between phenomena that in practice shape and influence each other on an ongoing basis. They are critical of universal definitions, such as the 'first commercial application of a new process or product' (Knights and McCabe, 2003: 39) that limit what we are to understand by innovation and prevent exploration of what they term 'innovation in context', an understanding of the change process within which innovation occurs (see also the study by Alvesson and Sveningsson, 2008). Similarly with creativity, we can identify a link and overlap with notions of innovation and change in the translation of new ideas into tangible outputs, novel services or new operating arrangements (Bessant and Tidd, 2007: 40). The conceptual and theoretical challenge remains and, we contend, is an area likely to stimulate further debate and research into processes of change, creativity and innovation.

In turning our attention to more practical matters, the next two sections, first, examine how we may best manage creative employees and, second, consider lessons for steering change, creativity and innovation in certain preferred directions.

The practical challenge: managing creative employees

Creative employees are often regarded as different or idiosyncratic. Their inclination to disregard the bureaucratic chain of command, their preference towards independence and risk taking as well as their interest in complexity and novelty, characterize such employees. They are often labelled or perceived as 'intrapreneurs' (internal entrepreneurs) with a high level of autonomy and develop an individualistic mentality that does not sit well in traditional organizations. Organizations like Intel Corporation or 3M are living examples of companies who recognize that creativity comes from individuals and their teams. Such companies develop working practices to increase collaboration or initiate staff meetings where employees are allowed to confront each other about their ideas. What is important in these companies is the merit of the idea rather than ownership. As illustrated by Sternberg et al.'s (1997) model, creative employees often behave in a manner that is conceptually similar to that of financial investors who aim to 'buy low and sell high'. In other words, creative employees need to invest their creative potential in coming up with ideas which are initially low in value since they are new and unusual, but which have the potential to yield high levels of value in the future.

People working in creative industries are generally required to have a mix of different types of intellectual skills and abilities ranging from coming up with new ideas to promoting and selling these ideas to others. Sternberg et al. (1997) highlight the importance of the synthetic, analytic and practical abilities as precursors to long-term success and endurance. The 'synthetic' ability refers to the ability to perceive connections and refine opportunities. The 'analytic' ability is about employees' ability to judge the value or potential of an idea. The 'practical' refers to the ability to 'sell' an idea to others. As far as the employees' intellectual abilities are concerned, Sternberg (1999, 2007) and Sternberg and Lubart (1999) suggest that leaders should be responsible for mixing the talents needed over the life cycle of an idea or product development. For instance, in the idea-generation stage, synthetic abilities must be encouraged, whereas, after this stage, choosing which ideas to pursue demands analytic abilities. In the final selection of the most promising ideas practical issues must be considered to transform these ideas into reality.

It is generally assumed that creative employees do not focus on financial compensation but are more interested in the output of their efforts. Our research within the creative industries clearly highlights that employees are greatly concerned about the quality of their work and the ideas they generate – although financial concerns are by no means absent. Research has also shown that employees are more likely to be creative in pursuits they enjoy. If employees do not enjoy an activity, they will not invest the large amounts of time and energy required. Hence, managers need to match people with jobs that reflect their expertise, interests and skills in order to ignite intrinsic motivation.

Managing creative employees and sustaining creative work environments requires balance and understanding in providing an appropriate blend of autonomy, support and control. Increasingly, creative employees must act proactively in learning new techniques/tools/methodologies to keep pace with marketplace processes in continually updating their knowledge. On this issue, Nonaka and Tekeuchi (1995) propose that knowledge is the only reliable and lasting source of competitive advantage. They argue that successful companies are those which consistently create new knowledge, disseminate it widely throughout the organization and rapidly translate it into new products or services. As such, it is important to develop intellectual capital that will create new competencies. Creative organizations need to be skilled in creating, acquiring and transferring knowledge and in encouraging behaviours that stimulate the continual search for new knowledge (Nordström and Ridderstråle, 2007). This knowledge can then be used to create the 'new' and challenge traditional expectations. Furthermore, we argue that the generation and implementation of ideas is neither a mystical process limited to 'Eureka' or 'Aha!' moments, nor the privilege of the selected few working on their own. On the contrary, it is about developing ways for employees to perpetually search for ideas within or outside their organizations, recombine them and apply them to new problems or situations.

At the individual level, an attitude of curiosity and playfulness must be supported. It is the inquisitive nature of experimenting, mixing or breaking products, business models, theories or processes, which must be nurtured. It is also the methods for motivating and rewarding the generation of new ideas that must be mastered by leaders and managers in order to harness the creative potential for the mutual benefit of the individual, the group and the organization. At the team level, the characteristics of the team must be managed to ensure the right mix of knowledge, skills and abilities. It is the exchange of knowledge, the sharing of viewpoints and opinions that enrich the pool of ideas from which the team can choose. If organizations want to foster creative activities, promote innovative thinking and support cultures of change, they must recognize the centrality of people to these processes and the need to nurture environments favourable to such developments. Leaders or managers of these organizations must, therefore, pay close attention to the way they lead employees and develop an organizational culture and structure conducive to creativity, innovation and change.

Steering change, creativity and innovation: beyond the recipe approach

Despite a plethora of guidelines for managing processes of change, creativity and innovation and the various toolkits on effective change management (Cameron and Quinn, 2006; Carnall, 2007), the majority of major change transformations still fail (Alvesson and Sveningsson, 2008; Kotter, 1996). Why is this?

Perhaps, in part, it reflects the complex dynamic and political nature of major change initiatives. Perhaps it also reflects the tendency to view change as a single linear process going through a number of identifiable and predictable stages, whereas in practice change is far from linear and often occurs within a multiple-change rather than a single-change environment. In our view, far too little attention has been given to the multiple, dynamic and processual nature of change (Dawson, 2003a, 2003b). As Jeanie Duck (1998) highlights, managers have been too fast to view change in terms of sequential stages rather than in viewing change as an ongoing dynamic:

> *The problem is simple: we are using a mechanistic model, first applied to managing physical work, and superimposing it onto the new mental model of today's knowledge organization. We keep breaking change into small pieces and then managing the pieces. This is the legacy of Frederick Winslow Taylor and scientific management. But with change, the task is to manage the dynamic, not the pieces. The challenge is to innovate mental work, not to replicate physical work. The goal is to teach thousands of people how to think strategically, recognize patterns, and anticipate problems and opportunities before they occur ... The proper metaphor for managing change is balancing a mobile. Most organizations today find themselves undertaking a number of projects as part of their change effort. An organization may simultaneously be working on TQM, process reengineering, employee empowerment, and several other programs designed to improve performance. But the key to the change effort is not attending to each piece in isolation; it's connecting and balancing all the pieces. In managing change, the critical task is understanding how pieces balance off one another, how changing one element changes the rest, how sequencing and pace affect the whole structure. (Duck, 1998: 57–8)*

The art of balancing multiple changes and having a strategic and operational overview of the dynamics of change is important, but are there guidelines that we can draw from these studies that can be of practical use without undermining our theoretical understanding of change processes? In other words, can we draw on a more processual holistic understanding of change, creativity and innovation in identifying some heuristics that can aid members of organizations steer processes in certain preferred directions?

In promoting a process perspective we seek to go beyond simple linear recipe approaches in identifying broader temporal and contextual lessons for steering change, creativity and innovation in certain preferred directions. In this, we recognize that authority and power relations are not equal within organizations and that political process is an important shaper of outcomes. Nevertheless, to sidestep the practical dimension would be to support the separation between theories and practice that we questioned at the outset of this book.

There is a host of best-practice guidelines on how to manage change, and many of these have been criticized for being too simplistic, linear and acontextual. One of the more popular models for change management (referred to in Chapter 7) is the one developed by John Kotter (1996) who forwards an eight-stage model on how to successfully manage change. In many ways Kotter's (1995, 1996) work resembles some of the earlier work of Beer and Nohria (1988) and Beer et al. (1990a and 1990b), who identify key steps to effective change: In their article on the critical path to change the six steps they recommend comprise (Beer et al., 1990a)

1. Mobilize commitment to change through joint diagnosis of business problems.

2. Develop a shared vision on how to organize and manage for competitiveness.

3. Foster consensus for the new vision, competence to enact it and cohesion to move it along.

4. Spread revitalization to all departments without pushing it from the top.

5. Institutionalize revitalization through formal policies, systems and structures.

6. Monitor and adjust strategies in response to problems in the revitalization process.

We would criticize these simple checklist approaches for their linearity. The complex dynamic nature of change is generally downplayed or side-stepped and these approaches pay little attention to context and political process. The focus of our approach has been on the complex nature of change, creativity and innovation that makes the distillation of simple recipes impractical. Whilst we do not wish to present a set of prescriptions on 'how to manage' these processes, like Alvesson and Sveningsson (2008) we do feel that a broader set of guidelines can be uncovered from processual research in this area. The 10 general lessons that emerge from our research are as follows:

1. There are no universal prescriptions on how best to manage processes of change, creativity or innovation, nor are there simple recipes to competitive success. We recognize that this will not prevent continuing company demand for such solutions and therefore stress the importance of being aware of the serious limitations of n-step guides. We would also call for practising managers and employees in general to challenge – where possible and practicable – the assumptions behind linear packages for 'company success'. This is perhaps why notwithstanding our current knowledge and experience of, for example, organizational change – 'the brutal fact is that about 70% of all change initiatives fail' (Beer and Nohria, 1998).

2. Strategies that promote change, creativity and innovation should be sensitive to the socio-cultural environment, temporal contextual conditions

and the shifting character of expectations in the views and reactions of employee groups and key political players. Political sensitivity and astuteness (the ability to manoeuvre through shifting terrain) are often well-honed skills in those individuals and groups (change agents, trade unionists, and the like) who are able to shape these processes in certain preferred directions.

3. As frequently stated in the literature – major change takes time. Changing the attitudes and behaviour of employees, generating commitment and support for change, creativity and innovation is a long-term goal. Moreover, any radical large-scale strategic and/or operational change requires considerable planning – including numerous revisions and modifications to planned changes – and is unlikely to be marked by a line of continual improvement.

4. Individual and group experience will vary in context and over time and there are no silver bullet guarantees for acceptance nor universal panacea to overcoming resistance to changes in the way work is organized and managed. For example, if the individual or group that questions change are viewed as an obstacle then they are unlikely to respond to or experience change in a positive way. Similarly, casting a jaundiced eye on a 'failed' project that has not enabled the translation of new ideas into commercial products may result in negative employee experience and thereby inadvertently support the assumption that the problem rests with employees and not with other elements of the organization. Such a view can create a self-fulfilling prophecy that can be hard to overcome, especially if this position appeals to commonsense assumptions about why individuals and groups resist change. This clearly highlights the importance and need for continuous critical reflection in order to question take-for-granted assumptions.

5. It is important to learn from all experiences (the good, the bad and the ugly) and not simply to focus attention on so-called 'success' stories or the views of those in dominant positions. Such stories are often *post-hoc* rationalized accounts constructed to convey a certain preferred message to an intended audience. As such, the experiences and views of different groups and individuals at various levels within an organization are all potential sources of knowledge for understanding and shaping processes of change, creativity and innovation. We can generally learn more from failure than the reconstructed (selective and partisan) stories of success.

6. Employees should be trained in new techniques and procedures when needed and as required. The misalignment of training programmes with initiatives that seek to develop new skills and encourage new behaviours is not uncommon in organizations and can be a major influence on employee experience.

7. Communication is central to managing change, promoting creativity and supporting the innovation process, but it also needs to be understood in

context. As supported by much of the literature, employee communication should be ongoing and consistent. However, within organizations there are often a number of competing narratives that co-exist at any given time, and these can undermine and misdirect attention and create environments of mistrust and uncertainty. The choice of what, when and how to communicate as well as the releasing of disconfirming information are often political issues. Communication is an important vehicle both for those seeking to steer processes in certain preferred directions and for those wishing to resist the intentions of others.

8. A simple lesson is that recipe approaches which promote well-defined programmes that support unitary notions of culture and context are ultimately misplaced. There is nothing so impracticable as a packaged prescriptive linear initiative that purports to provide the blueprint for commercial success.

9. We would contend that managing processes of change, creativity and innovation is ultimately a political process that draws on sources of power in achieving stated objectives. Or, to put it another way, political processes are central in gathering support, mobilizing resources and shaping outcomes.

10. The final lesson is perhaps the most straightforward lesson of all, and that is that managing change, creativity and innovation requires the utilization of an array of skills and competencies in the continual adaptation to changing contextual circumstances. It is complex, demanding and difficult as it involves orchestrating interweaving and sometimes contradictory processes towards a set of objectives, that may themselves be refined and changed over time. These processes have an ongoing history that is never static but open to change as the past is rewritten in the context of the present and in the light of future expectations. For us, this draws attention to the value of a processual approach in understanding the theory and practice of change, creativity and innovation.

Conclusion

This chapter has set out to challenge the reader through presenting some more contentious and debatable ideas behind the theory and practice of change, creativity and innovation. Focus was given to the way we view the world – whether as comprising fixed entities or fluid processes – and how this view can influence our predisposition to certain types of theory development. Those who see the world as 'things' as fixed objects, tend to look towards more variance-based models and contingency-type approaches that may seek to gain 'fit' between the operating structures of an organization and the business market within which it operates. Those who adopt a more processual perspective (the predisposition of the authors) tend to view organizations as in a continual state of becoming, of complex flows and dynamic processes that can at times present an illusion of stability, or what Lewin (1951) refers to as 'quasi-stationary equilibrium'. Unlike our previous chapters, we have given more space to exploring some of these notions of process, the links between agency and structure (structuration theory) and the concept of dualities. Turning to the work of Pettigrew and colleagues (2003), we examined some of the findings from the dual methods research into new forms of organizing. Following on from these discussions, we then examined some of the more practical dimensions to managing change, creativity and innovation. This commenced with an exploration of the problems and issues in managing creative employees from which we expanded our presentation to outline some practical guidelines around a more process-based view of organizations. Although this chapter has raised as many questions as it has answered, we hope it provides food for thought and further discussion on these key contemporary issues of change, creativity and innovation.

RESOURCES, READINGS AND REFLECTIONS

CASE STUDY 11.1   MANAGING CHANGE: THE EXPERIENCE OF THE TAYLOR GROUP BY PATRICK DAWSON

The Taylor Group is a family business which is now run by the fourth generation. Over time the business has experienced growth, decline, diversification and contraction. In the 1980s, it grew to embrace manufacturing and plastics in the context of growing business activity within the Silicon Glen corridor that links Glasgow and Edinburgh. Since 2000, the electronics and communications industry has experienced a fall in demand that resulted in a contraction of operations for the Taylor Group. They currently face a challenging environment in which the future strategic direction of the company has to be considered and questions on how best to manage change remain to the fore. As such, the Taylor Group provides a good example of managing change within both the context of growth – with businesses developing in Glasgow, Cumbernauld and Dundee during the 1980s and 1990s – and decline in the 2000s (for example, a decision has been made to close the original iron foundry).

A period of growth and acquisition
During the heyday of manufacturing growth in Britain, the iron foundry business flourished. Growth and development of this enterprise provided a secure business foundation and operations peaked in the early 1980s prior to the decline of UK heavy engineering. At this stage, the company examined export opportunities, particularly in America and mainland Europe. Although the company did

(Continued)

(Continued)

have some success in this venture, exchange rate fluctuations, combined with the fact that most of these countries had their own iron-founding base, meant that this expansion did not provide a lasting solution to the decline in business. The export market did at least slow the process of contraction, although as Robbie Taylor reflects:

> In the early 1980s we saw the inevitable decline in heavy engineering and we were competing by exporting and by considering service as the sort of key differentiator rather than technology. Exporting helped quite a lot; we exported into mainland Europe and North America and had a reasonable amount of success there. But, these countries had their own domestic foundry industry, it's a low value-added component and so it was difficult to compete. And then we had all the vagaries of the exchange rates, etc. So I then had a choice to make: whether to continue to run this family iron foundry business that was in steady decline as far as demand was concerned and to eke out a living (and I thought I probably could through to retirement), or to spread the portfolio and to look at taking the business in a different direction. And strangely as it may sound, joining a family business, whilst it sounds wonderful, also creates other tensions. And the tension for me was, would I have made a success of my business career unless I got this sort of golden opportunity to join a family business. And so, anyway, I decided that I really wanted to spread the portfolio and go into uncharted waters and find excitement in the business world. We looked at a sheet-metal business without success. Then we made an approach to NEI (New England Instrument) Plc who had a die-casting operation which they hardly knew existed, based in Dundee. We made a direct approach and they were happy to move the business on. They hadn't invested in the business: it was servicing one or two NEI subsidiaries; it was servicing the electrical industry – that's plugs and sockets, and the like. But they had more important things on their mind than this small operation in Dundee. So we were able to purchase it and very quickly, with some investment and increasing the profile of the business, it radically improved its performance.

At this time (1986), the die-casting operation in Dundee had the legacy of a militaristic style of management. It operated along hierarchical lines with a classic Taylorite command-and-control administrative structure that contrasted sharply with the approach that had evolved within their iron foundry business. Although there were key cultural change issues to be approached, the acquisition proved to be a good business decision. The commercial success of this venture into manufacturing raised an interest in scanning for other business opportunities. In their appetite for acquisitions, the Taylor Group discovered that NEI had another tool-making and plastic-moulding business within its portfolio based in Glasgow. They decided to purchase the business and set up a greenfield site in

Cumbernauld to service the burgeoning electronics sector in Scotland. However, this acquisition proved more problematic and it did not provide the commercial benefits they had experienced with their newly acquired die-casting operation in Dundee:

> Plastic moulding wasn't as easy to make money at as we had thought. Certainly the acquisition wasn't as smooth as with die-casting, mainly because I think that we weren't large enough to have purchasing leverage over the suppliers of the raw material. And the raw material represented 40–45 per cent of your sales cost and being petroleum based it fluctuated like hell and we never made any real money in plastics. We found that with every new order we acquired it required substantial capital investment at the backend of the process – things like screen-printing or whatever. So we ran that business for a while and we began to get a little disenchanted. It was sucking in cash and it wasn't making profit. Then IBM spoke to one of its major suppliers down south, a plc, and said we want you to have a location servicing us in Scotland. They decided that the best way to do that was rather than set up a greenfield site was to look at what was already in existence. They reviewed seven companies and chose us and I was delighted to sell.

At this stage, the Board was reluctant to pursue any further acquisitions, particularly into uncharted territories. Confidence in making the right business decisions had taken a blow and a more conservative culture prevailed. Business scanning did however continue and a number of sheet-metal operations that also serviced the growing electronics sector were considered. Eventually, the Taylor Group was successful in securing a relatively robust business. Located in Livingstone, the sheet-metal business that they acquired serviced a wider range of electronic clients than their die-casting operation and hence there was a good synergy between the two. In 1992, the Livingstone operation employed 100 people with an annual turnover of £3 million. In the eight years that followed, the business grew rapidly with an increase in turnover of around 300 per cent and employment rose from 100 to just over 200 personnel. However, during 2000/1, an American company indicated an interest in the business. They wanted a platform in Europe and the Livingstone operation would service their needs. The company was sold onto them. As Robbie Taylor explains:

> I mean you might wonder why? But we were coming to the conclusion ourselves that manufacturing was more and more difficult, more and more competitive. Eastern Europe was now quite a threat and unless you had some real value-added in your technology then people were moving stuff around the world for cheaper prices. We felt that the days of manufacturing plants in the UK were numbered. So we were quite happy to sell. So

(Continued)

(Continued)

this left us with the original iron-founding business, which was a shadow of its former self, and the die-casting plant.

A period of decline and reassessment

Selling the business in 2001 involved a lot of time and energy, with the result that the die-casting operation was largely left to its own devices. The die-casting plant in Dundee that produces volume precision zinc and aluminium castings for the general electronics sector was performing well and so it was left alone. Up until the downturn in the electronics and telecommunications industry in 2001–2, the company experienced continual growth with good profits that were reinvested in plant, equipment and people. However, the slump in the business market caused heavy losses, resulting in a fall in turnover of over 40 per cent. In 2002/3 the company managed to break even, but to do so the company needed to reduce costs and this was achieved through a 30 per cent reduction in staff. Within the context of employee redundancy, low profitability, reduction in turnover, and an uncertain and fragile business market with consequent job insecurity for employees, the company maintained a commitment to the training and development of all their employees. Currently the workforce comprises approximately two male to every female employee, and an average length of service of 12 years.

The guiding principles

Throughout this period, entrepreneur and 'mingle mania nomad' Robbie Taylor remained committed to a philosophy of open communication and a culture that encourages employee involvement and commitment. This is highlighted in a document referred to as the 'guiding principles' (see Figure 11.1) and is further supported by regular contact with all employees and a small management team. Although a previous decision to appoint a new managing director had inadvertently hindered this objective:

> Without thinking I advertised and put in a new managing director that looked good, he was good, very competent. But this was a small operation and it was running through difficult times, we were trying to cut overheads and the demand in the marketplace was low. It took me 18 months to realize what was happening by having a new managing director there who really didn't have enough to do. It was a small plant with difficult market conditions, so he was policing like hell every single move the small team here were making. That put us back. He understood the values of the guiding principles of our business but he had too much time on his hands and didn't realize that what he was doing was suppressing innovation and excitement. People lost their will … So I came to an agreement, an arrangement with him, and he left. It was time to do things differently; it is too small an operation for a full-time managing

Taylor Group Guiding Principles

"Making customers feel confident, valued and special"

Tel: 01382 826763

Company Ethos

We want our customers to feel confident valued and special. We know what they think of us because we ask them every year in our annual customer survey and every employee is encouraged to visit at least one customer or supplier every year to find out at first hand what our customers want. This helps us to anticipate the need for change so that we can stay ahead of competitors and exceed customer expectations.

We invest in our people through training. We listen to their opinions on the future through our annual employee survey and their views contribute to the direction of our business. Personal development is monitored through our appraisal scheme.

We look beyond our organisation to find ways to improve our service and learn from others including our competitors. We all have a responsibility to be creative and innovative and to discover new and better ways to work.

We maintain a conducive and safe workplace and are proud to invite customers to visit our sites on our open days, using our operating facilities as a shop window to demonstrate our capabilities.

One measure of our success is our profitability and we are committed to reinvesting in the business and sharing with all employees the benefits of the success that they create.

Taylor Group Diecastings Ltd
St Mary's Road
Dundee
DD3 9DL

www.tgdiecasting.co.uk

FIGURE 11.1 Example of company guiding principles

(*Source*: Taylor Group Diecasting. See also http://www.tgdiecasting.co.uk/principles.htm)

Our Guiding Principles make us think more deeply about our company, our colleagues and to understand the part that we all play in the overall success of the business.

They set a climate within the business that engenders greater trust and honesty, allowing everybody to air their views, make suggestions, use their initiative and take responsibility.

Our ultimate goal is : -

To provide a standard of service that competitors envy and on which customers can rely.

The Way We Work

The company is accountable for setting a climate that encourages exceptional contribution:

1. We treat all employees with equal respect and let them get on with the job
2. We compete by investing in people
3. We balance the demands of all who influence our business
4. We listen to new ideas and take action
5. We encourage trial and error in pursuit of our goals
6. We give people what they need to do their job
7. We encourage dynamic, open communication with all stakeholders inside and outside our business

Signature:

The Way I Work

I matter to the business because

1. I take responsibility for my work
2. I work hard and learn new skills to improve our service
3. I address customer, supplier, colleague and other stakeholder needs
4. I continually try to improve the way we do things
5. I am honest about my mistakes and learn from them
6. I use all available resources to help us exceed customer expectations
7. I take pride in doing a good job because that is the basis of a good reputation

Signature:

FIGURE 11.1 Continued

director so what do we do? So I made the management team those below. To the management team I said: 'Hey, you've got the guiding principles, you've got the corporate policy, get on with it'. And that was really interesting. And that's got some strengths and some weaknesses to it. And that's how we are operating the plant today. And they love it. They've got responsibility and they have transformed the business in very difficult times.

Maintaining a culture of employee involvement and commitment in periods of decline and contraction has not been easy. Currently the business operates on a fairly flat management structure and through practices promoted by the guiding principles seeks to ensure employee engagement and commitment to the future of operations at Dundee. For a number of years there has been a profit-sharing scheme; for example, if the company were to make a 6 per cent margin as profit on sales then 9 per cent of this profit would be shared out among employees. This additional income has been distributed pro rata to people's earnings, although recently an attempt to change the way these profits are distributed has raised some interesting issues (but alas, not ones that we have space to deal with here). Suffice to say, the Taylor Group has experienced considerable change over time and have developed and repositioned in response to changes in business fluctuations and proactive strategies for change. Some of the business opportunities have proven very successful (as commercial ventures), whilst others have not produced anywhere near their anticipated earnings. So this leaves us with the key question: what is it that we can draw from these experiences on the practice of managing creativity, innovation and change?

Some reflections from a business practitioner and entrepreneur
Some answers to questions on the practice of managing change posed to Robbie Taylor are presented below. There was no prior warning about the type of questions that were to be asked and, hence, the answers were neither prepared nor was there time for prolonged consideration within the interview setting. The questions asked were as follows:

1. How important is management and how important is leadership to company change?
2. What in your experience are the key issues and concerns raised by employees during times of change?
3. What are the main lessons on managing change that can be drawn from your experience of the Taylor Group?
4. How important is the size of the company to the way change can be managed?
5. Do you agree that complacency can be a barrier to change and innovation during times of company success?
6. How difficult is it to sustain change in times of economic downturn?
7. What in your view are the key elements to managing change?

(Continued)

(Continued)

Stop! Think about these questions and make some brief notes before reading the sections that follow. Remember, there is no single right answer to these questions – the main aim is to stimulate thinking and critical reflection. It may also be fun!

Change management questions

Below are Robbie Taylor's (RT) responses to the questions posed following a discussion of the business 'highs' and 'lows' of the Taylor Group.

How important is management and how important is leadership to company change?
RT: I think that management is a process and that it is less important than leadership. I think that leadership is there to inspire, to motivate, to create, to churn, to present the company with all sorts of ideas that will influence strategy, and so on. And I think that the behaviour of leadership inculcates the sort of ultimate culture of the business. I believe that the way that people behave, particularly the leader, determines the culture of the business. I don't know how to rate it, other than to say that leadership is far, far more important than management *per se*. But of course you do need management and managers, and I don't think that the leader should try and manage. I think he has got to create a climate in which others enjoy managing the business. A leader should not be seen as typically the person who is making all the decisions. I think the leader is there to stimulate decision making and to influence decision making.

There is an issue in leading an organization and that is in fact determining what is most important to be doing and to be seen to be doing. And it is far too easy to do the things that you like to do, and the things that you're comfortable doing, and the things that you've always done. It's far more difficult and you have to develop quite a discipline to do the things that actually you need to be doing and to be seen to be doing.

What in your experience are the key issues and concerns raised by employees during times of change?
RT: That they have not got enough time to cope with the changes that you are asking them to become involved in. They themselves don't like the uncertainty. If you take one major change in our business – of endeavouring to trust everybody in that business – you push responsibility further and further and further throughout the organization, managers wonder what their role is and if this goes too far will they have a role? Of course, over the years, with flattening the structure, we don't have some of the senior managers that we used to have and so you can understand their concerns. They have witnessed what happens when you liberate an organization. All I can say is that they have to learn to change with it, so that they find a role for themselves, a new role, if the change that we are introducing threatens their current position.

I think the other issue of change is that they are concerned because change in many instances brings new responsibilities to people, gives authority to people, brings in new blood, and people are always a bit suspicious of that and what impact it will have on them. I think these are all natural emotions.

What are the main lessons on managing change that can be drawn from your experience of the Taylor Group?
RT: I don't have a structured answer to this. Without a doubt the most important thing about change is to involve the team in your thinking. Although it is not fully developed let them influence it, let them feel that they are a part of the change process. Ensure evidence of something that they have suggested is a part of this whole change. Get them on-side and certainly, as far as my business is concerned, I suggest one thing that I think that we do better than many, which is that we are always warming people up for a change because they know about the latest order, or the latest failures, or the way the economy is running, or the performance of the business, or where we are investing money. By doing this, they get a more holistic view of the business world rather than their own little fiefdom. In doing this, I'm trying to make everyone a business man or woman in their own right, by sharing all my concerns. Some of them don't like having difficult news fed to them, but it is the only way that they can take responsibility and think about it and then come back and respond. In responding they can influence the way change occurs. But the more you do it the more people become accustomed to it.

How important is the size of the company to the way change can be managed?
RT: I'm sure it has a bearing. Today we are talking about an organization with 22 people. If you recall, within the organization in the early to mid-90s we had an organization with five plants and just over 300 employees. It was a little more difficult in the larger organization to get a complete buy-in. But equally, I would go back to this size of organization and say that it didn't work here because then the general manager didn't really believe it would work. He paid lip-service, so if you extrapolate that on to one of your larger national or international businesses, then I think that the change process can work as long as each time you're cascading it, you're cascading it to like-minded general managers, or departmental managers, or whatever, and some will be better at it than others, just as in our group some were better at it than others. And I suppose in a larger organization potentially you can resource it a lot more effectively. You know, you can throw a lot more resources at it. I have to say that the written word is the least effective way of inculcating any change in values.

Do you agree that complacency can be a barrier to change and innovation during times of company success?
RT: I think this is absolutely right and that we all fall into this trap. I think the business has to decline for you to wake up and see that 'Woops, we have relaxed and

(Continued)

we need to do something about it.' [Interviewer: 'We have to be pushed out of our comfort zone'.] Without a doubt and that's why I think this mingle mania, this benchmarking, this travelling to see how other people do it – not necessarily in your own sector – is so critical because it makes you ask questions and it makes you listen to the answers.

How difficult is it to sustain change in times of economic downturn?
RT: Dare I say this? I think your question shows a misunderstanding of change and economic cycles. There's one thing in terms of changing, tinkering and playing around with the edges and I think it was Tom Peters who said, it is not all about one big change it's about hundreds of little changes. I think that is partly correct in good times but I have to say that the biggest and most radical changes that we have brought about in our businesses is when we hit the tough times. Because the status quo is no longer good enough and I find that in the tough times people are on-side, they are ready for radical changes because they can see the chasm, they can see the precipice. They think, Christ, we have to do something quite different in order to recover … When they actually see the big picture, it acts as a stimulus for increased involvement in change, and that's got to be helpful.

What in your view are the key elements to managing change?
RT: This is going to sound trite, but of course the great barrier to managing change is people. People are often looking for a respite and they don't see change as a necessary element of the business, this constant innovation. I don't think you should assume that change is something that you do for yourself or that you have to find some new ways of doing things. What you have to do is go out and look at like industries within your own sector, look at organizations outwith your own sector, and plagiarize whatever you think will work within your own business. And I think that is where the majority of our change has come from. The difficulty as an entrepreneur is that your management staff say: 'Oh okay, it's another fad'. And sometimes they are fads and, hey, a load of them do end up in the bucket. But you absolutely must never, ever give up experiment-ing, shifting the emphasis, or whatever. As I said to you earlier, I think the worst thing in a business is the moment you sit back and relax and say 'Things are going well'. This is the very time – although you often can't see it – that you should be involved in some very radical change within your business.

A lot of change is implemented as an act of faith. I think it is very difficult to sit down and rationalize and sell the concept of certain changes to your Board because you just don't know. You have to put your toe in the water, you've got to become acquainted with whatever it is you're endeavouring to do, before you can truly articulate what the ultimate benefits will be. So a lot of change must be done as an act of faith and you must leave space and time within your busy schedule to play with change or with new ideas, and to get out there and look out how other people do things.

The way to manage change is to be able to let go of whatever you've just recently created. You shouldn't see it as your baby that you're going to hang on to and control. Once you've introduced it let it go. If by way of letting it go some-times it fails, it's because others are not convinced and they may well be right. Those changes that you let go that do have a life of their own, is because you have persuaded others that it's worthwhile.

Theoretically I'm very interested at the moment in change being brought about by giving younger people their heads. I think that as we get older we do become more set in our ways and I try desperately not to be. We have these assumptions and prejudices and we have all this experience, which can prevent us from thinking more freely when it comes to change. I think that youngsters don't carry that baggage and that we should bring them into the whole process of change management at a very early stage.

Hands-on exercise

Students are allocated to small groups and are required to reflect on and dis-cuss the answers given above. Each group is expected to evaluate the answers of RT and, through drawing on the knowledge and experience of group mem-bers, draft 10 key lessons on managing change. Reflect on these lessons by con-sidering what you would have done the same and what you would have done differently if you were managing this company. Finally, compare your lessons with Kotter's eight-stage model on how to successfully manage change.

Team debate exercise

Debate the following statement:

> **Research generates theory, theory informs practice and practice stimulates research.**

Divide the class into groups. Each group should reflect on the contribution of theory to practice, on the importance of researching practice in developing concepts and theories, and on the dynamic link or inevitable separation between the two. One group should argue as convincingly as possible why the-ory and practice will always be distinct and separate. The other group should argue why there should always be a close link between theory and practice. Each group should be prepared to defend their position.

References

Alvesson, M. and Sveningsson, S. (2008) *Changing Organizational Culture: Cultural Change Work in Progress*. London: Routledge.

Anderson, P. and Tushman, M. (1990) 'Technological discontinuities and dominant designs: a cyclical model of technological change', *Administrative Science Quarterly*, 35: 604–33.

Beer, M., Eisenstat, R. and Spector, B. (1990a) *The Critical Path to Corporate Renewal.* Boston, MA: Harvard Bussiness School Press.

Beer, M., Eisenstat, R. and Spector, B. (1990b) '*Why change programs do not produce change*', *Harvard Business Review*, November–December.

Beer, M. and Nohria, N. (1998) 'Cracking the code of change', *Harvard Business Review*, 78 (3): 133–41.

Bessant, J. and Tidd, J. (2007) *Innovation and Entrepreneurship.* Chichester: John Wiley.

Burns, T. and Stalker, G.M. (1961) *The Management of Innovation.* London: Tavistock.

Burnes, B. (2000) *Managing Change: A Strategic Approach to Organizational Dynamics.* 3rd edn. London: Pitman.

Burnes, B. (2000) *Managing Change: A Strategic Approach to Organizational Dynamics,* 3rd edn. London: PLT man.

Cameron, K. and Quinn, R. (2006) *Diagnosing and Changing Organizational Culture: Based on the Competing Values Framework*, revd edn. San Francisco: Jossey-Bass.

Carnall, C. (2007) *Managing Change in Organizations*, 5th edn. Harlow: Financial Times Prentice Hall.

Child, J. (1972) 'Organization structure, environment and performance: the role of strategic choice', *Sociology*, 6: 1–22.

Child, J. (1997) 'Strategic choice in the analysis of action, structure, organizations and environment: retrospect and prospect', *Organization Studies*, 18: 43–76.

Dawson, P. (2003a) *Understanding Organizational Change: The Contemporary Experience of People at Work.* London: Sage.

Dawson, P. (2003b) *Reshaping Change: A Processual Perspective.* London: Routledge.

DeSanctis, G. and Poole, M.S. (1994) 'Capturing the complexity in advanced technology use: adaptive structuration theory', *Organization Science*, 5 (2): 121–47.

Dubinskas, F. (1994) 'On the edge of chaos', *Journal of Management Inquiry*, 3: 355–67.

Duck, J. (1998) 'Managing change: the art of balancing', *Harvard Business Review on Change.* Boston, MA: Harvard Business School Press. pp. 55–81.

Giddens, A. (1984) *The Constitution of Society – Outline of the Theory of Structuration.* Cambridge: Polity Press.

Hatch, M.J. and Cunliffe, A. (2006) *Organization Theory: Modern, Symbolic and Postmodern Perspectives*, 2nd edn. Oxford: Oxford University Press.

Hayes, J. (2007) *The Theory and Practice of Change Management*, 2nd edn. Basingstoke: Palgrave.

Knights, D. and McCabe, D. (2003) *Organization and Innovation: Guru Schemes and American Dreams.* Milton Keynes: Open University Press.

Kotter, J. (1995) 'Leading change: why transformation efforts fail', *Harvard Business Review*, 73 (2): 59–67.

Kotter, J. (1996) *Leading Change.* Harvard: Harvard Business School Press.

Kotter, J. (2002) *The Heart of Change: Real Life Stories of How People Change their Organizations.* Boston, MA: Harvard Business School Press.

Lewin, K. (1951) *Field Theory in Social Science.* New York: Harper & Row.

MacIntosh, N.B. and Scapens, R.W. (1990) 'Structuration theory in management accounting', *Accounting, Organizations and Society*, 15: 455–77.

Nonaka, I. and Takeuchi, H. (1995) *The Knowledge Creating Company: How Japanese Companies Create the Dynamics of Innovation.* New York: Oxford University Press.

Nordström, K. and Ridderstråle, J. (2007) *Funky Business Forever: How to Enjoy Capitalism.* London: Financial Times Prentice Hall.

Orlikowski, W.J. (1992) 'The duality of technology: rethinking the concept of technology in organisations', *Organization Science*, 3: 398–427.

Pettigrew, A.M. (1985) *The Awakening Giant: Continuity and Change in Imperial Chemical Industries.* Oxford: Blackwell.

Pettigrew, A. (2003) 'Innovative forms of organizing: progress, performance and process', in A. Pettigrew, R. Whittington, L. Melin, C. Sanchez-Runde, F. van den Bosch, W. Ruigrok and T. Numagami (eds), *Innovative Forms of Organizing.* London: Sage. pp. 331–51.

Pettigrew, A. and Massini, S. (2003) 'Innovative forms of organizing: trends in Europe, Japan and the USA in the 1990s', in A. Pettigrew, R. Whittington, L. Melin, C. Sanchez-Runde, F. van den Bosch, W. Ruigrok and T. Numagami (eds), *Innovative Forms of Organizing.* London: Sage. pp. 1–32.

Pettigrew, A., Whittington, R., Melin, L., Sanchez-Runde, C., van den Bosch, F., Ruigrok, W. and Numagami, T. (eds) (2003) *Innovative Forms of Organizing.* London: Sage.

Romanelli, E. and Tushman, M. (1994) 'Organizational transformation as punctuated equilibrium: an empirical test', *Academy of Management Journal,* 37: 1141–66.

Stacey, R. (1992) *Managing Chaos: Dynamic Business Strategies in an Unpredictable World.* London: Kogan Page.

Sternberg, R.J. (ed.) (1999) *Handbook of Creativity.* New York: Cambridge University Press.

Sternberg, R.J. (2007) *Wisdom, Intelligence, and Creativity Synthesized.* New York: Cambridge University Press.

Sternberg, R.J. and Lubart, T.I. (1991) 'An investment thoery of creativity and its developement', *Human Developement,* 34: 1–31.

Sternberg, R.J. and Lubart, T.I. (1999) 'The concept of creativity: prospects and paradigms', in R.J. Sternberg (ed.), *Handbook of Creativity.* New York: Cambridge University Press.

Sternberg, R.J., O'Hara, L.A. and Lubart, T.I. (1997) 'Creativity as investment', *California Management Review,* 40 (1): 8–21.

Tsoukas, H. and Chia, R. (2002). 'On organizational becoming: rethinking organizational change', *Organization Science,* 13 (5): 567–82.

Van de Ven, A. and Poole, M. (2005) 'Alternative approaches for studying organizational change', *Organization Studies,* 26: 1377–404.

Whetten, D. A. (2006) 'Albert and Whetten revisited: strengthening the concept of organizational identity', *Journal of Management Inquiry,* 15 (3): 219–34.

Whittington, R. and Melin, L. (2003) 'The challenge of organizing/strategizing', in A. Pettigrew, R. Whittington, L. Melin, C. Sanchez-Runde, F. van den Bosch, W. Ruigrok and T. Numagami (eds), *Innovative Forms of Organizing.* London: Sage. pp. 35–48.

Recommended reading

- Buchanan, D. and Dawson, P. (2007) 'Discourse and audience: organizational change as multi-story process', *Journal of Management Studies,* 44: 669–86.

- Child, J. (1997) 'Strategic choice in the analysis of action, structure, organizations and environment: retrospect and prospect', *Organization Studies,* 18: 43–76.

- Hatch, M.J. and Cunliffe, A. (2006) *Organization Theory: Modern Symbolic and Postmodern Perspectives,* 2nd edn. Oxford: Oxford University Press.

- Pettigrew, A., Whittington, R., Melin, L., Sanchez-Runde, C., van den Bosch, F., Ruigrok, W. and Numagami, T. (eds) (2003) *Innovative Forms of Organizing*. London: Sage.

- Tsoukas, H. and Knudsen, C. (2005) *The Oxford Handbook of Organization Theory*. Oxford: Oxford University Press.

- Van de Ven, A. and Poole, M. (2005) 'Alternative approaches for studying organizational change', *Organization Studies*, 26: 1377–404.

12

Conclusion

Introduction

Over the last few years the market for literature on management has expanded rapidly ... Yet, it is noteworthy that, in spite of this growth in the provision of formal management education, a minority of the management literature currently in production is of the scholarly or textbook variety. Indeed it seems that scholarly works on management now represent the marginal fringes of the market for management books. (Collins, 2000: 19)

We have set out to present a scholarly yet readable book on change, creativity and innovation. As we noted from the outset, these subjects are often treated as separate domains for academic research and educational study. In our view, however, there is a need to look beyond these self-imposed definitional barriers and to at least attempt a more holistic and integrative approach in examining our theoretical and practical understanding of these areas. Whilst we recognize the limits to such an endeavour, we hope that we have gone some way to opening up these areas for broader discussion and debate. Two key arguments that we have returned to throughout the book are: first, the need for more critical reflection and awareness of the assumptions that lie behind new theories and management fashions. Second, the need to cross discipline boundaries in considering and reflecting upon business practice and organization theory – in order to learn from the way in which these influence each other in the development of new knowledge.

Throughout the book we have presented a range of theories, models and techniques that cover a range of disciplines and perspectives. We also emphasize our concerns with simple recipe-type prescriptions in highlighting our preference for more critical process-based approaches. We claim that, in practice, these simple management recipes have not stood the test of time and that the failure to deliver practical long-term solutions spotlights the problem of management books that identify and codify supposedly best-practice strategies for achieving organizational effectiveness based on commonsense interpretations of organizational life. In drawing on the early work of Pettigrew (1985), we show how there has been a growing support for studies which are both critical and processual, where the 'established priorities and values are not assumed to be legitimate' (Alvesson and Willmott, 1996: 31) and where power, status and political struggles are not simply viewed as disruptive to the 'rational' management of an organization (Knights and Murray, 1994: 3). For example, Hatch argues that this movement away from more stability-oriented frameworks to change-centred perspectives – that emphasize the dynamic and processual aspects of organizing – are required to make sense of innovation and change (1997: 350–2); whilst Collins argues for more reflective approaches to the study of change that are able to accommodate contradiction and complexity rather than the tendency to focus on consensus and stability (1998: 193). Although there remains disagreement within this group of scholars on key aspects of such an approach (for example, with regard to factors such as power, politics and identity), there is support for the general assumptions underlying a processual perspective (see, for example, Alvesson and Sveningsson, 2008; Buchanan and Dawson, 2007; Dawson, 1994; Knights and McCabe, 2003; Pettigrew et al., 2003; Tsoukas and Chia, 2002). We hope that this book has gone some way to presenting the debates within and across alternative positions in a clear and illuminating way, and to fulfilling our opening objective of presenting a 'more holistic approach that is able to cut across boundaries and disciplines in furthering our knowledge and understanding of change, creativity and innovation'.

In the sections that follow, we commence with an overview of some of the changing contextual conditions that organizations face and how these influence the generation of new ideas, their development into new products and services, and their uptake and use. From this we turn our attention to identifying factors that foster and support change and creativity in the business drive for innovation. The chapter concludes that whilst there can never be a comprehensive definitive theory of our domains of interest, there is a lot we can do to further our knowledge and understanding of change, creativity and innovation.

Changing contextual conditions: from urban factories to networked communities

Resistance to new ideas and their translation and uptake does not always occur in the most likely contexts, and yet there are certain types of environments that may be more conducive to change, creativity and innovation than others. As mentioned at the outset of this book, the steam engine that fuelled the Industrial Revolution and led to a rapid expansion in international trade and commerce was the result of bringing together existing expertise and knowledge in the creation of something new and innovative. The control mechanisms associated with the watch-making industry, the pressure boiler that was linked with the brewing industry, and the technology associated with cannon production (and in particular the honing of barrels) all combined in the innovative design of the first steam engine. This development was further refined and used by Stevenson in the construction of a steam train that could transport passengers and freight over a railway network and, as a consequence, these changes formed part of an Industrial Revolution that literally revolutionized the social and economic face of Britain. The reconfiguration of existing technology and expertise in the design and development of something, that whilst not new in terms of its component parts, was revolutionary in terms of its impact on the world of commerce and trade, acted as a driver for radical change.

The creation of new towns and urban centres with the more rapid transportation of materials and the growth in the textile industry, stimulated change on a massive scale. The mass manufacture of goods that would previously be handcrafted but could now be produced by the new machines of the Industrial Revolution enabled the rise of a new consumer market and the growth in the middle class. In an industrial world fuelled by change, new ideas flourished alongside convention and tradition. In other words, there was room for creativity whilst, at the same time, the old structures, established aristocracy and political economy continued to operate and was never fully replaced. Adaptation and accommodation occurred over time, with the new influencing and redefining and not simply replacing or discarding all that went before. In different environments and in different ways, it is these processes of change, creativity and innovation that push new frontiers, accommodate, redefine and adapt. It is an ongoing process that is variously constrained and enabled by the conditions and context within which these dynamics occur.

Since the turn of the century, innovations in the way companies do business, the growth of e-commerce management and e-business (Chaffey, 2003), globalization (Michie, 2003) and developments in information and communication technologies (Preece et al., 2000), have all contributed to a sense of dynamism and urgency in the search for solutions to the 'problem' of increased competition (Gostick and Telford, 2003). Typically, leading-edge companies have moved away from mass-production systems towards more varied customized techniques that provide greater product and service differentiation, and allow for the creation and maintenance of more creative work environments. Modern customers expect customization and choice, and companies have responded by creating organizations that support creative employees, that can react quickly to market forces in producing a continually changing range of goods and services, and that view innovation and change as integral to company survival.

The emergence of new telecommunication infrastructures through the application of new transmission technologies, such as in the use of satellites and optical-fibre cables, is providing new configurations for worldwide information distribution and processing systems. In using these new information channels, an increasing amount of business is completed away from traditional retail outlets and outside of the conventional office or factory. The use of email, video-conferencing systems and the internet have changed not only the way many of us work, but also other activities such as banking and shopping. New organizational forms have emerged based around the use of information and communication technologies: for example, through the shift to electronically-assisted relationships with partner firms, the tight coupling of customer-supplier relations in using a particular form of electronic data exchange, and the development of federated organizations. These developments have stimulated change and innovation in a wide range of organizations in a broad range of sectors.

In business activities the processing of information is a critical activity and it is in these areas that developments in technology are beginning to present a range of new options in the way that work can be managed and organized. For example, the development of international multimedia digital networks, the arrival of new electronic journals, the development of on-line archives within museums, galleries and libraries, and the use of overseas-based call centres, are just a few of the technology-related innovations which suggest the possibility for radical change in the operation of information-centred organizations. Outside of the conventional concept of a physical place of work, is the idea of the portable electronic office, where individuals can work from mobile devices spread across dispersed localities that need not be tied to any particular work-space. This is the notion of the virtual organization where the office and factory building becomes redundant as employees spend periods in virtual space car-rying out their daily activities and work tasks. It is within this context of changes in international trade and business, developments in advanced communication and information technologies and the development of new management tech-niques, that companies are seeking new ideas to tackle the old problem of sus-taining company survival and achieving competitive advantage.

Fostering change and creativity in the drive for innovation and change

Creating and supporting a culture of change and creativity is increasingly central to businesses operating in highly competitive markets. In the case of creative industries, governments have been slow to recognize the import of this sector as a key poten-tial engine for powering economic growth. Over the last decade, this position has changed and a number of governmental policies have been developed to further promote activities within creative industries in Europe and North America. The implications of this sector for jobs and the generation of national wealth remain open to debate, yet most agree that this is an emergent and dynamic market that warrants serious attention and consideration in the development of economic policy.

In fostering change in organizations we would argue that whilst the planning of technical configurations is important and the procedures and timing of train-ing, implementation and uptake are key aspects, it is more generally the human and behavioural contingencies rather than technical problems that derail change initiatives. To put it another way, structural or technical change without behaviour change ultimately results in a no-change scenario. Pinch and Bijker (2000) illustrate this in their example of the development of the bicycle in which pneumatic tyres were originally viewed as an 'unsavoury' and contro-versial innovation. When this development was first launched people ques-tioned the aesthetics of the air tyre and rejected its use as a means of reducing vibration. As stated at the time: 'the appearance of the tyres destroys the sym-metry and graceful appearance of a cycle, and this alone is, we think, sufficient to prevent their coming into general use' (Pinch and Bijker, 2000). However, when it was later launched as a speed innovation – in being successfully mounted on racing bikes – it finally became accepted by the general public. So what does this tell us? Well, the history of pneumatic tyres draws our attention to an important social lesson; namely, that technical innovations do not by themselves bring about the expected behavioural change or social acceptance that may have been envisaged at the time of their development and launch. So it is not just about getting the technical side of innovations right, it is about getting people to accept new ideas, to see the value of these creative innovations and to recognize the need for change. On this count, it is perhaps as much about managing interpretations and meanings as it is about identifying new structures and procedures around creativity and innovation at work. As Collins (1998: 193) concludes in his critique of the literature:

> *A key and recurrent practical theme which has emerged from this theoretical analysis and reflection, is that in attempting to manage change in open social systems, systems which are driven by confusion and complexity, only the brave or foolish would claim to have the definitive answer to any particular problem. While little is certain in matters of human interaction, what does seem clear is that in organizations finding 'the answer' to a particular problem or event – whether the answer arrived at is more-or-less accurate or flawed – is less important than the ability to marshal and solicit support for your preferred viewpoint. Yet this process of marshalling support for your preferred worldview or for your preferred course of action is only possible when we can begin to understand how and why people might see the world differently from us. Only when we can approach managerial problems from this perspective can we begin to understand the different, and often competing views which people bring to bear on work-place problems, and only then can we hope to work to convince them of the validity of our preferred view.*

Finding the balance between rushing a new initiative or embarking on a change programme with too little planning and paying too much attention to detailed preparation (that may limit choice and flexibility), is not always easy to judge. If large amounts of effort are put into the planning process it is important to ensure that the plans themselves do not become the focus of attention. However, when too little time is given to planning considerations change agents often find themselves caught up in constant fire-fighting and crisis management, rather than with the actual management of change. In other words, organizations that embark on change and ignore the planning process often run into difficulties. Conversely, those companies that spend too long preparing the perfect plan can stifle change initiatives through non-action or an inability to adapt to the various twists and turns that will arise during the implementation process. What is required is ongoing reflective analysis of the planning process with recognition that even with the best-laid plans, the unexpected and unforeseen will occur.

Within the context of fast and rapid change, change can become an end in itself without due consideration of the reasons for change. It is important for companies to hold back and take a breath, in critically assessing when not to change as well as when to change. A lot of time, energy and money can be spent on developing and implementing programmes of change that are neither necessary nor helpful to the strategic positioning of a company. Change initiatives that are viewed by employees as unnecessary (a white elephant) can generate employee cynicism and promote growing employee weariness to even the thought of future change initiatives. Change fatigue among employees is a growing issue in many organizations and, as such, it is important to know when not to engage with a particular change initiative as well as when change is important.

A related consideration centres on an accurate critical assessment of the origin and purpose of change. As already noted, change for change's sake is generally of no value and is only likely to generate employee discontent. Similarly, change strategies that simply imitate market trends may do little to secure an organization's competitive market position as it is simply following the benchmarks set by others. A key question therefore centres on the relationship of a proposed change initiative to the future strategic direction of a company. During the 1980s and 1990s, a lot of companies embarked on a whole raft of efficiency-driven change initiatives in order to consolidate their market position and to cut costs, whereas in today's environment, the need for more creative strategies (doing the right thing and being effective) is of critical importance for companies in fast-moving markets and industries. Today, recognizing the importance of creating and sustaining environments conducive to creative processes is sometimes lost in the pressure to maintain costs within highly competitive and dynamic markets. The pressures for change are multi-directional and therefore critical analysis of when, what and how to change needs to be ongoing.

In fostering change and creativity it is important to keep an open mind and to be aware of all viewpoints. The failure of change agents and key decision makers to listen to others and to critically reflect on their position and the possible future trajectories for the organization can severely limit creativity and reinvention. It is perhaps ironic that success can breed complacency, myopia and a reluctance to listen to less powerful voices that can often be the engine for change. Too often it is wrongly assumed that strategies that worked in the past and served as the foundation for companies' current 'success' will be the necessary driver for future strategic advantage. The need to reinvent and appraise change strategies rather than to simply imitate others or refine initiatives that have been successful in the past, is central to our argument about the overlapping links between the concepts of change, creativity and innovation. Failure to recognize this is therefore another key issue that we would identify as crucial to organizations.

In attempting to foster a culture of creativity, the individual is often identified as the first essential building block. Studies have focused on the social and psychological factors that promote creative thinking among individuals. The ability to tolerate ambiguity, take risks, be non-conformist yet confident in oneself, have all been identified as cognitive elements that comprise the creative individual. However, individuals also require a rich body of knowledge and need to be motivated to achieve high creative outputs. It is not enough to have the skills and cognitive make-up to be creative if there is no motivation or will to be creative. Consequently, we often discover creative processes occurring within group environments through the influence of interpersonal interactions and group support (musicians who form a band provide a good example of this). In the case of a business setting, creative ideas and their translation into practice generally require the co-ordination and co-operation of people from different areas and backgrounds (functions and departments), often across sites and perhaps involving external collaborators, as well as those at different hierarchical levels. To this end, the characterization and composition of teams affect interpersonal interactions and the effectiveness of team creativity. Managing the dynamics of teams is challenging but there are a number of techniques that can be employed to enhance team creativity, such as the nominal group technique, brainstorming and brainwriting. In other words, although it is possible to develop team creativity and improve individual and group skills, what remains essential is the creation and maintenance of an environment conducive to creative endeavours.

Creating a culture that promotes the generation and implementation of ideas is seen as essential to sustaining creativity, innovation and change. Managing people in the development and use of appropriate leadership skills is seen as an integral part of this process, as well as the organizational setting, company structure, resource provisions and operating procedures. Even with the vast number of studies on leadership and culture, the key question remains on how in practice do you develop and sustain creative environments in organizations? To this seemingly simple question there are no simple answers. On one level, we can describe how structures, systems and resources can be managed to promote and support an environment within which creative processes may flourish; on another, we draw attention to the practical difficulties of developing a culture that fosters creativity and yet, at the same time, promotes the social cohesion necessary for turning ideas into new products or services. To put it another way, whilst we can identify potential changes needed in order to facilitate creativity within organizations, we are not able to predefine or manage culture through prescriptive means as in practice, we can never be certain of the outcomes of such changes. In identifying the centrality of these intangible elements, we need to be aware of the limits of our understanding in the tools and techniques that we describe, whilst at the same time recognizing that we do have some knowledge that can help us create and sustain environments in which there is a far greater probability that change, creativity and innovation will occur as an ongoing dynamic.

Concluding remarks

In this book we have argued that change, creativity and innovation lie both within and outside the explicit and measurable, it includes the intangible, such as tacit knowledge, the ill-defined and the unexpected. Tangible elements, such as structures, procedures and regulations, may enable space for 'free thinking' or they may create 'prisons of conformity' that discredit alternative views or multiple perspectives. Individuals may actively seek environments in which creativity and open-mindedness are encouraged, where resources and a culture of curiosity support innovative activities. Working in teams, individuals may find further factors that facilitate or limit imaginative thoughts and different contextual environments that variously inhibit or aid the translation of new ideas into practical outcomes. Project deadlines, budget constraints and the need to conform to quality regulations can all serve to shape these processes, and the effects of these contextual influences on change, creativity and innovation often comprise the anticipated, the unplanned for and the unforeseen. Managing change is a complex unfolding dynamic that requires planning, political acumen, flexibility and improvisation, whilst the intangible nature of creativity speaks to the centrality of context in fostering this social process. Both come together in the translation of new ideas into new products, services or ways of thinking. To phrase it differently, change, creativity and innovation represent a complex dynamic of overlapping processes that are shaped by the changing contextual conditions in which they occur.

Taken as a whole, we have sought to introduce the reader to new concepts, theories and studies that provide insight and understanding to processes of change, creativity and innovation. These are areas of great import not only to the world of business, but to our own understanding and interpretation of the world we inhabit. Although there can be no definitive theory that can capture all the nuances and underlying forces associated with these phenomena, we hope that we have enabled greater insight into the nature of these processes. From our perspective, it is in seeking answers to questions that may not be answerable, but that may in the seeking improve our understanding that is at the heart of education and an essential part of student life in the ongoing pursuit of knowledge.

References

Alvesson, M. and Sveningsson, S. (2008) *Changing Organizational Culture: Cultural Change Work in Progress*. London: Routledge.

Alvesson, M. and Willmott, H. (1996) *Making Sense of Management: A Critical Introduction*. London: Sage.

Buchanan, D. and Dawson, P. (2007) 'Discourse and audience: organizational change as multi-story process', *Journal of Management Studies*, 44: 669–86.

Chaffey, D. (2003) *E-Business and E-Commerce Management*, 2nd edn. London: Financial Times Prentice Hall.

Collins, D. (1998) *Organizational Change: Sociological Perspectives*. London: Routledge.

Collins, D. (2000) *Management Fads and Buzzwords: Critical–Practical Perspectives*. London: Routledge.

Dawson, P. (1994) *Organizational Change: A Processual Approach*. London: Paul Chapman Publishing.

Gostick, A. and Telford, D. (2003) *Integrity Advantage: Creating and Sustaining a Competitive Advantage in Business*. Layton, UT: Gibbs M. Smith Inc.

Hatch, M.J. (1997) *Organization Theory: Modern Symbolic and Postmodern Perspectives*. Oxford: Oxford University Press.

Knights, D. and McCabe, D. (2003) *Organization and Innovation: Guru Schemes and American Dreams*. Maidenhead: Open University Press.

Knights, D. and Murray, F. (1994) *Managers Divided: Organisation Politics and Information Technology Management*. Chichester: John Wiley.

Michie, J. (2003) *The Handbook of Globalisation*. Cheltenham: Edward Elgar.

Pettigrew, A.M. (1985) *The Awakening Giant: Continuity and Change in Imperial Chemical Industries*. Oxford: Blackwell.

Pettigrew, A., Whittington, R., Melin, L., Sanchez-Runde, C., van den Bosch, F., Ruigrok, W. and Numagami, T. (eds) (2003) *Innovative Forms of Organizing*. London: Sage.

Pinch, T. and Bijker, W. (2000) 'The social construction of facts and artifacts: or how the sociology of science and the sociology of technology might benefit each other', in D. Preece, I. McLoughlin and P. Dawson (eds), *Technology, Organizations and Innovation: Critical Perspectives on Business and Management. Vol. 11: Theories, Concepts and Paradigms*. London: Routledge.

Preece, D., McLoughlin, I. and Dawson, P. (eds) (2000) *Technology, Organizations and Innovation: Critical Perspectives on Business and Management, Vols I–IV*. London: Routledge.

Index

Note: Page numbers in *italic type* refer to figures. Page numbers in **bold type** refer to case studies.